NORTH CAROLINA SLAVES
AND
FREE PERSONS OF COLOR

CHOWAN COUNTY

VOLUME TWO

William L. Byrd, III

HERITAGE BOOKS
2008

HERITAGE BOOKS
AN IMPRINT OF HERITAGE BOOKS, INC.

Books, CDs, and more—Worldwide

For our listing of thousands of titles see our website
at
www.HeritageBooks.com

Published 2008 by
HERITAGE BOOKS, INC.
Publishing Division
100 Railroad Ave. #104
Westminster, Maryland 21157

International Standard Book Numbers
Paperbound: 978-0-7884-2460-1
Clothbound: 978-0-7884-7576-4

For William Paul Huffman

Contents

Introduction ____ *vii*

Acknowledgements ____ *ix*

Chapter One ____ *1*

Chowan County ____ **1**

Criminal Actions ____ 1

Chapter Two ____ *23*

Chowan County ____ **23**

Civil Actions ____ 23

Chapter Three ____ *341*

Chowan County ____ **341**

Miscellaneous Records ____ 341

Chapter Four ____ *347*

Chowan County ____ **347**

Miscellaneous Records - CRX ____ 347

Appendix A ____ *355*

Glossary of Legal Terms ____ **355**

Table of Cases ____ *363*

Civil and Criminal Actions ____ **363**

Index ____ *379*

Introduction

The records in this book were transcribed from original papers located in the North Carolina State Archives. Most of these papers are listed under general headings such as "Slaves and Free Negroes, " or "Slaves and Free Persons of Color." Occasionally they are listed under the heading of "Miscellaneous Records."[1]

This particular group of papers were selected from the North Carolina county of Chowan. Not a few of these records are torn and faded. In some cases, part of the original text is missing, and many of the names of individuals are almost indecipherable. Nevertheless, every attempt has been made to transcribe these papers as accurately as possible.

Included are a variety of Civil and Criminal actions pertaining to slaves and free persons of color. The interactions between both Blacks and Whites are displayed on an antagonistic and intimate level, and are dramatically played out through crime and punishment. The criminal cases are filled with intrigue involving murder, felonies, trading with slaves and harboring slaves.

The different sections of this book are broken down into the following categories: Civil Actions, from 1757-1819, and Criminal

---

[1] Thornton W. Mitchell, "Preliminary Guide to Records Relating to Blacks in the North Carolina State Archives," ***Archives Information Circular*** 17(June 1980): 3-4.

Actions, from 1777-1817, Miscellaneous Records containing Gun Permits, Sales of Slaves and Hiring of Slaves, and other Miscellaneous Records containing more Criminal Actions . Chowan County was formed in 1670. It began as a precinct in Albemarle County. It was named in honor of the Chowan Indians, who lived in the northeastern part of the Colony. Chowan County is bounded by Albemarle Sound, Chowan River, and Bertie, Hertford, Gates, and Perquimans counties. The county seat, Edenton, was established in 1720, and has continued to be the county seat since that time. Part of Tyrell, Hertford and Gates were formed from Chowan.[2]

---

[2] David Leroy Corbitt, ***The Formation of the North Carolina Counties: 1663-1943*** (Raleigh: Division of Archives and History, 1950) 65-66

Acknowledgements

All acknowledgements regarding this book belong to the staff of the North Carolina State Archives. Without their help and courteousness it would not have been possible.

Chapter One

Chowan County

Criminal Actions

North Carolina State Archives
Chowan County Records
Records of Slaves and Free Persons of Color
C.R.024.928.27

State Vs. Negro Sam
Criminal Action [1777]
Chowan County Records
Felony

State of North Carolina }

Whereas complaint has been made to me this day by John Serimshell that some time ago he was Robbed on board his Boat of Fourteen Pounds Current money of this State; and that he has good Reasons to believe that a Negro named Sam on board of Capt. Walk's Brig was the Person who Robbed him of the said Money

These are therefore in the Name of the Said State to command you to take the Body of the said Negro, and bring him before me or some other Justice of the Peace of this County to answer the above Complaint for which this shall be your Sufficient Authority, Given under my Hand & Seal this 22nd day of May 1777.

To any Lawful Officer } Joseph Hewet[?]
To Execute & Return }

****

State Vs. Negro Frank
Criminal Action [1782]
Chowan County Records
Felony (Assault)

State of North Carolina }
Chowan County }

Whereas Complaint hath this Day hath been made unto me by Mary Kelly that a Certain Negroe Man Slave called Frank belonging to Henry O'Neil of the Town of Edenton did about the Hours of One or Two O'Clock this Morning come to the House of the said Mary Kelly & Break open the door thereof & did forcibly enter it & Abuse & otherwise Maltreat the said Mary Kelly to the Manifest Danger of her Life.

These are therefore in the Name of the State to Command you to take the said Negroe Man Slave Frank & bring him before me or some other Justice of the Peace for said County & for so doing this shall be your Warrant, Given under my Hand & Seal this 22nd April 1782.

To any Lawfull Officer to Execute & Return & for want of Such to
Jonathan Boulton Chas. Johnson. JP

Executed and the within Named Negroe Frank in Custody
Jona. Boulton

****

State Vs. Henry D. Watson
Criminal Action [1783]
Chowan County Records
Selling Liquor to a Slave

Chowan County
Criminal Actions

State Vs. Henry D. Watson
Warrant
Executed P. James Garrett

Chowan County Sessions

Complaint has been made to me by Joseph Blount, that Henry Drake Watson, has harboured, entertained & Sold liquors to a Negro Slave belonging to him

These are to Command you in the Name of the State to take & bring before me the said Watson to answer the above Complaint

Given under my hand & Seal this 8th day of Septr. 1783

To James Garrett to Execute & Return
Michl Payne, JP

****

State Vs. Jacob Dowdey
Criminal Action [1783]
Chowan County Records
Trading with a Negro

State Warrant Vs. Jacob Dowdey
Executed
James Forros[?]

Chowan County }
Edenton } SS

Whereas complaint hath been made to me by Nathaniel Allen Esqr that Jacob Dowdey has been bargaining with a Negro man of his nam'd George contrary to Law.

These are therefore in the name of the State to command you to bring the Sd. Jacob Dowdey before me or some other Justice of the Peace to answer the above complaint. Given under my hand this 29th June 1783.

To any Lawfull }
Officer to Execute }
L. Dickinson

****

Chowan County
Criminal Actions

State Vs. Elizabeth Plummer
Criminal Action [1785]
Chowan County Records
Trading with a Slave

State of No. Car.
Chowan County

Before us Samuel Dickinson & Stephen Cabarrus Esquires Justices of the Peace for the County aforesaid, appeared Martha Martin who maketh oath that some time last fall she heard Elizabeth Plummer of Benton say that she bought from a Certain Negro fellow Belonging to Michl. Payne Esquire two piggs which this deponent saw in her possession and that two or three days after, she saw the said Elizabeth Plummer buy and receive in the Night of the said Negro fellow a shoulder of Bacon and a quantity of wheat which the deponent supose to be a bushel and half, the deponent further declares that she saw the Sd. Elizabeth Plummer some time after buy of the same Negro Fellow two other piggs and a quantity of tallow which she the deponent suposes to be fifteen or twenty pounds Wt and further the deponent Saith not. Sworn before us this 21st day of June Anno Dom. 1785.
S. Dickinson
S. Cabarrus

****

State Vs Negro John
Criminal Action [1787]
Chowan County Records
Murder

Trial of Negro John
The Property of S. Johnston Esqr
Octr. 15th 1787

Summoned: Micheal Payne, Stephen Cabarrus, & Nathaniel Allen, Esquires

Chowan County
Criminal Actions

Wm. Littlejohn, Samuell Butler, Alexander Black, & Thomas King, Freeholders owners of Slaves
Sayeth Henry Bond, D Shff

State of North Carolina }
Chowan County }

To the Sheriff of the County aforesaid, Greeting:
You are hereby Commanded to Summon Three Justices of the Peace and four Freeholders Owners of Slaves to Meet at the Court House in Edenton at Twelve O'Clock this forenoon to sett and try Negro John the property of Samuel Johnston Esqr. charged with Murdering a Negroe Slave Called Sandy the property of Josiah Collins Esqr. for so doing this shall be your Sufficient Authority. Given under my Hand and Seal this 15th day of October 1787.
Michl. Payne

****

State Vs. Negroes July, Jack & James
Criminal Action [1790]
Chowan County Records
Breaking & Entering

At a Court Called and held at the Court House in Edenton Pursuant to the several Acts of Assembly made for the trial of Slaves the 23rd day of August 1790 for the trial of Negro July the property of William Carter & Jack the property of John Beasley's Estate and negro James the property of Mrs. Penelope Cooley -- charged with having broken open the store house of Smith and Shaw & stole from thence, one piece of printed linnin, one bedstick, fourteen yds of strip'd Holland, five pair of mens shoes, three pewter Trapotts, one pound Coarse white thread and about one Barrell of northward Rum.

Present
Edmund Blount }
William Barritz } Esqrs, Justices
Nathl. Allen }

Saml.Butler }

Jos. H. Eellbeck } Freeholders & Owners
Alexr. Black }of Slaves
Robert Egan }

The Court Qualified agreeable to Law & proceeded to the Trial of the said negroes July & James & Jack and after hearing the Evidences against them do adjudge the said July, James & Jack to be Guilty of the Crimes they stand Charged with and that they be Committed to the Gaol untill tomorrow & that between the hours of Eleven & Twelve tomorrow they & Each of them shall receive thirty nine Lashes on their bare back at the Whipping post & then be recommitted to Prison till Thursday & then between the hours of Eleven & Twelve they shall receive Twenty one Lashes each at the Whipping post on their bare backs & that the Sheriff see this Judgment faithfully Executed.

Edmd. Blount, Wm. Barritz, Nathl. Allen, Saml. Butler, Alex Black & Robert Egan.

****

State Vs. Daniel Leary
Criminal Action [1794]
Chowan County Records
Assault

Pros - Cyrus Marsh
Sworn & Sent
Jos. Blount, No Bill
Jos Beasley, Foreman

State of North Carolina }
Chowan County } Sept. Term 1794

The Jurors for the State on their oath present that Daniel Leary of the said County, Cordwainer on the 3rd day of August 1794 with force & arms in the County aforesaid one Negroe Jim the property of Penelope Barker widow & at that time in the employ of Cyrus Marsh in the peace of God & the said State then and there being did make an assault with a certain pair knife which he the said Daniel in his right hand then & there held and **[?]** the said Negroe Jim with the said Knife -- then and there did stick into the body of the said Jim the property as aforesaid of Cyrus did then & there beat wound & ill treat & other ways injure to the said Jim the property as aforesaid then & there did to the great damage of the said Jim & his Owners as aforesaid to the evil example of all others in the like [?] against the peace & Dignity of the State.

****

State Vs. Negro Rages
Criminal Action [1794]
Chowan County Records
Breaking & Entering

Chowan SS

Whereas complaint hath been made on oath to me this 13th November by Mr. Cyrus Marsh, that last Sunday Night the 9th Instant his Shop was broke open, and his Chest was opened at same time, & there was between fifty and Sixty Dollars Value in paper Currency taken out of his Chest at that time, belonging to him and that he has reason to believe that a Negro Named Rages belonging to Doctr Ramcke has taken the same.

These are therefore in the name of the State to command you to make diligent search in all suspected places in the day time where he may secret his property and the money or any part of it having found that you bring it and the person in whose possession you find it before me or some other Justice of the peace, in or Order they may be dealt with as the Law directs.

Given under my hand and Seal this day above written.

To the Constable of }
Edenton to Execute }
& return }
Wm. Littlejohn, JP

****

State Vs. Rufus Stafford
Criminal Action [1795]
Chowan County Records
Trading with Slaves

Chowan County
Criminal Actions

State Vs. Rufus Stafford
Jas Bond Pros:
& Witness
Sworn & Sent, Norfleet
A True Bill
John Little, Foreman

State of North Carolina } December Term 1795
Chowan County }

The Jurors for the State & County aforesaid on their Oath present that Rufus Stafford, Merchant on the 17th of Decemr. 1795 in the County aforesaid did sell to a certain Negro Slave named **[Blank]** the property of some person unknown a small quantity of Rum without the said Slave having any permission in writing from his Master or Mistress in contempt of the Act of Assembly in such case made and provided to the advancement of bad Morals Evil & Immorality to the evil example of all others in the like case offending and against the peace and dignity of the State.
[?] Atto

****

State Vs. Thomas Simmons
Criminal Action [1795]
Chowan County Records
Petty Larceny

State Vs. Simons, et als
Petty Larceny
Pros, Wm Hayes, Witness, Alex Millen
Sworn & sent, E Norfleet
A True Bill, John Little, Foreman

State Vs Thos Simons & Jos Wilkins
Subpoena, Executed so says Chas Roberts, Sheriff

State of North Carolina
To the Sheriff of Chowan County, Greeting:

Chowan County
Criminal Actions

You are hereby commanded to summon Isacker Branch & John Clemons personally to be and appear before the Justices of our Inferior Court of Pleas and Quarter Sessions, at the Court House in Edenton on Wednesday the 14th of September, then and there to testify and the truth to say in behalf of Thos. Simons & Joseph Wilkins in a certain matter of controversy in said Court depending, and then and there to be traversed between the State & Thomas Simons & Joseph Wilkins; and this you shall in no wise omit, under the penalty by law enjoined. Witness Elisha Norfleet Clerk of the said Court, at Edenton the 13th day of September in the XX year of our Independence, Anno Dom. 1796
E Norfleet, CC

State Vs. Thomas & Joseph Wilkins
Subpoena
Executed so says Chas Roberts, Sheriff

State of North Carolina
To the Sheriff of Chowan County, Greeting:
You are hereby commanded to summon Elizabeth Simons personally to be and appear before the Justices of our Inferior Court of Pleas and Quarter Sessions, at the Court House in Edenton immediately, then and there to testify and the truth to say in behalf of Thomas Simons & Joseph Wilkins in a certain matter of controversy in the said Court depending, and then and there to be traversed between the State, and Thos Simons & Joseph Wilkins Defendants; and this you shall in no wise omit, under the penalty by law enjoined. Witness Elisha Norfleet Clerk of the said Court, at Edenton the 13th day of Decr. In the 21st year of our Independence, Anno Dom. 1796.
E Norfleet

State Vs Thomas Simons & Jos: Wilkins
March Term 1796
Executed by W.H. Boyce, DShff

State of North Carolina
To the Sheriff of Hertford County, Greeting:
You are hereby commanded to summon Polly Hayes, Elisha Perry, Robert Perry & Winefred Hayes personally to be and appear before the Justices of

our Inferior Court of Pleas and Quarter Sessions, at the Court House in Edenton on the second Monday of March next, then and there to testify and the truth to say in behalf the State in a certain matter of controversy in said Court depending, and then and there to be Traversed between the State, and Thomas Simons & Joseph Wilkins, and this you shall in no wise omit, under the penalty by law enjoined. Witness Elisha Norfleet, Clerk of the said Court, at Edenton the XIX day of December in the XX year of our Independence, Anno, Anno Dom. 1795.
E Norfleet, CC

State Vs Thomas Simons & Joseph
Capias
Returnable Immediately
Dismist, March 97
Executed so says Chas Roberts, Sheriff

State of North Carolina
To the Sheriff of Chowan County, Greeting:
We command you to take the bodies of Thomas Simons & Joseph Wilkins Planters if to be found in your bailiwick, and them safely keep, so that you have them before the Justices of the County Court of Pleas and Quarter Sessions now setting at the Court House in the County of Chowan Immediately, then and there to answer unto the Court on behalf of the State to a Certain Bill of Indictment & herein fail not, and have you then and there this writ, and how you have executed the same. Witness Elisha Norfleet Clerk of the said Court, at Edenton this 16th day of December in the year of our Lord 1795.
E Norfleet, CC

North Carolina }
Chowan County } Decemr. Term 1795

The Jurors for the State on their Oath present that Thomas Simmons & Joseph Wilkins, Planters on the eleventh day of December one thousand seven hundred & ninety five with force & Arms in the County aforesaid one Negroe boy called Joe and one Negroe Girl called Cherry the property of Winifred Hayes, widow, of the value of sixpence then & there being

found, feloniously did steal, take & carry away against the peace & dignity of the State.
J Hamilton for State.

****

State Vs. Bet, a Slave
Criminal Action [1796]
Chowan County Records
Arson

State of North Carolina }
Chowan County }

To the keeper of the common Gole of the Edenton District I herewith send you the Body of Negro Bet the property of Samuel Dickinson of Chowan County Charged with having set fire to the House of her Master Saml. Dickinson on the night of **[Blank]** day of January 1796

And I do hereby command you in the name of the State to receive her in your said Gaol, and there safely keep without bail or mainprize till she be from there Discharged by due course of Law.
Given under my hand & Seal this 26th day of December 1796.
Jacob Blount (Seal)

****

State Vs Isaac, a Negro
Criminal Action [1797]
Chowan County Records
Taken up as Emancipated

Notice
Negroe Isaac Vs State

North Carolina
Chowan County

To Caleb Bundey you are hereby Summoned to appear at the County Court of Chowan in Edenton the second Monday in June next then and there to

make your Rite know to a Certain Negrow man nam'd Isaac who is taken up as emancipated Negrow.
Edenton 30th May 1797
Chas. Roberts, Shff

****

State Vs. Negro Peter
Criminal Action [1797]
Chowan County Records
Hiring his own Time

Information have been made by Mr. Blount to the Grand Jury that a Negroe Man Peter Belonging to Mr. D. Clunea[?] hires his Time of his Master

---

State of North Carolina } Chowan County Court
} March Term 1797

To the Sheriff of Chowan County, It is Ordered that you take up Negroe Peter belonging to Marquis Declughny, secure & keep him safely so that you have him before the next County Court to be held at the Court House in Edenton on the second Monday in June next there to be tried on a Bill Presented against him at the above term, agreeable to an act of the Genl Assembly &c &c and that you give his Master Notice according to Law.
By Order, E Norfleet, CC

State Vs Negroe Peter
Marquis DeClughny
June Term 1797

Executed, Chas Roberts, Sheriff
I Promis to Be Security for the within Negro Peter's Appearance when Called for
Holloday Walton

Presentment of Negroe Peter

Chowan County Criminal Actions

Jesse Blount
Sworn & Sent
E Norfleet

North Carolina }
Chowan County } March Term 1797

The Jurors for the State on their Oath present that Negroe Peter, the property & Slave of the Marquis DeClugny, Gentleman is permitted by the said DeClugny his Master to hire his own time contrary to the Act of Assembly in such Case made & provided & against the peace & Dignity of the State
J Hamilton for State
A True Bill
Samuel Hoskins, Foreman

****

State Vs. Negro Dick
Criminal Action [1800]
Chowan County Records
Taken up as Emancipated

State of North Carolina } Chowan County

To Francis White & Caleb White June Term 1800 you are hereby Summoned to appear at the Next County Court of Please & Quarter Sessions to be held for the County of Chowan on the second Monday in September next then & there to make known your Right & Title to a Certain Negro Man Slave Named Dick who is taken up as an Emancipated Negro and will be Tried at the aforesaid Term of September under the Act of Assembly in such Case made and Provided.
Chas Roberts, Shff

Caleb White and Francis White
Claim To Negro Dick
To September Term 1800

State of North Carolina }

Chowan County Criminal Actions

Chowan County SS. } September Term 1800

And now at this day towit on Monday the first day of this Term Came Francis White & Caleb White summoned by Charles Roberts Esquire Sheriff of Chowan County to appear before this Worshipful Court and make known their Claim, Right or Title to a Certain Negro man Slave named Dick Taken up as an Emancipated negro &c, Whereupon the said Francis and Caleb by William Slade their Attorney set forth declare and say, that they are informed and verily believe that the said Negro Dick was the property of Caleb White the Elder, the Father of these Claimants, & that the said Slave was in his infancy fraudulently & secretly taken away and detained, from the Possession & Service of the said Caleb White the Elder during his life, and hath always from the death of the said Caleb White to the Present time been kept and detained from the possession and Service of these Claimants, without their consent and agreement and against their will -- Nevertheless they have reason to hope and believe that they shall be able to Establish a good subsisting legal Title to the said Slave against there who now hold, or may hereafter hold the said Slave in their possession.

And these Claimants further say and aver that the said Negro Dick hath never from his nativity to the present time been Liberated, Set free, or let go at large by & with the privity or consent of the said Caleb White the Elder in his lifetime, Or by these Claimants since his death, all which they are ready to Verify, and pray that the said Negro may be Surrendered unto them, &c without [?] &c.

W. Slade, Atty for the Claimants.

Notice &c	19
3 Subpoenas	4.6
11 Cont 3/	1.13
Deter & E'n	11.3
	£3-7:9
W.S., Atto	2
Sheriff	16.10
	£6-4-7
Richd Haughton, Edward Hall	
Wm Hall	12

Chowan County
Criminal Actions

State Vs. Negro Dick

Saml Hoskins maketh oath that he served this notice on James White some time in the month of Augt. Last Sworn to in open Court the 12th day of Sept. 1800

Received of Mr. Francis White Executor of Caleb White and one of his heirs the sum of five pounds for filing a Claim in Chowan Court to the Negro Dick and obtaining Judgment in behalf of the Claimants
January Term 1800
W. Slade.

Wm. Slade Esquire Rect. For fee
Roberts, Sheriff
Negroe Dick

Recevd. Edenton June the 13th 1801 of Francis White the sum of Eighty Shillings it being for tending as a witness in the suit of Negrow Dick recvd. By me
William Slade

Wm Hall Receipt

The within sum I have charged in my accompt with my expences when I attend Court.

Wm Hall Receipt
This is allso Charged with my expence

Edenton September 19th 1801
Received of Francis White the sum of four shillings for attending as a witness in the Suit of Negro Dick Received by me
William Hall

****

State Vs. Negro Will

Chowan County
Criminal Actions

Criminal Action [1800]
Chowan County Records
Felony

Executed
John Fife[?], Const.

North Carolina }
Chowan County SS } September Term 1800

Upon the within Written Complaint & under the act of Assy 1793 a Charge of Petit Larceny is exhibited agt. The within named Negroe Will the property of James Neil for the taking, stealing & carrying away of two sheep the property of Chas. Roberts Esqr with force & arms in the County aforesaid on the 20th day of August 1800 against the peace & Dignity of the State.
J. Hamilton

State of No. Car. }
Chowan County }

Complaint having been made to me this day by Charles Roberts of the State & County aforesaid, that a negro man named Will the property of James Neil has feloniously stolen, taken and carried away from Mr. Jno. Blount's Plantation two sheep the property of Chas Roberts

Therefore Command you in the name of the State to take the body of said Negro Will & to bring him before me or some other Justice of the peace for the County aforesaid to answer the above Complaint and be dealt with agreeable to law.

Given under my hand & Seal this 12th Sept. 1800.
S. Cabarrus (Seal)
To any lawful Officer to Execute & Return.

Indictment an Warrant	" 6--
Trial &c	" 7 -- 6
Execution	" 3 --9
Atto	1.6.8
Sherif	" -- 8 --

The Court	} Fined	} Sci Fa	" 6
Vs	}Sci Fa	} Sheriff	" 5.4
Jas Neil	}		
Trial Of Will &c			£.11. 4
			2.11.11
			3. 7. **[Faded]**

****

State Vs. Negro Toney
Criminal Action [1812]
Chowan County Records
Felony

State of North Carolina }
Chowan County }

To any Lawfull Officer to Execute

Whereas William Jackson have Complained Before me Reuben Small one of the Justices of the Peace for said County that he had a boy Feloniously stolen and Carried away from him sometime last spring from the **[?]** of Thomas Matthias; which he has Just Cause to believe that a Certain Negroe by the name of Toney formerly the property of Col. John Bond Decd. took and Carried away the same, these are therefore to Command you to take the body of the said Negroe Toney and bring him before me or some other Justice of the Peace to answer the Complaints alledged against him, Given under my Hand and Seal this 10th Day of Novr. 1812.

Reuben Small (Seal)

Summon Henery P. Barrett, Jack Mieres, John Coffield, Senr., Seth Parker Junr.

Continue till Next Tuesday the 24th
Continued till the first -- R. Small
Caleb Nash -- Reuben Small
This 24th Nov 1812

Chowan County
Criminal Actions

Judgment to give Negroe Toney Twenty Stripes on his bear Back this 5th day Decr. 1812
Reuben Small

Warrant Vs. Toney

The Defendant prays the appeal and gives for Security
Test, Reuben Small
Thos Matthias

The State Vs. Negro Toney
Subpoena
For E. Jones, 1st March
March Term 1813
Executed, Hoskins, Shff

State of North Carolina
To the Sheriff of Chowan County, Greeting:
You are hereby commanded to summon Edmund Jones personally to be and appear before the Justices of the County of Chowan, at the Court House in Edenton, on the second Monday in March then and there to testify and the truth to say in behalf of Negro Toney in a certain matter of controversy in the said Court depending, and then and there to be tried, wherein the State is plaintiff, and Negro Toney belonging to Est Jno Bond defendant. And this you shall in no wise omit, under the penalty by law enjoined. Witness James Norfleet, Clerk of the said Court, at Edenton the 14th day of December in the XXX7th year of our Independence, Anno Dom. 1812
Jas Norfleet.

State Vs. Negro Toney
Subpoena
Decr. Term 1812
Executed by Edmd Jones

State of North Carolina.
To the Sheriff of Chowan County, Greeting:

Chowan County
Criminal Actions

You are hereby commanded to summon Henry Bennett & his Negro Jack personally to be and appear before the Justices of our County Court of Pleas and Quarter Sessions, at the Court House in Edenton, immediately, then and there to testify and the truth to say, in behalf of the State in a certain matter of controversy in the said Court depending, and then and there to be tried, wherein the State is Plaintiff, and Negro Tony is Defendant; and this you shall in no wise omit, under the penalty by law enjoined. Witness James Norfleet, Clerk of the said Court at Edenton, the 16th day of Decr. In the XXXVII year of our Independence, Anno Dom 1812
Jas Norfleet, Clk.

The State Vs Negro Toney
Subpoena
Reuben Small, 1st March
March Term 1813
Executed, Jas Skinner, DShff

State of North Carolina
To the Sheriff of Chowan County, Greeting:
You are hereby commanded to summon Reuben Small personal to be and appear before the Justices of the County Court of Pleas and Quarter Sessions at the next Court, to be held for the County of Chowan, at the Court House in Edenton, on the second Monday in March then and there to testify and the truth to say in behalf of Negro Toney in a certain matter of controversy in the said Court depending, and then and there to be tried, wherein the State is Plaintiff, and Negro Toney belonging to Est of Jno Bond defendant. And this you shall in no wise omit, under the penalty by law enjoined. Witness James Norfleet, Clerk of the said Court, at Edenton, the 14th day of December in the XXX7th year of our Independence, Anno Dom. 1812.
Jas Norfleet, Clk

****

State Vs. Negro Jack
Criminal Action [1814]
Chowan County Records
Hiring his own Time

Chowan County
Criminal Actions

State Vs. Negro Jack the property
Of William Ryhton
June Term 1814
Not to be found, E. Hoskins, Shff

State of North Carolina

To the Sheriff of Chowan County, Greeting:

You are hereby commanded to take the body of Negro Jack the property of William Righton if to be found in your Bailiwick, and him safely keep, so that you have him before the Justices of the County Court of Pleas and Quarter Sessions, at the next Court, to be held for the the County of Chowan, at the Court House in Edenton, on the second Monday in June next, then and there to answer unto the State by our Solicitor Thomas D Mardin Esqr on an Indictment preferred against him for hiring his own time Contrary to Law. Herein fail not and have you then and there this writ. Witness James Norfleet, Clerk of the said Court, at Edenton, the 16th day of March in the XXXVIII year of our Independence, Anno Dom 1814.
James Norfleet, Clk

****

State Vs William Jackson
Criminal Action [1817]
Chowan County Records
Crime not Given

State Vs. William Jackson
Subpoena
Stephen Elliot & Willis Elliot
March Term 1817
Not to be Found, Ephrm. Elliot

State of North Carolina

To the Sheriff of Chowan County, Greeting:

You are hereby commanded to summon Stephen Elliot and Willis Elliot personally to be and appear before the Justices of the County Court of Pleas and Quarter Sessions at the next Court, to be held for the County of Chowan, at the Court House in Edenton, on the second Monday in March next then and there to testify and the truth to say in behalf of the State in a

certain matter of controversy in said Court depending, and then and there to be tried, wherein the State is Plaintiff and William Jackson is Defendant. And this you shall in no wise omit, under the penalty by law enjoined. Witness William Norfleet, Clerk of the said Court, at Edenton, the 9th day of December in the XLI year of our Independence, Anno Dom 1817.
William Norfleet, Clk.

That the presentment in which the bill was found, Inst - at the [?] of the Copy of the Indictment the word "of" Re form" of the [?] it should read this way -- are there any persons other than those mentioned who can prove the fact or confession.

The Transcript with the above Aception is perfect.

MS.

Chapter Two

Chowan County

Civil Actions

North Carolina State Archives
Chowan County Records
Records of Slaves and Free Persons of Color
C.R.024.928.27

Jordan Vs. Winham
Civil Action [1757]
Chowan County Records

Jordan Vs. Winham
July Court 1757
J. Carleton
For Mr. Jones to copey

North Carolina } July Court 1757
Chowan County }

Chowan County
Civil Actions

William Winham late of Chowan County in the Province afsd. Planter was attached to answer to Charles Jordan of a Plea of Trespass with Force & Arms One Negroe Man the Servant of the said Charles named Frank he the said William assaulted & injured at Chowan County aforsd. So that of the said beating the Sd. Negroe Man Servant languished whereby the said Petr. Was deprived of his Service & the benefit of his Labour and whereupon the Sd. Petr by Jasper Charlton his Atty complained that the Sd. William on the Twenty fifth Day of April in the year of our Lord one thousand seven hundred & fifty seven at Chowan County Afsd. With Force & Arms & so forth in and against a Negroe Man Servant of him the Sd. Petr. An assault did make & him the said Negroe Man Servant named Jack did beat, bruise & evilly mistreat by means of which beating & bruising the said Negroe Man Servant languished from the said Twenty fifth Day of April until the fifth Day of May **[Faded]** following whereby the said Petr. Totally lost the Service of the said Servant during the Time aforesaid & other Injury to the Sd Petr. The Sd. William then & there did against the Peace of our Sovereign Lord the now King Whereupon the Sd. Plaintiff saith he is injured & hath Damages to the Value of **[Blank]** therefore sues.
J Charlton, Atty.

****

Swift Vs. Copland
Civil Action [1760]
Chowan County Records

Swift Vs. Copland
Writ
To January Infr Court, 1760
Executed by Rob Lenox
So Saith Witt**[?]**
Saml. Johnston, Atto

North Carolina } George the Second by the Grace of God
Chowan County } King of Great Britain &c

To the Sheriff of Chowan County Greeting: We Command you that you take the Body of Peter Copland if to be found in your Bailiwick so that you have his Body before the Justices of our Inferior Court of Pleas and

Quarter Sessions at our next Court to be held for our said County at the Court House in Edenton on the third Thursday in January next then and there to Answer to Samuel Swift of a Plea of Trespass on the Case &c Damage Ten Pounds Procl. Money Herein fail not & make due Return hereof & have you then & there this Writt, Witness Thomas Jones Clerk of our said Court the XLX Day of October Anno Dom 1760
Thos Jones, Clk

North Carolina }
Chowan County }

Know all men by these presents that we Peter Copland & Robert Lenox of the County & Province Afsd are held & firmly bound unto William Halsey Esquire high Sheriff of the County Afsd his heirs, Executors, Administrators or assigns in the Sum of Twenty Pounds Procl. Money -- To which payment well & truly to be made & done we bind our selves our heirs, Executors & administrators Jointly & Severally, firmly by these presents, Sealed & Dated this Eleventh Day of Novemr. Anno Dom 1760.

The Condition of this obligation is such that if the above bounden Peter Copland do & shall make his personall appearance before the Justices of our Inferior Court of Pleas & Quarter Sessions at our next Court to be held for the County of Chowan at the Court house in Edenton on the third Thursday in January next then & there to Answer Saml: Swift of a Plea of Trespass on the Case & Damage Ten Pounds Procl. Money, and there stand to & abide by the Judgment of the said Court and not depart the same without License first had & obtained that then the above obligation to be Void or else to be & remain in full force & Virtue
Sealed & Delivered in the presence of
Peter Copland (Seal)
Robt. Lenox (Seal)

****

Solomon King Vs. Daniel Marshal
Civil Action [1759]
Chowan County Records

King Vs. Marshal

Chowan County
Civil Actions

April Court 1759, Edenton
Barker, Atto
Executed So Saith Will Halsephor

North Carolina }

George the second by the Grace of God of Great Britain, France & Ireland, king & Defender of the Faith &c.

To the Sherif of Chowan County Greeting we Command you that you take the body of Daniel Marshal late of Edenton in Chowan County Cordwainer -- if to be found in your Bailiwick & him safely keep so that you have him before the Justices of our County Court to be held for the said County at the Court House in Edenton on the First Tuesday in April Next then & there to answer to Solomon King of a Plea that he Tender to him Six Pounds Eighteen Shillings Proclamation Money which to him he owes & unjustly Detains, Damage Eight Pounds Proclamation Money -- Herein Fail Not and have you there this Writ, Witness Thomas Jones Clerk of our Sd. County Court at Edenton the IV Day of April in the XXXII of our Reign 1759.
Thos Jones, Clerk

****

William Littlejohn Vs. Richard Michalls
Civil Action [1781]
Chowan County Records

Chowan County Inferior Court
William Littlejohn Vs. Richard Michalls
Assault
Issued the 20th of June 1781
Cumming, Atto
Came to hand the 20th of June 1782
Executed and Security so says Ed. Blount, Sheriff

State of North Carolina

To the Sheriff of Chowan County Greeting:

You are commanded to take the Body of Richard Michalls late of your County Mariner if to be found in your Bailiwick and him safely keep so that you have him before the Justices of the County Court of Pleas and

Chowan County
Civil Actions

Quarter Sessions to be held at the Court House in Edenton for the County of Chowan on the fourth Monday in June next then and there to answer unto William Littlejohn of a Plea wherefore with force and Arms he made an Assault on a certain Negroe man Slave named Mingoe the Property of the said William Littlejohn and him beat wounded and evilly treated to nearly lost one of his Eyes and his life was greatly dispaired of and other Enormities to him did to the great Injury of the said William Littlejohn and against the Peace of the State and so forth Damage fifty thousand Pounds &c. and have you then and there this Writ and have you Executed the same: Witness James Blount, Clerk of the said Court at Edenton this XX10th day of March Anno Domini 1781
W. Cumming, Atto
James Blount, CCC

****

John Robinson Vs. Henry O'Neal
Civil Action [1782]
Chowan County Records

State of North Carolina }
Chowan County } SS

John Robinson, Planter Complains of Henry O'Neal, Planter, for that whereas the said Henry O'Neal on the Twenty Seventh day of April in the Year of our Lord One Thousand Seven Hundred and Eighty two at the County aforesaid in the Town of Edenton with force and Arms and against the Peace did Enter the House of Henry Watson late of the said Town and then and there with Clubs and Swords did beat, bruise, Wound and inhumanly Treat one Negro Man Jack, wherefor the said Robinson saith he injured and hath damage to the Value of Forty Thousand Pounds and whereof He bruiseth, [?] and so forth.

John Do } Wai[?] Atty
Richard Roe } Pledges of Pros for the Pltff

Robinson Vs O'Neal
Writ
Came to hand the 2nd Day of May 1782

Executed & Bail so say Ed. Blount, Sheriff

State of North Carolina

To the Sheriff of Chowan County Greeting:

You are hereby Commanded to take the Body of Henry O'Neal if to be found in your Bailiwick and him safely keep so that you have him before the Justices of our County Court of Pleas and Quarter Sessions to be held for the County of Chowan at the Court House in Edenton on the fourth Monday in June next then and there to answer to John Robinson of a Plea of Trespass by force of Arms and against the Peace &C Damage Forty Thousand pounds, herein fail not & have you there this Writ, Witness James Blount Clerk of our said Court at Edenton this 2nd day of May 1782.
Signed by Law --- James Blount, Clk.

Robinson Vs O'Neal
To Sept Court
Summons for Wm. Watson

State of North Carolina

To the Sheriff of Chowan County, Greeting:

You are hereby Commanded to summons ~~William~~ Henry Watson personally to be and appear before the Justices of the County Court of Pleas and Quarter Sessions to be held for the County of Chowan at the Court House in Edenton on the fourth Monday of September next; then and there to testify, and the Truth to say, on behalf of John Robinson in a certain matter of controversy in the said Court depending, and then and there to be tried, between John Robinson Plaintiff, and Henry O'Neal Defendant; and this you shall in no wise omit; under the penalty of Fifty Pounds Current Money, Witness William Wilkins for James Blount Clerk of the said Court, at Edenton the XX[?] Day of June Anno Dom. 1782.
William Wilkins for Jas. Blount, Clk.

Robinson Vs O'Neal
To Sept. Court 1782
Summons for Parshall
Executed So Saith William Roberts.

State of North Carolina

Chowan County
Civil Actions

To the Sheriff of Chowan County, Greeting:
You are hereby Commanded to summons Benjamin Parshall personally to be and appear before the Justices of the County Court of Pleas and Quarter Sessions to be held for the County of Chowan at the Court House in Edenton on the fourth Monday of September next; then and there to testify, and the Truth to say, on behalf of John Robinson in a certain matter of controversy in said Court depending, and then and there to be tried, between John Robinson Plaintiff, and Henry O'Neal Defendant; and this you shall in no wise omit; under the penalty of Fifty Pounds Current Money, Witness William Wilkins for Jas. Blount, Clerk of the said Court, at Edenton the XXIII Day of June Anno Dom. 1782.
William Wilkins for Jas. Blount, Clk.

Robinson Vs O'Neal
To Sept. Court, 1782
Summons for Jos. Whedbee
Executed So Saith William Roberts.

State of North Carolina
To the Sheriff of Chowan County, Greeting:
You are hereby commanded to summons Joseph Whedbee personally to be and appear before the Justices of the County Court of Pleas and Quarter Sessions to be held for the County of Chowan at the Court House in Edenton on the fourth Monday in September next; then and there to testify and the Truth to say, on behalf of John Robinson in a certain Matter of Controversy in the said Court depending, and then and there to be tried, between John Robinson Plaintiff, and Henry O'Neal Defendant; and this you shall in no wise omit; under the Penalty of Fifty Pounds Current Money, Witness William Wilkins for James Blount, Clerk of the said Court, at Edenton the XXVII17th Day of June Anno Dom. 1782.
William Wilkins for Jas. Blount, Clk.

Robinson Vs O'Neal
To Sept. Court 1782
Summons for Dr. Dickinson
Executed So Saith William Roberts

State of North Carolina

Chowan County
Civil Actions

To the Sheriff of Chowan County, Greeting:
You are hereby commanded to summons Samuel Dickinson, Esqr. personally to be and appear before the Justices of the County Court of Chowan at the Court House in Edenton on the fourth Monday of September next; then and there to testify, and the Truth to say, on behalf of John Robinson in a certain Matter of Controversy in the said Court depending, and then and there to be tried, between John Robinson Plaintiff, and Henry O'Neal Defendant; and this you shall in no wise omit; inder the penalty of Fifty Pounds Current Money. Witness William Wilkins for Jas. Blount Clerk of the said Court, at Edenton, the XXIII Day of June Anno Dom. 1782
William Wilkins for Jas. Blount, Clk.

****

Ann Anderson Vs Samuel Kerr
Civil Action [1782]
Chowan County Records

Chowan County Sessions
December Court 1782

To the Worshipfull the Justices of the County Court of Pleas and Quarter Sessions for the County of Chowan now Sitting.

The Claim and Petition of Anne Anderson of Chowan County aforesaid Widow humbly Sheweth unto your Worships that Samuel Kerr Merchant is justly indebted unto her in the Sum of twelve hundred & seventy nine pounds seven shillings four pence Specie, Your Petitioner further sheweth that the said Samuel Kerr hath removed himself, from the United States of America and is Resident in the City of New York within the British Lines or in some of the Countries, Territories subject to the Dominion of the King of great Britain and hath entered to the Premises of the United States of America, Your Petitioner thyerefore humbly Prays that your Worships will be pleased to order that **[Faded]** may be summoned pursuant to the directives of the Act of Assembly in such case made & provided to inquire into the Justice of her Claim and that your Worships will grant her such further relief as she is intitled to by the said Act agreeable to equity and good concurrence, and your Petitioner will ever Pray &c.
Anne Anderson

Edenton 28th Feby 1766

Borrowed and Recd. Of Mrs Ann Anderson Two hundred pounds Sterling which I oblidge me & my heirs &c. to pay on demand with 5 Pr Annum: thereafter sell, paid, Witness My hand
Samuel Kerr

Portsmouth 2nd Decr. 1775

Dear Madam
Agreeable to your desire I herewith Send You Your Negroes Milly & her two Children, Fanny and her child and Betty; I return you my sincere thanks for the use of them and shall send you the rest as soon as I can procure carts. I hope to have the pleasure of Seeing you at Edenton next Month, till then I beg you'll make yourself easy on my Acct as I apprehend no other Danger but confinement in this neighbourhood till some alteration in matters, You may rest Assured that nothing shall prevail on me to take up arms & that I am ever Dear Madam.
Yr. Dutiful & grateful Grnd Son
Samuel Kerr

Mrs Kerr will send you an acct of the other articles here with this & I beg to refer you to her Letter.

To Mrs. Ann Anderson in Edenton

In Consequence of your Letter of this day Whereby you hire to me Twelve of your Slaves Viz, Salisbury, Cate, Hamlett, Taff, Bob, Isaac, Michael, Rose, Hannah, Milly, Mariam & Tereza & their increase during Yr Natural life I hereby oblige my self punctually to pray to you & your order Forty Pounds Viz. Money Pr Annum July & January equally, find them all necessarys pay their Tax &C. & receive you of all Charges Concerning them, **[?]** if I fail this shall enable You to Dispose of the said Slaves at Yr. Pleasure

I am more re4spectfully Madam, Your Most **[?]**
Edenton Decr. 1767

Samuel Kerr.

****

Thomas Harramond Vs. William McDonald
Civil Action [1790]
Chowan County Records

State of North Carolina

To Abner Neale Esqr. Commissioner Greeting:

Know Ye, That We, in confidence of your prudence and circumspection, do empower you to call and cause to come before you, (at such time and place as you shall appoint) Mrs. Elizabeth Tomlinson and her diligently examine on the Holy Evangelists of Almighty God, what she may know in a certain cause now depending in the County Court of Pleas and Quarter Sessions for the County of Chowan between Thomas Harramond Plaintiff and William McDonald Defendant as well on the part of the Plaintiff as the Defendant, And the examinations so by you to be taken, you are to send closed up under your Seal to the County Court of Pleas and Quarter Sessions for the County of Chowan at the Court House in Edenton on the 10th Monday in June next, together with this Writ. Witness Joseph Blount Clerk of the said Court, at Edenton the XXII Day of March in the X[?] Year of American Independence, and in the Year of our lord, one thousand, seven hundred and Ninety.
Jos. Blount, Clk.

Deposition of Mrs. Elizabeth Tomlinson

North Carolina
New Bern 5th June 1790

In obedience to a Commission to me directed from the Court of Chowan County to take the Deposition of Mrs. Elizabeth Tomlinson on behalf Thomas Lee Harrimond against William McDonald in a Suit there depending I have caused Mrs. Tomlinson to appear before and there being duly sworn on the Holy Evangelists deposeth and Saith that she was well acquainted with Mrs. Hardy who was a relation to this Deponant that about Twenty four Years ago when she was at the House of Mrs. Hardy, Henry Harriman being present as well as some of his Children Mrs. Hardy Called

up three of her Young Negroes named Venus, Ned and Prince and said she gave Venus to her Grandson Henry Harriman, Ned to Another Grandson Thomas Lee Harriman and Prince to her neice Nancy Brice and at the same time delivered one of them in the name of the whole to Henry Harriman her Son in Law on behalf of the Children observing that after her death, or before it she chose or thought proper the said Henry Harriman should take them in care for the Children to whom she had thus given, and this Deponant further says that no one was present at the time of the Gift but one Burns (Except the said Henry Harriman & the Children) and she also says that in two or three Months after this Gift she intermarried with a certain Samuel Black, but previous to the intermarriage, a few days, but this Deponant cannot remember how many, the said Mrs. Hardy at the request and on the advice of this Deponant committed to writing the Gift as before mentioned, expressing therein that in case of the death of Nancy Brice that the Negroe Prince was to go to her son Thomas Lee and this Deponant further says that the said Mrs. Hardy executed the said writing in her presence and committed it to her Care & gave as well as this deponant believes, a Copy of it to the said Burns and this Deponant further says that she does not know that Mr. Black knew of the Gift before his marriage, and this deponant further says that three or four Years after her intermarriage Mrs. Black came to New Bern where this Deponant lived and received of this Deponant the Writing or Memorandom before mentioned and further this deponant Saith Not.
Elizabeth Tomlinson
Sworn before me the day & date aforesaid.
Abner Neal, JP

****

Elizabeth Patterson Vs. Michael McKeel
Civil Action [1791]
Chowan County Records

Eliz. Patterson Vs. Michl. McKeel
Writ of Debt
Decem Term 1791
Issd. 29th Novemr 1791
Tho. Iredell, Atto for Pltff
Executed for William Roberts so says Michl Payne, DShff

Chowan County
Civil Actions

State of North Carolina }
Chowan County }

Elizabeth Patterson, Widow by Thos. Iredell her Atto complains of Michael McKeel in custody, &c. of a plea, that he render to the said Elizabeth Patterson the sum of **[?]** Pounds which he the said Michael McKeel owes to and unjustly detains from the Plaintiff for this cause, to wit, That whereas the aforesaid Michael McKeel in the County of Chowan and State aforesaid, by his certain writing obligatory, sealed with his seal, and dated the day of **[Blank]** bound himself to the said Elizabeth in the sum of One hundred Pounds to be paid to the Plaintiff, when the said Michael should be thereunto required; nevertheless the said Michael altho' often required, hath not yet paid the said sum, but doth neglect to pay the same, to the damage of the Plaintiff at One hundred pounds current money; and thereupon she brings Suit. Pledges, &c.
Thos Iredell, Atto for the Pltff.

State of North Carolina

To the Sheriff of Chowan County, Greeting:

You are hereby commanded to take the body of Michael McKeel (Taylor) if to be found in your bailiwick, and him safely keep, so that you have him before the Justices of the County Court of Pleas and Quarter Sessions to be held for the County of Chowan at the Court House in Edenton on the 2nd Monday in Decem. Next; then and there to answer to Elizabeth Patterson of a Plea that he render to her Fifty Pounds Specie which to her he owes & unjustly detains to her damage One hundred pounds. Herein fail not, and have you then and there this writ.

Witness Joseph Blount Clerk of the said Court, at Edenton the 17th day of Septemr in the **[?]** year of our Independence, Anno Dom. 1791.
Joseph Blount, Clk.

State of North Carolina

Know all Men by these Presents, That We Michael McKeel and James Farrow are held and firmly bound unto William Roberts, Sheriff of the County of Chowan in the Sum of One hundred pounds to which payment well and truly to be made, We bind ourselves, our Heirs, Administrators and Assigns, jointly and severally, firmly by these Presents.

Sealed with our Seals, and dated this Twentieth Day of October One thousand seven hundred and ninety one.

The Condition of this Obligation is such, That if the above bounden Michael McKeel do make his personal Appearance before the Justices of the County Court of Pleas and Quarter Sessions, to be held at the Court house in Edenton on the 11th Monday in December then and there to answer unto Elizabeth Patterson of a Plea of Debt and there stand and abide by the Judgment of the said Court, and not depart without Liberty first had and obtained, then the above Obligation to be void, otherwise to remain in full Force and Virtue.
Michl. McKeel (Seal)
James Farrow (Seal)
Signed, Sealed and Delivered in the Presence of
Michl Payne
I William Roberts of Chowan County, do hereby assign the above Obligation and Condition to Elizabeth Patterson the Plaintiff therein named, his Executors and Administrators, to be sued for according to the Statute in such Case made and provided. In Witness whereof, I have hereunto set my Hand and Seal, this 20th Day of October 1791.
For William Roberts
Michl. Payne, DShff

Patterson Vs McKeel
Declr
Chowan County
Dec. Term 1791

State of North Carolina

Know all Men by these Presents, That We Michael McKeel & John Frizzell are held and firmly bound unto William Roberts, Sheriff of the County of Chowan in the Sum of Seventy Pounds to which payment well and truly to be made, We bind ourselves, our Heirs, Administrators and Assigns, jointly and severally, firmly by these Presents. Sealed with our Seals, and dated this Eighth Day of February One thousand seven hundred and ninety two.

The Condition of this Obligation is such, That if the above bounden Michael McKeel do make his personal Appearance before the Justices of

the County Court of Pleas and Quarter Sessions, to be held at the Court House in Edenton on the 11th Monday in March then and there to answer unto Elizabeth Patterson of a Plea of Breach of Covenant & there stand and abide by the Judgment of the said Court, and not depart without Liberty first had and obtained, then the above Obligation to be void, otherwise to remain in full Force and Virtue.
Michl. X McKeel (Seal)
John Frazal (Seal)
Signed, Sealed and Delivered in the Presence of
Michl. Payne

I William Roberts of Chowan County, do hereby assign the above Obligation and Condition to Elizabeth Patterson the Plaintiff therein named, his Executors and Administrators, to be sued for according to the Statute in such Case made and provided. In Witness whereof, I have hereunto set my Hand and Seal, this Eighth Day of February 1792.
For William Roberts
Michl. Payne, DShff

E. Patterson, Writ Vs. M. McKeel, Breach of Covenant
March Term 1792
Issued 5th March 1792
T. Iredell Atto, Pltff
Executed for William Roberts
Michl. Payne, DShff

State of North Carolina
To the Sheriff of Chowan County, Greeting:
You are hereby commanded to take the body of Michael McKeel if to be found in your bailiwick, and him safely keep, so that you have him before the Justices of the County Court of Pleas and Quarter Sessions to be held for the County of Chowan at the Court House in Edenton on the 2nd Monday in March next; then and there to answer unto Elizabeth Patterson of a plea of Breach of Covenant, damage Seventy Pounds &c.

Herein fail not, and have you then and there this writ. Witness Joseph Blount Clerk of the said Court, at Edenton the 17th day of Decem Anno Dom 1791
Jos. Blount, Clk.

I promise to Pay on cause to be paid unto Elizabeth Paterson her order, Exrs., or assigns in the Just and Full Sum of twenty Five Pound Specie twelve Months after Date for Value received as Witness my Hand this First Day January 1785

His
Michel + McKeell
Mark

Test, AS Bryands
Joshua Simons

---

1 Note £31.5 8 years Interest 14-16	£46-1
1 do 25 2 years do 3	28
	£7.4.1
By A/C	£12-10
Order on Mr B	21
Mr Pattersons	20-5-2
53-15-2	£53-15-2
Bal due Mr Patterson	£20-5-10

Miss Elizabeth Patterson

Octor. 27th 1793 To Michael McKeel Dr.

To 1 butter	2.8
To 2 Bushels corn	10.0
To Cash	3.0.0
To 3 pints rum	0.3.0
To 30 days hire, Jack	12.0.0
To 3 cords wood	3.0.0
To Capt Cook	1.5.6
To Mr Cameron	1.4.0
	21.5.2
To Cash	2.0.0
	£23.5.2

Edenton December 11th 1793

I except the within Orders
His
Michl. + McKeel
Mark
July 22nd 1785 Recd. The Sum of Nine Pounds
In Part of the within, Ed. Blount
March 8th 1786 Recd. The sum of Six pounds one Shilling in Part Payment of the within as Pr anno Rendered one By Mr. McKeal
Ed. Blount
2s--96.1
Bal 15.1
5-19
£2s
Order Mr. McKeal

Sir/ please to pay Mr. Edmund Blount Twenty one Pounds Currency, it being due me for Negro hire for the year 1784, and Much Oblige.
Your humble Servant

Edenton Febr 20th 1785 - Elizabeth Patterson
For Mr. Michl McKeel

1782 Mrs Elizabeth Patterson
To Michael McKeel Dr

March 26th To 1 Gown pattern	£10.0
To 1 Skirt	2.10
	£12.10

Patterson Vs. McKeel
Judgt.

This Memorandum of an agreement made and entered into at Edenton this twenty fourth of March in the year of our Lord one thousand seven hundred & Eighty three by & [?] Elizabeth Patterson of the one part & Michael McKeel of the other part

Witnesseth

That the said Elizabeth Patterson for & in Consideration of the sum of Nineteen Pounds ten Shillings specie paid to her on the Twenty fifth day of December next insuing hath hired unto the said Michael McKeel a Certain Negroe fellow Called John by trade a Taylor until the said Twenty fifth of December next insuing the said Mrs. Eliz. Patterson to find his summer Cloathes & pay his levys, In Witness whereof We have hereunto set our hands & seals at Edenton the day & year above mentioned.

His
Michael + McKeel (Seal)
Mark

Signed & Sealed In Presence of
Willm. Blair
Elizabeth Patterson

****

Thomas Harramond Vs. James De Camp
Civil Action [1791]
Chowan County Records

Tho. S. Harramond Vs. James DeCamp
Commission
June Term 1791

State of North Carolina

To John Fonville Greeting:

Know Ye, That We, in confidence of your prudence and circumspection do empower you to call and cause to come before you, (at such day, time and place as you shall appoint) Elizabeth Tomlinson and her diligently examine on the Holy Evangelists of Almighty God, what they may know in a certain cause now depending in the County Court of Pleas and Quarter Sessions for the County of Chowan between Thomas Harramond Plaintiff and James DeCamp Defendant as well on the part of the Plaintiff as of the Defendant, And the examinations so by you to be taken, you are to send closed up under your Seal to the County Court of Pleas and Quarter Sessions for the County of Chowan at the Court House at Edenton on the 2nd Monday in June next, together with this Writ. Witness Joseph Blount

Clerk of the said Court, at Edenton the XXXth day of March in the XV12th year of American Independence, and in the year of our Lord one thousand seven hundred and Ninety One.
Jos. Blount

North Carolina
Newbern 6th June 1791

To Obedience to a Commission to me directed from the County of Chowan County to take the Deposition of Mrs. Elizabeth Tomlinson on behalf of Thomas Lee Harramond against James DeCamp in a suit there depending & have caused Mrs. Elizabeth Tomlinson to appeare before me and she being duly Sworn on the Holy Evangelists deposeth and Saith that she was well acquainted with Mrs. Hardy who was a relation to this deponant that about twenty four years ago when she was at the House of Mrs. Hardy, Henry Harramond Senr. Being present as well as some of his Children Mrs. Hardy Called up three of her young Negroes Named Venus, Ned, and Prince and said she gave Venus to her Grandson Henry Harramond & Ned to Another Grandson Thos. Lee Harramond and Prince to her Niece Fanny Brice and at the same time delivered one of them in the name of the whole to Henry Harramond Senr. Her son in Law on behalf of the Children Observing that after her Death or before it if she chose or thought proper the said Henry Harramond should take them in care for the Children to whom she had there given and this Deponant further says that she was present at the time of the gift but one Burns (Except the Sd.Henry Harramond and the Children) and she also says that in the two or three Months after this Gift she intermarried with a certain Samuel Black, but previous to the intermarriage, a few days but this Deponant cannot remember how many the Sd. Mrs. Hardy at the request and on the advice of this Deponant Committed it to writing, the Gift as before Mentioned expressing there in that in case of the Death of Nancy Brice that the Negroe Prince was to go to her son Tho. Lee and this Deponant further says that the said Mrs. Hardy executed the Sd. writing in her presence and Committed it to her care & gave as well as this Deponant believes a Copy of it to the Sd. Burns and this Deponant further says that she does not know that Mr. Black knew of the gift before his marriage and this Deponant says that three or four years after her intermarriage Mr. Black Came to Newbern where this Deponant liv'd and receiv'd of this Deponant the writing or memorandum before mentioned and further this Deponant Saith not.

Elizabeth Tomlinson
Sworn before me the day & date aforesaid
John Fonville, JP

****

Smith Vs. Jeffreys
Civil Action [1795]
Chowan County Records

Smith Vs. Jefferys
Bail Bond
Baill Bond of Christopher Jaffreys

North Carolina }
Pasquotank Province } SS

Know all Men by these Presents that we Christafor Jaffors, Joshua Markham [?] and Province Aforesaid are Firmly bound unto Robert Kalbors[?] Esqr precinct Marshall of the said Province Afforesaid in the full & just Sum of One thousand Pounds Current Money of the Province Aforesaid to which payment to well and Truly to be Made We Bind us & each of our Heirs, Exrs., Admnrs. Joyntly and Severally by these Present, Seald with our Seals and dated This the 9th Day of May 1795.

The Condition of this Obligation is such that if the above Bound Christafor Jaffreys Doth make his Personall Appearance at the next Court to be held for the said Government at the Court House in Edenton on the Last Tusday in July next then and there to Answer to suit brought against him by Burg[?] Smith and not Depart without the Leave of the said Court then this obligation to be void and of no Affect otherwise to stand and remain in full force, Power & vertue.
Christofor Jeffreys & Joshua Markham
Sind, Seald And Delivered in the Presents of
Ged[?] Rowll
His
Edward E Wharton
Mark

****

Chowan County
Civil Actions

Henry Harramond Vs. Daniel Young
Civil Action [1796]
Chowan County Records

Henry Harramond Vs. Daniel Young

North Carolina }
Newbern April 30th 1796 }

To Obedience to a Commission to me directed from the County of Chowan County to take the Deposition of Mrs. Elizabeth Tomlinson on behalf of Thomas Lee Harramond against James DeCamp in a suit there depending & have caused Mrs. Elizabeth Tomlinson to appeare before me and she being duly Sworn on the Holy Evangelists deposeth and Saith that she was well acquainted with Mrs. Hardy who was a relation to this deponant that about twenty four years ago when she was at the House of Mrs. Hardy, Henry Harramond Senr. Being present as well as some of his Children Mrs. Hardy Called up three of her young Negroes Named Venus, Ned, and Prince and said she gave Venus to her Grandson Henry Harramond & Ned to Another Grandson Thos. Lee Harramond and Prince to her Niece Fanny Brice and at the same time delivered one of them in the name of the whole to Henry Harramond Senr. Her son in Law on behalf of the Children Observing that after her Death or before it if she chose or thought proper the said Henry Harramond should take them in care for the Children to whom she had there given and this Deponant further says that she was present at the time of the gift but one Burns (Except the Sd. Henry Harramond and the Children) and she also says that in the two or three Months after this Gift she intermarried with a certain Samuel Black, but previous to the intermarriage, a few days but this Deponant cannot remember how many the Sd. Mrs. Hardy at the request and on the advice of this Deponant Committed it to writing, the Gift as before Mentioned expressing there in that in case of the Death of Nancy Brice that the Negroe Prince was to go to her son Tho. Lee and this Deponant further says that the said Mrs. Hardy executed the Sd. writing in her presence and Committed it to her care & gave as well as this Deponant believes a Copy of it to the Sd. Burns and this Deponant further says that she does not know that Mr. Black knew of the gift before his marriage and this Deponant says that three or four years after her intermarriage Mr. Black Came to Newbern where this Deponant liv'd and receiv'd of this Deponant the writing or memorandum before mentioned and further this Deponant Saith not, and this Deponant further Saith that Nancy Brice the above Mentioned did dye before the above mentioned Thomas Lee.

Signed Elizabeth Tomlinson
Sworn before me the day & date aforesaid
William Tisdale, JP

State of North Carolina, Tyrell County

By an order of Court to me directed We have met According to appointment at Mr. John Armistead's to take the Deposition of George Matthews he being duly Sworn on the Holy Evangelists of Almighty God Deposeth & Sayeth that in the year 1779 that Capt Richard Forbes told me that he had made a demand of a negroe boy Named Prince from Mr. Samuel Black who had married the Widow Hardy of Bertie County which negro Prince had been given to his Wife, Sister Nancy Brice, she died young being unmarried and by an Instrument of Writing which I saw that the above boy was given to Miss Nancy Brice by her aunt Mrs. Hardy but if she, Nancy, died without heir the boy was to go to Thomas Lee, Son of Mrs. Hardy and further this Deponant Sayeth not, Sworn to before me this Thirty first Day of March 1796.
George Matthews
William Fergason, JP

Mr John Hamelton the 16th day of April 1796 and Mrs. Young
Thomas Satterwhite
Colo. Hamilton, Edenton
John Hamilton, Esqr., Edenton
Executed on Mr John Hambleton the nineteenth day of March 1796

Sir

You are desired to attend at the Town of Plymouth, Tyrell County at Mr. George Matthews deposition will be taken of Mr. Armistead's House at 2 Oclock afternoon the Thirty First day this Month in a Suit Henry Harramond Agt. Daniel Young of Edenton March ye 19th 1796
Henry Harromond

Chowan County
Civil Actions

Sir,

The deposition of Mrs. McCartney and Mrs. Tomlinson are to be taken at Newbern Saturday the Thirtieth this month at the House of Capt Forbes at Twelve Oclock Noon in a Suit Henry Harramond Plaintiff & Capt Daniel Young is Defendant and you are desired to give your Attendance and am Yr Servt
April 16th 1796
Henry Harramond.

****

John Vs. John Johnston
Civil Action [1797]
Chowan County Records

John Vs. John Johnston

Samuel Johnston maketh Oath that he has known the Mother of the Plaintiff fifty years or thereabouts in the Capacity of a Slave in the Family of Penelope Dawson and her Father Gabriel Johnston deceased, that he has understood that he came to the possession of the said Gabriel Johnston by his intermarriage with the Widow of Geo. Phennery Esqr. who had been a Resident in one of the Bahama Islands but whether Mr. Phenny brought the Mother of the Plaintiff from the Bahamas or acquired her in this Country, this Deponant does not know nor did he ever hear till within a short time past that she or her Children set up any Pretentions to their Freedom.
Sam Johnston
Sworn to in open Court
April 11th 1797
Test Will Blair, Clk

****

Elisha Jones Vs. John Vail
Civil Action [1798]
Chowan County Records

Elisha Jones Vs. Jno Vail
To September Term, 1798

Chowan County
Civil Actions

WS

State of North Carolina } September Term 1798
Chowan County Court }

Elisha Jones Complains of John Vail in Custody &c for this Cause Towit That Whereas the said John Vail on the first day of April 1798 at Edenton, the County aforesaid was indebted to the said Elisha Jones in the sum of Fifty Pounds Current Money for work and Labour before that time done & performed by a Negro Man Slave of the said Elisha Jones, On board a Vessell of the said John Vail at his special instance & request, and the said John being so indebted in consideration there of afterwards Towit on the same day and year aforesaid at Edenton in the County aforesaid took up himself and faithfully the said Elisha, that he the said John, should well and Truly pay unto him the said Fifty pounds, he should be thereto afterward required, Nevertheless he hath not paid the same nor any part thereof altho Often requested so to do but hath hitherto refused & Still doth refuses to pay the same to the damage of the said Elisha Jones. Therefore he sues &c.
Pledges
Jno Den }
Richd Fen }

****

Icabod Jordan Vs. Levendure
Civil Action [1798]
Chowan County Records

Chowan County }

You are hereby Commanded to take the Body of Levendure and have him to appear before me or some other Justice for this County to answer a complaint of Icabod Jordan for trading with his Negro, herein fail not to make due Returns of this Warrant, Sworn under my hand this 27th, April 1798.
W J Skinner
To any Lawful Officer }
To Execute and Return }
I otherwise **[?]** to Serve this Warrant in the Behalf of me Jacob Jordan

---

Judgment in favour of the Plaintiff for the sum of ten pounds with Costs given this 19th May 1798
W. Skinner

The Defendant appeals for the above Judgmt. And gives Nicholas Stallings as Security
Nichl. Stallings
Executed by Willy Ming

****

Unknown Vs. Unknown
Civil Action [1798]
Chowan County Records

State of North Carolina }
Tyrell County }

Appeared Mathew Brickhous Before me and Declared on the holy Evangelist of Almighty God that he happened in Company with John Sedguike and he heard him say that his Wife had gave away Sundray Negroes to Sundray Children before he married her and them that his wife gave before he Married her he lay'd no Clame to but the Children that the Old wench had sence he was Married he Clamed as his own property and amongst the rest his wife gave a negro girl By the Name of Dinah to the wife of Samuel Spruill By the Name of Ann & Joseph Jinnett had taken his Negro away and he wanted Samuel Spruill to take his negro away and he said that he shood not as long as his Mother in law lived and said that Samuel Spruill left Corne Two years for the support of said negro as he was being it from his plantation up the greate River about forty yeares agoe.

His
Matthew M Brickhous
Marke

Sworn to Before me 15th day of December 1798
Henry Norman, JP

****

Sarah Hoskins Vs. William Badham
Civil Action [1799]
Chowan County Records

Sarah Hoskins Vs. William Badham
Case
To September Term, 1799
W.S.

Mr. William Badham
To Sarah Hoskins Dr.
To One Year hire of Negro Mingo ending 1st day of April 1798
£30.0.0

State of North Carolina } September Term 1799
Chowan County }

Sarah Hoskins Complaines of William Badham in Custody &c for his Cause Towit For that whereas the said William on the 1st day of January in the year of our Lord 1799 in the County of Chowan, was indebted to the said Sarah in the sum of thirty pounds Current money, for the hire of Negro Mingo for the year 1798 (towit said Negro, the said Sarah hired to the said William, at his Instance and request) and the said William being so indebted to the said Sarah, in consideration thereof took upon himself, and than and there Faithfully promised to the said Sarah, to pay her the aforesaid sum of Money which he should be thereto afterwards required, Nevertheless the said William not regarding his said Promise and [?] Contriving and fraudulently pretending how to injure and Defraud the said Sarah, hath not paid her the said sum of money, or any part thereof (Although often requested) but hath hitherto referred, & still doth refuse to her damage **[Blank]** &c.
W Slade for Pltffs Atto
Pledge &c.
John Doe }
Richd Fen }

****

Chowan County
Civil Actions

Mason Miller Vs. Honore Neil
Civil Action [1800]
Chowan County Records

Narr. In Case
M Miller agt Hon Neil
1806

Chowan County SS
March Term 1800

Mason Miller by his Atto complains of Honore Neil Mercht of a Pleas of Trespass &c wherefore & which the said Honore owes to the Pltff under the Act of Assy 1791. C. .4, wherein it is enacted that if any person shall entice or persuade any Servant or Slave to absent him or herself from his or her owners Service or who shall harbour or maintain under any pretence whatever any runaway servant or Slave shall for any such offense forfeit & pay to the owner of such Servant or Slave the Sum of £50 &c & whereas the said Mason Complains that the said Honore did on the **[Blank]** day of **[Blank]** prior to the **[?]** of the writ entice & persuade two Negroes called Robin & George the property of the Pltff to absent themselves from the said Mason's Service & harboured & maintained the said Robin & George Negroes aforesaid for the space of Months contrary to the said Act of Assy &c. Nevertheless &c whereupon &c the said Mason avers **[?]** according to **[?]** & thereupon the said Mason Causes Suit &c of the in the Court **[?]**.
J H Hamilton
J Doe }
R Roe }

Narr indebt
Under state
Mason Miller Vs. Honore Neil, 1800

North Carolina } March Term 1800
Chowan County }

Mason by his Atto complains of Honore Neil, Mercht, of a Plea of Trespass on the Case &c wherefore ~~Which the said Honore owes to Plff~~

under the act of Assy, 1791.C.4 wherein it is enacted that if any person shall entice or persuade any Servant or Slave to absent him or herself from his or her owners Service or who shall harbour or maintain under any pretence whatever any runaway Servant or Slave shall for every such offense forfeit & pay the owner of such Servant or Slave the ~~Sum of Fifty~~ &c Damage &c and whereas the said Mason complains that the said Honore did on the **[Blank]** day of **[Blank]** prior to Inspection of the Writ entice & persuade two negroes called Robin & George the property of the Plaintiff did absent themselves from the said Mason's Service & harboured & maintained the said Robin & George, Negroes aforesaid for the space of Months contrary to said Act of Assy & Nevertheless whereupon the said Mason avers & **[Blank]** according **[?]** to said Writ & thereupon the said Mason brings suit to the Worshipfull Court.
JH Hamilton
Jno Doe }
R Roe }

****

Charles Roberts, Sheriff Vs. Negro Dick
Civil Action [1801]
Chowan County Records

Charles Roberts, Sheriff Vs. Negro Dick
Subpoena
March 1807
Executed on William Hall
Jno Fife, Constable

State of North Carolina
To the Sheriff of Chowan County, Greeting:
You are hereby commanded to summon William Hall & Edward Hall personally to be and appear before the Justices of the County Court of Pleas and Quarter Sessions now fitting for the County of Chowan, at the Court House in Edenton, Immediately, then and there to testify and the truth to say, in behalf of the Reputed owners of Negro Dick in a certain matter of controversy in the said Court depending, and then and there to be tried, wherein Charles Roberts, Sheriff & als are Plaintiffs and Negro Dicks owners are Defendants. And this you shall in no wise omit, under the penalty by law enjoined. Witness Elisha Norfleet, Clerk of the said

Chowan County
Civil Actions

Court, at Edenton, the 12th day of March in the 25th year of our Independence, Anno Dom. 1801
E Norfleet, Clk

Filed March 9th
1802

State of North Carolina }
Hertford County } May Term 1801

Present the Worshipfull Lewis Brown. Isaac Carter, Godwin Cotton and others there Follows

Be it Remembered that hereto fore Viz on February Term in the year of our Lord One Thousand Seven hundred & ninety nine before the Justices of the County Court of Pleas & quarter Sessions held for Hertford County came Richard Williamson by Peter Brown his Attorney & brought here in to Court his Certain Bill against William Bynum of the said County in a Plea that he render unto him One Negro boy Slave Named West of the Value of Three hundred pounds which from him he unjustly detains to his damage One hundred pounds (no declaration filed in Writing) and now at this day to wit on the Fourth Monday in February in the year of Our Lord One thousand Seven hundred and ninety nine at the Court House in Winton before the Court aforesaid came the said William Bynum by James H. Keys his Attorney and plead now [?] and Act of Lein Release (No plea filed in Writing) and of this he puts himself on the country and the said Richard Williamson does so likewise, afterwards the proceedings was Continued by the parties aforesaid until the fourth Monday in May in the year of Our Lord One thousand eight hundred and One when before the Court aforesaid at the Court House in Winton Came the aforesaid Richard Williamson as well as the aforesaid William Bynum by their Attorneys aforesaid and the Jurors being summoned & Sworn to by the issue aforesaid say Upon their Oath that the Defendant does detain the Negro West of the Value of two hundred & thirty seven Pounds six shillings that there is no release and that the Act of [?] does not bar and assess the Plaintiff's Damage to [?] Costs, Therefore it is Considered that the said Richard Williamson Receive against the said William Bynum his said damage Assessed by the Jury and the Sum of five pounds Sixteen Shillings and Sixpence Adjudged by the Court for his Charges and that the said Richard Williamson have execution thereof, whereupon the said William

Bynum being dissatisfied prayed an Appeal to the Superior Court to be held for the District of Edenton at the Court House in Edenton on the sixth day of October next and tendered bond with Charles Skenner & Ethelred Bull Security in the sum of five Hundred pounds entry of which & the execution thereof being made it was Ordered that all proceedings there in before Mentioned be Stayed,
Copy
Test, N Harrell, Clk

West &C to	.14
Tax /2 Suba /	8
3 Cent 3/ Trial 7/6	16
Appl of Afd Bond 6/	14
Tax on Appl	10
Shff	14
PB Atto	2
	£5.16.6

****

Benjamin Coffield Vs. John B. Bennet
Civil Action [1802]
Chowan County Records

Benjamin Coffield Vs. John B. Bennett
Writ in Case
March Term 1803
Issd 12th Feby, Tax 5/ Pd
Executed Chas Roberts, Shff

State of North Carolina
To the Sheriff of Chowan County, Greeting:
We command you to take the body of John B. Bennett if to be found in your bailiwick, and him safely keep, so that you have him before the Justices of the County Court of Pleas and Quarter Sessions, to be held at the Court House in Edenton, in the County of Chowan on the second Monday in March next, then and there to answer unto Benjamin Coffield of a plea of Trespass on the Case &c Damage one Hundred pounds &c.

Herein fail not, and have you then and there this Writ, and how you have executed the same. Witness Elisha Norfleet, Clerk of the said Court, at Edenton, this XVIIIth day of December in the year of our Lord, 1802 and in the XXV[?] year of our Independence.
E Norfleet, Clk.

I promise to Be Security for the Costs of this Suit under the Act of Assembly February 1803
Abraham Norfleet

Mr. B. Coffield
I have just received by your boy Jack three Barrells of Corn which makes 50 Bblls that I have received & remain Dear Sir your most Obt. Servt.
August 5th 1802
Jno. B. Bennett.

Mr. John B. Bennett to Benj Coffield	Dr.
1802	
Augt. 2 To 12 Barrels of Corn @ 3	18.0.0
Augt 4th to 21 Barrels of Corn @ 3	31.10.0
Augt 5th To 17 Barrells of Corn @ 3	25.10.0
	£75.0.0

Intrest 10 Months £3.15
75
£78.15

Judgment	£78.15.0
P. Tax	5
Writ & Tax	19
2 Continu 3/	6
2 Subpoenas 1/6	3
Deter & [?]	11.3
	£1.19.3
Atto	2
Sheriff	16.6
	£4.15.9

A Small, John Coffield

****

Nathaniel Brinn Vs. Jethro Benton et als
Civil Action [1802]
Chowan County Records

Nathaniel Vs Jethro Benton
Vends Expons
December Term 1802
Satisfies Jethro Sumner
Rec'd the within Judgment for Nathl Brinn
Saml McGuire

State of North Carolina, Chowan County
To the Sheriff of Gates County, Greeting:
Whereas we by our Writ have commanded you, that of the goods and chattels, lands and tenements of Jethro Benton & Miles Benton if to be found in your bailiwick, you should cause to be made the sum of Fifty one Pounds Eighteen Shillings & two pence whereof the said Jethro Benton & Miles Benton are convicted and liable, as appears to us of record, besides your own fees for this service; and that you should have those monies before the Justices of our Inferior Court of Pleas and Quarter Sessions, at our next Court, to be held for the county of Chowan, at the Court House in Edenton, on the second Monday in Septr next; then and there to render to the said Nathaniel Brinn his debt, damages and costs as aforesaid; and you at that day returned on the said writ to you directed, that you had levied on two Negroes & no Sale for the want of a bid: We do therefore command you, that you again expose to sale the property aforesaid, by you levied on, so that you have the money aforesaid before our Justices of our Inferior Court of Pleas and Quarter Sessions, to be held at the Court House in Edenton, [?] year of the Independence of the said State Anno Dom 1802.
Issued the 22nd day of September 1802
E. Norfleet

Judjment	£47.3
Clerk	£2.2.3
JH Plf's Atto	2
Sheriff Chowan	16.8
	4.18.11

52.1.11

****

Charles Roberts Vs. Arthur Howe
Civil Action [1807]
Chowan County Records

Charles Roberts Vs Arthur Howe
Fi Fa
March Term 1807

State of North Carolina
To the Coroner of Chowan County, Greeting:
You are hereby commanded, that of the goods and Chattels, lands and tenements of Arthur Howe (if to be found in your bailiwick) you cause to be made the sum of Three Hundred & Sixty Pounds Ten Shillings & Four pence which lately in the County Court of Pleas and Quarter Sessions held for Chowan County, Charles Roberts recovered against said Arthur Howe for debt, and also the sum of Four Pounds five Shillings & nine pence for his damages, by reason of the detention of the said debt, and for the costs and charges by him in his Suit expended, whereof the said Arthur Howe is convicted and liable as to us appears of record. And have you the said monies before the Justices of the said Court, to be held for the said County, at the Court House in Edenton, on the second Monday in March next, then and there to render to the said Charles Roberts for his debt, damages and costs and charges aforesaid. And have you then and there this Writ. Witness Elisha Norfleet, Clerk of the said Court, the 11th day of December in the XXXIth year of the Independence of the said State, Anno Dom. 1806
E Norfleet, Clk

Mr. Elisha Norfleet, Clerk of County Court

Dear Sir,
I am willing to pay Intrest on Mr. Robert's Judgment against me, as he has stay'd the Execution, you will therefore pleas to Enter it on the Docket -- the Intrest to be paid from the 1st Day of Judgment.
March 13th 1807

Chowan County
Civil Actions

Arthur Howe

Levied on the following property Belonging to Arthur Howe at the Instance of Charles Roberts Vizt. Negroes, Nancy, Joan, Dave, the following House Hold Furniture, One Bed, two Matrasses, two Bed Steads, one Dish, one Tea Table, Spits & Kitchen Furniture, one Horse, and on the Surplus of the property which is Mortgaged to Docter John Beasley after paying up his Debt & Stayed by Consent of the Plaintiff.
Myles O'Malley

Judgment	£360.10.4
Interest	6
	£366.10.4
Clerk	£1.15.3
Atto JBS	2
Coroner PPL	0.10.6

****

Edward Tilghman Vs. James Granbery
Civil Action [1803]
Chowan County Records

Edwd. Tilghman Vs. James Granbery
Vends Expons
June Term 1803
Stayde By the Plaintiff's Agent
Chas Roberts, Shff

State of North Carolina
To the Sheriff of Chowan County, Greeting:
Whereas we by our writ have commanded you, that of the goods and chattels, lands and tenements of James Granbury, Esqr. if to be found in your bailiwick, you should cause to be made the sum of two Hundred Pounds with Interest from 14th Novr. 1800 untill paid whereof the said James Granbery is convicted and liable, as appears to us of record, besides your own fees for this service; and that you should have those monies

before the Justices of our Inferior Court of Pleas and Quarter Sessions, at our next Court, to be held for the County of Chowan at the Court House in Edenton on the second Monday in Septr 1802 next; then and there to render to the said Edward Tilghman Assignee for his debt, damages, and costs as aforesaid; and you at that day returned on the said Writ to you directed, that you had levied on Negroes Frank, Esther & Betty, Children of Bess & Sale Postponed by the agent of Pltff: We do therefore command you, that you again expose to sale the property aforesaid, by you levied on, so that you have the money aforesaid before our Justices of our Inferior Court of Pleas and Quarter Sessions, to be held at the Court in Edenton on the second Monday in June next; to render to the said Edward Tilghman Assignee for his debt, damages and costs as aforesaid. Herein fail not; and have you then and there this Writ. Witness Elisha Norfleet, Clerk of the said Court, at Edenton the XXVI day of March in the XX**[?]** year of the Independence of the said State Anno Dom 1803. Issued the 16th day of May 1803
E. Norfleet, Clk

Judgment £200 with Int. from 14th Novr. 1800 untill paid
Clerk & Tax £1.17.9

****

Nehemiah Batemans Vs. William Rombough
Civil Action [1804]
Chowan County Records

Nehemiah Batemans Vs Wm Rombough
Vends Expons
September Term 1804
Countermanded By A Miller **[Millen?]**
Chas Roberts, Shff

State of North Carolina
To the Sheriff of Chowan County, Greeting:
Whereas we by our writ have commanded you, that of the goods and chattels, lands and tenements of William Rombough if to be found in your bailiwick, you should cause to be made the sum of Sixty Pounds Fifteen Shillings for Debt & three & nine pounds for this writ whereof the said William Rombough is convicted and liable, as appears to us of record,

besides your own fees for this service; and that you should have those monies before the Justices of our Inferior Court of Pleas and Quarter Sessions, at our next Court, to be held for the County of Chowan, at the Court House in Edenton, on the second Monday next; then and there to render to the said Nehemiah Batemans Executers for their debt, damages and costs as aforesaid; and you at that day returned on the said Writ to you directed, that you had levied on one Negroe Boy Named George & not sold by consent: We do therefore command you, that you again expose to sale the property aforesaid, by you levied on, so that you have the money aforesaid before our Justices of or Inferior Court of Pleas and Quarter Sessions, to be held at the Court House in Edenton, on the second Monday in September next; to render to the said Nehemiah Batemans Executors for his debt, damages and costs as aforesaid. Herein fail not; and have you then and there this writ. Witness Elisha Norfleet, Clerk of the said Court, at Edenton, the 16th day of June in the 28th year of the Independence of the said State, Anno Dom 1804. Issued 16th day of August 1804.
E Norfleet, Clk

Judgment	£60.15
Clerk for this ats	3.9
	£60.18.9
Satisfied to E Norfleet $78.75	39.7.6
	£21.11.3

****

Daniel McClannen Vs. John B. Griffin
Civil Action [1804]
Chowan County Records

Daniel McClannen Vs. John B. Griffin
September Term 1804

Chowan County SS.
September Term 1804

Daniel McClannen complains of John B Griffin in custody &c. for that whereas on the **[Blank]** day of **[Blank]** in the year 1804 the said John for and in consideration of the sum of £125 currency to him in hand paid by the said Daniel did bargain & sell unto him the said Daniel a certain

negro Slave without making known to the said Daniel the unsoundness & debility called Lelvey in consequence of which consideration money the said Slave, John implied warranted the said negro to be sound & firm & became bound to make satisfaction to the said Daniel if the said Negro Slave was unsound at the time of the sale -- Now the said Negro woman Slave was unsound at the time of sale which was entirely unknown to the said Daniel and nevertheless the said John, altho often requested refuses to make compensation to the said Daniel for the deceit & imposition in the said sale, Wherefore he brings suit &c.
Jos. Skinner, Clk

****

Robert Jordan Vs. Samuel Dickinson
Civil Action [1806]
Chowan County Records

Robt. Jordan Vs. Saml. Dickinson
Acct of sale of 3 Negroes

Sir, I find a Mistake in the Settlement between you and Mr Williams, I find a Mistake of five pounds which I Expect was on acct, the Negro boy Lennon **[Lennox?]** which I have sent on to Mr Blauer to stop it out of the £25 pounds, I suppose you did Not acct for in your Settlement, you will pleas settle the business with Mr Blauer and in so doing you will oblige your, C. Etheridge
Acct 12th 1806

Sales of Three Negroes Sold by Executors belonging to the Estate of Samuel Dickinson Esqr Acct to Satisfy Robert Jordan's [?] against the said Estate, Edenton 8th August 1805

George To Mrs. Eliz P. Dickinson			£25.10
Perthena To	""	""	20.10
Frank	""	""	26.1.0
			£72.1.0
Judgment & Cost			67.6.3
Due Exrs			£4.14.9

72: 1.0
<u>62.3.0</u>
<u>£9.18.0</u>
<u>4.14.9</u>
£5.3.3

****

John Oxley Vs. David Gaskins et als
Civil Action [1807]
Chowan County Records

Oxley Vs. Gaskins
Vend Exp, Fi Fa
Chowan Supr Court
March Term 1808
Sattisfyed, Wm. Watson, Bertie

State of North Carolina
To the Sheriff of **[Blank]** County, Greeting:
Whereas, we by our writ, commanded you that of the goods and chattels, lands and tenements of David Gaskins, Johnston Demsey & James Mohun (in your bailiwick) you should cause to be made the sum of Twenty eight pounds nine shillings & two pence which lately in our Superior Court of Law at Edenton, John Oxley recovered against them as well for Damages which he sustained by reason of certain trespasses &c. as for the costs and charges by him in his suit in that behalf expended, whereof the said David, Johnston & James are convicted and liable at to us appears of record; besides your own fees for that service, and that you should have the said money before the Judges of our said Court, at Edenton, on the 1st Monday after the 4th Monday of September next, after the fourth day of April in the year of our Lord one thousand eight hundred and seven to render to the said John Oxley his damages, costs and Charges aforesaid: And you at that day returned on the said writ, that you had levied the same on one Negro boy which remains in your hands unsold for want of Bidders. We do therefore command you, that you again expose to sale the chattels by you so as aforesaid levied upon, so that you have the said money and 9 shillings for accruing costs, before the Judges of our said Court, at Edenton, on the first Monday after the fourth Monday of March next, and

we do command you further, that of the goods and chattels, land and tenements of the said David, Johnston & James in your bailiwick, you cause to be made the residue of the said damages, costs and charges, and that you have the said money before the Judges of our said Court, at Edenton, on the day aforesaid, to render to the said John Oxley his damages, costs and charges aforesaid; and have you then and there this writ. Witness William Blair, Clerk of our said Court, at Edenton, the Ninth day of October in the XXXIInd year of our Independence, Anno Domimi 1807
Will Blair, Clk

Damages	£4.0.0
Clk & Tax	5.6.
Atto, WS	5.0.0
Sheriff	2.15
Witness	11.8.2
	£28.9.2
Accruing Costs	9
	£28.18.2

Recd on this Exor £5.15 Clks fees

****

Josiah Collins Vs. Arthur Howe
Civil Action [1807]
Chowan County Records

Jos: Collins Vs. Arthur Howe
Vends Expons
March Term 1807

Of the sum of one
State of North Carolina
To the Sheriff of Chowan County, Greeting:
Whereas we by our writ have commanded you, that of the goods and chattels, lands and tenements of Arthur Howe in your baliwick, you should cause to be made the sum of Two hundred pounds to be discharged on payment of one hundred pounds, with Interest from the first May 1799 till paid whereof the said Arthur Howe is convicted and liable, as appears to us of record, Besides your own fees for this service; and that you should have

those monies before the Justices of our Inferior Court of Pleas and Quarter Sessions, at our next Court, to be held for the County of Chowan at the Court House in Edenton on the second Monday in September next; then and there to render to the said Josiah Collins his debt, damages and costs as aforesaid; and you at that day returned on the said writ to you directed, that you had levied on one Boy by the Name of Step & the Sale postponed by Docter Beasley, who is the Plaintiff infact, untill further Orders we do therefore command you, that you again expose to sale the property aforesaid, by you levied on, so that you have the money aforesaid before our Justices of our Inferior Court of Pleas and Quarter Sessions, to be held at the Court House in Edenton on the second Monday in March next; to render to the said Josiah Collins for his debt, damages and costs as aforesaid. Herein fail not, and have you then and there this writ. Witness Elisha Norfleet, Clerk of the said Court, at Edenton the 11th day of December in the XXXIth year of the Independence of the said State Anno Dom. 1806. Issued 26th day February 1807.
E. Norfleet, Clk

The Sale of Negro Boy Step for bid by Jno Blount which Claims the said boy by Mortgage and Josiah Collins who says he is Pltff acknowledges himself Satisfied & all Cost paid by Jno Blount
Will Roberts, DShff

Judgment £200 to be discharged on the payment of the sum of 100 with Interest from 1st May 1799 till paid

Clerk	2.2
Atto	2
Shff	10.6

****

Officers Vs. John McFarland et als
Civil Action [1807]
Chowan County Records

Officers Vs. McFarland
Vend Exp

Chowan County
Civil Actions

Fi Fa for Costs
Chowan Supr Court
March Term 1808
Not Satisfied for want of bidders
Gab. Bailey, Sheriff, Pasquotank

State of North Carolina

To the Sheriff of Pasquotank County, Greeting:

Whereas John McFarland & William Stott (in your bailiwick) you should cause to be made the sum of Nine Pounds ten Shillings which lately in our Superior Court of Law at Edenton, was taxed & adjudged to the Officers of our said Court as the Costs and charges of a suit there brought by the said John McFarland against John Wilroy whereof the said John McFarland & William Stott are convicted and liable as to us appears of record; besides your own fees for that service, and that you should have the said money before the Judges of our said Court, at Edenton, on the Sixth day of October next, after the XIXth day of April in the year of our Lord one thousand eight hundred and six to render to the said Officers their costs and charges aforesaid: and you at that day returned on the said writ, that you had levied the same on One negro belonging to the said William Stott which remains in your hands unsold for want of Bidders We do therefore command you, that you expose to sale the chattels by you so as aforesaid levied upon, so that you have the said money and 19 shillings for accruing costs, before the Judges of our said Court, at Edenton, on the first Monday after the fourth Monday of March next, and we do command you further, that of the goods and chattels, lands and tenements of the said John McFarland & William Stott in your bailiwick, you cause to be made the residue of the said costs and charges, and that you have the said money before the Judges of our said Court, at Edenton, on the day aforesaid, to render to the said Officers their costs and charges aforesaid; and have you then and there this writ. Witness William Blair, Clerk of our said Court, at Edenton, the ninth day of October in the XXXIInd year of our Independence, Anno Domini 1807.

Will Blair, Clk.

Clerk & Tax	£3.17
Attorney	5
Sheriff	13
	£9.10

Accruing Costs 19
£10.9

****

Edwin Lisles Vs. John B. Hunter
Civil Action [1807]
Chowan County Records

Lisle H. Ramsay, Pltff in fact vs. Hunter
Vend Exp, Fi Fa
Chowan Supr. Court
September Term 1807

The within named property advertised Agreeable for want of Bidders
H Smithwick

State of North Carolina
To the Sheriff of Martin County, Greeting:
Whereas, we by our writ, commanded you that of the goods and chattels, lands and tenements of John B. Hunter (in your Bailiwick) you should cause to be made the sum of Ninety five pounds sixteen shillings & six pence which lately in our Superior Court of Law at Edenton, Edwin Lisles recovered against him as well for Damages which he sustained by reason of the now performance of certain promises &c. as for the costs and charges by him in his suit in that behalf expended, whereof the said John B. Hunter is convicted and liable as to us appears of record; besides your own fees for that Service, and that you should have said money before the Judges of our said Court, at Edenton, on the Sixth day of October next, after the XIXth day of April in the year of our Lord one thousand eight hundred and six to render to the said Edwin Lisles for his damages, costs and charges aforesaid: And you at that day returned on the said writ, that you had levied the same on two Negroes by the name of Tom & Merrick which remain in your hands unsold for want of Bidders. We do therefore command you, that you expose to sale the goods and chattels by you so as aforesaid levied upon, so that you have the said money and 14 shillings for accruing costs, before the Judges of our said Court, at Edenton, on the first Monday after the fourth Monday of September next, and we do command you further, that of the goods and chattels, lands and tenements of the said John B. Hunter in your bailiwick, you cause to be made the residue of the

said damages, costs and charges, and that you have the said money before the Judges of our said Court, at Edenton, on the day aforesaid, to render to the said edwin Lisles his damages, costs and charges aforesaid; and have you then and there this writ. Witness William Blair in the XXXI1st year of our Independence, Anno Domini 1807.
Will Blair, Clk.

Judgment	£85.10.6
Clerk & Tax	4.13.0
Attorney	5
Sheriff & Cryer	0.13.0
	95.16.6
Accruing Costs	£96.10.6

Lisles H. Ramsay in fact Vs. Jno. B. Hunter als
Vend Exp, Fi Fa
Chowan Supr. Court
September Term 1808
Satisfy as to all but the Sheriff Tomeson
H Smithwick

State of North Carolina
To the Sheriff of Martin County, Greeting:
Whereas, we by our writ commanded you that of the goods and chattels, lands and tenements of John B. Hunter (in your bailiwick) you should cause to be made the sum of Ninety five pounds sixteen shilling & six pence which lately in our Superior Court of Law in Edenton, Edwin Lisles recovered against him as well for damages which he sustained by reason of the nonperformance of certain promises &c. as for the costs and charges him in his suit in that behalf expended, whereof the said John B. Hunter is convicted and liable as to us appears of record; besides your own fees for that service, and that you should have the said money before the Judges of our said Court, at Edenton, on the 1st Monday after the 4th Monday of March next after the ninth day of October in the year of our Lord one thousand eight hundred and seven to render to the said Edwin Lisles his damages, costs and charges aforesaid: and you at that day returned on the said writ, that you had levied the same on Two negroes by the names of Tom & Merrick which remain in your hands unsold by reason of the

forbearance of the Plaintiff. We do therefore command you, that you expose to sale the goods and chattels by you so as aforesaid levied upon, so that you have the said money and 28 shillings & three pence for accruing costs, before the Judges of our said Court, at Edenton, on the first Monday after the fourth Monday of September next, and we do command you further, that of the goods and chattels, land and tenements of the said John B. Hunter in your bailiwick, you cause to be made the residue of the said damages, costs and charges, and that you have the said money before the Judges of our said Court, at Edenton, on the day aforesaid, to render to the said Edwin Lisles his damages, costs and charges aforesaid; and have you then and there this writ. Witness James Iredell, Clerk of our said Court, at Edenton, the Ninth day of April in the XXXIInd year of out Independence, Anno Dom. 1808.
Jas Iredell, Clk.

Judgment	£85.10.6
Clk & Tax due Mr. Blair	4.13
Atto P.B.	5
Shff & Cryer	13
	£95.16.6
Accruing Costs owed J.J. Clk	1.8.3
	£97.4.9

Windsor 29th Apl. 1808 an acct of the above Judgment One Hundred & fifty Dollars by me for Henry Ramsay
JP Morgan

Lisles H Ramsay in fact Vs. Hunter
Vend Exp, Fi Fa
Chowan Supr. Court
March Term 1808
Stayd by order of the Plaintiff's Agent
H. Smithwick

State of North Carolina
To the Sheriff of Martin County, Greeting:

Chowan County Civil Actions

Whereas, we by our writ, commanded you that of the goods and chattels, lands and tenements of John B Hunter (in your bailiwick) you should cause to be made the sum of Ninety five pounds sixteen shillings & six pence which lately in our Superior Court of Law at Edenton, Edwin Lisles recovered against him as well for Damages which he sustained by reason of the non performance of certain promises &c. as for the costs and charges by him in his suit that behalf expended, whereof the said John B. Hunter is convicted and liable as to us appears of record; besides your own fees for that Service, and that you should have the said money the Judges of our said Court, at Edenton, on the sixth day of October next, after the XXIth day of April in the year of our Lord one thousand eight hundred and Six to render to the said Edwin Lisles his damages, costs and charges aforesaid: And you at that day returned on the said writ, that you had levied the same on Two negroes by the names of Tom & Merrick which remain in your hands unsold for want of Bidders, We do therefore command you, that you again expose to sale the goods and chattels by you so as aforesaid levied upon, so that you have the said money and 19 shillings for accruing costs, before the Judges of our said Court, at Edenton, on the first Monday after the fourth Monday of March next, and we do command you further, that of the goods and chattels, lands and tenements of the said John B. Hunter in your bailiwick, you cause to be made the residue of the said damages, costs, and charges, and that you have the said money before the Judges of our said Court, at Edenton, on the day aforesaid, to render to the said Edwin Lisles his damages, costs and charges aforesaid; and have you then and there this writ. Witness William Blair, Clerk of our said Court, at Edenton, the Ninth day of October in the XXXIInd year of our Independence, Anno Domini 1807.
Will Blair, Clk

Judgment	£85.10.6
Clk & Tax	4.13
Attorney	5
Shff & Cryer	13
	£95.16.6
Accruing Costs	19
	£96.15.6

****

Chowan County Civil Actions

Lewis Bond Vs. Benajah Nicholls et als
Civil Action [1807]
Chowan County Records

Bond Vs. Nicholls
Vend Exp, Fi Fa
Chowan Supr. Court
March Term 1808
Sattisfied, Wm. H Greens

State of North Carolina

To the Sheriff of Bertie County, Greeting:

Whereas, we by our writ, commanded you that of the goods and chattels, lands and tenements of Benajah Nicholls and William Ashburn (in your bailiwick) you should cause to be made the sum of Two hundred & ninety one pounds which lately in our Superior Court of Law at Edenton, Lewis Bond recovered against them for Debt & also the sum of Fifty six pounds fourteen shillings as well for damages which he sustained by reason of the detention of that Debt as for the the costs and charges by him in his suit in that behalf expended, whereof the said Binajah Nicholls & William Ashburn are convicted and liable as to us appears of record; besides your own fees for that service, and that you should have the said money before the Judges of our said Court, at Edenton, on the 1st Monday after the 4th Monday of September next, after the fourth day of April in the year of our Lord one thousand eight hundred and Seven to render to the said Lewis Bond his Debt damages, costs and charges aforesaid: And you at that day returned on the said writ, that you had levied the same on two negro women by the names of Tamer & Moll, the property of B. Nicholls which remain in your hands unsold for want of Bidders. We do therefore command you, that you again expose to sale the chattels by you so as aforesaid levied upon, so that you have the said money and 9 shillings for accruing costs, before the Judges of our said Court, at Edenton on the first Monday after the fourth Monday of March next, and we do command you further, that of the goods and chattels, lands and tenements of the said Binajah & William in your bailiwick, you cause to be made the residue of the said Debt, damages, costs and charges, and that you have the said money before the Judges of our said Court, at Edenton, on the day aforesaid, to render to the said Lewis Bond his Debt, damages, costs and charges aforesaid; and have you then and there this writ. Witness William

Blair, Clerk of our said Court, at Edenton, the Ninth day of October in the XXXIInd year of our Independence, Anno Domini 1807.
Will Blair, Clk.

[Top Line Torn]

Damages	**[Torn]**
Clerk	2.9
Atto, WAL	5
Cryer	5.0.6
Costs below	5.11.6
	£56.14
Accruing Costs	9
	£3.48.3

N. B. all the costs except 9/ & £150 of the
Judgment have been paid on a former Exp
Recd on this Exp £9 Clks fees
J.J. Clk.

****

William Gregory Vs. John B. Hunter et als
Civil Action [1807]
Chowan County Records

Gregory Vs Hunter als
Vend Exp, Fi Fa
Chowan Supr. Court
September Term 1807

The within named property Advertised Agreeable to Law Exposed for sale not Sold for want of Bidders
H Smithwick

State of North Carolina
To the Sheriff of Martin County, Greeting:
Whereas, we by our writ, commanded you that of the goods and chattels, lands and tenements of John B. Hunter & Henry Hunter (in your bailiwick) you should cause to be made the sum of One Hundred pounds which lately in our Superior Court of Law at Edenton, William Gregory recovered

against them for Debt and also the sum of seventeen pounds sixteen shillings as well for his damages sustained by reason of the detention of that Debt as for the costs and charges by him in his suit in that behalf expended, whereof the said John B. Hunter & Henry Hunter are convicted and liable as to us appears of record; besides your own fees for that service, and that you should have the said money before the Judges of our said Court, at Edenton, on the Sixth day of April next, after the XIXth day of October in the year of our Lord one thousand eight hundred and five to render to the said William Gregory his Debt, damages, costs and charges aforesaid: And you at that day returned on the said writ, that you had levied the same on Two Negroes George & Dan which remain in your hands unsold for want of Bidders. We do therefore command you, that you again expose to sale the goods and chattels by you so as aforesaid levied upon, so that you have the said money and five shillings for accruing costs before the Judges of our said Court, at Edenton, on the first Monday after the fourth Monday of September next, and we do command you further, that of the goods and chattels, lands and tenements of the said John and Henry in your bailiwick, you cause to be made the residue of the said Debt, damages, costs and charges, and that you have the said money before the Judges of our said Court, at Edenton, on the day aforesaid, to render to the said William Gregory his Debt, damages, costs and charges aforesaid; and have you then and there this writ. Witness William Blair, Clerk of our said Court, at Edenton, the fourth day of April in the XXXIst year of our Independence, Anno Domini 1807.
Will Blair, Clk.

Debt	£100
Damages	£8.15
Clerk & tax	3.1
Attorney	5
Sheriff	1
	17.16
	£117.16
Accruing Costs	5
	£118.1

Gregory Vs Hunter
Vend Exp, Fi Fa

Chowan Supr. Court
September Term 1808

The within named property Advertised Agreeable to Law & not sold for want of Bidders
H Smithwick

State of North Carolina
To the Sheriff of Martin County, Greeting:
Whereas, we by our writ commanded you that of the goods and chattels, lands and tenements of John B. Hunter and Henry Hunter (in your bailiwick) you should cause to be made the sum of One hundred pounds which lately in our Superior Court of Law at Edenton, William Gregory recovered against them for Debt and also the sum of seventeen pounds sixteen shillings as well for his damages sustained by reason of the detention of that Debt as for the costs and charges by him in his suit in that behalf expended, whereof the said John B. Hunter & Henry Hunter are convicted and liable as to us appears of record; besides your own fees for that service, and that you should have the said money before the Judges of our said Court, at Edenton, on the sixth day of April next, after the XIXth day of October in the year of our Lord one thousand eight hundred and five to render to the said William Gregory his Debt, damages, costs and charges aforesaid: And you at that day returned on the said Writ, that you had levied the same on Two negroes by the names of George and Dan which remain in your hands unsold for want of Bidders. We do therefore command you, that you again expose to sale the goods and chattels by you so as aforesaid levied upon, so that you have the said money and 23 shillings & three pence for accruing costs, before the Judges of our said Court, at Edenton, on the first Monday after the fourth Monday of September next, and we do command you further, that of the goods and chattels, lands and tenements of the said John B. and Henry in your bailiwick, you cause to be made the residue of the said Debt, damages, costs and charges, and that you have the said money before the Judges of our said Court, at Edenton, on the day aforesaid, to render to the said William Gregory his Debt, damages, costs and charges aforesaid; and have you then and there this writ. Witness James Iredell, Clerk of our said Court, at Edenton, the ninth day of April in the XXXIInd year of our Independence, Anno Dom. 1808
Jas. Iredell, Clk.

Debt	£100
Damages	8.15
Tax due Wm. Blair	3.1
Atto JBL	5
	£117.16
Accruing costs due J.J. Clk	1.3.3
	£118.19.3

Gregory Vs. Hunter
Vend Exp, Fi Fa
Chowan Supr. Court
March Term 1809

The within named property Advertised Agreeable to Law Stayd by order of Mr. John Arnestead
H Smithwick

State of North Carolina
To the Sheriff of Martin County, Greeting:
Whereas, we by our writ commanded you that of the goods and chattels, lands and tenements of John B. Hunter & Henry Hunter (in your bailiwick) you should cause to be made the sum of One Hundred Pounds which lately in our Superior Court of Law at Edenton, William Gregory recovered against them for Debt and also the sum of Seventeen pounds sixteen Shillings as well for his Damages &c as for the costs and charges by him in his suit in that behalf expended, whereof the said John B. Hunter & Henry Hunter are convicted and liable as to us appears of record; besides your own fees for that service, and that you should have the said money before the Judges of our said Court at Edenton, on the sixth day of April next, after the XIXth day of October in the year of our Lord one thousand eight hundred and Five to render to the said William Gregory his Debt, damages, costs and charges aforesaid: And you at that day returned on the said writ, that you had levied the same on Two negroes by the names of George & Dan which remain in your hands unsold for want of Bidders. We do therefore command you, that you expose to sale the goods and chattels by you so as aforesaid levied upon, so that you have the said money and 32 shillings for Accruing costs, before the Judges of our said Court, at Edenton, on the first Monday after the fourth Monday of March next, and

we do command you further, that of the goods and chattels, lands and tenements of the said John & Henry in your bailiwick, you cause to be made the residue of the said Debt damages, costs and charges, and that you have the said money before the Judges of our said Court, at Edenton, on the day aforesaid, to render to the said William his Debt, damages, costs and charges aforesaid; and have you then and there this writ. Witness James Iredell, Clerk of our said Court, at Edenton, the 8th day of October in the XXXIIIst year of our Independence, Anno Dom. 1808.
Jas. Iredell, Clk.

Debt	£100
Damages	8.15
Tax due Wm Blair	3.1
Atto JBL	5
Shff	1
	£117.16
Accruing costs due J.J. Clk	1.12.6
	£119.8.6

Gregory Vs. Hunter als
Vend Exp, Fi Fa
Chowan Supr. Court
September term 1809

Thw within named property Advertised agreeable to Law Exposed for sale not sold for want of Bidders
H Smithwick

State of North Carolina
To the Sheriff of Martin County, Greeting:
Whereas, we by our writ commanded you that of the goods and chattels, lands and tenements of John B. Hunter and Henry Hunter (in your bailiwick) you should cause to be made the sum of One hundred pounds which lately in our Superior Court of Law at Edenton, William Gregory recovered against them for Debt and also the sum of Seventeen pounds sixteen shillings as well for his damages &c for the costs and charges by him in his suit in that behalf expended, whereof the said John B. Hunter & Henry Hunter are convicted and liable as to us appears of record; besides

your own fees for that service, and that you should have the said money before the Judges of our said Court, at Edenton, on the sixth day of April next, after the XIXth day of October in the year of our Lord one thousand eight hundred and five to render to the said William Gregory his Debt, damages, costs and charges aforesaid: And you at that day returned on the said writ, that you had levied the same on Two negroes by the names of George & Dan which remain in your hands unsold by reason of the forebearance of the Plaintiff. We do therefore command you, that you expose to sale the goods and chattels by you so as aforesaid levied upon, so that you have the said money and 41 shillings & 9d for accruing costs, before the Judges of our said Court, at Edenton on the first Money after the fourth Monday of September next, and we do command you further, that of the goods and Chattels, lands and tenements of the said John B. & Henry in your bailiwick, you cause to be made the residue of the said Debt, damages, costs and charges, and that you have the said money before the Judges of our said Court, at Edenton, on the day aforesaid, to render to the said William Gregory his Debt, damages, costs and charges aforesaid; and have you then and there this writ. Witness James Iredell, Clerk of our said Court, at Edenton , the 7th day of April in the XXXIIIst year of our Independence, Anno Dom. 1809
Jas. Iredell, Clk.

Debt	£100
Damages	8.15
Tax Due W. Blair Late Clk	3.1
Atto JBL	5
Sheriff	1
	£117.16
Accruing Costs due J.J. Clk	2.1.9
	£119.17.9

Gregory Vs Hunter
Vends Exp, Fi Fa
Chowan Supr Court
March Term 1810

The within named property advertised agreeable to Law Exposed for Sale Not Sold for want of Bidders

H Smithwick, Shff

State of North Carolina

To the Sheriff of Martin County, Greeting:

Whereas, we by our writ commanded you that of the goods and Chattels, lands and tenements of John B. Hunter & Henry Hunter (in your bailiwick) you should cause to be made the sum of One hundred pounds which lately in our Superior Court of Law at Edenton, William Gregory recovered against them for Debt as also the further sum of Seventeen pounds sixteen shillings as well for his Damages &c as for the costs and charges by him in his suit in that behalf expended, whereof the said John B. Hunter & Henry Hunter are convicted and liable as to us appears of record; besides your own fees for that service, and that you should have the said money before the Judges of our said Court, at Edenton, on the sixth of April next, after the 19th day of October in the year of our Lord one thousand eight hundred and five to render to the said William Gregory his Debt, damages, costs and charges aforesaid: And you at that day returned on the said writ, that you had levied the same on Two negroes by the names of George & Dan which remain in your hands unsold, for want of Bidders. We do therefore command you, that you expose to sale the goods and chattels by you so as aforesaid levied upon, so that you have the said money and 51 shillings for accruing costs, before the Judges of our said Court, at Edenton, on the first Monday after the fourth Monday of March next, and we do command you further, that of the goods and chattels, lands and tenements of the said John B. and Henry in your bailiwick, you cause to be made the residue of the said Debt, damages, costs and charges, and that you have the said money before the Judges of our said Court, at Edenton, on the day aforesaid, to render to the said William his Debt, damages, costs and charges aforesaid; and have you then and there this writ. Witness James Iredell, Clerk of our said Court, at Edenton, the 7th day of October in the XXIVth year of our Independence, Anno Dom. 1809.

Jas. Iredell, Clk

Debt & Damages	£108.15
Tax due Wm Blair late Clk	3.1
Atto	5
Sheriff	1
	£117.16
Accruing Costs due J.J. Clk	2.11

£120.7

Gregory Vs. Hunter
Vends Exp, Fi Fa
Satisfyed, H Smithwick, Shff
Chowan Supr. Court
September Term 1810

State of North Carolina
To the Sheriff of Martin County, Greeting:
Whereas, we by our writ commanded you, that of the goods and chattels, lands and tenements of John B. Hunter & Henry Hunter (in your bailiwick) you should cause to be made the sum of One hundred Pounds which lately in our Superior Court of Law at Edenton, William Gregory recovered against them for Debt, as also the further sum of Seventeen pounds sixteen shillings as well for his Damages &c as for the costs and charges by him in his suit in that behalf expended, whereof the said John B Hunter & Henry Hunter are convicted and liable as to us appears of record; besides your own fees for that service, and that you should have the said money before the Judges of our said Court, at Edenton, on the Sixth day of April next, after the 19th day of October in the year of our Lord one thousand eight hundred and five to render to the said William Gregory his Debt, damages, costs and charges aforesaid: And you at that day returned on the said writ, that you had levied the same on Two negroes by the names of George and Dan which remain in your hands unsold, for want of Bidders. We do therefore command you, that you expose to sale the goods and chattels by you so as aforesaid levied upon, so that you have the said money and 60 shillings & 3 pence for accruing costs, before the Judges of our said Court, at Edenton, on the first Monday after the fourth Monday of September next, and we do command you further, that of the goods and chattels, lands and tenements of the said John B. and Henry in your bailiwick, you cause to be made the residue of the said Debt, damages, costs and charges, and that you have the said money before the Judges of our said Court, at Edenton, on the day aforesaid, to render to the said William his Debt, damages, costs and charges aforesaid; and have you then and there this writ. Witness James Iredell, Clerk of our said Court, at Edenton, the 7th day of April in the XXXIVth year of our Independence, Anno Dom. 1810
Jas. Iredell, Clk

Debt & Damages	£108.15
Tax due Wm Blair late Clk	3.1
Atto	5
Sheriff	1
	117.16
Accruing Costs due J.J. Clk	3.0.3
	£120.16.3

Received into the Office £6 of the Clerks fees

****

Josiah Collins Vs. John Leary Jr.
Civil Action [1807]
Chowan County Records

Josiah Collins Jr. Vs. John Leary Jr.
Vends Exp
September Term 1807

State of North Carolina
To the Sheriff of Chowan County, Greeting:
Whereas we by our writ have commanded you, that of the goods and chattels, lands and tenements of John Leary Junr. In your bailiwick, you should cause to be made the sum of seventy Eight Pounds Ten Shillings & three Pence with Interest from 13th March 1804 till paid whereof the said John Leary Junr. Is convicted and liable, as appears to us of record, besides your own fees for this service; and that you should have those monies before the Justices of our inferior Court of Pleas and Quarter Sessions, at our next Court, to be held for the County of Chowan at the Court House in Edenton on the second Monday in **[Blank]** next; then and there to render to Josiah Collins Junr. His debt, damages and costs as aforesaid; and you at that day returned on the said writ to you directed, that you had levied on Negroe Boy Miles & not sold for want of Bidders, We do therefore command you, again to expose to sale the property aforesaid, by you levied on, so that you have the money aforesaid before our Justices of our Inferior Court of Pleas and Quarter Sessions, to be held at the Court House in Edenton on the second Monday in September next; to render to the said Josiah Collins Junr. For his debt, damages and costs as aforesaid. Herein fail not, and have you then and there this writ. Witness Elisha Norfleet

Clerk of the said Court, at Edenton the 13th day of June in the XXXIst year of the Independence of the said State, Anno Dom. 1807
E Norfleet, Clk

Execution	£78.2.3	156.22
Interest from 13th March 1804 to 9th October 1805		
18 months 25 days		14.76
		170.98
Payment P Rect to TB		100
Interest from 9th October 1805 till paid		70.98

Payment £78.2.3 with Int from 13th March 1804 till pd.
Clerk 6.9
Costs 5.12.9

****

William Wilson & Co. Vs Thomas C. Ferebe
Civil Action [1807]
Chowan County Records

Wilson Vs Williams, Admr.
Chowan Supr. Court
September Term 1807
Currituck

State of North Carolina
To the Sheriff of Currituck County, Greeting:
Whereas, we by our writ, commanded you that of the goods and chattels, lands and tenements Thomas C. Ferebee (in your bailiwick) you should cause to be made the sum of Twelve hundred & twenty four pounds sixteen shillings & six pence which lately in our Superior Court of Law at Edenton, William Wilson and Company recovered against him as well for damages which they sustained by reason of the non performance of certain promises &c as for the costs and charges by them in their suit in that behalf expended, whereof the said Thomas Ferebee is convicted and liable as to us appears of record; besides your own fees for that service, and that you should have the said money before the Judges of our said Court, at

Edenton, on the 1st Monday after the 4th Monday of March next, after the XIXth day of October in the year of our Lord one thousand eight hundred and six to render to the said William Wilson & Company their damages, costs and charges aforesaid: And you at that day returned on the said writ, that you had levied the same on Ten negroes & the plantation whereon Thomas C. Ferebee lives which remain in your hands unsold for want of Bidders, we do therefore command you, that you again expose to sale the goods and chattels, Lands & tenements by you so as aforesaid levied upon, so that you have the said money and 14 shillings for accruing costs, before the Judges of our said Court, at Edenton, on the first Monday after the fourth Monday of September next, and we do command you further, that of the goods and chattels, lands and tenements of the said Thomas C. Ferebee in your bailiwick, you cause to be made the residue of the said damages, costs and charges, and that you have the said money before the Judges of our said Court, at Edenton, on the day aforesaid, to render to the said William Wilson & Company damages, costs and charges aforesaid; and have you then and there this writ. Witness William Blair, Clerk of our said Court, at Edenton, the fourth day of April in the XXXIth year of our Independence, Anno Domini 1807.
Will Blair, Clk

Judgment	£1211.9.0
Clerk	£2.15
Atto	5
Shff & Cryer	3.6
Costs below	5.8.6
	13.7
	1224.16.6
Accruing Costs	14
	£1225.10.6

W.B. the sum of £720.10.6 will satisfy this Exor £500 having been paid by a draught on Philadelphia & the Attorney's fee satisfied on a former Exor
W.B., Clk

****

Caleb Winslow Vs. James Sowell
Civil Action [1807]

Chowan County
Civil Actions

Chowan County Records

Caleb Winslow Vs James Sowell
Vends Exp
March Term 1808
Chowan County
Not Sold for want of Bidders
Matt Deans, Shff
Hertford

State of North Carolina

To the Sheriff of Hertford County, Greeting:

Whereas we by our writ have commanded You, that of the goods and chattels, lands and tenements of James Sowell in your bailiwick, you should cause to be made the sum of Twenty Seven Pounds Eight Shillings & 4d adjudged to Caleb Winslow for his Costs whereof the said James Sowell is convicted and liable, as appears to us of record, besides your own fees for this service; and that you should have those monies before the Justices of our Inferior Court of Pleas and Quarter Sessions at our next Court, to be held for the County of Chowan at the Court House in Edenton on the second Monday in December next; then and there to render to the said Caleb Winslow his debt, damages and costs as aforesaid; and you at that day returned on the said writ to you directed, that you had levied on Two Negroes & not Sold for want of Bidders. We do therefore command you, that you again expose to sale the property aforesaid, by you levied on, so that you have the money aforesaid before our Justices of our Inferior Court of Pleas and Quarter Sessions, to be held at the Court House in Edenton on the second Monday in March next; to render to the said Caleb Winslow for his debt, damages and costs as aforesaid. Herein fail not, and have you then and there this writ. Witness Elisha Norfleet, Clerk of the said Court, at Edenton the 17th day of December in the XXXIInd year of the Independence of the said State, Anno Dom. 1807

E Norfleet, Clk.

Clerk & Tax	£3.17.2
Atto JBS	2
Sheriff	1.2.6
Enoch Parker, Wits	12.14.8
John Fullington	7.14
	£27.8.4

Chowan County
Civil Actions

Caleb Winslow Vs. Jas. Sowell
Vends Exp
June Term 1808
Not Sold for want of Bidders
Matt Deans**[?]**, Shff
Hertford

State of North Carolina

To the Sheriff of Hertford County, Greeting:

Whereas we by our writ have commanded you, that of the goods and Chattels, lands and tenements of James Sowell in your bailiwick, you should cause to be made the sum of Twenty Seven pounds seven **[Torn]** Costs whereof the said James Sowell is convicted and liable, as appears to us of record, besides your own fees for this service, and that you should have those monies before the Justices of our Inferior Court of Pleas and Quarter Sessions, at our next Court, to be held for the County of Chowan at the Court House in Edenton on the second Monday in June next; then and there to render to the said Caleb Winslow for his Costs, his damages as aforesaid; and you at that day returned on the said writ to you directed, that you had levied on Two Negroes & not Sold for want of Bidders. We do command you, that you again expose to sale the property aforesaid, by you levied on, so that you have the money aforesaid before our Justices of our Inferior Court of Pleas and Quarter Sessions, to be held at the Court House in Edenton on the second Monday in June next; to render to the said Caleb Winslow for his damages and costs as aforesaid. Herein fail not, and have you then and there this writ. Witness Elisha Norfleet, Clerk of the said Court, at Edenton the 18th day of March in the XXXIInd year of the Independence of the said State, Anno Dom, 1808. Issued the 5th day of March 1808.
E. Norfleet

Clerk & Tax	£4.6.5
Atto JBS	2
Shff	1.2.6
Enoch Parker, Wits	12.14.8
John Fullington	7.14
	£27.17.7

Chowan County Civil Actions

Caleb Winslow Vs Jas Sowell
Vends Exp
September Term 1808
Hertford

State of North Carolina

To the Sheriff of Hertford County, Greeting:

Whereas we by our writ have commanded you, that of the goods and chattels, lands and tenements of James Sowell in your bailiwick, you should cause to be made the sum of Twenty Eight pounds Six shillings and ten pence adjudged to Caleb Winslow for costs of Suit whereof the said James Sowell is convicted and liable as appears to us of record, besides your own fees for this service; and that you should have those monies before the Justices of our Inferior Court of Pleas and Quarter Sessions, at our next Court, to be held for the County of Chowan, at the Court House in Edenton, on the second Monday in **[Blank]** next; then and there to render to the said Caleb Winslow his debt, damages and costs as aforesaid; and you at that day returned on the said writ to you directed, that you had levied on two Negroes & not sold for want of Bidders. We do therefore command you, that you again expose to sale the property aforesaid, by you levied on, so that you have the money aforesaid before our Justices of our Inferior Court of Pleas and Quarter Sessions, to be held at the Court House in Edenton, on the second Monday in December next; to render to the said Caleb Winslow for his debt, damages and costs as aforesaid. Herein fail not, and have you then and there this writ. Witness Elisha Norfleet, Clerk of the said Court, at Edenton, the 17th day of September in the XXXIInd year of the Independence of the said Stste, Anno Dom. 1808
E Norfleet

Satisfyed the sum of thirty nine dollars & 50 cents in part of the within execution
Matt Deans, DShff

Clerk & Tax	£4.15.8
Atto JBS 40/ Shff 22/6	3.2.6
Enoch Parker, Witness	12.14.8
John Fullington	7.14
T Coffield Claims this	£28.6.10

Chowan County
Civil Actions

Caleb Winslow Vs. James Sowell
Vends Espons
December Term 1808
Not Sold for want of Bidders but Satisfyed
20/ Matt Deans[?] Davis, DShff
Hertford

State of North Carolina

To the Sheriff of Hertford County, Greeting:

Whereas we by our writ have commanded you, that of the goods and chattels, lands and tenements of James Sowell in your bailiwick, you should cause to be made the sum of Twenty Nine Pounds five shillings & 4d adjudged to Caleb Winslow for Costs of Suit whereof the said James Sowell is convicted and liable as appears to us of record, besides your own fees for this service; and that you should have those monies before the Justices of our Inferior Court of Pleas and Quarter Sessions, at our next Court, to be held for the County of Chowan, at the Court House in Edenton, on the second Monday in **[Blank]** next; then and there to render to the said Caleb Winslow his costs as aforesaid; an you at that day returned on the said writ to you directed, that you had levied on two Negroes & not Sold for want of Bidders. We do therefore command you, that you again expose to sale the property aforesaid, by you levied on, so that you have the money aforesaid before our Justices of our Inferior Court of Pleas and Quarter Sessions, to be held at the Court House in Edenton, on the second Monday in March next; to render to the said Caleb Winslow for his debt, damages and costs as aforesaid. Herein fail not, and have you then and there this writ. Witness Elisha Norfleet, Clerk of the said Court, at edenton, the 17th day of december in the XXXIInd year of the Independence of the said State, Anno Dom. 1808.
E. Norfleet

Clerk & Tax	£5.4.11
Atto & Shff	3.2.6
Enoch Parker	12.14.8
John Fullington & T. Coffield	7.14.0
	£28.16.1

The Sum of $39.50 was Satisfied on a former Vends Ex
19.15 - £9.1.1

State of North Carolina

To the Sheriff of Hertford County, Greeting:

Whereas we by our writ have commanded you, that of the goods and chattels, lands and tenements of James Sowell in your bailiwick, you should cause to be made the sum of Twenty Seven pounds & nine shillings & three pence adjudged to Caleb Winslow for costs of suit whereof the said James Sowell is convicted and liable as appears to us of record, besides your own fees for this service; and that you should have those monies before the Justices of our Inferior Court of Pleas of and Quarter Sessions, at our next Court, to be held for the County of Chowan, at the Court House in Edenton, on the second Monday in **[Blank]** next; then and there to render to Caleb Winslow his debt, damages and costs as aforesaid; and you at that day returned on the said writ to you directed, that you had levied on two Negroes & not Sold for want of Bidders. We do therefore command you, that you again expose to sale the property aforesaid, by you levied on, so that you have the money aforesaid before our Justices of our Inferior Court of Pleas and Quarter Sessions, to be held at the Court House in Edenton, on the second Monday in September next; to render to the said Caleb Winslow for his debt, damages and costs as aforesaid. Herein fail not, and have you then and there this writ. Witness Elisha Norfleet, Clerk of the said Court, at Edenton, the 17th day of June in the XXXII year of the Independence of the said State, Anno Dom.

E Norfleet

Caleb Winslow Vs. James Sowell
Vends Expons
June Term 1809
Not Sold for want of Bidder
J Carb[?]
Hertford

State of North Carolina

To the Sheriff of Hertford County, Greeting:

Whereas we by our writ have commanded you, that of the goods and chattels, lands and tenements of James Sowell in your bailiwick, you should cause to be made the sum of Twenty Nine pounds Fourteen Shillings & seven pence which Caleb Winslow recovered agt them for Cost of Suit whereof the said James Sowell is convicted and liable as

appears to us of record, besides your own fees for this service; and that you should those monies before the Justices of our Inferior Court of Pleas and Quarter Sessions, at our next Court, to be held for the County of Chowan, at that day returned on the said writ to you directed, that you had levied on two Negroes & not Sold for want of Bidders. We do therefore command you, that you again expose to sale the property aforesaid, by you levied on, so that you have the money aforesaid before our Justices of our Inferior Court of Pleas and Quarter Sessions, to be held at the Court House in Edenton, on the second Monday in June next; to render to the said Caleb Winslow for his costs as aforesaid. Herein fail not, and have you then and there this writ. Witness Elisha Norfleet, Clerk of the said Court, at Edenton, the 18th day of March in the XXXIInd year of the Independence of the said State, Anno Dom. 1809
E Norfleet.

Clerk	£6.3.5
Atto & Shff	3.2.6
E Parker P CW	12.14.8
John Fullington	7.14
	£29.14.7
	22.15
The Sum of has been satesfied as appears	£6.19.7

Caleb Winslow Vs. James Sowell
Vends Expons
September Term 1809
Hertford

Satisfied by the sale of Negro Arthur, said by Matt Deans former deputy Shff to be one of the negroes mentioned in this Ven Exp.
Lewis Walters, Shff

State of North Carolina
To the Sheriff of Hertford County, Greeting:
Whereas we by our writ have commanded you, that of the goods and chattela, lands and tenements of James Sowell in your bailiwick, you should cause to be made the sum of Thirty pounds 3/10 which Caleb Winslow recovered for Costs of a Suit said James Sowell [?] agt. Him & failed therein, whereof the said James Sowell is convicted and liable as

appears to us of record, besides your own fees for this service; and that you should have those monies before the Justices of our Inferior Court of Pleas and Quarter Sessions, at our next Court, to be held for the County of Chowan, at the Court House in Edenton, on the second Monday in **[Blank]** next; then and there to render to the said Caleb Winslow his costs as aforesaid; and you at that day returned on the said writ to you directed, that you had levied on two negroes & not Sold for want of Bidders. We do therefore command you, that you again expose to sale the property aforesaid, by you levied on, so that you have the money aforesaid before our Justices of our Inferior Court of Pleas and Quarter Sessions, to be held at the Court House, in Edenton, on the second Monday in September next; to render to the said Caleb Winslow for his debt, damages and costs as aforesaid. Herein fail not, and have you then and there this writ. Witness Elisha Norfleet, Clerk of the said Court, at Edenton, the 15th day of June in the XXXIInd year of the Independence of the said State, Anno Dom. 1809
E Norfleet, Clk

Clerk	£6.12.8
Atto & Sheriff	3.2.6
E Parker P CW	12.14.8
John Fullington T. Coffield	7.14
	£30.3.10
The sum of	22.15
Has been satisfied	£7.8.10

Caleb Winslow Vs. James Sowell
Vends Expons
March 1809
Not Sold for want of Bidders
Matt Deans, DShff
Hertford

Sowell Vs. Winslow
Witness Tickets

Peter B. Marten claims	£4.10
C.W. for E.P. & R. Keating	3.2.8
R. Keating for EP [?]	13.8

E Parker for his Ticket	3.5.8
	£11.12
C Winslow for EP ticket Supr Court	1.2
	£12.14

C Winslow Vs Jas Sowell
Bill of Witness
No. 44 Septr 1809

Recd. Feby 1st 1810 of E Norfleet Clerk Chowan County Court the within mentioned Twelve pounds one shilling it being for Enoch Parkers witness Ticketts in the within Suit.
Caleb Winslow

Jas. Sowell } Nonsuit. I sowell liable
Caleb Winslow } the costs

Enoch Parker witness 1 Ticket		£1.9.8
	1 do	1.1.8
	1 do	17.8
	1 do	1.1.8
PB Marten has [?]		£4.10.8
E Parker assigned Robt Keating		17.8
		13.8
		17.8
		13.8
		1.2
		4.4.8
E Parker by R Keating		13.8
E Parker filed by him		3.5.8
		£12.14.8
John Fullington to T Coffield		7.14
		£20.8.8
Paid Tho Coffield		7.14
Pd J.N. for R. Keating		13.8
Pd C. Winslow foe E Parker		12.1.0

****

Chowan County
Civil Actions

Herbert Pride Vs. John Drew the Elder
Civil Action [1807]
Chowan County Records

Pride Vs Drew
Vends Expons, Fi Fa
Chowan Supr Court
September Term 1807

Exposed the Negroes within named as levied on for sale, on the 1st day of October 1807 but could have no sale for want of Bidders
Wm. H Green, Shff
Bertie

State of North Carolina
To the Sheriff of Bertie County, Greeting:
Whereas, we by our writ, commanded you that of the goods and chattels, lands and tenements of John Drew the Elder (in your bailiwick) you should cause to be made the sum of Four hundred pounds four shillings & seven pence which lately in our Superior Court of Law at Edenton, Herbert Pride recovered against him as well for his damages which he sustained by reason of the non performance of certain promises before that time made to him by the said John Drew as for the costs and charges by him in his suit in that behalf expended, whereof the said John Drew the Elder is convicted and liable as to us appears of records; besides your own fees for that service, and that you should have the said money before the Judges of our said Court, at Edenton, on the 1st Monday after the 4th Monday of March next, after the XIXth day of October in the year of our Lord one thousand eight hundred and Six to render to the said Herbert Pride his damages, costs and charges aforesaid: And you at that day returned on the said writ, that you had levied the same on Negroes Sam, Lewis, David, Joe & Exi which remain in your hands unsold for want of Bidders. We do therefore command, that you expose to sale the goods and chattels by you so as aforesaid levied upon, so that you have the said money and five shillings for accruing costs, before the Judges of our said Court, at Edenton on the first Monday after the fourth Monday of September next, and we do command you further, that the goods and Chattels, lands and tenements of the said John Drew the Elder in your bailiwick, you cause to be made the residue of the said damages, costs and charges, and that you have the said money before the Judges of our said Court, at Edenton, on the day

aforesaid, to render to the said Herbert Pride damages, costs and charges aforesaid; and have you then and there this writ. Witness William Blair, Clerk of our said Court, at Edenton, the fourth day of April in the XXXIst year of our Independence, Anno Domini 1807.
Will Blair, Clk.

Judgment	£388.8.7
Clerk & Tax	5.1
Atto	5
Shff & Cryer	1.15
	£400.4.7
Accruing Costs	5
	£400.9.7

Pride Vs Drew
Vends Expons, Fi Fa
Als. Issued
Chowan Supr. Court
September term 1807

Exposed the negroes within named as levied on for sale on the 1st day of October but could have no sale for want of Bidders
Wm H Green, Shff
Bertie

State of North Carolina
To the Sheriff of Bertie County, Greeting:
Whereas, we by our writ, commanded you that of the goods and chattels, lands and tenements of John Drew the Elder (in your bailiwick) you should cause to be made the sum of One Hundred & thirteen pounds eighteen shillings & six pence which lately in our Superior Court of Law at Edenton, Herbert Pride recovered against him as well for his damages which he sustained by reason of the non performance of certain promises &c. as for the costs and charges by him in his Suit in that behalf expended, whereof the said John Drew the Elder is convicted and liable as to us appears of record; besides your own fees for that service, and that you should have the said money before the Judges of our said Court, at Edenton, on the 1st Monday after the 4th Monday of September next, after the XIXth day of October in the year of our Lord one thousand eight

hundred and six to render to the said Herbert Pride his damages, costs and charges aforesaid: And you at that day returned on the said writ, that you had levied the same on negroes Sam, Lewis, Davis, Joe & Exi which remain in your hands unsold for want of Bidders. We do therefore command you, that you expose to sale the goods and chattels by you so as aforesaid levied upon, so that you have the said money and 5 shillings for accruing costs, before the Judges of our said Court, at Edenton, on the 1st Monday after the fourth Monday of September next, and we do command you further, that of the goods and chattels, lands and tenements of the said John Drew the Elder in your bailiwick, you cause to be made the residue of the said damages, costs and charges, and that you have the said money before the Judges of our said Court, at Edenton, on the day aforesaid, to render to the said Herbert Pride his damages, costs and charges aforesaid; and have you then and there this writ. Witness William Blair, Clerk of our said Court, at Edenton, the fourth day of April in the XXXIst year of our Independence, Anno Domini 1807.
Will Blair, Clk.

Judgment	£102.2.6
Clk & Tax	5.1.0
Atto	5
Shff & Cryer	1.15.0
	113.18.6
Accruing Costs	5
	£114.3.6

Pride als Vs. Drew
Vends Expons, Fi Fa
Chowan Supr. Court
March Term 1808
Not Sold for want of Bidders
Wm. H. Green
Bertie

State of North Carolina
To the Sheriff of Bertie County, Greeting:
Whereas, we by our writ, commanded you that of the goods and chattels, lands and tenements of John drew the Elder (in your bailiwick) you should cause to be made the sum of Four hundred pounds four shillings & seven

pence which lately in our Superior Court of Law at Edenton, Herbert Pride recovered against him as well for his damages which he sustained by reason of the non performance of certain promises before that time made to the said Herbert by the said John as for the costs and charges by him in his Suit in that behalf expended, whereof the said John Drew the Elder is convicted and liable as to us appears of record; besides your own fees for that service, and that you should the said money before the Judges of our said Court, at Edenton, on the 1st Monday after the fourth Monday of March next, after the XIXth day of October in the year of our Lord one thousand eight hundred and Six to render to the said Herbert Pride his damages, costs and charges aforesaid: And you at that day returned on the said writ, that you had levied the same on negroes Sam, Lewis, David, Joe & Exi which remain in you hands unsold for want of Bidders. We do command you, that you expose to sale the goods and Chattels by you so as aforesaid levied upon, so that you have the said money and 14 shillings for accruing costs, before the Judges of our said Court, at Edenton, on the first Monday after the fourth Monday of March next, and we do command you further, that of the goods and chattels, lands and tenements of the said John Drew the Elder in your bailiwick, you cause to be made the residue of the said damages, costs and charges, and that you have the said money before the Judges of our said Court, at Edenton, on the day aforesaid, to render to the said Herbert Pride his damages, costs and charges aforesaid; and have you then and there this writ. Witness William Blair, Clerk of our said Court, at Edenton the ninth day of October in the XXXIInd year of our Independence, Anno Domini 1807.
Will Blair, Clk

Judgment	£388.8.7
Clerk & Tax	5.1.0
Attorney	5
Shff & Cryer	1.15
	£400.4.7
Accruing Costs	14
	£400.18.7

Pride Vs Drew
Vends Expons, Fi Fa
Chowan Supr court
March Term 1808

Satisfied, Wm H. Green, Shff
Bertie

State of North Carolina

To the Sheriff of Bertie County, Greeting:

Whereas, we by our writ, commanded you that of the goods and chattels, lands, and tenements of John Drew the Elder (in your bailiwick) you should cause to be made the sum of One hundred & thirteen pounds eighteen shillings & six pence which lately in our Superior Court of law at Edenton, Herbert Pride recovered against the said John as well for his damages which he sustained by reason of the non performance of certain promises &c. as for the costs and charges by him in his Suit in that behalf expended, whereof the said John Drew the Elder is convicted and liable as to us appears of record; besides your own fees for that service, and that you should have the said money before the Judges of our said Court, at Edenton, on the 1st Monday after the fourth Monday of March next, after the XIXth day of October in the year of our Lord one thousand eight hundred and Six to render the said Herbert Pride his damages, costs and charges aforesaid: And you at that day returned on the said writ, that you had levied on Negroes Sam, Lewis, David, Joe & Exi which remain in your hands unsold for want of Bidders. We do therefore command you, that you again expose to sale the goods and chattels by you so as aforesaid levied upon, so that you have the said money and 14 shillings for accruing costs, before the Judges of our said Court, at Edenton, on the first Monday after the fourth Monday of March next, and we do command you further, that of the goods and chattels, lands and tenements of the said John Drew the Elder in your bailiwick, you cause to be made the residue of the said damages, costs and charges, and that you have the said money before the Judges of our said Court, at Edenton, on the day aforesaid, to render to the said Herbert Pride his damages, costs and charges aforesaid; and have you then and there this writ. Witness William Blair, Clerk of our said Court, at Edenton, the ninth day of October in the XXXIInd year of our Independence, Anno Domini 1807.

Will Blair, Clk

Judgment	£102.2.6
Clerk & Tax	5.1.0
Attorney JTC	5
Shff & cryer	1.15
Accruing Costs	1.4.0

£114.12.6

Recd on this Exor £10.15 Atto's fees, Recd the Atto's fee from Ja. Iredell
Herbert Pride

Pride Vs. Drew
Vends Exp, Fi Fa
Chowan Supr. Court
September Term 1808
Sattisfied, Wm H Green, Shff
Bertie

Sheriff will make sale on Saturday the 11th day of June 1808

State of North Carolina

To the Sheriff of Bertie County, greeting:

Whereas, we by our writ commanded you that of the goods and chattels, lands and tenements of lands & tenements of John Drew the Elder (in your Bailiwick) you should cause to be made the sum of Four hundred pounds four shillings & seven pence which lately in our Superior Court of Law at Edenton, Herbert Pride recovered against him as well for his damages which he sustained by reason of the non performance of certain promises before that time made to the said Herbert by the said John as for the costs and charges by him his Suit in that behalf expended, whereof the said John Drew the Elder is convicted and liable as to us appears of record; besides your own fees for that service, and that you should have the said money before the Judges of our said Court, at Edenton on the 1st Monday after the 4th Monday of September next, after the XIXth day of October in the year of our Lord one thousand eight hundred and Six to render to the said Herbert Pride his damages, costs and charges aforesaid: And you at that day returned on the said writ, that you had levied the same on negroes Sam, Lewis, David, Joe & Exi which remain in your hands unsold for want of Bidders. We do therefore command you, that you expose to sale the goods and chattels by you so as aforesaid levied upon, so that you have the said money and 23 shillings & three pence for accruing costs, before the Judges of our said Court, at Edenton, on the first Monday after the fourth Monday of September next, and we do command you further, that of the goods and chattels, lands and tenements of the said John in your bailiwick, you cause to be made the residue of the said damages, costs and charges, and that you have the said money before the Judges of our said Court, at

Edenton, on the day aforesaid, to render to the said Herbert Pride his damages, costs and charges aforesaid; and have you then and there this writ. Witness James Iredell, Clerk of our said Court, at Edenton, the 9th day of April in the XXXIInd year of our Independence, Anno Dom. 1808.
Jas. Iredell, Clk

Judgment	£388.8.7
Clk & Tax due Wm Blair	5.1
Atto	5
Shff & Cryer	1.15
	£400.4.7
Accruing costs due J.J.	1.3.3
	£401.7.10

****

William Shaw Vs. John Norcom
Civil Action [1807]
Chowan County Records

Wm Shaw Vs John Norcom
Fi fa
March Term 1808
Satisfied & paid the Plaintiff
E Hoskins, Shff,
Chowan

Recd 17th March 1808 the Amt of the within Judgment & damages in full from the Sheriff
Wm Shaw

State of North Carolina
To the Sheriff of Chowan County, Greeting:
You are hereby commanded, that of the goods and Chattels, lands and tenements of John Norcom (if to be found in your bailiwick) you cause to be made the sum of Fifty Pounds which lately in the County Court of Pleas and Quarter Sessions, held for Chowan County, William Shaw recovered against Sd. John Norcom for debt, , and also the sum of Seven pounds Ten Shillings & 9d for his damages, by reason of the detention of the said debt, and for the costs and charges by him in his suit expended, whereof the said

Chowan County
Civil Actions

John Norcom is convicted and liable as to us appears of record. And have you the said monies before the Justices of the said Court, to be held for the said County, at the Court House in Edenton, on the second Monday in March next, then and there to render to the said William Shaw for his debt, damages and costs and charges aforesaid. And have you then and there this writ. Witness Elisha Norfleet, Clerk of the said Court, the 17th day of december in the XXXII year of the Independence of the said State, Anno Dom. 1807
E Norfleet, CS

I do hereby agree, in case I should fail to pay to Edmd Hoskins, Shff of Chowan by the first day of March Court the Amt of a Judgment & Cost against myself, in favor of Wm Shaw of Nixonton that he may sell at public Sale before Mrs Horniblows door for ready Money, one Negroe Boy Stephen without advertising him to discharge the said Judgmt & Court
3rd March 1808
John Norcom

Judgment	£50
Damages	3.5
Clerk	£1.15.3
JBS Atto	2
Shff WR	10.6
	4.5.9
	57.10.9
Exrs & Court	1.16.3
Recd fifty pounds	£59.7.0

****

Josiah Collins Vs. John McCrae et als
Civil Actions [1807]
Chowan County Records

Josiah Collins Vs Jno McCrae als
Vends Exp
December Term 1807
The 6th Decr 1807
To late to hand
James Hoskins, Shff

Chowan County
Civil Actions

Tyrell

State of North Carolina

To the Sheriff of Tyrell County, Greeting:

Whereas we by our writ have commanded you, that of the goods and chattels, lands and tenements of Jno McCrae & Henry Flury in your bailiwick, you should cause to be made the sum of two hundred & seventy three pounds £273.13 whereof the said McCrae & Flury are convicted and liable, as appears to us of record, besides your own fees for this service; and that you should have those monies before the Justices of our Inferior Court of Pleas and Quarter Sessions, at our next Court, to be held for the County of Chowan at the Court House in Edenton on the 2nd Monday in December next; then and there to render to the said Josiah Collins his debt, damages and costs as aforesaid; and you at that day returned on the said writ to you directed, that you had levied on one negro boy named Prince and one horse riding chair & Harness. We do therefore command you, that you again expose to sale the property aforesaid, by you levied on, so that you have the money aforesaid before our Justices of our Inferior Court of Pleas and Quarter Sessions, to be held at the Court House in edenton on the 2nd Monday in December next; to render to the said Josiah Collins for his debt, damages and costs as aforesaid. Herein fail not, and have you then and there this writ. Witness Elisha Norfleet, Clerk of the said Court, at Edenton the 17th day of Septr in the XXXIInd year of the Independence of the said State, Anno Dom. 1807. Issued the 3rd day of Novr 1807.
E Norfleet, Clk

Judgment £268.8 to be discharged on payments of £117.5 with Int. from 25th Octr. 1804 & the further sum of £16.19 with Int. 24th Novr 1803 untill paid & all costs

Clerk	£2.7
Atto	2
Shff	10
	£5.5

****

Nathan Creecy Vs. Simion Simons
Civil Action [1807]
Chowan County Records

Chowan County
Civil Actions

Nathan Creecy als Vs. Simion Simons
Vends Exp
December Term 1807
Satisfied to Wm Roberts, former Sheriff
Mr Blount

State of North Carolina

To the Sheriff of **[Blank]** County, Greeting:

Whereas we by our writ have commanded you, that of the goods and chattels, lands and tenements of Simion Simons in your bailiwick, you should cause to be made the sum of forty six pounds 11/2 which Nathan Creecy lately recovered whereof the said Simion Simons is convicted and liable, as appears to us of record, besides your own fees for this service; and that you should have those monies before the Justices of our Inferior Court of Pleas and Quarter Sessions, at our next Court, to be held for the County of Chowan at the Court House in Edenton on the 2nd Monday in December next; then and there to render to the said Nathan Creecy his debt, damages and costs as aforesaid; and you at that day returned on the said writ to you directed, that you had levied on one negro man named Mingo & not sold by consent. we do therefore command you, that you again expose to sale the property aforesaid, by you levied on, so that you have the money aforesaid before our Justices of our Inferior Court of Pleas and Quarter Sessions, to be held at the Court House in Edenton on the 2nd Monday in December next; to render to the said Nathan Creecy for his debt, damages and costs as aforesaid. Herein fail not, and have you then and there this writ. Witness Elisha Norfleet, Clerk of the said Court, at Edenton the 17th day of September in the XXXIInd year of the Independence of the said State, Anno Dom. 1807. Issued 31st day of October 1807
E Norfleet.

Judgment	£41
Costs	5.17.11

****

Littlejohn Blount Vs. Lewis Bond
Civil Action [1808]
Chowan County Records

Chowan County
Civil Actions

Littlejohn Blount Vs Lewis Bond
Vends Exp
March Term 1809

Satisfied all cost & paid in the Office the Clk & Atto fees by sale of corn, the negroe and horses sold by Constable Jones by prior levies
Hoskins, Shff

State of North Carolina

To the Sheriff of Chowan County, Greeting:

Whereas we by our writ have commanded you, that of the goods and chattels, lands and tenements of Lewis Bond in your bailiwick, you should cause to be made the sum of one hundred thirty three pounds 18/b to be discharged on payment of £66: 19:3 with Interest, which Littlejohn Blount recovered agt. Said Lewis Bond & the costs whereof the said Lewis Bond is convicted and liable as appears to us of record, besides your own fees for this service; and that you should have those monies before the Justices of our Inferior Court of Pleas and Quarter Sessions, at our next Court, to be held for the County of Chowan, at the Court House in Edenton, on the second Monday in **[Blank]** next; then and there to render to the said Littlejohn Blount his debt, damages and costs as aforesaid; and you at that day returned on the said writ to you directed, that you had levied on the crop of Corn & one Negroe Fellow named Ben & two horses & stayed by the plaintiffs. We do therefore command you, that you again expose to sale the property aforesaid, by you levied on, so that you have the money in March next; to render to the said Littlejohn Blount for his debt, damages ans costs as aforesaid. Herein fail not, and have you then and there this writ. Witness Elisha Norfleet, Clerk of the said Court, at Edenton, the 17th day of December in the XXXIInd year of the Independence of the said State, Anno Dom. 1808.
E. Norfleet

Judgment£33:18: 6 to be discharged by paying the sum of £66: 19:3 with Int from 15th June 1807 to be paid.

Clerk	£2.10.3
Atto WAL	2
Shff	4.13.6
	£5: 3: 9

****

Chowan County
Civil Actions

Benjamin Coffield Vs. James W. Langley
Civil Action [1808]
Chowan County Records

Benj Coffield, Assignee Vs Jas Langly
Vends, Expons
September Term 1808
Satisfied & paid
Pltff Amt of Judgment
E Hoskins, Shff

State of North Carolina

To the Sheriff of Chowan County, Greeting:

Whereas we by our writ have commanded you, that of the goods and chattels, lands and tenements of James W. Langley in your bailiwick, you should cause to be made the sum of thirty four pounds Twelve shillings which Benjamin Coffield, assignee recovered agt. Him for Debt & the costs, whereof the said James W. Langley is convicted and liable as appears to us of record, besides your own fees for this service; and that you should have those monies before the Justices of our Inferior Court of Pleas and Quarter Sessions, at our next Court, to be held for the County of Chowan, at the Court House in Edenton, on the second Monday in June next; then and there to render to the said Benjamin Coffield, assignee, his debt, damages and costs as aforesaid; and you at that day returned on the said writ to you directed, that you had levied on Boy Jacob & the sale for **[?]** by the Plaintiff. We do therefore command you, that you again expose to sale the property aforesaid, by you levied on, so that you have the money aforesaid before our Justices of our Inferior Court of Pleas and Quarter Sessions, to be held at the Court House in Edenton, on the second Monday in September next; to render to the said Benjamin Coffield, Assignee & for his debt, damages and costs as aforesaid. Herein fail not, and have you then and there this writ. Witness Elisha Norfleet, Clerk of the said Court, at Edenton, the 17th day of June in the XXXIInd year of the Independence of the said State, Anno Dom. 1808.
E. Norfleet

Judgment	£30:18
Damages by way of Int	3:14
Clerk	6/9

Recd. The above Judgt. & Interest in full 17 Sept 1808
Benj. Coffield

****

Phillip McGuire & Benjamin Coffield Vs. John Dickinson
Civil Action [1808]
Chowan County Records

Phillip McGuire & Benjamin Coffield Vs. John Dickinson
Vends Expons
September Term 1808
Thos Coffield rect for John Fullington's Tickets
The Sale forbourn by the Plaintiff

State of North Carolina
To the Sheriff of Chowan County, Greeting:
Whereas we by our writ have commanded you, that of the goods and chattels, lands and tenements of John Dickinson in your bailiwick, you should cause to be made the sum of Fifty one pounds fifteen Shillings which Phillip McGuire & Benj Coffield, real Plff recovered agt. Him for debt and the costs of sixty, whereof the said John Dickinson is convicted and liable as appears to us of record, besides your own fees for this service; and that you have those monies before the Justices of our Inferior Court of Pleas and Quarter Sessions, at our next Court, to be held for the County of Chowan, at the Court House in Edenton, on the second Monday in June next; then and there to render to the said Benjamin Coffield, real Plaintiff his debt, damages and costs as aforesaid; and you at that day returned on the said writ to you directed, that you had levied on Man Tom the property of John Dickinson & forbourn by the plaintiff. We do therefore command you, that you again expose to sale the property aforesaid, by you levied on, so that you have the money aforesaid before our Justices of our Inferior Court of Pleas and Quarter Sessions, to be held at the Court House in Edenton, on the second Monday in September next; to render to the said Benjamin Coffield, Real Plaintiff for his debt, damages and costs as aforesaid. Herein fail not and have you then and there this writ. Witness Elisha Norfleet, Clerk of the said Court, at Edenton, the 17th day of June in the XXXIInd year of the Independence of the said State, Anno Dom. 1808.
E Norfleet

Judgment	£50
Damage	1.15
Clerk	6/9

Recd of Elisha Norfleet Seven pounds fourteen Shillings it being for amount of John Fullington's Tickets in the Suit James Sowel sued out agt Caleb Winslow, Septr 3rd 1808
Thos Coffield

Phillip McGuire & Ben: Coffield, Real Plff Vs. John Dickinson
December Term 1808

State of North Carolina
To the Sheriff of Chowan County, Greeting:
Whereas we by our writ have commanded you, that of the goods and chattels, lands and tenements of John Dickinson as before Required in your bailiwick, you should cause to be made the sum of Fifty one Pounds Fifteen Shillings which Phillip McGuire & Benj Coffield, real Plff recovered agt him and costs, whereof the said John Dickinson is convicted and liable as appears to us of record, besides your own fees for this service; and that you should have those monies before the Justices of our Inferior Court of Pleas and Quarter Sessions, at our next Court, to be held for the County of Chowan, at the Court House in Edenton, on the second Monday in **[Blank]** next; then and there to render to the said Benjamin Coffield, Real Plaintiff, his debt, damages and costs as aforesaid; and you at that day returned on the said writ to you directed, that you had levied on Man Tom the property of John Dickinson & forbourn by the Plaintiff. We do therefore command you, that you again expose to sale the property aforesaid, by you levied on, so that you have the money aforesaid before our Justices of our Inferior Court of Pleas and Quarter Sessions, to be held at the Court House in Edenton, on the second Monday in December next; to render to the said Benjamin Coffield, real Plff for his debt, damages and costs as aforesaid. Herein fail not, and have you then and there this writ. Witness Elisha Norfleet, Clerk of the said Court, at Edenton, the 17th day of September in the XXXII year of the Independence of the said State, Anno Dom. 1808.
E Norfleet

Judgment	£50
Damages	1.15
Clerk	13.6

Amt of Judgmt Satisfied & paid to John Coffield
13/6 cost paid in the Office
E Hoskins, Shff

****

William Saunders & Nathan Creecy Vs. Townsend Elliot
Civil Action [1808]
Chowan County Records

Wm. Saunders & N. Creecy, Real Plff Vs. Townsend Elliot
Vends, Expons
September Term 1808
Sale to on the 12th

State of North Carolina
To the Sheriff of Chowan County, Greeting:
Whereas we by our writ have commanded you, that of the goods and chattels, lands and tenements of Townsend Elliot in your bailiwick, you should cause to be made the sum of thirty seven pounds five shillings and four pence whereof the said Townsend Elliot is convicted and liable as appears to us of record, besides your own fees for this service; and that you have those monies before the Justices of our Inferior Court of Pleas and Quarter Sessions, at our next Court, to be held for the County of Chowan, at the Court House in Edenton, on the second Monday in September next; then and there to render to the said Wm. Saunders & Nathan Creecy, Real Plaintiff his debt, damages and costs as aforesaid; and you at that day returned on the said Writ to you directed, that you had levied on a Grist Mill and Negro man Jack. We do therefore command you, that you again expose to sale the property aforesaid, by you levied on, so that you have the money aforesaid before our Justices of our Inferior Court of Pleas and Quarter Sessions, to be held at the Court House in Edenton, on the second Monday in September next; to render to the said Townsend Elliot for his debt, damages and costs as aforesaid. Herein fail not, and have you then and there this writ. Witness Elisha Norfleet, Clerk of the said Court, at

Edenton, the 17th day of June in the XXXIInd year of the Independence of the said State, Anno Dom. 1808
E Norfleet

Judgment	£30.18.7
Clerk	6/9
	£37.5.4

Not sold for want of time to advertise the Mill & Negroe Jack sold by Virtue of an Excr. To the Shff of Perquimans prior to my Levy
E. Hoskins, Shff

Wm Sanders & Nathan Creecy, Real Plff Vs Elliot
Vends Exp
Septr Term 1808
Sale to be on the 12th

State of North Carolina

To the Sheriff of Chowan County, Greeting:

Whereas we by our writ have commanded you, that of the goods and chattels, lands and tenements of Townsend Elliot in your bailiwick, you should cause to be made the sum of Fifty Eight Pounds Fourteen Shillings & six pence & thirty seven shillings 82d for damage & the Costs whereof the said Townsend Elliot is convicted and liable as appears to us of record, besides your own fees for this service; and that you should have those monies before the Justices of our Inferior Court of Pleas and Quarter Sessions, at our next Court, to be held for the County of Chowan, at the Court House in Edenton, on the second Monday in June next; then and there to render to the said William Saunders & Nathan Creecy, Real Plff his debt, damages and costs as aforesaid; and you at that day returned on the said writ to you directed, that you had levied on his Grist Mill & a Negro Jack & Forbourn. We do therefore command you, that you again expose to sale the property aforesaid, by you levied on, so that you have the money aforesaid before our Justices of our Inferior Court of Pleas and Quarter Sessions, to be held at the Court House in Edenton, on the second Monday in September next; to render to the said Nathan Creecy, Real Plff for his debt, damages and costs as aforesaid. Herein fail not, and have you then and there this writ. Witness Elisha Norfleet, Clerk of the the said Court, at Edenton, the 17th day of June in the XXXIInd year of the Independence of the said State, Anno Dom. 1808.

Chowan County
Civil Actions

E. Norfleet

Judgment	£58.14.6
Damage	1.17.2
Clerk	6/9

The Mill not sold for want of time. Negroe Jack Sold by Virtue of an Execution to the Shff of Perquimans prior to my levy.
E. Hoskins, Shff

****

Gray & Blount Vs. James Langley
Civil Action [1808]
Chowan County Records

Gray & Blount, Indorsees
Vends Expons
September Term 1808
Satisfied
Chowan

State of North Carolina
To the Sheriff of Chowan County, Greeting:
Whereas, we by our writ commanded you that of the goods and chattels, lands and tenements of James W. Langley (in your bailiwick) you should cause to be made the sum of one hundred & thirty three Pounds seventeen shillings which lately in our County Court of Pleas & Quarter Sessions held for the County of Chowan Gray & Blount recovered against James W Langley for debt, and the further sum of Four pounds Twelve Shillings & six pence for the costs and charges by them in their suit in that behalf expended, whereof the said James W Langly is convicted and liable as to us appears of record; besides your own fees for that service, and that you should have the said money before the Justices of our said Court, at Edenton, on the second Monday next, after the **[Blank]** day of **[Blank]** in the year of our Lord one thousand eight hundred and 1808 to render to the said Gray & Blount their debt, damages, costs and charges aforesaid: And you at that day returned on the said writ, that you had levied the same on two Negroes, Joe & Isaac which remain in your hands unsold. We do therefore command you, that you expose to sale the goods and chattels

above named by you so as aforesaid levied upon, so that you have the said money and **[Blank]** shillings for accruing costs, before the Justices of our said Court, at Edenton, and we do command you further, that of the goods and chattels, lands and tenements of the said James W Langley in your bailiwick, you cause to be made the residue of the said damages, costs and charges, and that you have the said money before the Judges of our said Court, at Edenton, on the day aforesaid, to render to the said Gray & Blount damages, costs and charges aforesaid, and have you then and there this writ. Witness Elisha Norfleet, Clerk of our said Court, at Edenton, the 17th day of June the XXXIInd year of our Independence, Anno Dom. 1808
E. Norfleet

Judgment	£133.17
Costs, Pd.	£4:5:9
For als Fi Fa	6/9

Recd from Edmd Hoskins, Shff the within Judgt in full
Gray & Blount

****

Benjamin Coffield Vs. Josiah Skinner
Civil Action [1808]
Chowan County Records

Benj Coffield Vs Josiah Skinner
Vends Expons
December Term, 1808

State of North Carolina
To the Sheriff of Chowan County, Greeting:
Whereas we by our writ have commanded you, that of the goods and chattels, lands and tenements of Josiah Skinner in your bailiwick, you should cause to be made the sum of one hundred & Twenty five pounds with interest from 12th June 1807 untill paid, whereof the said Josiah Skinner is Convicted and liable as appears to us of record, besides your on fees for this service; and that you should have those monies before the Justices of our Inferior Court of Pleas and Quarter Sessions, at our next Court, to be held for the County of Chowan, at the Court House in Edenton, on the second Monday in **[Blank]** next; then and there to render

to the said Benj Coffield, assignee, his debt, damages and costs as aforesaid; and you at that day returned on the said writ to you directed, that you had levied on a Negro Man George & forborne by the Plff. We do therefore command you, that you again expose to sale the property aforesaid, by you levied on, so that you have the money aforesaid before our Justices of our Inferior Court of Pleas and Quarter Sessions, to be held at the Court House in Edenton, on the second Monday in December next; to render to the said Benjamin Coffield for his debt, damages and costs as aforesaid. Herein fail not, and have you then and there this writ. Witness Elisha Norfleet, Clerk of the said Court, at Edenton the 17th day of September in the XXXIII year of the Independence of the said State, Anno Dom. 1808.
E Norfleet

Judgment£125 with Interest from 12 June 1807 til paid

Judgment	
Clerk	£1:15:3
Atto	2
Shff	10.6
Als Vends Expons	6/9

The sum of £50 & 35/3 of the Clk's fees has been paid P return

---

Satisfied & paid the Judgmt to John Coffield P order. Clks Fees paid
E. Hoskins, Shff

Recd from Edmd Hoskins, Shff eighty five pounds 12/6 in full of this Judgmt & Interest 15th Decr. 1808
Thomas Coffield for John Coffield

Mr Edm Hoskins, Sir, pay the Balance of the Execution that is in your Hands that is against Josiah Skinner to Mr John Coffield
Benj Coffield
Jany 8th 1809
James Iredell for Jos B Skinner

Benj Coffield, assignee Vs. Josiah Skinner
Vends Expons
Als

December Term 1810

Satesfied the Atto fee & pd to the Pltff as Pr Receit Clks fee pd in the office
E. Hoskins, Shff

State of North Carolina
To the Sheriff of Chowan County, Greeting:
Whereas we by our writ have commanded you, that of the goods and chattels, lands and tenements of Josiah Skinner in your bailiwick, you should cause to be made the sum of one hundred Twenty five pounds which Benj Coffield, assignee recovered agt Josiah Skinner, whereof the said Josiah Skinner is convicted and liable, as appears to us of record, besides your own fees fir this service; and that you should have before the Justices of our Inferior Court of Pleas and Quarter Sessions, at our next Court, to be held for the County of Chowan at the Court House in Edenton on the 2nd Monday in Septr. Next; then and there to render to the said Benjamin Coffield, assignee & his debt, damages and costs as aforesaid; and you at that day returned on the said writ to you directed, that you had levied on one Negro Man George & forborne by the Plff. We do therefore command you, that you again expose to sale the property aforesaid, by you levied on, so that you have the money aforesaid before our Justices of our Inferior Court of Pleas and Quarter Sessions, to be held at the Court House in Edenton on the 2nd Monday in December next; to render to the said Benj Coffield, Assignee & his debt, damages and costs as aforesaid. Herein fail not, and have you then and there this writ. Witness Elisha Norfleet, Clerk of the said Court, at Edenton the 12th day of September in the XXXV year of the Independence of the said State, Anno Dom. 1810. Issued the 10th day of October 1810.
E. Norfleet

Judgment £125 with Interest from 12th 1807 till paid

Atto JBS (BC)	2
Clerk for this Exp & Cont	6/9
Sheriff	10.6

There was Satesfied September 1808 the sum of Fifty pounds to the Pltff
Recd the Atto fee forty Shillings
Benj Coffield

****

Chowan County
Civil Actions

Joseph Blount Vs James Hathaway
Civil Action [1808]
Chowan County Records

Joseph Blount, Assignee Vs James Hathaway, Esquire
Vends Expons
December Term 1808
Satisfied and paid the Pltff
E. Hoskins, Shff
Chowan

State of North Carolina
To the Sheriff of Chowan County, Greeting:
Whereas we by our writ have commanded you, that of the goods and chattels, lands and tenements of James Hathaway Esqr. in your bailiwick, you should cause to be made the sum of Seventy Seven Pounds 6/8 Which Joseph Blount, Assignee recovered agt. Said James Hathaway & for the Costs of Suit, whereof the said James Hathaway is convicted and liable as appears to us of record, besides your own fees for this service; and that you should have those monies before the Justices of our Inferior Court of Pleas and Quarter Sessions, at our next Court, to be held for the County of Chowan, at the Court House in Edenton, on the second Monday in September next; then and there to render to the said Joseph Blount, assignee &c his debt, damages and costs as aforesaid; and you at that day returned on the said writ to you directed, that you had levied on one Negroe Woman and three children and forborne by the Plaintiff. We do therefore command you, that you again expose to sale the property aforesaid, by you levied on, so that you have the money aforesaid before our Justices of our Inferior Court of Pleas and Quarter Sessions, to be held at the Court House in Edenton, on the second Monday in December next; to render to the said Joseph Blount, Assignee &c for his debt, damages and costs as aforesaid. Herein fail not, and have you then and there this writ. Witness Elisha Norfleet, Clerk of the said Court, at Edenton, the 17th day of September in the XXXIInd year of the Independence of the said State, Anno Dom.
E. Norfleet

Judgment & Damages	£72.7.2
Clerk	£2.6

Sheriff & Coroner Bertie 13.6

Recd 5th October 1808 Seventy Two pounds 7/2 for the Judgment on this Execution -- from Edmund Hoskins Esqr Shff of Chowan
Jos Blount

****

Thomas Stewart Vs. John Drew et als
Civil Action [1808]
Chowan County Records

Stewart vs Drew et als
Vends Expons, Fi Fa
Chowan Supr Court
September Term 1808
Sattisfied, Wm H Green, Shff
Bertie

State of North Carolina
To the Sheriff of Bertie County, Greeting:
Whereas, we by our writ commanded you that of the goods and chattels, lands and tenements of John Drew Junr., Jonathan Jacocks and David Goodman (in your bailiwick) you should cause to be made the sum of Ninety three pounds fifteen shillings which lately in our Superior Court of Law at Edenton, Thomas C. Stewart recovered against them for damages which he sustained by reason of certain promises &c. and also the further sum of Eleven pounds nineteen shillings for the costs and charges by him in his Suit in that behalf expended, whereof the said John, Jonathan & David are convicted and liable as to us appears of record; besides your own fees for that service, and that you should have the said money before the Judges of our said Court, at Edenton, on the 1st Monday after the 4th Monday of March next, after the 9th day of October in the year of our Lord one thousand eight hundred and seven to render to the said Thomas C. Stewart his damages, costs and charges aforesaid: And you at that day returned on the said writ, that you had levied the same on three negroes & two yoke of Oxen which remain in your hands unsold for want of Bidders. We do therefore command you, that you expose to sale the goods and chattels by you so as aforesaid levied upon, so that you have the said money and 9 shillings & 3d for accruing costs, before the Judges of our

said Court, at Edenton, on the first Monday after the fourth Monday of September next, and we do command you further, that of the goods and chattels, lands and tenements of the said John Drew, Jonathan Jacocks & David Goodman in your bailiwick, you cause to be made the residue of the said damages, costs and charges, and that you have the said money before the Judges of our said Court, at Edenton, on the day aforesaid, to render to the said Thomas C. Stewart his damages, costs and charges aforesaid; and have you then and there this writ. Witness James Iredell, Clerk of our said Court, at Edenton, the 9th day of April in the XXXIInd year of our Independence, Anno Dom. 1808.
Jas. Iredell, Clk

Damages	£93.15
Wm Blair former Clk	1.8
Jas Iredell, Clk	5
Atto W.C.	5
Costs below	5.6
	£105.14
Accruing costs du J.J. Clk	9.3
	£106.3.3

Recd W.B. & fees & 14/3 J.J.

****

Thomas Saterfield Vs. James Bond
Civil Action [1808]
Chowan County Records

Den ex Den Thos Saterfield Vs Roe & James Bond
Vends Expons
March Term 1808
Chowan

State of North Carolina
To the Sheriff of Chowan County, Greeting:
Whereas we by our writ have commanded you, that of the goods and chattels, lands and tenements of James Bond in your bailiwick, you should cause to be made the sum of Eleven pounds Fourteen Shillings & ten pence whereof the said James Bond is convicted and liable, as appears to us of record, besides your own fees for this service; and that you should have

those monies before the Justices of our Inferior Court of Pleas and Quarter Sessions, at our next Court, to be held for the County of Chowan at the Court House in Edenton on the second Monday in Decr. Next; then and there to render to Thomas Saterfield his costs as aforesaid; and you at that day returned on the said writ to you directed, that you had levied on James Bond Interest in a Negro Man named Jack & not sold for want of Time. We do therefore command you, that you again expose to sale the property aforesaid before our Justices of our Inferior Court of Pleas and Quarter Sessions, to be held at the Court House in Edenton on the second Monday in March next; to render to the said Thomas Saterfield for costs as aforesaid. Herein fail not, and have you then and there this writ. Witness Elisha Norfleet, Clerk of the said Court, at Edenton the 17th day of December in the XXXIInd year of the Independence of the said State, Anno Dom. 1807. Issued the 7th day of Jany 1808.
E. Norfleet

The within Mentioned Negroe Jack was sold which satisfyed in part of a Vends, Expons at the instance of the [?] the Court Vs. Jas. Bond which did not satisfy the same
Edmd Hoskins, Shff

Clerk & Tax	£2.14.6
JBS Atto	5
Sheriff	1.15
Phill McGuire	2.5.4

****

Lewis Bond Vs. Reuben Small
Civil Action [1809]
Chowan County Records

Lewis Bond Vs Reuben Small
Fi Fa
December Term 1809

Satisfied & paid in the Office Clk & Atto fees & Mr Thompson say £5.7.9
E Hoskins, Shff

State of North Carolina

Chowan County Civil Actions

To the Sheriff of Chowan County, Greeting:
We command you, that of the goods and chattels, lands and tenements of Reuben Small Esqr as before required Negro Boy Squire was levied on (if to be found in your bailiwick) you cause to be made the sum of Nine pounds one Shilling & Seven pence which was lately in our County Court of Pleas and Quarter Sessions, held for Chowan County, at the Court House in Edenton, adjudged to Lewis Bond for the costs of a Suit, he sued out agt said Lewis & was nonsuited for costs and charges in the said suit expended, whereof the said Reuben Small Esqr is liable, as appears to us of record. And have you the said monies, besides your fees for this service, before our said Court, at Edenton aforesaid, on the second Monday in December next, then and there to render to the Officers of the Court the costs and charges aforesaid. Herein fail not, and have you then and there this writ. Witness Elisha Norfleet, Clerk of the said Court, the 14th day of september Anno Dom. 1809
E. Norfleet

Clerk	£2.16.3
Atto WAL	2
Sheriff	1.2
Mr Thompson	11.6
Due to E.H.} J.N. for M. Beckley	1.14.4
For E Simpson	17.6
	£9.1.7

Lewis Bond Vs Reuben Small
Vends Expons
September Term 1809
Forborne
E Hoskins, Shff

State of North Carolina
To the Sheriff of Chowan County, Greeting:
Whereas we by our writ have commanded you, that of the goods and chattels, lands and tenements of Reuben Small in your bailiwick, you should cause to be made the sum of Eight pounds fourteen shillings & Ten pence which was adjudged to Lewis Bond for the costs of Suit wherein Reuben Small was nonsuited, whereof the said Reuben Small is convicted and liable as appears to us of record, besides your own fees for this service;

and that you should have those monies before the Justices of our Inferior Court of Pleas and Quarter Sessions, at our next Court, to be held for the County of Chowan, at the Court House in Edenton, on the second Monday in **[Blank]** next; then and there to render to the said Lewis Bond for his costs as aforesaid; and you at that day returned on the said writ to you directed, that you had levied on one Negroe Boy named Squire, & not sold for want of Bidders. We do therefore command you, that you again expose to sale the property aforesaid, by you levied on, so that you have the money aforesaid before our Justices of our Inferior Court of Pleas and Quarter Sessions, to be held at the Court House in edenton, on the second Monday in September next; to render to the said Lewis Bond for his costs as aforesaid. Herein fail not, and have you then and there this writ. Witness Elisha Norfleet, Clerk of the said Court, at Edenton, the 15th day of June in the XXXIInd year of the Independence of the said State, Anno Dom. 1809.
E Norfleet

Judgment	
Clerk	£2.9.6
Atto WAL	2
Sheriff	1.2
Wm Thompson	11.6
Moses Buckley	1.14.4
JN for Evan Simpson	17.6
John Bond	

****

Jackson Hoyle Vs John Dickinson
Civil Action [1809]
Chowan County Records

Jackson Hoyle, Tredwell & Allen, Infant Vs John Dickinson
Vends Expons
Forborne by the Plttf's Atto
E. Hoskins, Shff

State of North Carolina
To the Sheriff of Chowan County, Greeting:

Chowan County
Civil Actions

Whereas we by our writ have commanded you, that of the goods and chattels, lands and tenements of John Dickinson in your bailiwick, you should cause to be made the sum of two hundred & sixty one pounds ten shillings, Debt & five pounds 13/8 costs, whereof the said John Dickinson is convicted and liable as appears to us of record, besides your own fees for this service; and that you should have those monies before the Justices of our Inferior Court of Pleas and Quarter Sessions, at our next Court, to be held for the County of Chowan, at the Court House in Edenton, on the second Monday in **[Blank]** next; then and there to render to the said Jackson S. Hoyle recovered for his debt, damages and costs as aforesaid; and you at that day returned on the said writ to you directed, that you had levied on, Negroe Boy Ralfe & Sd. John's right of the Brick House Plantation & was forborned by Pltffs atto. We do therefore command you, that you again expose to sale the property aforesaid, by you levied on, so that you have the money aforesaid before our Justices of our Inferior Court of Pleas and Quarter Sessions, to be held at the Court House in Edenton, on the second Monday in december next; to render to the said Jackson S Hoyle, Tredwell & Allen, Real Pltff for debt, damages and costs as aforesaid. Herein fail not, and have you then and there this writ. Witness Elisha Norfleet, Clerk of the said Court, at Edenton, the 14th day of September in the XXXIVth year of the Independence of the said State, Anno Dom. 1809.
E Norfleet

Judgment£261 to be discharged on payment of the sum of 130.16.6 Interest from 13th May 1808 till paid

Clerk	£2.3.6
Atto WAL	2
Sheriff	13.6
H. Gorham	0.16.8
	5.13.8

****

Margaret Norfleet Vs. James Jones
Civil Action [1809]
Chowan County Records

Norfleet Vs. Jones

Writ
September Term 1809
Chowan
Executed, E. Hoskins, Shff
Iredell Atto

I am Security for the costs of this Suit
Jas. Iredell (Seal)

State of North Carolina
To the Sheriff of Chowan County, Greeting:
You are hereby commanded to take the body of James Jones if to be found in your bailiwick, and him safely keep, so that you have him before the Justices of the County Court of Pleas and Quarter Sessions, to be held at the Court House in Edenton, in the County of Chowan, on the second Monday of September next, then and there to answer unto Margaret Norfleet of a plea that he render to her a certain negro man slave named Charles of the value of Three hundred pounds which from her hr unjustly detains to her damage fifty pounds. Herein fail not, and have you then and there this writ, and how you have executed the same. Witness Elisha Norfleet, Clerk of the said Court, at Edenton, this second Monday of June in the year of our Lord, 1809 and in the XXXIInd year of American Independence
E. Norfleet

Writ of Tax	£1.4
4 Subp 1/6	0.6.0
1 Coms	0.2.4
2 Seals of Court 2/6	0.5.0
3 Contens 3/	0.9.0
Deter & Exr	0.11.3
	£2.17.7
Atto JB & WAL	2
Sheriff	1.5.6
	6.3.1

****

Officers Vs. Evans et als
Civil Action [1809]

Chowan County
Civil Actions

Chowan County Records

Officers Vs Evans & als
Vends Expons, Fi Fa for costs
Chowan Supr Court
September term 1809
Balling Fetter, DShff
Hertford

State of North Carolina

To the Sheriff of Hertford County, Greeting:

Whereas, we by our writ commanded you that of the goods and chattels, lands and tenements of Eden Evans, James Moore & N. Harrell (in your bailiwick) you should cause to be made the sum of Seven pounds eight shillings & five pence which lately in our Superior Court of Law at Edenton, was taxed & adjudged to the officers of our said Court as the costs & charges of a Suit there brought by the said Eden Evans against James Odham, whereof the said Eden Evans, James Moore & N. Harrell are convicted and liable as to us appears of record; besides your own fees for that service, and that you should have the said money before the Judges of our said Court, at Edenton, on the first Monday after the fourth Monday of September next, after the 9th day of April in the year of our Lord one thousand eight hundred and eight to render to the said Officers their costs and charges aforesaid: And you at that day returned on the said writ, that you had levied the same on one feather bed of Eden Evans, & one negro woman of the Estate of Nathan Harrell which remain in your hands unsold, for want of Bidders. We do therefore command you, that you expose to sale the goods and chattels by you so as aforesaid levied upon, so that you have the said money and 18 shillings & 6d for accruing costs, before the Judges of our said Court, at Edenton, on the first Monday after the fourth Monday of September next, and we do command you further, that of the goods and chatells, lands and tenements of the said Eden, James & N. Harrell in your bailiwick, you cause to be made the residue of the said costs and charges, and that you have the said money before the said Judges of our said Court, at Edenton, on the day aforesaid, to render to the said Officers their costs and charges aforesaid; and have you then and there this writ. Witness James Iredell, Clerk of our said Court, at Edenton, the 7th day of April in the XXXIInd year of our Independence, Anno Dom. 1809.
Jas. Iredell

Wm Blair late Clk	£6.7.6
J.J. Clk	18.3
Cryer	2.8
	£7.8.5
Accruing Costs due J.J. Clk	18.3
	£8.6.8

Recd WBS fees & my own £8.4 J.J. Clk

****

Cross Vs. Mumford
Civil Action [1809]
Chowan County Records

Cross & als Vs Mumford
Fi Fa
Chowan Supr Court
March Term 1810
Came to hand the 25th day of Jany
Satisfied

T Gilmore, Shff
I have retained the Sheriffs fees of nineteen shillings & six pence inserted in this Bill of Costa
T. Gilmore, Shff

State of North Carolina
To the Sheriff of Cumberland County, Greeting
We command you that you distrain Robinson Mumford late of your said County, by all his goods & chattels, lands & tenements so that neither he nor any person by him lay hands on them untill you shall have other commands from us therefore, and that of the rents, issues and profits you account to the Judge of our Superior Court of Law to be holden in and for the County of Chowan at the Court House in the Town of Edenton on the first Monday after the Fourth Monday of March next, so as to compel the said Robinson Mumford to render to Richard T. Cross, Edward Cross, Luten Lewis & Margaret his Wife a certain negro woman slave of the name of Violet of the price of two hundred pounds which from them he unjustly detains; And we also command you that of the goods, chattels, lands & tenements of the said Robinson Mumford in your bailiwick you

cause to be made the sum of Sixty pounds seven shillings & nine pence which lately in our said Court the said Richard T. Cross, Edward Cross, Luten Lewis and Margaret his Wife recovered against him as well for their damages which they sustained by reason of the detention of the said negro slave, as for the costs & charges in & about their Suit in that behalf by them laid out & expended, whereof the said Robinson Mumford is convicted & liable as to us appears of record, besides your own fees for this service -- Herein fail not & have you the said money before the Judge of our said Court at Edenton on the day aforesaid to render to the said Richard T. Cross, Edward Cross, Luten Lewis & Margaret his wife their damages, costs & charges aforesaid, & how you shall have executed this Writ you are then and there to make known to our said Court -- Witness James Iredell Clerk of our said Court at Edenton the seventh day of October in the XXXIVth year of American Independence & in the year of our Lord One thousand eight hundred and Nine.
Jas. Iredell

Damages	£4.3
William Blair late Clk	2.6
J.J. Clk	2.0.3
Atto	5
Sheriff	19.6
Abel Cross Wife	7.2
	£60.27.9

We Acknowledge the receipt of the Negro Woman Slave Violet Mentioned in this Execution, from Robinson Mumford the Defendant given under our hands this 25th day of jany 1810

Edwd Cross for Richard Cross
Edwd Cross for himself

The damages of Forty Three pounds is paid to Plaintiffs
29th March 1810
T. Cross, Edwd Cross

****

William Littlejohn Vs. Moses Sumner
Civil Action [1809]
Chowan County Records

Chowan County Civil Actions

Littlejohn Vs. Sumner
Vends Expons, Fi Fa
Chowan Supr Court
Lewis Walters, Shff
Hertford

State of North Carolina

To the Sheriff of Hertford County, Greeting:

Whereas, we by our writ commanded you that of the goods and chattels, lands and tenements of Moses Sumner (in your bailiwick) you should cause to be made the sum of One hundred and thirty one pounds eleven shillings & three pence which lately in our Superior Court of Law at Edenton, William A. Littlejohn recovered against him for Debt & damages sustained by reason of the detention of that Debt and also for the costs and charges by him in his suit in that behalf expended, whereof the said Moses Sumner is convicted and liable as to us appears of record; besides your own fees for that service, and that you should have the said money before the Judges of our said Court, at Edenton, on the first Monday after the Fourth Monday of September next, after the seventh day of April in the year of our Lord one thousand eight hundred and Nine to render to the said William A. Littlejohn his debt, damages, costs and charges aforesaid: And you at that day returned on the said writ, that you had levied the same on three negroes which remain in your hands unsold for want of Bidders. We do therefore command you, that you expose to sale chattels by you so as aforesaid levied upon, so that you have the said money and 9 shillings for accruing costs, before the Judges of our said Court, at Edenton, on the first Monday after the fourth Monday of March next, and we do command you further, that of the goods and chattels, lands and tenements of the said Moses Sumner in your bailiwick, you cause to be made the residue of the said Debt, damages, costs at edenton, on the day aforesaid, to render to the said William A. Littlejohn his Debt, damages, costs and charges aforesaid; and have you then and there this writ. Witness James Iredell, Clerk of our said Court, at Edenton, the, the 7th day of April in the XXXIVth year of our Independence, Anno Dom. 1809.
Jas. Iredell

Recd. February 26th 1810 of Bolling Felton Deputy Sheriff Hertford County one hundred & thirty three pounds twelve shillings & six pence in full of the within Debt, damage & Interest.

Debt	£125
Damages	2.6
	£127.6
Ja. Iredell, Clk	2.9.6
Atto WAL	2
Shff	10.6

N.B. the Debt £125 bears interest from 7th April 1809 till paid according to act of assembly
Jas. Iredell, Clk

The Judgment is payable to Miles Rayner
J.J. , Clk

****

John Haughton Vs. Thomas Vail
Civil Action [1810]
Chowan County Records

John Haughton, assignee Vs. Thomas Vail
Vends Expons
September Term 1810
Forborne by the Plff
E Hoskins, Shff

State of North Carolina
To the Sheriff of Chowan County, Greeting:
Whereas we by our writ have commanded you, that of the goods and chattels, lands and tenements of Thomas Vail in your bailiwick, you should cause to be made the sum of Fifty five Pounds with Interest Costs of Suit, which John Haughton assignee recovered agt. Him, whereof the said Thomas Vail is convicted and liable as appears to us of record, besides your own fees for this service; and that you should have those monies before the Justices of our inferior Court of Pleas and Quarter Sessions, at our next Court, to be held for the County of Chowan, at the Court House in Edenton, on the second Monday in June next; then and there to render to the said John Haughton, Assignee &c his debt, damages and costs as aforesaid; and you at that day returned on the said writ to you directed, that

you had levied on Negroes Rachael & Jim & was forborne. We do therefore command you, that you again expose to sale the property aforesaid, by you levied on, so that you have the money aforesaid before our Justices of our Inferior Court of Pleas and Quarter Sessions, to be held at the Court House in Edenton, on the second Monday in September next; to render to the said John Haughton his debt, damages and costs as aforesaid. Herein fail not, and have you then and there this writ. Witness Elisha Norfleet, Clerk of the said Court, at Edenton, the 16th day of June in the in the XXXIV year of the Independence of the said State, Anno Dom. 1810.
E. Norfleet

Judgment £55 with Interest from 14th September 1809 till paid

Damage	1.0.2
Clerk	2.8.9
Atto TBH	2
Shff	0.10.6

****

John Coffield Vs. Jesse Hassell
Civil Action [1810]
Chowan County Records

John Coffield, Assignee Vs Jesse Hassell, & als
Vends Expons
June Term 1810

Satisfied & paid the Pltff Amot. Of Judgmt & Damages, Cost paid in the office, E Hoskins, Shff.

State of North Carolina
To the Sheriff of Chowan County, Greeting:
Whereas we by our writ have commanded you, that of the goods and chattels, lands and tenements of Jesse Hassell in your bailiwick, you should cause to be made the sum of Ninety two pounds Ten Shillings; which John Coffield Assignee &c recovered agt. Jessey Hassell & for debt, whereof the said Jessey Hassell & is convicted and liable as appears to us of record, besides your own fees for this service; and that you should have

those monies before the Justices of our Inferior Court of Pleas and Quarter Sessions, at our next Court, to be held for the County of Chowan, at the Court House in Edenton, on the second Monday in December, then next; then and there to render to the said John Coffield, assignee &c his debt, damages and costs as aforesaid; and you at that day returned on the said writ to you directed, that you had levied on a Negro Woman Rose & Boy George the property of Jesse Hassell, the sale forborne by the Pltff. We do therefore command you, that you again expose to sale the property aforesaid, by you levied on, so that you have the money aforesaid before our Justices of our Inferior Court of Pleas and Quarter Sessions, to be held at the Court House in Edenton, on the second in June next; to render to the said John Coffield, assignee &c for his debt, damages and costs as aforesaid. Herein fail not, and have you then and there this writ. Witness Elisha Norfleet, Clerk of the said Court, at Edenton, the 17th day of March in the XXXIV year of the Independence of the said State, Anno Dom. 1810
E Norfleet, Clk

Judgment	£92.10
Damages	3.14.0
Clerk	0.6.9

Recd payment in full of the above Judgt. & Int.
14 June 1810, Thos. Coffield

****

Robert Bowne Vs. Reuben Small
Civil Action [1810]
Chowan County Records

Robert H.Bowne Vs Reuben Small
September Term 1810
Forborne by the Plttf's Atto
E Hoskins, Shff

State of North Carolina
To the Sheriff of Chowan County, Greeting:
Whereas we by our writ have commanded you, that of the goods and chattels, lands and tenements of Reuben Small Esqr. in your bailiwick, you

should cause to be made the sum of Sixty five pounds 5/4 and costs of Suit, which Robert H Bowne recovered against him, whereof the said Reuben Small is convicted and liable as appears to us of record, besides your own fees for this service; and that you should have those monies before the justices of our Inferior Court of Pleas and Quarter Sessions, at our next Court, to be held for the County of Chowan, at the Court House in Edenton, on the second Monday in June then next; then and there to render to the said Robert H. Bowne his debt, damages and costs as aforesaid; and you at that day returned on the said writ to you directed, that you had levied on one Negroe woman Simon, one Negroe Girl and one boy named Squire & not sold for want of Bidders. We do therefore command you, that you again expose to sale the property aforesaid, by you levied on, so that you have the money aforesaid before our Justices of our Inferior Court of Pleas and Quarter Sessions, to be held at the Court House in edenton, on the second Monday in September next; to render to the said Robert H Bowne for his debt, damages and costs as aforesaid. Herein fail not, and have you then and there this writ. Witness Elisha Norfleet, Clerk of the said Court, at Edenton, the 16th day of June in the XXXIV year of the Independence of the said State, Anno Dom. 1810.
E Norfleet, Clk

This execution draws Interest from the time of the Judgt., Reuben Small.

Judgment £61 with Interest from the 15th Decr. 1809

Damage	4.5.4
Clerk	2.11.9
Atto JBS	2
Sheriff	0.16.6
	70.13.7

R H Bowne Vs. Reuben Small
Vends Expons
December Term 1810
Amot. Of Cost Satisfied & paid in the Office Clk
& Atto fee, E. Hoskins, Shff

State of North Carolina
To the Sheriff of Chowan County, Greeting:

Chowan County
Civil Actions

Whereas we by our writ have commanded you, that of the goods and chattels, lands and tenements of Reuben Small Esqr. in your baliwick, you should cause to be made the sum of Seventy one pounds & 4d which Robert H Bowne lately recovered agt. Him whereof the said Reuben Small is convicted and liable, as appears to us of record, besides your own fees for this service; and that you should have those monies before the Justices of our Inferior Court of Pleas and Quarter Sessions, at our next Court, to be held for the County of Chowan at the Court House in Edenton on the 2nd Monday in **[Blank]** next; then and there to render to the said Robert H Bowne his debt, damages and costs as aforesaid; and you at that day returned on the said writ to you directed, that you had levied on Negroe Simon, one Negroe Girl, and one Boy named Squire and not sold for want of Bidders. We do therefore command you, that you again expose to sale the property aforesaid, by you levied on, so that you have the money aforesaid before the Justices of our Inferior Court of Pleas and Quarter Sessions, to be held at the Court House in Edenton on the 2nd Monday in December next; to render to the said Robert H Bowne for his debt, damages and costs aforesaid. Herein fail not, and have you then and there this writ. Witness Elisha Norfleet, Clark of the said Court, at Edenton the 12th day of September in the XXXV year of the Independence of the said State, anno Dom. 1810. Issued the 19th day of October 1810.
E. Norfleet, Clk

Judgt. & Int. forborne, by John Coffield real Plaintiff, Cost Satisfied
E. Hoskins, Shff

Judgment £61 with Int from 15th December 1809 till paid

Damage	4.5.4
Clerk	2.18.6
Atto JBS	2
Sheriff	0.16.6

Robert H Bowne vs Reuben Small
Vends Expons
March 1811

State of North Carolina
To the Sheriff of Chowan County, Greeting:

Whereas we by our writ have commanded you, that of the goods and chattels, lands and tenements of Reuben Small Esqr in your bailiwick, you should cause to be made the sum of Seventy one Pounds Seven Shillings & one penny which Robert H Bowne lately recovered agt him, whereof the said Reuben Small is convicted and liable, as appears to us of record, besides your own fees for this service; and that you should have those monies before the Justices of our Inferior Court of Pleas and Quarter Sessions, at our next Court, to be held for the County of Chowan at the Court House in Edenton on the 2nd Monday in **[Blank]** next; then and there to render to the said Robert H Bowne his debt, damages and costs aforesaid; and you at that day returned on the said writ to you directed, that you had levied on Negroe Simon, one Negroe Girl & one Boy named Squire & forborne by John Coffield, Real Plaintiff. We do therefore command you, that you again expose to sale the property aforesaid, by you levied on, so that you have the money aforesaid before our Justices of our Inferior Court of Pleas and Quarter Sessiond, to be held at the Court House in Edenton on the 2nd Monday in March next; to render to the said Robert H Bowne or J.C. for his debt, damages and costs as aforesaid. Herein fail not, and have you then and there this writ. Witness Elisha Norfleet, Clerk of the said Court, at Edenton the 15th day of December in the XXXVI year of the Independence of the said State, Anno Dom. 1810. Issues the 2nd day of Jany 1811.
E. Norfleet, Clk

Judgment	£61 with Int from Decr. 1809 till paid	
Damages		4.5.4
Costs		5.15.0
Clerk for this		0.6.9
		71.76.19

Robert H Bowne, Assignee Vs Reuben Small
Vends Expons
June Term 1811

State of North Carolina
To the Sheriff of Chowan County, Greeting:
Whereas we by our writ have commanded you, that of the goods and chattels, lands and tenements of Reuben Small Esqr in your bailiwick, you should cause to be made the sum of Seventy one pounds thirteen shillings

& Ten pence which Robert H Bowne lately recovered agt. Sd. Reuben Small, whereof the said Reuben Small is convicted and liable, as appears to us of record, besides your own fees for this service; and that you should have those monies before the Justices of our Inferior Court of Pleas and Quarter Sessions, at our next Court, to be held for the County of Chowan at the Court House in Edenton on the 2nd Monday in **[Blank]** next; then and there to render to the said Robert H Bowne for his debt, damages and costs aforesaid; and you at that day returned on the said writ to you directed, that you had levied on Negroe Simon, one Negroe Girl & one Boy named Squire & Forborned by John Coffield, Real Plaintiff. We do therefore command you, that you again expose to sale the property, by you levied on, so that you have the money aforesaid before our Justices of our Inferior Court of Pleas and Quarter Sessions, to be held at the Court House in Edenton on the 2nd Monday in June next; to render to the said Robert H Bowne for his debt, damages and costs aforesaid. Herein fail not, and have you then and there this writ. Witness Elisha Norfleet, Clerk of the said Court, at Edenton the 4th day of March in the XXXVth year of the Independence of the said State, Anno Dom. 1811.
E. Norfleet, Clk

Satisfied all costs and twenty Pounds & 1d and paid to Plaintiff
Jas. Skinner, Shff

Receivd twenty Pound and 7d in part of the within Judgment June the 12th 1811
Thos Coffield

Judgment £61 with Interest from 15th Decr. 1809 till paid	
Damages	£4.5.4
Costs	5.15.0
Clerk 2 **[?]** Vends Expons	0.13.6

Robert H Bowne, Assignee, John Coffield, real Plaintiff Vs Reuben Small
Vends Expons
Issued 4th Jany
March Term 1812
Suspended by the Pltff
E. Hoskins, Shff

Chowan County
Civil Actions

State of North Carolina

To the Sheriff of Chowan County, Greeting:

Whereas we by our writ have commanded you, that of the goods and chattels, lands and tenements of Reuben Small in your bailiwick, you should cause to be made the sum mof Sixty one pounds which Robt. H. Bowne recovered against him for debt as also the sum of £10.13.10 Damages, Cost and charges whereof the said Reuben Small is convicted and liable, as appears to us of record, besides your own fees for this service; and that you should have those monies before the Justices of our Inferior Court of Pleas and Quarter Sessions, at our next Court, to be held for the County of Chowan at the Court House in Edenton on the 2nd Monday in June next; then and there to render to the said Robert H Bowne, his debt, damages and costs as aforesaid; and you at that day returned on the said writ to you directed, that you had levied on One Negro woman named **[Blank]**, one small Girl named **[Blank]** and one boy named Squire. We do therefore command you, that you again expose to sale the property aforesaid, by you levied on, so that you have the money aforesaid before our Justices of our Inferior Court of Pleas and Quarter Sessions, to be held at the Court House in Edenton on the 2nd Monday in March next; to render to the said Robert H Bowne for his debt, damages and costs as aforesaid. Herein fail not, and have you then and there this writ. Witness James Norfleet, Clerk pf the said Court, at Edenton the 13th day of decemr in the XXX6 year of the Independence of the said State, Anno Dom 1811.

Jas. Norfleet, Clk

Judgment £61 Int from 15th Decr 1809

Damage	£4.5.4
Clerk	0.6.9
	4.12.1

£20 pd. Has been pd. On the above at June 1811

Robt. H. Bowne, Assignee & John Coffield, Plaintiff
Vends Expons
44.5
Issued 13th April
June Term 1812
Satisfied, Jas Skinner, DShff
Rect 13/6 J.W., Clk

Chowan County
Civil Actions

State of North Carolina
To the Sheriff of Chowan County, Greeting:
Whereas we by our writ have commanded you, that of the goods and chattels, lands and tenements of Reuben Small in your bailiwick, you should cause to be made the sum of Sixty One pounds which Robert H. Bowne recovered against him for Debt as also the sum of £4.12.1 Cost, Damages &c, whereof the said Reuben Small is convicted and liable, as appears to us of record, besides your own fees for this service; and that you should have those monies before the Justices of our Inferior Court of Pleas and Quarter Sessions, at our next Court, to be held for the County of Chowan at the Court House in Edenton on the 2nd Monday in March next; then and there to render to the said Robert H. Bowne his debt, damages and costs as aforesaid; and you at that day returned on the said writ to you directed, that you had levied on Negro woman named Betty, on small girl named Ann and one boy named Squire and suspended by John Coffield, Real Plaintiff. We do therefore command you, that you again expose to sale the property aforesaid, by you levied on, so that you have the money aforesaid before our Justices of our Inferior Court of Pleas and Quarter Sessions, to be held at the Court House in Edenton on the second Monday in June next; to render to the said Robert H. Bowne for his debt, damages and costs as aforesaid. Herein fail not, and have you then and there this writ. Witness James Norfleet, Clerk of the said Court, at Edenton the 12th day of March in the XXXIth year of the Independence of the said State, Anno Dom. 1812.
Jas Norfleet, Clk

Recd Satisfaction in full this the 2nd day of June 1812
Thos Coffield & John Coffield

Judgment £61 Int from 15th Decr. 1809
Damage 4.5.4
Clerk 0.13.6
£20.0.7 was paid at June Term 1811

****

Henry Wills Vs William Blair
Civil Action [1810]
Chowan County Records

Henry Wills Vs Wm Blair
Vends Expons
December Term 1810
Perquimans
Levied on Negroe Woman Suck

State of North Carolina
To the Sheriff of Perquimans County, Greeting:
Whereas we by our writ have commanded you, that of the goods and chattels, lands and tenements of William Blair, Esqr. in your bailiwick, you should cause to be made the sum of Seventy seven Pounds five Shillings & 11d which Henry Wills recovered agt. William Blair, whereof the said William Blair is convicted and liable, as appears to us of record, besides your own fees for this service; and that you should have those monies before the Justices of our Inferior Court of Pleas and Quarter Sessions, at our next Court, to be held for the County of Chowan at the Court House in Edenton on the 2nd Monday in September next; then and there to render to the said Henry Wills, his debt, damages and costs as aforesaid; and you at that day returned on the said writ to you directed, that you had levied on, Jef, John, Mary, Will and Pompy to satisfy these three Executions & not sold for want of Bidders. We do therefore command you, that you again expose to sale the property aforesaid, by you levied on, so that you have the money aforesaid before our Justices of our Inferior Court of Pleas and Quarter Sessions, to be held at the Court House in Edenton on the 2nd Monday in December next; to render to the said Henry Wills for his debt, damages and costs aforesaid. Herein fail not, and have you then and there this writ. Witness Elisha Norfleet, Clerk of the said Court, at Edenton the 12th day of September in the XXV year of the Independence of the said state, Anno Dom. 1810. Issued the 22nd day of Septr. 1810.
E. Norfleet.

Not sold for want of Bidders
Wm Felton, DShff

Judgment	£71.0.8
Clerk	£3.14.9
Atto JBS WAL	2
Shff	0.10.6

Henry Wills Vs Will Blair, Esqr.
Vends Expons
March Term 1811
Not sattesfied for want of bidders
Wm Felton, DShff
Perquimans

State of North Carolina
To the Sheriff of Perquimans County, Greeting:
Whereas we by our writ have commanded you, that of the goods and chattels, lands and tenements of William Blair, Esqr. in your bailiwick, you should cause to be made the sum of Seventy Seven Pounds fifteen Shillings & two pence which Henry Wills recovered agt. William Blair for Debt, & Cost. Whereof the said William Blair is convicted and liable, as appears to us of records, besides your own fees for this service; and that you should have those monies before the Justices of our Inferior Court of Pleas and Quarter Sessions, at our next Court, to be held for the County of Chowan at the Court House in Edenton on the 2nd Monday in **[Blank]** next; then and there to render to the said Henry Wills his debt, damages and costs as aforesaid; and you at that day returned on the said writ to you directed, that you had levied on Negroe woman Suck & not sold for want of Bidders. We do therefore command you, that you again expose to sale the property aforesaid, by you levied on, so that you have the money aforesaid before the Justices of our Inferior Court of Pleas and Quarter Sessions, to be held at the Court House in Edenton on the 2nd Monday in March next; to render to the said Henry Wills for his debt, damages and costs as aforesaid. Herein fail not, and have you then and there this writ. Witness Elisha Norfleet, Clerk of the said Court, at Edenton the 15th day of December in the XXXVth year of the Independence of the said state, Anno Dom. 1810. Issued the 30th day of Jany 1811.
E. Norfleet, Clk

Judgment	£71.0.8
Clerk	£4.4.0
Atto JBS	2
Shff	0.10.6
6.14.6	

Henry Wills Vs. William Blair

Chowan County
Civil Actions

Vends Expons
September Term 1811
Perquimans

State of North Carolina

To the Sheriff of Perquimans County, Greeting:

Whereas we by our writ have commanded you, that of the goods and chattels, lands and tenements of William Blair Esqr., in your bailiwick, you should cause to be made the sum of Seventy Seven pounds fifteen shillings & two pence, which Henry Wills Receiv'd against William Blair, whereof the said William Blair is convicted and liable, as appears to us of record, besides you own fees for this service; and that you should have those monies before the Justices of our Inferior Court of Pleas and Quarter Sessions, at our next Court, to be held for the County of Chowan at the Court House in Edenton on the 2nd Monday in September next; then and there to render to the said Henry Wills his debt, damages and costs as aforesaid; and you at that day returned on the said writ to you directed, that you had levied on Negro woman Suck and not sold for want of Bidders. We do therefore command you, that you again expose to sale the property aforesaid, by you levied on, so that you have the money aforesaid before our Justices of our Inferior Court of Pleas and Quarter Sessions, to be held at the Court House in Edenton on the 2nd Monday in September next; to render to the said Henry Wills for his debt, damages and costs aforesaid. Herein fail not, and have you then and there this writ. Witness Elisha Norfleet, Clerk of the said Court, at Edenton the 12th day of June in the XXX5th year of the Independence of the said state, Anno Dom. 1811
E. Norfleet, Clk

Judgment	£71.0.8
Clerk	£5
Atto	2
Shff	0.10.6

Received of the above from Mr Blair

Jany 10th 1811	£55
June 22nd	15
	£70

Henry Wills

Chowan County
Civil Actions

Henry Wills Vs William Blair
Vends Expons
June Term 1811
Perquimans

State of North Carolina

To the Sheriff of Perquimans County, Greeting:

Whereas we by our writ have commanded you, that of the goods and chattels, lands and tenements of William Blair, Esqr. in your bailiwick, you should cause to be made the sum of Seventy Seven Pounds fifteen Shillings & two Pence which Henry Wills Recovered against William Blair, whereof the said William Blair is convicted and liable, as appears to us of record, besides your own fees for this service; and that you should have those monies before the Justices of our Inferior Court of Pleas and Quarter Sessions, at our next Court, to be held for the County of Chowan at the Court House in Edenton on the 2nd Monday in March then next; then and there to render to the said Henry Wills for his debt, damages and costs as aforesaid; and you at that day returned on the said writ to you directed, that you had levied on Negroe woman Suck and not sold for want of Bidders. We do therefore command you, that you again expose to sale the property aforesaid, by you levied on, so that you have the money aforesaid before our Justices of our Inferior Court of Pleas and Quarter Sessions, to be held at the Court House in Edenton on the 2nd Monday in June next; to render to the said Henry Wills for his debt, damages and costs aforesaid. Herein fail not, and have you then and there this writ. Witness Elisha Norfleet, Clerk of the said Court, at Edenton the 14th day of March in the XXVth year of the Independence of the said State, Anno Dom. 1811
E. Norfleet, Clk

Came to hand the 15th of May 1811 Not Satisfyed for want of Time.
Myles Elliott, Shff

Judgment	£71.0.8
Clerk	£4.10.9
Atto	2
Sheriff	0.10.6
	£7.1.3

Henry Wills Vs William Blair

Chowan County
Civil Actions

Vends Expons
Issued 24 October
December Term 1811

State of North Carolina

To the Sheriff of Perquimans County, Greeting:

Whereas we by our writ have commanded you, that of the goods and chattels, lands and tenements of William Blair in your bailiwick, you should cause to be made the sum of Seventy Seven pounds which Henry Wills recovered agt. Him for Debt as also the sum of Seven Pounds 10/6 for costs and charges, whereof the said William Blair is convicted and liable, as appears to us of record, besides your own fees for this service; and that you should have those monies before the Justices of our Inferior Court of Pleas and Quarter Sessions, at our next Court, to be held for the County of Chowan at the Court House in Edenton on the 2nd Monday in September next; then and there to render to the said Henry Wills his debt, damages and costs as aforesaid; and you at that day returned on the said writ to you directed, that you had levied on Negro woman Suck and not sold for want of Bidders. We do therefore command you, that you again expose to sale the property aforesaid, by you levied on, so that you have the money aforesaid before our Justices of our Inferior Court of Pleas and Quarter Sessions, to be held at the Court House in Edenton on the 2nd Monday in December next; to render to the said Henry Wills for his debt, damages and costs as aforesaid. Herein fail not, and have you then and there this writ. Witness Elisha Norfleet, Clerk of the said Court, at Edenton the 2nd Monday of September in the XXX6 year of the Independence of the said state, Anno Dom. 1811
E. Norfleet, Clk

Not Satisfyed for want of Bidders
Myles Elliott, Shff

Judgment	£71.0.8
June 10th 1811 was paid £55	
June 22 1811 was paid 15	70
	£1.0.8
Clerk	5.9.3
Attorney	2
Sheriff	0.10.6

Chowan County
Civil Actions

Henry Wills Vs William Blair
Vends Expons
54.7
Issued 9th January
March Term 1812

State of North Carolina

To the Sheriff of Perquimans County, Greeting:

Whereas we by our writ have commanded you, that of the goods and chattels, lands and tenements of William Blair in your bailiwick, you should cause to be made the sum of Seventy Seven pounds Debt and £7.19.9 Cost which Henry Wills recovered against him, whereof the said William Blair is convicted and liable, as appears to us of record, besides your own fees for this service; and that you should have those monies before the Justices of our Inferior Court of Pleas and Quarter Sessions, at our next Court, to be held for the County of Chowan at the Court House in Edenton on the 2nd Monday in Decemr. Next; then and there to render to the said Henry Wills his debt, damages and costs as aforesaid; and you at that day returned on the said writ to you directed, that you had levied on Negro Woman Suke and not sold for want of Bidders. We do therefore command you, that you again expose to sale the property aforesaid, by you levied on, so that you have the money aforesaid before our Justices of our Inferior Court of Pleas and Quarter Sessions, to be held at the Court House in Edenton on the 2nd Monday in March next; to render to the said **[Blank]** for his debt, damages and costs as aforesaid. Herein fail not, and have you then and there this writ. Witness James Norfleet, Clerk of the said Court, at Edenton the 2nd Monday of December in the XXX6 year of the Independence of the said State, Anno Dom. 1811.
Jas Norfleet, Clk

Not satisfyed for want of Bidders
Myles Elliott, Shff

Levied on the Lands of William Blair where he now lives and Negro Jef, Ben, Pomp, Jacob, Will, Atlas, Edmund, John, Jude, Pat, Marian, Serener, Sook, Abram & Mariah, 3 Head of horses, 2 Mules, 1 Yoke of Oxen and sundry of household furniture Levied on the 6th of March 1812
Myles Elliott, Shff

Judgment	£71.0.8
June 10th 1811 cash £55	
EN Former Clerk	5.9.3
J. N. Clerk	0.9.3
Attorney JBS	2
Sheriff	0.10.6

****

Benners Vail Vs William Blair
Civil Action [1810]
Chowan County Records

Benners Vail, Assignee Vs. Wm. Blair, Esqr.
Vends Expons
December 1810
Perquimans

State of North Carolina

To the Sheriff of Perquimans County, Greeting:

Whereas we by our writ have commanded you, that of the goods and chattels, Lands and tenements of William Blair Esqr. in your bailiwick, you should cause to be made the sum of one hundred & seventy Seven Pounds 3/6 Debt & five pounds six shillings Costs -- Which Benners Vail, assignee &c Recovered agt. William Blair, whereof the said William Blair is convicted and liable, as appears to us of record, besides your own fees for this service; and that you should have those monies before the Justices of our Inferior Court of Pleas and Quarter Sessions, at our next Court, to be held for the County of Chowan at the Court house in Edenton on the 2nd Monday in September next; then and there to render to the said Benners Vail his debt, damages and costs as aforesaid; and you at that day returned on the said writ to you directed, that you had levied on, John, Mary, Will & Pompy to satisfy these three Executions, & is not sold for want of Bidders. We do therefore command you, that you again expose to sale the property aforesaid, by you levied on, so that you have the money aforesaid before our Justices of our Inferior Court of Pleas and Quarter Sessions, to be held at the Court House in Edenton on the 2nd Monday in December next; to render to the said Benners Vail, Assignee &c for his debt, damages and costs as aforesaid. Herein fail not, and have you then and there this writ. Witness Elisha Norfleet, Clerk of the said Court, at Edenton the 12th day of

September in the XXXV year of the Independence of the said State, Anno Dom. 1810. Issued the 22nd day of Sept. 1810.
E Norfleet, Clk

Levied on Mulatto Boy Atlas & not sold for want of Bidders.
Wm. Felton, DShff

Judgment£177.3.6 to be discharged on payment of the sums -- 88.11.9 with Interest from 15 July 1807 till paid

Clerk	£3.6.0
WAL Atto	2

Benners Vail, Assignee Vs William Blair, Esqr.
Vends Expons
June Term 1811
Perquimans

State of North Carolina
To the Sheriff of Perquimans County, Greeting:
Whereas we by our writ have commanded you, that of the goods and chattels, lands and tenements of William Blair Esqr. in your bailiwick, you should cause to be made the sum of one hundred & Seventy Seven pounds 3/6 & Costs which Benners Vail, Asssignee &c Recovered agt. William Blair for debt, whereof the said William Blair is convicted and liable, as appears to us of record, besides your own fees for this service; and that you should have those monies before the Justices of our Inferior Court of Pleas and quarter Sessions, at our next Court, to be held for the County of Chowan at the Court House in Edenton on the 2nd Monday in **[Blank]** next; then and there to render to the said Benners Vail his debt, damages and costs aforesaid; and you at that day returned on the said writ to you directed, that you had levied on Mulatto Boy Atlas and not sold for want of Bidders. We do therefore command you, that you again expose to sale the property aforesaid, by you levied on, so that you have the money aforesaid before our Justices of our Inferior Court of Pleas and Quarter Sessions, to be held at the Court House in Edenton on the 2nd Monday in June next; to render to the said Benners Vail, Assignee &c for his debt, damages and costs as aforesaid. Herein fail not, and have you then and there this writ. Witness Elisha Norfleet, Clerk of the said Court, at Edenton the 14th day of

March in the XXXVth year of the Independence of the said state, Anno Dom. 1811
E. Norfleet, Clk

Came to hand the 29th of May 1811, Not Satisfyed for want of Time.
Myles Elliott, Shff

Judgment £177.3.6 to be discharged on the payment of the sum 88.11.9 with Interest from 15th June 1807 till paid.

Clerk	£3.15.3
Atto	2

Benners Vail Vs Wm. Blair
Vends Expons
September Term 1811
Perquimans

State of North Carolina
To the Sheriff of Perquimans County, Greeting:
Whereas we by our writ have commanded you, that of the goods and chattels, lands and tenements of William Blair Esqr. in your bailiwick, you should cause to be made the sum one hundred & Seventy Seven pounds 3/6 & Costs which Benners Vail, Assignee &c Recovered against William Blair for Debt, whereof the said William Blair is convicted and liable, as appears to us of record, besides your own fees for this service; and that you should have those monies before the Justices of our Inferior Court of Pleas and Quarter Sessions, at the next Court, to be held for the County of Chowan at the Court House in Edenton on the 2nd Monday in **[Blank]** next; then and there to render to the said Benners Vail, Assignee &c his debt, damages and costs as aforesaid; and you at that day returned on the said writ to you directed, that you had levied on Mulatto Boy Atlas and not sold for want of Bidders. We do therefore command you, that you again expose to sale the property aforesaid, by you levied on, so that you have the money aforesaid before our Justices of our Inderior Court of Pleas & Quarter Sessions, to be held at the Court house in Edenton on the second Monday in September next; to render to the said Benners Vail for his debt, damages and costs as aforesaid. Herein fail not, and have you then and there this writ. Witness Elisha Norfleet, Clerk of the said Court, at

Edenton the 12th day of June in the XXX5th year of the Independence of the said state, Anno Dom. 1811.
E. Norfleet, Clk

Not Satisfied for the want of Bidders
Myles Elliott, Shff

Judgment£177.3.6 to be discharged on payment 88.11.9 with Interest from 5th June 1807 till Pd.

Clerk	£4.4.6
Atto	2

Benners Vail, Assignee Vs William Blair
Vends Expons
Issued 24th October
December Term 1811

State of North Carolina
To the Sheriff of Perquimans County, Greeting:
Whereas we by our writ have commanded you, that of the goods and chattels, lands and tenements of William Blair in your bailiwick, you should cause to be made the sum of One hundred and Seventy Seven pounds 3/6 which Benners Vail, Assignee recovered against him for Debt, as also the Sum of Six pounds 4/6 for Cost & Charges whereof the said William Blair is convicted and liable, as appears to us of record, besides your own fees for this service; and that you should have those monies before the Justices of our Inferior Court of Pleas and Quarter Sessions, at our next Court, to be held for the County of Chowan at the Court House in edenton on the 2nd Monday in September next; then and there to render to the said Benners Vail, Assignee his debt, damages and costs as aforesaid; and you at that day returned on the said writ to you directed, that you had levied on Mulatto Boy Atlas and not sold for want of Bidders. We do therefore command you, that you again expose to sale the Property aforesaid, by you levied on, so that you have the money aforesaid, before our Justices of our Inferior Court of Pleas & Quarter Sessions, to be held at the Court House in Edenton on the 2nd Monday in December next; to render to the said Benners Vail, Assignee for his debt, damages and costs as aforesaid. Herein fail not, and have you then and there this writ. Witness Elisha Norfleet, Clerk of the said Court, at Edenton the 2nd

Monday of September in the XXX **[Blank]** year of the Independence of the said state, Anno Dom. 1811
E. Norfleet

Not Satisfyed for want of Bidders
Myles Elliott, Shff

Judgment177.3.6 to be discharged on payment of 88.11.9 with Int from 15th June 1807.

Clerk	4.13.9
Attorney WAL	2

Benners Vail, Assignee Vs William Blair
Vends Expons
53.7
Issued 9th January
March Term 1812

State of North Carolina
To the Sheriff of Perquimans County, Greeting:
Whereas we by our writ have commanded you, that of the goods and chattels, lands and tenements of William Blair in your bailiwick, you should cause to be made the sum of One hundred and Seventy Seven pounds 3/6 which Benners Vail, Assignee recovered against him as also the sum of £6.13.9 for costs whereof the said William Blair is convicted and liable, as appears to us of record, besides your own fees for this service; and that you should have those monies before the Justices of our Inferior Court of Pleas and Quarter Sessions, at our next Court, to be held for the County of Chowan at the Court House in Edenton on the 2nd Monday in December next; then and there to render to the said Benners Vail, Assignee his debt, damages and costs as aforesaid; and you at that day returned on the said writ to you directed, that you had levied on Mulatto boy Atlas and not sold for want of Bidders. We do therefore command you, that you again expose the property aforesaid, by you levied on, so that you have the money aforesaid before the Justices of our Inferior Court of Pleas and Quarter Sessions, to be held at the Court House in Edenton on the 2nd Monday in March next; to render to the said Benners Vail for his debt, damages and costs as aforesaid. Herein fail not, and have you then and there this writ. Witness James Norfleet, Clerk of the said

Chowan County
Civil Actions

Court, at Edenton the 13th day of December in the XXX6 year of the Independence of the said State, Anno Dom. 1811.
Jas. Norfleet, Clk

No sold for want of Bidders
Myles Elliott, Shff
Levied on the Lands of William Blair where he now lives & Negroes Jeff, Ben, Jacob, Will, Atlas, Edmon, John, Jude, Pat, Marian, Serener, Sook, Abram, Mariah 3 head of cattle of horses, 2 mules, 1 yoke of Oxen & Sundry of house hold furniture the 6th of March 1812
By Myles Elliott, Shff

Judgments £177.3.6 to be discharged on payments of 88.11.9 Int. from 15th June 1807.

E.N. Former Clk	£4.13.9
J. N. Clerk	9.3
WAL Attorney	2
	7.3.0

Benners Vail, Assignee Vs William Blair
Vends Expons
Als Pls
63.8
Issued 10th April
June Term 1812
Recd £7.12.3, J.N. Clk

State of North Carolina
To the Sheriff of Perquimans County, Greeting:
Whereas we by our writ have commanded you, that of the goods and chattels, lands and tenements of William Blair in your bailiwick, you should cause to be made the sum of One hundred and seventy seven pounds 3/6 which Benners Vail, Assignee recovered against him as also the sum of £6.13.9 for costs &c whereof the said William Blair is convicted and liable, as appears to us of record, besides your own fees for this service; and that you should have those monies before the Justices of our Inferior Court of Pleas and Quarter Sessions, at our next Court, to be held for the County of Chowan at the Court House in Edenton on the 2nd Monday in March next; then and there to render to the said Benners Vail,

Assignee his debt, damages and costs as aforesaid; and you at that day returned on the said writ to you directed, that you had levied on mulattoe Boy Atlas and not sold for want of Bidders, also the land where William Blair lives and negroes Jeff, Ben, Pomp, Jacob, Will, Edmund, John, Jude, Pat, Marian, Serener, Sook, Abraham & Mariah, 3 head of horses, 2 Mules, 1 yoke of Oxen and household furniture. We do therefore command you, that you again expose to sale the property aforesaid, by you levied on, so that you have the money aforesaid before our Justices of our Inferior Court of Pleas and Quarter Sessions, to be held at the Court House in Edenton on the 2nd Monday in June next; to render to the said Benners Vail for his debt, damages and costs as aforesaid. Herein fail not, and have you then and there this writ. Witness James Norfleet, Clerk of the said Court, at Edenton the 12th day of March in the XXX6 year of the Independence of the said State, Anno Dom. 1812.
Jas Norfleet, Clk

Recd of Myles Elliott Sheriff the sum of Two Hundred & Thirty Dollars & Seventy Cent in full for a Judgment and Interest that I obtained against William Blair in the County Court of Chowan June 5th 1812
B. Vail

Satisfyed in full the 5th of June 1812
Myles Elliott, Shff

Judgment £177.3.6 to be discharged on payment of 88.11.9 Int from 15th June 1807

EN former Clk	£4.13.9
M Clk	18.6
WAL Attorney	2
	£7.12.3

****

Benj. Coffield & Fred Creecy Vs. John Dickinson
Civil Action [1810]
Chowan County Records

Benjamin Coffield & Fred: Creecy, Real Pltff Vs. John Dickinson
Fi Fa
June Term 1810

Forborne by the Pltff
E. Hoskins, Shff
$179.20

State of North Carolina

To the Sheriff of Chowan County, greeting:

We command you, that of the goods and chattels, lands and tenements of John Dickinson, John B. Blount & Jas R. Bent (if to be found in your bailiwick) you cause to be made the sum of One hundred & thirty four pounds which Ben Coffield, Frederick Creecy, Real Pltff lately in our County Court of Pleas and Quarter Sessions, held for Chowan County, at the Court House in Edenton, recovered against them for Debt, as also the sum of Seven pounds & three Pence for his damages, costs and charges in the said Suit expended, whereof the said John Dickinson, John B. Blount & James R. Bent is convicted and liable as to us appears of record. And have you the said Monies before the Justices of our said Court, on the second Monday in June next, then and there to render to the said Frederick Creecy his Debt & costs and charges aforesaid. Herein fail not, and have you then and there this writ. Witness Elisha Norfleet, Clerk of the said Court, at Edenton, the 17th day of March in the XXXIV year of our Independence, Anno Dom. 1810.
E. Norfleet, Clk

Judgment £134 to be discharged on payment of the sum of £65 with Interest from 10th Novr 1806 till paid $30--00 Int

Clerk	£2.2.3
Atto JBS	4
Sheriff	0.18.0

****

James Ming Vs Thomas Saterfield
Civil Action [1810]
Chowan County Records

James Ming Vs. Thomas Saterfield
Vends Expons
June Term 1810

State of North Carolina

To the Sheriff of Chowan County, Greeting:
Whereas we by our writ have commanded you, that of the goods and chattels, lands and tenements of Thomas Saterfield if in your bailiwick, you should cause to be made the sum of Thirty Seven Pounds10/ with Interest which James Ming Recovered agt him for Debt & the Sum of Five Pounds 12/8 for costs whereof the said Thomas Saterfield is convicted and liable as appears to us of record, besides your own fees for this service; and that you should have those monies before the Justices of our inferior Court of Pleas and Quarter Sessions, at our next Court, to be held for the County of Chowan, at the Court House in Edenton, on the second Monday in March, then next; then and there to render to the said James Ming his debt, damages and costs as aforesaid; and you at that day returned on the said writ to you directed, that you had levied on Negroe Boy Jack, and forborne by the Pltff. We do therefore command you , that you again expose to sale the property aforesaid, by you levied on, so that you have the money aforesaid before our Justices of our Inferior Court of Pleas and Quarter Sessions, to be held at the Court House in Edenton, on the second Monday in June next; to render to the said James Ming for his debt, damages and costs as aforesaid. Herein fail not, and have you then and there this writ. Witness Elisha Norfleet, Clerk of the said Court, at Edenton, the 17th day of March in the XXXIV year of the Independence of the said State, Anno Dom. 1810.
E. Norfleet, Clk

Satisfied to the Plaintiff and paid Clerk Fees
Jas Skinner, DShff

Judgment £37.10 with Interest from 15th March 1809 till paid 2.16.3
£40.6.3

Clerk	2.3.6
Do for LM atto fee	2
Sheriff JS	0.16.6
J. Norfleet for JBW	0.12.8

****

Elliot Vs. Stallings
Civil Action [1810]
Chowan County Records

Chowan County
Civil Actions

Elliot als Vs. Stallings
Vends Expons
Fi Fa
Chowan Supr. Ct.
March Term 1811
Gates

State of North Carolina

To the Sheriff of Gates County, Greeting:

Whereas, we by our writ commanded you, that of the goods and chattels, lands and tenements of Simon Stallings (in your bailiwick) you should cause to be made the sum of fifty one Pounds thirteen Shillings & five pence which lately in our Superior Court of Law at Edenton, Miles Elliott recovered against him as well for damages sustained by reason of the non performance of certain promises &c as for the costs and charges by him in his Suit in that behalf expended, whereof the said Simon Stalling is convicted and liable as to us appears of record; besides your fees for that service, and that you should have the said money before the Judges of our said Court, at Edenton, on the first Monday after the fourth Monday of March next, after the Seventh day of October in the year of our Lord one thousand eight hundred and him to render to the said Miles Elliott his damages, costs and charges aforesaid: And you at that day returned on the said writ, that you had levied the same on One [?] one negro boy and all the houshold furniture belonging to Simon Stallings which remain in your hands unsold for want of a Bid. We do therefore command you, that you expose to sale the goods and chattels by you so as aforesaid levied upon, so that you have the said money and 18 1/2 shillings for accruing costs, before the Judges of our said Court, at Edenton, on the first Monday after the fourth Monday of March next, and we do command you further, that of the goods and chattels, lands and tenements of the said Simon Stallings in your bailiwick, you cause to be made the residue of the said damages, costs and charges, and that you have the said money before the Judges of our said Court, at Edenton, on the day aforesaid, to render to the said Miles Elliott his damages, costs and charges aforesaid; and have you then and there this writ. wItness Thos H Skinner, Clerk of our said Court, at Edenton, the 6th day of October in the XXXVth year of our Independence, Anno Dom. 1810

Thos H Skinner, Clk

The within property said to be levied on by a former execution as recited in this execution was so levied by the former Shff, the immediate predecessor

to Richd. Barnes now Shff of Gates; it either wasted or destroyed so as I cannot find any part of it - nor no other property real or personal belonging to the within named defendant.
Wm. Oodman[?], DShff

Damages	£10.13.3
Clk JJ	2.5.3
Atty	2
Shff	1.19.0
Costs Below	25.10.9
Stephen Elliott writ	1.16.6
Willis Elliott Do	2.0.8
Myles Elliott Junr.	1.14.0
Wm Jackson	0.12.4
James Haughton	1.5.4
Wm White	1.16.4
	51.13.5
Accruing Costs JJ	0.9.3
Do T.H. S.	0.9.3
	£52.11.11

****

Benjamin & John Coffield Vs. Thomas Vail
Civil Action [1810]
Chowan County Records

B. Coffield & John Coffield, Real Plaintiff Vs. Thomas Vail
Vends Expons
September Term 1810
Satisfied

State of North Carolina
To the Sheriff of Chowan County, Greeting:
Whereas we by our writ have commanded you, that of the goods and chattels, lands and tenements of Thomas Vail in your bailiwick, you should cause to be made the sum of Fifty Pounds with Interest, which Ben Coffield & John Coffield, real Pltff recovered agt. Him & the Damages & Costs, whereof the said Thomas Vail is convicted and liable as appears to us of record, besides your own fees for this service; and that you should

have those monies before the Justices of our Inferior Court of Pleas and Quarter Sessions, at our next Court to be held for the County of Chowan, at the Court House in Edenton, on the second Monday in June then next; then and there to render to the said John Coffield, Real Pltff his debt, damages and costs as aforesaid; and you at that day returned on the said writ to you directed, that you had levied on Negroes Rachel & Jim & forborne by F. Creecy. We do therefore command you, that you again expose to sale the property aforesaid, by you levied on, so that you have the money aforesaid before our Justices of our Inferior Court of Pleas and Quarter Sessions, to be held at the Court House in Edenton, on the second Monday in September next; to render to the said John Coffield for his debt, damages and costs as aforesaid. Herein fail not, and have you then and there this writ. Witness Elisha Norfleet, Clerk of the said Court, at Edenton, the 16th day of June in the XXXIV year of the Independence of the said State, Anno Dom. 1810.
E. Norfleet, Clk

Rec'd from Edmd. Hoskins, Shff the within Judgt & Int in full
Thos Coffield

Judgment £50 with Interest from 18th March 1809 till paid 412 6 to 3 Octr 1810. 18th March 1809 till paid

Damage	2.50
Clerk	0.13.6
	57.11.0
Coms &c	1.16.3
	£59.7.3

John Coffield Vs. Thomas Vail
Vends Expons
Issued 24th October
Decembr Term 1811
Judgt Suspended, Cost Satisfied
E. Hoskins, Shff

State of North Carolina
To the Sheriff of Chowan County, Greeting:
Whereas we by our writ have commanded you, that of the goods and chattels, lands and tenements of Thomas Vail in your bailiwick, you should

cause to be made the sum of Fifty pounds 16/ which John Coffield recovered agt. Him for Debt as also the sum of Eight pounds 10/ for Damages, Costs &c, whereof the said Thomas Vail is convicted and liable, as appears to us of record, besides your own fees for this service; and that you should have those monies before the Justices of our Inferior Court of Pleas and Quarter Sessions, at our next Court, to be held for the County of Chowan at the Court House in Edenton on the 2nd Monday in September next; then and there to render to the said John Coffield his debt, damages and costs as aforesaid; and you at that day returned on the said writ to you directed, that you had levied on Negro woman Rachael and forborne by the Plaintiff. We do therefore command you, that you again expose to sale the property aforesaid before our Justices of our Inferior Court of Pleas and Quarter Sessions, to be held at the Court House in Edenton on the 2nd Monday in decemr. Next; to render to the said John Coffield for his debt, damages and costs as aforesaid. Herein fail not, and have you then and there this writ. Witness Elisha Norfleet, Clerk of the said Court, at Edenton the 2nd Monday day of September in the XXX6 year of the Independence of the said State, Anno Dom. 1811
E. Norfleet, Clk

Judgment £50.16 Int from 12 Decr. 1810

Damage	£2.5.7
Clerk	2.17
Attorney JBS	2
Sheriff	0.13.6
JB [?] writ	1.0.8

John Coffield Vs. Thomas Vail als
Vends Expons
67.3
Issued 10th Jany
March Term 1812
Satisfied, E. Hoskins, Shff

State of North Carolina
To the Sheriff of Chowan County, Greeting:
Whereas we by our writ have commanded you, that of the goods and chattels, lands and tenements of Thomas Vail in your bailiwick, you should cause to be made the sum of Fifty Pounds 16/ for debt as also the sum of

£8.16.9 Cost &c which John Coffield recovered against him whereof the said Thomas Vail is convicted and liable; as appears to us of records, besides your own fees for this service; and that you should have those monies before the Justices of our Inferior Court of Pleas and Quarter Sessions, at our next Court, to be held for the County of Chowan at the Court House in Edenton on the 2nd Monday in Decemr next; then and there to render to the said John Coffield his debt, damages and costs aforesaid; and you at that day returned on the said writ to you directed, that you had levied on Negro woman Rachael and Suspended. We do therefore command you, that you again expose to sale the property aforesaid, by you levied on, so that you have the money aforesaid before our Justices of our Inferior Court of Pleas and Quarter Sessions, to be held at the Court House in Edenton on the 2nd Monday in March next; to render to the said John Coffield for his debt, damages and costs as aforesaid. Herein fail not, and have you then and there this writ. Witness James Norfleet, Clerk of the said Court, at Edenton the 13th day of Decemr in the XXX6th year of the Independence of the said State, Anno Dom. 1811
Jas. Norfleet, Clk

Rec'd payment in full of the within Execution
Thos Coffield & John Coffield.

Judgments £50.16 Int. from 12th decr. 1810

Damage	£2.5.7
EN former Clk	2.17.0
JN Clerk	6.9
JBS Attorney	2
Shff	13.6
EN for [?] ticket	1.0.8

****

Job Parker Vs. Reuben Small
Civil Action [1810]
Chowan County Records

Job Parker Vs Reuben Small
Vends Expons
September Term 1810

Chowan County
Civil Actions

State of North Carolina

To the Sheriff of Chowan County, Greeting:

Whereas we by our writ have commanded you, that of the goods and chattels, lands and tenements of Reuben Small in your bailiwick, you should cause to be made the sum of Five Shillings which Job Parker recovered agt. Him and the sum of Eleven pounds 13/4 for Costs & charges, whereof the said Reuben Small is convicted and liable as appears to us of record, besides your own fees for this service; and that you should have those monies before the Justices of our Inferior Court of Pleas and Quarter Sessions, at our next Court, to be held for the County of Chowan, at the Court House in Edenton, on the second Monday in September next; then and there to render to the said Job Parker for his Damages his debt, damages and costs as aforesaid; and you at that day returned on the said writ to you directed, that you had levied on negro man Simon & not sold for want of Bidders. We do therefore command you, that you again expose to sale the property aforesaid, by you levied on, so that you have the money aforesaid before the Justices of our Inferior Court of Pleas and Quarter Sessions, to be held at the Court House in Edenton, on the second Monday in September next; to render to the said Job Parker for his debt, damages and costs as aforesaid. Herein fail not, and have you then and there this writ. Witness Elisha Norfleet, Clerk of the said Court, at Edenton, the 16th day of June in the XXXVI year of the Independence of the said State, Anno Dom. 1810

E. Norfleet

Judgment	£5
Clerk	2.18.6
Atto J.N .	2
Shff E.H Js M	2.96
Phil McGuire 30/ M Bunch 26/2.16	2.16
Caleb Nash	1.9.4
	11.18.4
	6.9
	12.5.1

Job Parker Vs. Reuben Small
Vends Expons
September Term 1810

State of North Carolina

To the Sheriff of Chowan County, Greeting:

Whereas we by our wrut have commanded you, that of the goods and chattels, lands and tenements of Reuben Small Esqr. in your bailiwick, you should cause to be made the sum of Four pounds Eighteen shillings & three pence which Job Parker recovered agt. Him Damages & costs whereof the said Reuben Small is convicted and liable as appears to us of record, besides your own fees for this service; and that you should have those monies before the Justices of our Inferior Court of Pleas and Quarter Sessions, at our next Court, to be held for the County of Chowan, at the Court House in Edenton, on the second Monday in **[Blank]** next; then and there to render to the said Job Parker his debt, damages and costs as aforesaid; and you at that day returned on the said writ to you directed, that you had levied on, negro Man Simon & not sold for want of Bidders. We do therefore command you, that you again expose to sale the property aforesaid, by you levied on, so that you have the money aforesaid before the Justices of our Inferior Court of Pleas and Quarter Sessions, to be held at the Court House in Edenton, on the second Monday in September next. To render to the said Job Parker for his debt, damages and costs as aforesaid. Herein fail not, and have you then and there this writ. Witness Elisha Norfleet, Clerk of the said Court, at Edenton, the 16th day of June in the XXXVI year of the Independence of the said State, Anno Dom. 1810.
E. Norfleet

Judgment	6d
Clerk	2.5
JN atto	2
Shff JS	0.19.6
Nancy Taxsey	5.5.0
Joseph Taxsey	6.9
Elliott Taxsey	

Job Parker Vs. Reuben Small
Vends Expons
Als
December Term 1810
Satisfied & paid the Judgt & Clk fee in the office
E. Hoskins, Shff
Rec'd my fee, Jas. Norfleet

Chowan County
Civil Actions

State of North Carolina

To the Sheriff of Chowan County, greeting:

Whereas we by our writ have commanded you, that of the goods and Chattels, lands and tenements of Reuben Small Esqr. in your bailiwick, you should cause to be made the sum of Five pounds Eleven Shillings & 9d which Job Parker lately recovered agt. Him whereof the said Reuben Small is convicted and liable, as appears to us of record, besides your own fees for this service; and that you should have those monies before the Justices of our Inferior Court of Pleas and Quarter Sessions, at our next Court, to be held for the County of Chowan at the Court House in Edenton on the 2nd Monday in December next; then and there to render to the said Job Parker his debt, damages and costs as aforesaid; and you at that day returned on the said writ to you directed, that you had levied on Negro man Simon & not sold for want of Bidders. We do therefore command you, that you again expose to sale the property aforesaid, by you levied on, so that you have the money aforesaid before our Justices of our Inferior Court of Pleas and Quarter Sessions, to be held at the Court House in Edenton on the 2nd Monday in December next; to render to the said Job Parker for his debt, damages and costs as aforesaid. Herein fail not, and have you then and there this writ. Witness Elisha Norfleet, Clerk of the said Court, at Edenton the 2nd day of September in the XXXV year of the Independence of the said State, Anno Dom. 1810. Issued the 19th day of October 1810.
E. Norfleet

Judgment	0.0.6d
Clerk	2.11.9
Atto JN	2
Sheriff JS	0.19.6
	5.11.9

Job Parker Vs. Reuben Small
Vends Expons
December term 1810
Satisfied & paid in the office
E. Hoskins, Shff
Rec'd my fee, Jas. Norfleet

State of North Carolina

Chowan County
Civil Actions

To the Sheriff of Chowan County, greeting:
Whereas we by our writ commanded you, that of the goods and chattels, lands and tenements of Reuben Small in your bailiwick, you should cause to be made the sum of Twelve Pounds 5/1 for Damages & Costs which Job Parker recovered agt. Him whereof the said Reuben Small is convicted and liable, as appears to us of record, besides your own fees for this service; and that you should have those monies before the Justices of our Inferior Court of Pleas and Quarter Sessions, at our next Court, to be held for the County of Chowan at the Court House in Edenton on the 2nd Monday in December next; then and there to render to the said Job Parker his debt, damages and costs as aforesaid; and you that day returned on the said writ to you directed, that you had levied on, negro Man Simon & Not sold for want of Bidders. We do therefore command you, that you expose to sale the property aforesaid, by you levied on, so that you have the money aforesaid before our Justices of our Inferior Court of Pleas and Quarter Sessions, to be held at the Court House in Edenton on the 2nd Monday in December next; to render to the said Job Parker for his debt, damages and costs aforesaid. Herein fail not, and have you then and there this writ. Witness Elisha Norfleet, Clerk of the said Court, at Edenton the 12th day of September in the XXXV year of the Independence of the said state, Anno Dom. 1810. Issued the 19th day of October 1810.
E. Norfleet, Clk

Judgment	£0.5.0
Clerk	3.5.3
Atto JN	2
Shff, EH JS	2.9.6
JN Phillip McGuire	1.10.0
Mich Bunch	1.6.0
Caleb Nash	1.9.4
	12.5.1

****

Nixen Carter & Co. Vs. John Shaw als
Civil Action [1810]
Chowan County Records

Chowan County
Civil Actions

Nixen Carter Vs. John Shaw
Vends Expons
September Term 1810
Forborne by a suspendance from the Judge
Gabl. Bailey, Shff
Pasquotank

State of North Carolina

To the Sheriff of Pasquotank County, Greeting:

Whereas by our writ have commanded you, that of the Goods and Chattels, Lands and tenements of John Shaw, Wm. Gregory, John Boyd & William Shaw, if to be found in your Baliwick, you cause to be made the sum of two hundred & fifty seven pounds which Nixen Carter & Co. Recovered against them for Damage, and the further sum of Seven pounds Seventeen Shillings & nine pence for costs whereof the said John Shaw, William Gregory, John Boyd & William Shaw are convicted and are liable as appears of Record besides your own fees for this service and that you should have those monies before the Justices of our Sd. Court of Pleas & Quarter Sessions, at our next Court to be held at the Court House in Edenton on the 2nd Monday in June then next; then and there to Render to the said Nixen R. Carter & their Damage, Costs & Charges as aforesaid: and you at that day Returned on the said Writ to you directed, that you had levied on two ware House Store of goods, Some Negroes and Stack of Different Kinds Belonging to William Shaw & William Gregory and not sold By Orders of the Plaintiffs Agent. We do therefore command that you again expose to sale the property aforesaid by you levied on, so that you have the money aforesaid before our Justices of the Court of Pleas and Quarter Sessions to be held at the Court House in Edenton on the second Monday in September next to Render to the said Nixon Carter & Co. for their Damage, Costs and Charges aforesaid. Herein fail not, and have you then and there this writ. Witness Elisha Norfleet, Clerk of the said Court at Edenton the 16th June in the year 1810
E. Norfleet

Judgment £267 Int. from 6th June 1809 to 10th June 1810

Clerk	3.5.3
Atto	4
Sheriff	12.6

49
Nixen Carter & Co. Vs John Shaw als
Vends Expons
September Term 1810
Forborne by a [?] from the Judge
Gabl. Bailley, Shff
Pasquotank

State of North Carolina
To the Sheriff of Pasquotank County Greetings:
Whereas we by our writ have commanded you that of the goods and chattels, Lands & tenements of John Shaw, Wm. Gregory, John Boyd and William Shaw (if to be found in your bailiwick) you cause to be made the sum of two hundred & six pounds, Seven Shillings & six pence which Nixen Carter & Company Recovered against them from Damage, and the further sum of of Seven pounds Seventeen Shillings & nine pence for Costs whereof the said John Shaw, William Gregory, John Boyd & William Shaw are convicted and are liable as appears of record besides your own fees for this service, and that you should have those monies before the Justices of our said Court of Pleas & Quarter Sessions, at our next Court to be held at the Court House in Edenton on the 2nd Monday in June then next; then and there to Render to the said Nixon Carter & Co. their damage, Costs & Charges as aforesaid: and you at that day returned on the Said writ to you directed, that you had levied on two ware house Stores of goods, some Negroes and Stock of Different Kinds Belonging to William Shaw & William Gregory and not sold by Order of the Plaintiffs Agent. We do therefore command you, that you again expose to sale the Property aforesaid by you levied on, so that you have the money aforesaid before our Justices of the Court of Pleas and Quarter Sessions to be held at the Court House in Edenton on the second Monday in September next to Render to the said Nixen Carter & Co. for their Damage, Costs and Charges aforesaid. Herein fail not, and have you then and there this writ. Witness Elisha Norfleet, Clerk of the said Court at Edenton the 16th day of June in the year 1810.
E. Norfleet, Clk

Judgment £206.7.6 Interest from 6th June 1809 to June 1810

Clerk	3.5.3
Atto	4

Shff 0.12.6

****

Joseph B. Skinner Vs. Henry A. Donaldson als
Civil Action [1810]
Chowan County Records

Jos. B. Skinner, Atty Vs Henry Donaldson & als
Vends Expons
September Term 1810

State of North Carolina

To the Sheriff of Chowan County, Greeting:

Whereas, we by our writ commanded you that of the goods and chattels, lands and tenements of Henry A. Donaldson & Duncan McDonald (in your bailiwick) you should cause to be made the sum of two thousand three hundred & sixty six Pounds 1/6 to be pd. By £1183.0.9 with Int. from 1st May 1807 which lateley in our Court of Pleas & Quarter Sessions, Joseph B. Skinner attorney &c recovered against Sd. Henry A Donaldson & Duncan McDonald for debts, for the costs and charges by him in his Suit in that behalf expended, whereof the said Henry & Duncan are convicted and liable as to us appears of record; besides youe own fees for that service, and that you should have the said money before the Justices of our said Court, at Edenton, on the 16th day of **[Blank]** next, after the **[Blank]** day of **[Blank]** in the year of our Lord one thousand eight hundred and **[Blank]** to render to the said Joseph B. Skinner, Atty &c for his debt, damages, costs and charges aforesaid: And you at that day returned on the said writ, that you had levied on five negroes, Fanny, Esther, Reddick, Henry, Mills, one Horse & chair & Sundry Household & Kitchen furniture of Henry A Donaldson Subject to Clendening & Adams & not sold, which remain in your hands unsold. We do therefore command you, that you expose to sale the goods and chattels of Henry A Donaldson by you so as aforesaid levied upon, so that you have the said Money and 13/6 shillings for accruing costs, before the Justices of our said Court, at Edenton, on the 2nd Monday in September next, and we do command you further, that of the goods and chattels, land and tenements of the said Duncan McDonald if in your bailiwick, you cause to be made the residue of the said debt, damages, costs and charges, and that you have the said money before the Justices of our said Court, at Edenton, on the day aforesaid, to render to the said

Joseph B. Skinner, Atty &c damages, costs and charges aforesaid; and have you then and there this writ. Witness Elisha Norfleet, Clerk of our said Court, at Edenton, the 16th day of June in the XXXIV year of our Independence, Anno Dom. 1810
E. Norfleet, Clk

Septr. 12th 1810 received of Henry A Donaldson by John M. Roberts the sum of one thousand seven hundred & sixty dollars Eighty seven Cents in part of this Execution for which I have given him a duplicate receipt of this date
Jos. B. Skinner

Judgment £2366.1.6 to be discharged on 1183.0.9 with interest from may 1807 till paid. There was a payment on 18th Jany 1808 of the sum off £331.5 to the Plff
Clerk 13/6

****

Clendening & Adams Vs. Henry A. Donaldson
Civil Action [1810]
Chowan County Records

1810 Clendening & Adams Vs. Henry A Donaldson
Vends Expons
September Term 1810

State of North Carolina
To the Sheriff of Chowan County, Greeting:
Whereas, we by our writ commanded you that of the goods and chattels, lands and tenements of Henry A Donaldson (in your bailiwick) you should cause to be made the sum of two hundred & fifty four Pounds Eighteen Shillings & ten pence which lateley in our Court of Pleas & Quarter Sessions Clendening & Adams recovered against said Henry A Donaldson for Damage for the costs and charges by them in their Suit in that behalf expended, whereof the said Henry A Donaldson is convicted and liable as to us appears of record; besides your own fees for that service, and that you should have the said money before the Justices of our said Court, at Edenton, on the **[Blank]** day of **[Blank]** next, after the **[Blank]** day of **[Blank]** in the year of our Lord one thousand eight hundred and **[Blank]** to

render to the said Clendining & Adams for their damages, costs and charges aforesaid: And you at that day returned on the said writ, that you had levied the same on five negroes, Fanny, Esther, Reddick, Henry & Mills, one horse & chair & Sundry House hold & Kitchen Firniture & on sundry goods; forborne which remain in your hands unsold. We do therefore command you, that you expose to sale the goods and chattels of Henry A Donaldson by you so as aforesaid levied upon, so that you have the said money and 2d shillings for accruing costs, before the Justices of our said Court, at Edenton, on the 2nd Monday in September next, and we do command you further, that of then goods and chattels, lands and tenements of the said Henry A Donaldson in your bailiwick, you cause to be made the residue of the said damages, costs and charges, and that you have the said money before the Justices of our said Court, at Edenton, on the day aforesaid, to render to the said Clendening & Adams their damages, costs and charges aforesaid; and have you then and there this writ. Witness Elisha Norfleet, Clerk of our said Court, at Edenton, the 16th day of June in the XXXIV year of the Independence, Anno Dom. 1810
E. Norfleet, Clk

Septr 12th 1810 received of H.A. Donaldson by John M. Roberts the amount of the within execution for which I have given a duplicate Receipt to the Defendant of this date
Jos. B. Skinner

Judgment	£254.18.10
Clerk	0.13.6

Clendening & Adams Vs Henry A Donaldson
Vends Expons
June 1810
Forborne by JB Skinner, Atto

State of North Carolina
To the Sheriff of Chowan County, Greeting:
Whereas we by our writ have commanded you, that of the goods and chattels, lands and tenements of Henry A Donaldson in your bailiwick, you should cause to be made the sum of Two hundred & fifty four Pounds 18/10 which Clendening & Adams Recovered against him whereof the said Henry A Donaldson is convicted and liable as appears to us of record,

besides your own fees for this service; and that you should have those monies before the Justices of our Inferior Court of Pleas and Quarter Sessions, at our next Court, to be held for the County of Chowan, at the Court House in Edenton, on the second Monday in June, then next; then and there to render to the said Clendening & Adams his debt, damages and costs as aforesaid; and you at that day returned on the said writ to you directed, that you had levied on five negroes, Fanny, Esther, Reddick, Henry & Mills, one Horse & Chair & sundry House hold & Kitchen Furniture & on Sundry goods & forborne. We do therefore command you, that you again expose to sale the property aforesaid, by you levied on, so that you have the money aforesaid before our Justices of our Inferior Court of Pleas and Quarter Sessions, to be held at the Court House in Edenton, on the second Monday in June next; to render to the said Clendening & Adams for his debt, damages and costs as aforesaid. Herein fail not, and have you then and there this writ. Witness Elisha Norfleet, Clerk of the said Court, at Edenton, the 17t[h] day of March in the XXXIV year of the Independence of the said State, Anno Dom. 1810
E. Norfleet

Judgment	£254.18.10
Clerk	0.6.9

****

Gardner Vs. Dickinson
Civil Action [1811]
Chowan County Records

Henry Gardner Vs John Dickinson
Vends Expons
March Term 1811
Judgt forborne by the Pltff, Cost Satesfied
Paid in the office all except Shff's fee
E. Hoskins, Shff

State of North Carolina
To the Sheriff of Chowan County, Greeting:
Whereas we by our writ have commanded you, that of the goods and chattels, lands and tenements of John Dickinson in your bailiwick, you should cause to be made the sum of Ninety three pounds seven shillings

Debt & £13.18.4 Damage & Costs which Henry Gardner lateley Recovered against him, whereof the said John Dickinson is convicted and liable, as appears to us of record, besides your own fees for this service; and that you should have those monies before the justices of our Inferior Court of Pleas and Quarter Sessions, at our next Court, to be held for the County of Chowan at the Court House in Edenton on the 2n[d] Monday in December next; then and there to render to the said Henry Gardner his debt, damages and costs as aforesaid; and you at that day returned on the said writ to you directed, that you had levied on two Negroe Girls & forborne by the Pltff Peggy & Nancy. We do therefore command you, that you again expose to sale the property aforesaid, by you levied on, so that you have the money aforesaid before our Justices of our Inferior Court of Pleas and Quarter Sessions, to be held at the Court House in Edenton on the 2nd Monday in March next; to render to the said Henry Gardner for his debt, damages and costs as aforesaid. Herein fail not, and have you then and there this writ. Witness Elisha Norfleet, Clerk of the said Court, at Edenton the 15th day of December in the XXXVth year of the Independence of the said state, Anno Dom. 1810. Issued the 8th day of February 1811.
E. Norfleet, Clk

Judgment £93.7.0 with Interest from 21st September 1810 till paid

Damage	£8.8.0	
Clerk	2.3.6	
Atto WAL	2	
Shff	0.13.6	
JN for JBW Ticket	4.8	
T. Jones	8.8	£13.18.4

All Costs Satisfied, E. Hoskins, Shff

Henry Gardner Vs John Dickinson
Vends Expons
June Term 1811

Satisfied & paid the Judgt to the Pltff as P Receit on this Fi Fa, Clerks fee paid in the office
E. Hoskins, Shff

State of North Carolina
To the Sheriff of Chowan County, Greeting:

Whereas we by our writ have commanded you, that of the goods and chattels, lands and tenements of John Dickson in your bailiwick, you should cause to be made the sum of Ninety three pounds Seven Shillings Debt and £8.14.9 Damage & Costs which Henry Gardner recovered of him, whereof the said John Dickinson is convicted and liable, as appears to us of record, besides your own fees for this service; and that you should have those monies before the Justices of our Inferior Court of Pleas and Quarter Sessions, at our next Court, to be held for the County of Chowan at the Court House in Edenton on the 2nd Monday in **[Blank]** next; then and there to render to the said Henry Gardner his debt, damages and costs as aforesaid; and you at that day returned on the said writ to you directed, that you had levied on two Negroe Girls, Peggy & Nancy & forborne by the Pltff. We do therefore command you, that you again expose to sale the property aforesaid, by you levied on, so that you have the money aforesaid before our Justices of our Inferior Court of Pleas and Quarter Sessions, to be held at the Court House in Edenton on the 2nd Monday in June next; to render to the said Henry Gardner for his debt, damages and costs as aforesaid. Herein fail not, and have you then and there this writ. Witness Elisha Norfleet, Clerk of the said Court, at Edenton the 14th day of March in the XXXVth year of the Independence of the said State, Anno Dom. 1811. Issued the 22nd day of March 1811.
E. Norfleet, Clk

Rec'd from Edmd Hoskins, Shff one hundred & four pounds fourteen Shillings in full of this judgt & Interest
His
Henry X Gardner
Mark
Micj Bunch

Judgment £93.7.0 with Interest from 21st Septr 1810 till paid

	£96.6.0
	8.8.0
	£104.14.0
Damage	£8.8.0
Clerk	0.6.9

Henry Gardner Vs Matthias E Sawyer als
Vends Expons

Chowan County
Civil Actions

Issued 6th October
December Term 1813

State of North Carolina

To the Sheriff of Perquimans County, Greeting:

Whereas we by our writ have commanded you, that of the goods and chattels, lands and tenements of John Dickinson, Townsend Elliott & Mathias E. Sawyer in your bailiwick, you should cause to be made the sum of One hundred & ten pounds which Henry Gardner recovered against them for debt also £1.5.3 cost, whereof the said John, Townsend & Mathias are convicted and liable, as appears to us of record, besides your own fees for this service; and that you should have those monies before the Justices of our Inferior Court of Pleas and Quarter Sessions, at our next Court, to be held for the County of Chowan at the Court House in Edenton on the 2nd Monday in September next; then and there to render to the said Henry Gardner his debt, damages and costs as aforesaid; and you at that day returned on the said writ to you directed, that you had levied on the Equitable Interest of Land and negroes now in possession of Townsend Elliott and not sold for want of Bidders. We do therefore command you, that you again expose to sale the property aforesaid, by you levied on, so that you have the money aforesaid before our Justices of our Inferior Court of Pleas and Quarter Sessions, to be held at the Court House in Edenton on the 2nd Monday in December next; to render to the said Henry Gardner for his debt, damages and costs as aforesaid. Herein fail not, and have you then and there this writ. Witness James Norfleet, Clerk of the said Court, at Edenton the 16th day of September in the XXXII year of the Independence of the said State, Anno Dom. 1813
James Norfleet, Clk

Not Satisfied for want of Bidders
Myles Elliott, Shff
Recd my fees in full to this term
Myles Elliott

Judgment £110 to be paid by £55 with Int. from 1st Jany 1809
Clk 1.14.6

Henry Gardner Vs Mathias E. Sawyer & als
Vends Expons

Chowan County
Civil Actions

Issued 10th January
March Term 1814

State of North Carolina
To the Sheriff of Perquimans County, Greeting:
Whereas we by our writ have commanded you, that of the goods and chattels, lands and tenements of John Dickinson, Townsent Elliott & Mathias E. Sawyer in your bailiwick, you should cause to be made the sum of Two hundred & twenty dollars which Henry Gardner recovered against them for debt also the sum of £3.45 costs, whereof the said John, Townsend & Mathias is convicted and liable, as appears to us of record, besides your own fees for this service; and that you should have those monies before the Justices of our Inferior Court of Pleas and Quarter Sessions, at our next Court, to be held for the County of Chowan at the Court House in Edenton on the 2nd Monday in December next; then and there to render to the said Henry Gardner his debt, damages and costs as aforesaid; and you at that day returned on the said writ to you directed, that you had levied on the equitable Interest of Land and negroes now in the possession of Townsend Elliott and not sold for want of Bidders. We do therefore command you, that you again expose to sale the property aforesaid, by you levied on, so that you have the money aforesaid before our Justices of our Inferior Court of Pleas and Quarter Sessions, to be held at the Court House in Edenton on the 3rd Monday in March next; to render to the said Henry Gardner for his debt, damages and costs as aforesaid. Herein fail not, and have you then and there this writ. Witness James Norfleet, Clerk of the said Court, at Edenton the 16th day of december in the XXXII year of the Independence of the said State, Anno Dom. 1813
James Norfleet, Clk

The Balance of the within debt has been stilled by Myles Elliott Esqr., Sheriff of Perquimans -- March 14th [?] say fifty one Dolars M. Sawyer & three cents

Judgment $200 to be paid by $110 with Interest from 1st January 1809
Clk 4.38
92
30

****

Chowan County
Civil Actions

Samuel Tredwell Vs. James W. Langley
Civil Action [1811]
Chowan County Records

24
Samuel Tredwell Vs. James Langley
Vends Expons
September term 1810
Forborne by the pltff
E. Hoskins, Shff

State of North Carolina

To the Sheriff of Chowan County, Greeting:

Whereas we by our writ have commanded you, that of the goods and chattels, lands and tenements of James W Langley in your bailiwick, you should cause to be made the sum of one hundred & seventy Pounds 18/ which Saml Tredwell recovered agt. Him for debt, whereof the said James W. Langley is convicted and liable as appears to us of record, besides your own fees for this service; and that you should have those monies before the Justices of our Inferior Court of Pleas and Quarter Sessions, at our next Court, to be held for the County of Chowan, at the Court House in Edenton, on the second Monday in March 1810 next; then and there to render to the said Samuel Tredwell his debt, damages and costs as aforesaid; and that you at that day returned on the said writ to you directed, that you had levied on negroes, Joe & York & forborne. We do therefore command you, that you again expose to sale the property aforesaid, by you levied on, so that you have the money aforesaid before our Justices of our Inferior Court of Pleas and Quarter Sessions, to be held at the Court House in Edenton, on the second Monday in September next; to render to the said Samuel Tredwell for his debt, damages and costs as aforesaid. Herein fail not, and have you then and there this writ. Witness Elisha Norfleet, Clerk of the said Court, at Edenton, the 16th day of June in the XXXVI year of the Independence of the said State, Anno Dom. 1810.
E. Norfleet, Clk

Judgment £170.18.0 October discharged on payment of £85.9 with Interest from 12th September 1806 till paid
Clerk £6.9

Chowan County Civil Actions

25
Samuel Tredwell Vs. Jas. W. Langley
Vends Expons
September Term 1810
Forborne by the Pltff
E. Hoskins, Shff

State of North Carolina
To the Sheriff of Chowan County, Greeting:
Whereas we by our writ have commanded you, that of the goods and chattels, lands and tenements of James W Langley in your bailiwick, you should cause to be made the sum of one hundred & sixty Pounds with Int- which Samuel Tredwell Recovered agt him whereof the said James W Langley is convicted and liable as appears to us of record, besides your own fees for this service; and that you should have those monies before the Justices of our Inferior Court of Pleas and Quarter Sessions, at our next Court, to be held for the County of Chowan, at the Court House in Edenton, on the second Monday in March 1810 next; then and there to render to the said Samuel Tredwell his debt, damages and costs as aforesaid; and you at that day returned on the said writ to you directed, that you had levied on Negroes Joe & York & forborne. We do therefore command you, that you again expose to sale the property aforesaid, by you levied on, so that you have the money aforesaid before our Justices of our Inferior Court of Pleas and Quarter Sessions, to be held at the Court House in Edenton, on the second Monday in September next; to render to the said Samuel Tredwell for his debt, damages and costs as aforesaid. Herein fail not, and have you then and there this writ. Witness Elisha Norfleet, Clerk of the said Court, at Edenton, the 16t[h] day of June in the XXXVI year of the Independence of the said State, Anno Dom. 1810.
E. Norfleet, CS

Judgment £160 to be discharged on the payment of the sum £80 with Interest from 12th March 1807 till paid.
Clerk £6.9

26
Samuel Tredwell Vs James W. Langley
Vends Expons
September Term 1810

Forborne by the Pltff
E. Hoskins, Shff

State of North Carolina
To the Sheriff of Chowan County, Greeting:
Whereas we by our writ have commanded you, that of the goods and chattels, lands and tenements of James Tredwell in your bailiwick, you should cause to be made the sum of Thirty Pounds 18/, whereof the said James W. Langley is convicted and liable as appears to us of record, besides your own fees for this service; and that you should have those monies before the Justices of our Inferior Court of Pleas and Quarter Sessions, at our next Court, to be held for the County of Chowan, at the Court House in Edenton, on the second Monday in March 1810 next; then and there to render to the said Samuel Tredwell his debt, damages and costs as aforesaid; and you at that day returned on the said writ to you directed, that you had levied on negroes Joe & York & forborne. We do therefore command you, that you again expose to sale the property aforesaid, by you levied on, so that you have the money aforesaid before our Justices of our Inferior Court of Pleas and Quarter Sessions, to be held at the Court House in Edenton, on the second Monday in September next; to render to the said Samuel Tredwell for his debt, damages and costs as aforesaid. Herein fail not, and have you then and there this writ. Witness Elisha Norfleet, Clerk of the said Court, at Edenton, the 16th day of June in the XXXIV year of the Independence of the said State, Anno Dom. 1810.
E. Norfleet, CS

Judgment £30.18.10 to be discharged on payment of the sum of 15.9.5 with Interest from 20th June 1807 till paid
Clerk £6.9

25
Saml. Tredwell Vs Jas. W. Langley
Vends Expons
December Term 1810
Judgt forborne by the Pltffs Atto
E. Hoskins, Shff

State of North Carolina
To the Sheriff of Chowan County, Greeting:

Whereas we by our writ have commanded you, that of the goods and chattels, lands and tenements of James W Langley in your bailiwick, you should cause to be made the sum of one hundred & seventy Pounds Eighteen Shillings, which Samuel Tredwell Recovered against him for debt, whereof the said James W Langley is convicted and liable, as appears to us of record, besides your own fees for this service; and that you should have those monies before the Justices of our Inferior Court of Pleas and Quarter Sessions, at our next Court, to be held for the County of Chowan at the Court House in Edenton on the 2nd Monday in **[Blank]** next; then and there to render to the said Samuel Tredwell his debt, damages and costs as aforesaid; and you at that day returned on the said writ to you directed, that you had levied on Negroes Joe & York and forborned. We do therefore command, that you again expose to sale the property aforesaid, by you levied on, so that you have the money aforesaid before our Justices of our Inferior Court of Pleas and Quarter Sessions, to be held at the Court House in Edenton on the 2nd Monday in December next; to render to the said Samuel Tredwell for his debt, damages and costs as aforesaid. Herein fail not, and have you then and there this writ. Witness Elisha Norfleet, Clerk of the said Court, at Edenton the 12th day of September in the XXXIV year of the Independence of the said state, Anno Dom. 1810. Issued the 4th day of October 1810.
E. Norfleet, CS

Judgment £170.18.0 to be discharged on payment of 85.9 with Interest from 12th September 1806 till paid.
Clerk £0.13.9

26
Saml Tredwell Vs James W. Langley
Vends Expons
December 1810
Forborne by the Atto
E. Hoskins, Shff

State of North Carolina
To the Sheriff of Chowan County, Greeting:
Whereas we by our writ have commanded you, that of the goods and chattels, lands and tenements of James W Langley in your bailiwick, you should cause to be made the sum of one hundred and sixty Pounds which

Samuel Tredwell Recovered agt. James W Langley whereof the said James W Langley is convicted and liable, as appears to us of record, besides your own fees for this service; and that you should have those monies before the Justices of our Inferior Court of Pleas and Quarter Sessions, at our next Court, to be held for the County of Chowan at the Court House in Edenton on the 2nd Monday in **[Blank]** next; then and there to render to the said Samuel Tredwell his debt, damages and costs aforesaid; and you at that day returned on the said writ to you directed, that you had levied on Negroes Joe & York & was forborned. We do therefore command you, that you again expose to sale the property aforesaid, by you levied on, so that you have the money aforesaid before our Justices of our Inferior Court of Pleas and Quarter Sessions, to be held at the Court House in Edenton on the 2nd Monday in December next; to render to the said Samuel Tredwell for his debt, damages and costs as aforesaid. Herein fail not, and have you then and there this writ. Witness Elisha Norfleet, Clerk of the said Court, at Edenton the 12th day of september in the XXXIV year of the Independence of the said state, Anno Dom. 1810. Issued the 4th day of October 1810.
E. Norfleet, CS

Judgment £160 to be discharged on payment of the sum of 80 with Intrest from 12th March 1807 till paid
Clk 0.13.6

27
Saml Tredwell Vs James W Langley
Vends Expons
December Term 1810
Forborne by the Pltffs Atto
E. Hoskins, Shff

State of North Carolina
To the Sheriff of Chowan County, Greeting:
Whereas we by our writ have commanded you, that of the goods and chattels, lands and tenements of James W Langley in your bailiwick, you should cause to be made the sum of Thirty Pounds Eighteen Shillings & ten Pence which Samuel Tredwell Recovered agt. James W Langley whereof the said James W Langley is convicted and liable, as appears to us of record, besides your own fees for this service; and that you should have

those monies before the Justices of our Inferior Court of Pleas and Quarter Sessions, at our next Court, to be held for the County of Chowan at the Court House in Edenton on the 2nd Monday in **[Blank]** next; then and there to render to the said Samuel Tredwell his debt, damages and costs as aforesaid; and you at that day returned on the said writ to you directes, that you had levied on Negroes Joe & York & forborne. We do therefore command you, that you again expose to sale the property aforesaid, by you levied on, so that you have the money aforesaid before our Justices of our Inferior Court of Pleas and Quarter Sessions, to be held at the Court House in Edenton on the 2nd Monday in December next; to render to the said Samuel Tredwell for his debt, damages and costs as aforesaid. Herein fail not, and have you then and there this writ. Witness Elisha Norfleet, Clerk of the said Court, at Edenton the 12th day of september in the XXXIV year of the Independence of the said State, anno Dom. 1810. Issued the 4th day of October 1810.
E. Norfleet, CS

Judgment £30.18.10 to be discharged on payment of 15.9.5 with Interest from 20th June 1807 til paid.
Clerk 0.13.6

57
Samuel Tredwell Vs Jas. W Langley
Vends Expons
March Term 1811
Judgt. Satisfied to Wm Martin, Real Pltff
Clks fee paid in the office
E. Hoskins, Shff

State of North Carolina
To the Sheriff of Chowan County, Greeting:
Whereas we by our writ have commanded you, that of the goods and chattels, lands and tenements of James W Langley in your bailiwick, you should cause to be made the sum of one hundred & seventy pounds Eighteen Shillings which Samuel Tredwell Recovered agt him for debt with Interest, whereof the said James W Langley is convicted and liable, as appears to us of record, besides your own fees for this service; and that you should have those monies before the Justices of our Inferior Court of Pleas and Quarter Sessions, at our next Court, to be held for the County of

Chowan at the Court House in Edenton on the 2nd Monday in **[Blank]** next; then and there to render to the said Samuel Tredwell his debt, damages and costs as aforesaid; and you at that day returned on the said writ to you directed, that you had levied on Negroes Joe & York & forborne. We do therefore command you, that you again expose to sale the property aforesaid, by you levied on, so that you have the money aforesaid before our Justices of our Inferior Court of Pleas and Quarter Sessions, to be held at the Court House in Edenton on the 2nd Monday in March next; to render to the said Samuel Tredwell for his debt, damages and costs as aforesaid. Herein fail not, and have you then and there this writ. Witness Elisha Norfleet, Clerk of the said Court, at Edenton the 15th day of december in the XXXVth year of the Independence of the said state, Anno Dom. 1810.
Issued the 25th day of January 1811
E. Norfleet, CS

Judgment £170.18.0 to be discharged on payment of 85.9.0 with Interest from 12th September 1806 till paid.
Clerk £1.0.3

58
Samuel Tredwell Vs James W. Langley
Vends Expons
March Term 1811
Satisfied to Wm Martin, Real Plfft the balance of this Judgt
Clks fee paid in the office
E. Hoskins, Shff

State of North Carolina
To the Sheriff of Chowan County, Greeting:
Whereas we by our writs have commanded you, that of the goods and chattels, lands and tenements of James W Langley in your bailiwick, you should cause to be made the sum of one hundred & sixty Pounds to be discharged on paymt of £80 with Interest which Samuel Tredwell Recovered agt him, whereof the said James W Langley is convicted and liable, as appears to us of record, besides your own fees for this service; and that you should have those monies before the Justices of our Inferior Court of Pleas and Quarter Sessions, at our next Court, to be held for the County of Chowan at the Court House in Edenton on the 2nd Monday in **[Blank]** next; then and there to render to the said Samuel Tredwell his

debt, damages and costs aforesaid; and you at that day returned on the said writ to you directed, that you had levied on Negroes Joe & York & was forborne. We do therefore command you, that you again expose to sale the property aforesaid, by you levied on, so that you have the money aforesaid before our Justices of our Inferior Court of Pleas and Quarter Sessions, to be held at the Court House in Edenton on the 2nd Monday in March next; to render to the said Samuel Tredwell for his debt, damages and costs as aforesaid. Herein fail not, and have you then and there this writ. Witness Elisha Norfleet, Clerk of the said Court, at Edenton the 15th day of December in the XXXVth year of the Independence of the said state, Anno Dom. 1810. Issued the 25th day of Jany 1811.
E. Norfleet, CS

Judgment £160 to be discharged by paymt of the sum of 80 Int from 12th March 1807 till paid
Clerk £1.0.3

59
Samuel Tredwell vs James W Langley
Vends Expons
March Term 1811
Judgt Satisfied to Wm Martin
Satisfied by a sale of Negroes
Bid off by Wm Martin
Clks fees pd in the office
E. Hoskins, Shff

State of North Carolina
To the Sheriff of Chowan County, Greeting:
Whereas we by our writ have commanded you, that of the goods and chattels, lands and tenements of James W Langley in your bailiwick, you should cause to be made the sum of Thirty pounds Eighteen Shillings & ten pence which Samuel Tredwell Recovered agt him, whereof the said James W Langley is convicted and liable, as appears to us of record, besides your own fees for this service; and that you should have those monies before the Justices of our Inferior Court of Pleas and Quarter Sessions, at our next Court, to be held for the County of Chowan at the Court House in Edenton on the 2nd Monday in **[Blank]** next; then and there to render to the said Samuel Tredwell his debt, damages and costs as

aforesaid; and you at that day returned on the said writ to you directed, that you had levied on Negroes Joe & York & forborne. We do therefore command you, that you again expose to sale the property aforesaid, by you levied on, so that you have the money aforesaid before our Justices of our Inferior Court of Pleas and Quarter Sessions, to be held at the Court House in Edenton on the 2nd Monday in March next; to render to the said Samuel Tredwell for his debt, damages and costs aforesaid. Herein fail not, and have you then and there this writ. Witness Elisha Norfleet, Clerk of the said Court, at Edenton the 15th day of December in the XXXVth year of the Independence of the said state, Anno Dom. 1810. Issued the 25th day of January 1811
E. Norfleet, CS

14 June 1810 Amot. Of this Judgt & No. 57 & 58	218.19 **[Torn]**
By payment to Wm A Littlejohn	150.0 **[Torn]**
	68.19.5
Int to 30th Jany 1811	2.11.9
Clk fees & Shffs	4.3.3
	£75.14.3

Judgment £30.18.10 to be discharged on payment 15.9.5 with Interest from 20th June 1807 till paid
Clerk £1.0.3

Edmund Hoskins, Esquire
Sheriff of Chowan County

I assign and transfer my right & title & Claim and Ont**[?]** in and to the within order to Wm Martin
Feby 28th 1811
Jas Norfleet

Mr Hoskins,

Mr James Norfleet has paid me One hundred and thirty nine dollars and 43/100 which which we calculated to be the balance due on the executions against James W. Langley at the Suit of Samuel Tredwell (Francis **[?]** Rennant's Administrator, real Plaintiff) You will therefore that amount from Mr Langley on the said Executions for the benefit of Mr Norfleet
Wm A Littlejohn, Atto for Plaintiff

Edenton 24th decr. 1810

Nathl Allens Exor Vs James W Langley
Judgt, pd Plfs Atto by the hand of Henry A Donaldson on the 14th June 1810 £150

****

James Saterfield Vs. John Norcom et als
Civil Action [1811]
Chowan County Records
48
Jas. Saterfield, Assignee Vs. John Norcom et als
Vends Expons
September Term 1811
Forborne by the Pltff
E. Hoskins, Shff

State of North Carolina

To the Sheriff of Chowan County, Greeting:

Whereas we by our writ have commanded you, that of the goods and chattels, lands and tenements of John Norcom & Edmund Norcom in your bailiwick, you should cause to be made the sum of Forty two Pounds Ten Shillings with Int. & costs-which James Saterfield, Assignee Recovered agt. John Norcom & Edmund Norcom for debt, whereof the said John Norcom & Edmund Norcom are convicted and liable, as appears to us of record, besides your own fees for this service; and that you should have those monies before the Justices of our Inferior Court of Pleas and Quarter Sessions, at our next Court, yo be held for the County of Chowan at the Court House in Edenton on the 2nd Monday in **[Blank]** next; then and there to render to the said James Saterfield his debt, damages and costs as aforesaid; and you at that day returned on the said writ to you directed, that you had levied on Negroe Man London & forborne by the Pltff. We do therefore command you, that you again expose to sale the property aforesaid, by you levied on, so that you have the money aforesaid before our Justices of our Inferior Court of Pleas and Quarter Sessions, to be held at the Court House in Edenton on the 2nd Monday in September next; to render to the said James Saterfield, Assignee for his debt, damages and costs as aforesaid. Herein fail not, and have you then and there this writ. Witness Elisha Norfleet, Clerk of the said Court, at Edenton the 12th day of

June in the XXXVth year of the Independence of the said state, Anno Dom. 1811.
E. Norfleet, Clk

Judgment £ 42.10 with Interest from 9th May 1807	
Clk	1.15.3
Shff MOM	18.0

****

McCotter & Muil Vs. John Dickinson
Civil Action [1811]
Chowan County Records

McCotter & Muil Vs John Dickinson
Vends Expons
June Term 1811

Satisfied & paid Amot. Of Judgt to James Muel, Clks fees paid in the office, E. Hoskins, Shff

State of North Carolina
To the Sheriff of Chowan County, Greeting:
Whereas we by our writ have commanded you, that of the goods and chattels, lands and tenements of John Dickinson in your bailiwick, you should cause to be made the sum of Ninety Six Pounds four Shillings & six pence McCotter & Muil Recovered agt him, whereof the said John Dickinson is convicted and liable, as appears to us of record, besides your own fees for this service; and that you should have those monies before the Justices of our Inferior Court of Pleas and Quarter Sessions, at our next Court, to be held for the County of Chowan at the Court House in Edenton on the 2nd Monday in March then next; then and there to render to the said McCotter & Muil his debt, damages and costs as aforesaid; and you at that day returned on the said writ to you directed, that you had levied on three Negroes, Nancy, Peggy & Nelly & forborne by Plff. We do therefore command you , that you again expose to sale the Property aforesaid, by you levied on, so that you have the money aforesaid before our Justices of our Inferior Court of Pleas and Quarter Sessions, to be held at the Court House in Edenton on the 2nd Monday in June next; to render to the said McCotter & Muil for his debt, damages and costs as aforesaid. Herein fail

not, and have you then and there this writ. Witness Elisha Norfleet, Clerk of the said Court, at edenton the 4th day of March in the XXXVth year of the Independence of the said state, Anno Dom. 1811. Issued the 22nd day of March 1811
E. Norfleet, CS

Judgment £96.4.6 Interest from 26th Feby 1810 till pd.
Clerk £2.2.0
Sheriff 0.10.6

McCotter & Muil Vs John Dickinson
Vends Expons
June Term 1811

Satisfied & paid Amot of Judgt to James Muil, Clks fee pd in the office
E. Hoskins, Shff

State of North Carolina
To the Sheriff of Chowan County, Greeting:
We command you, that of the goods and chattels, lands and tenements of John Dickinson, & you levied on three Negroes, Nelly, Peggy & Nancy & forborne, you will again expose to sale the same (if to be found in your bailiwick) you cause to be made the sum of Sixty pounds five Shillings, which was lately in our County Court of Pleas and Quarter Sessions, held for Chowan County, at the Court House in Edenton, adjudged to McCotter & Muil for Debt & the sum of two pounds 12/6 for costs and charges in the said Suit expended, whereof the said John Dickinson is liable, as appears yo us of record. And have you the said Monies, besides your fees for this service, before our said Court, at Edenton aforesaid, on the second Monday in June next, then and there to render to the said McCotter & Muil their debt, costs and charges aforesaid. Herein fail not, and have you then and there this writ. Witness Elisha Norfleet, Clerk of the said Court, the 14th day of March Anno Dom. 1811
E. Norfleet, CS

Judgment £60.5.0 Intst from 7th Decr 1807 till paid
Clerk 2.2.0
Shff 0.10.6

Chowan County
Civil Actions

****

James W. Langley Vs. Edward Reily
Civil Action [1811]
Chowan County Records

Jas W Langley & Jno Coffield Vs Edward Reily
Vends Expons
June Term 1811
Satisfied & payd the Judgt. To John Coffield as P Rec't
E. Hoskins, Shff
Sold the Houses for $50.25

State of North Carolina
To the Sheriff of Chowan County, Greeting:
Whereas we by our writ have commanded you, that of the goods and chattels, lands and tenements of Edward Reily in your bailiwick, you should cause to be made the sum of Forty Six Pounds Ten Shillings which James W Langley Recovered agt. him for Damage, whereof the said Edward Reily is convicted and liable, as appears to us of record, besides your own fees for this service; and that you should have those monies before the Justices of our Inferior Court of Pleas and Quarter Sessions, at our next Court, to be held for the County of Chowan at the Court House in Edenton on the 2nd Monday in **[Blank]** next; then and there to render to the said James W Langley his debt, damages and costs as aforesaid; and you at that day returned on the said writ to you directed, that you had levied on, one small Negroe Girl & one Store House on Water Street & Forborne by John Coffield. We do therefore command you, that you again expose to sale the property aforesaid, by you levied on, so that you have the money aforesaid before our Justices of our Inferior Court of Pleas and Quarter Sessions, to be held at the Court House in Edenton on the 2nd Monday in June next; to render to the said John Coffield for his debt, damages and costs as aforesaid. Herein fail not, and have you then and there this writ. Witness Elisha Norfleet, Clerk of the said Court, at Edenton the 14th day of March in the XXXVth year of the Independence of the said state, Anno Dom. 1811. Issued the 22nd day of March 1811.
E. Norfleet, CS

Judgment	£46.10.0
Clerk	6.9

Rec'd from Edmnd Hoskins, Shff the above Judgt of Forty Six pounds ten shillings in full
John Coffield & Thos Coffield

Mr Edmund Hoskins
Pleas to pay Mr William Nichols the amount of the Judgment Jas W. Langley, Jas Norfleet Reall Plff & Edward Reily when collected, and oblige
Yours &c
Jas Norfleet
$93---Int from 11 Decr 1810
Jany 21st 1811

****

Henry A. Donaldson Vs. Charles Haughton
Civil Action [1811]
Chowan County Records

Henry A Donaldson Vs Chas. Haughton
Vends Expons
June Term 1811
Judgt forborne by Saml. Tredwell
E. Hoskins, Shff

State of North Carolina
To the Sheriff of Chowan County, Greeting:
Whereas we by our writ have commanded you, that of the goods and chattels, lands and tenements of Charles Haughton in your bailiwick, you should cause to be made the sum of one hundred & Twenty five pounds with Interest, which Henry A Donaldson lately Recovered, whereof the said Charles Haughton is convicted and liable, as appears to us of record, besides your own fees for this service; and that you should have those monies before the Justices of our Inferior Court of Pleas and Quarter Sessions, at our next Court, to be held for the County of Chowan at the Court House in Edenton on the 2nd Monday in March then next; then and there to render to the said Henry A Donaldson his debt, damages and costs as aforesaid; and you at that day returned on the said writ to you directed, that you had levied on Negroe Girl Nancy & forborne. We do therefore command you, that you again expose to sale the property aforesaid, by you

you levied on, so that you have the money aforesaid before our Justices of our Inferior Court of Pleas and Quarter Sessions, to be held at the Court House in Edenton on the 2nd Monday in June next; to render to the said Henry A Donaldson for his debt, damages and costs as aforesaid. Herein fail not, and have you then and there this writ. Witness Elisha Norfleet, Clerk of the said Court, at Edenton the 14th day of March in the XXXvth year of the Independence of the said state, Anno Dom. 1811. Issued the 22nd day of March 1811.
E. Norfleet, CS

Judgment £125 with Interest from 23rd May 1810 till paid
Clerk £0.6.9

Henry A Donaldson Vs Chas. Haughton
Vends Expons
September Term 1811

State of North Carolina
To the Sheriff of Chowan County, Greeting:
Whereas we by our writ have commanded you, that of the goods and Chattels, lands and tenements of Charles Haughton in your bailiwick, you should cause to be made the sum of One hundred & Twenty five pounds with Interest, which henry A Donaldson lately Recovered agt. Said Charles Haughton, whereof the said Charles Haughton is convicted and liable, as appears to us of record, besides your own fees for this service; and that you should have those monies before the Justices of our Inferior Court of Pleas and Quarter Sessions, at our next Court, to be held for the County of Chowan at the Court House in Edenton on the 2nd Monday in **[Blank]** next; then and there to render to the said Henry A Donaldson his debt, damages and costs as aforesaid; and you at that day returned on the said writ to you directed, that you had levied on Negroe Girl Nancy & forborne. We do therefore command you, that you again expose to sale the property aforesaid, by you levied on, so that you have the money aforesaid before our Justices of our Inferior Court of Pleas and Quarter Sessions, to be held at the Court House in Edenton on the 2nd Monday in September next; to render to the said Henry A Donaldson for his debt, damages and costs as aforesaid. Herein fail not, and have you then and there this writ. Witness Elisha Norfleet, Clerk of the said Court, at Edenton the 12th day of June in the XXXvth year of the Independence of the said state, Anno Dom. 1811.

E. Norfleet, CS

Mr Blair promised to pay the Interest from Judgment until paid -- When this Execution is settled I wish him to be reminded of it.
H. Wills

Judgment £125 with Interest from 23rd May 1810 till paid
Clerk 0.13.6 Rec'd

****

Knox Vs. Johnson et als
Civil Action [1811]
Chowan County Records

Knox Vs. Johnson & als
Fi Fa
Chowan Supr Ct
September 1811
Bertie

State of North Carolina
To the Sheriff of Bertie County, Greeting:
Whereas, we by our writ commanded you, that of the goods and chattels, lands and tenements of William H. Johnston, Lewis Thompson and William Hentore (in your bailiwick) you should cause to be made the sum of One thousand and eighty three pounds fourteen shillings & nine pence which lately in our Superior Court of Law at Edenton, Andrew Knox recovered against them, as well for Debt & as for the costs and charges by him in his Suit in that behalf expended, whereof the said William W. Johnston, Lewis Thompson and William Hentore**[?]** are convicted and liable as to us appears of record; besides your own fees for that service, and that you should have the said money before the Judges of our said Court, at Edenton, on the first Monday after the fourth Monday of March next, after the 6th day of October in the year of our Lord one thousand eight hundred and ten to render to the said Andrew Knox his Debt, damages, costs and charges aforesaid: And that you at that day returned on the said writ, that you had levied the same on Three Negroes which remain in your hands unsold, for want of Bidders. We do therefore command you, that you again expose to sale the goods and chattels by you so as aforesaid levied

upon, so that you have the said money and 9 1/4 shillings for accruing costs, before the Judges of our said Court, at Edenton, on the first Monday after the fourth Monday of September next, and we do command you further, that of the goods and chattels, lands and tenements of the said William W. Lewis and William in your bailiwick, you cause to be made the residue of the said Debt, damages costs, and charges, and that you have the said money before the Judges of our said Court, at Edenton, on the day aforesaid, to render to the said Andrew Knox his Debt, damages, costs and charges aforesaid; and have you then and there this writ. Witness Thos H Skinner, Clerk of our said Court, at Edenton, the 6th day of April in the XXXVth year of our Independence, Anno Dom. 1811.
Tho: H: Skinner, Clk

Forborne by the Plaintiff and not to Issue before further orders
Thos. Coffield

Judgt. £1080-15-9 with Int on £950-15 from 7th Apl 1811 till Pd.

J.J.	£19.9
[?]	13.6
Atty	2
	£3-17-3

W.B. then has been paid Oct 2nd 1810) of the Judgt.
£906-10

****

Reuben Small Vs. Samuel McGuire
Civil Action [1811]
Chowan County Records

R. Small Vs McGuire
Vends Expons
Chowan Supr. Ct
September 1811
Chowan

Not Satisfied for want of Bidders
James Skinner, Shff

State of North Carolina

Chowan County
Civil Actions

To the Sheriff of Chowan County, Greeting:

Whereas, we by our writ commanded you, that of the goods and chattels, lands and tenements of Samuel McGuire (in your bailiwick) you should cause to be made the sum of Three Pounds and two Shillings which lately in our Superior Court of Law at Edenton Reuben Small recovered against him for Debt & also the further sum of Sixteen pounds three Shillings and four pence for the costs and charges by him in his Suit in that behalf expended, whereof the said Samuel McGuire is convicted and liable as to us appears of record; besides your own fees for that service, and that you should have the said money before the Judges of our said Court, at Edenton, on the first Monday after the fourth Monday of March next, after the 6th day of October in the year of our Lord one thousand eight hundred and ten to render to the said Reuben Small his Debt, costs and charges aforesaid: And you at that day returned on the said writ, that you had levied the same on One Negro Man named Luke which remains in your hands unsold for want of Bidders. We do therefore command you, that you expose to sale the goods and chattels by you so as aforesaid levied upon, so that you have the said money and 63 shillings & 9d for accruing costs, before the Judges of our said Court, at Edenton, on the first Monday after the fourth Monday of September next, and we do command you further, that of the goods and chattels, lands and tenements of the said Samuel McGuire in your bailiwick, you cause to be made the residue of the said Debt, costs and charges, and that you have the said money before the Judges of our said Court, at Edenton, on the day aforesaid, to render to the said Reuben his Debt, costs and charges aforesaid; and have you then and there tis writ. Witness Thomas H. Skinner, Clerk of our said Court, at Edenton, the 6th day of April in the XXXVth year of our Independence, anno Dom. 1811.

Thos H Skinner, Clk

Judgt.	£2-19-8
Int	2-4
	3-2
THS	2-2-6
Atto	4
Costs below	10-0-10
	£19-5-4
Accruing Costs due THS	13-6
	£19-18-10

Recd £4 - in full of my fees in the County & Superior Courts - £2 being relinguished by me
Ja. Iredell

****

Stephen Smith Vs. William Harris
Civil Action [1811]
Chowan County Records

40
Steph Smith Vs Wm Harris
Vends Expons
March Term 1812
Forborne by John Coffield, Real Pltff
Jas Skinner, Shff
Chowan

State of North Carolina
To the Sheriff of Chowan County, Greeting:
Whereas, we by our writ commanded you, that of the goods and chattels, lands and tenements of William Harris, Henry Flury, James Hathaway and King Luten (in your bailiwick) you should cause to be made the sum of Forty nine pounds eighteen Shillings and six pence which lately in our Superior Court of Law at Edenton Stephen Smith recovered against them for Debt and damages & also the further sum of Fourteen pounds fifteen Shillings for the costs and charges by him in his Suit in that behalf expended, whereof the said William, Henry, James & King are convicted and liable as to us appears of record; besides your own fees for that service, and that you should have the said money before the Judges of our said Court, at Edenton, on the first Monday after the fourth Monday of September next, after the 7th day of April in the year of our Lord one thousand eight hundred and ten to render to the said Stephen Smith his Debt, damages, costs and charges aforesaid: And you at that day returned on the said writ, that you had levied the same on a Negro Boy named Lawrence which remains in your hands unsold by reason of the Forbearance of T. Coffield, Real Plaintiff. We do therefore command you, that you expose to sale the goods and chattels by you so as aforesaid levied upon, so that you have the said money and 17/6 shillings & 9d for accruing costs, before the Judges of our said Court, at Edenton, on the first Monday

after the fourth Monday of March next, and we do command you further, that of the goods and chattels, lands and tenements of the said William, Henry, James & King in your bailiwick, you cause to be made the residue of the said Debts & damages, costs and charges, and that you have the said money before the Judges of our said Court, at Edenton, on the day aforesaid, to render to the said Stephen, his Debt, damages, costs and charges aforesaid; and have you then and there this writ. Witness Henry A. Donaldson, Clerk of our said Court, at Edenton, the 4th day of October in the XXXVI year of our Independence, Anno Dom 1811.
Hy A. Donaldson, Clk

Judgmt. When stayed	£47.2
Interest	2.16.6
	£49.18.6
JJ former Clk	3.17
THS late Clk	13.6
Had Clk	6.9
Atto JN	6
Costs below	4.15.6
	15.12.9
	£65.11.3

30
Step Smith Vs Wm Harris
Vends Expons
September Term 1812

Satisfied & paid the Pltff Coffield his Judgt & cost Pr Receipt on this Vend Expons, E. Hoskins, Shff
Chowan

State of North Carolina
To the Sheriff of Chowan County, Greeting:
Whereas, we by our writ commanded you, that of the goods and chattels, lands and tenements of William Harris, Henry Flury, James Hathaway & King Luten (in your bailiwick) you should cause to be made the sum of Forty Nine pounds eighteen shillings and six pence which lately in our Superior Court of Law at Edenton, Stephen Smith recovered against them for Debt and Damages and also the sum of Fourteen pounds fifteen

shillings for the costs and charges by him in his Suit in that behalf expended, whereof the said William, Henry, James & King are convicted and liable as to us appears of record; besides your own fees for that service, and that you should have the said money before the Judges of our said Court, at Edenton, on the first Monday after the fourth Monday of September next, after the 7th day of April in the year of our Lord one thousand eight hundred and ten to render to the said Stephen Smith his debt, damages, costs and charges aforesaid: And you at that day returned on the said writ, that you had levied the same on a Negro Boy named Lawrence which remain in your hands unsold by reason of the forbearance of J. Coffield, Real Plaintiff. We do therefore command you, that you expose to sale the goods and chattels by you so as aforesaid levied upon, so that you have the said money and 24 1/2 shillings for accruing costs, before the Judges of our said Court, at Edenton, on the first Monday after the fourth Monday of September next, and we do command you further, that of the goods and chattels, lands and tenements of the said William, Henry, James & King in your bailiwick, you cause to be made the residue of the said Debt, damages, costs, at Edenton, on the day aforesaid, to render to the said Stephen Smith his debt, damages, costs and charges aforesaid; and have you then and there this writ. Witness Henry A. Donaldson, Clerk of our said Court, at Edenton, the 1st day of April in the XXXVIth year of our Independence, Anno Dom. 1812.
Hy. A. Donaldson, Clk

Judgment when stayed	£47.2
Interest	2.16.6
	£49.18.6
J.J. former Clk	£3.17
THS late Clk	13.6
H AD Clk	13.6
Atto J.N.	6
Costs below	4.15.6
	15.19.6
	£65.18
	Coms 40/6

Recd Satisfaction from Edwd Hoskins, Shff in full of the above Judgt Int and Cost 8 Octr 1812
£71.18.0
John Coffield

****

Benjamin Coffield Vs. Norman King
Civil Action [1811]
Chowan County Records

37
Benjamin Coffield , Assignee Vs. Norman King als
Vends Expons
5.2
Issued 3rd January
March Term 1812

Satisfied and paid in the office Clerk and Atto fees
Jas Skinner, Dshff

State of North Carolina
To the Sheriff of Chowan County, Greeting:
Whereas we by our writ have commanded you, that of the goods and chattels, lands and tenements of Norman King and James Jackson in your bailiwick, you should cause to be made the sum of Thirty five pounds for debts as also the sum of Six Pounds 9/ 9d Damages, Costs &c, whereof the said Norman and James are convicted and liable, as appears to us of record, besides your own fees for this service; and that you should have those monies before the Justices of our Inferior Court of Pleas and Quarter Sessions, at our next Court, to be held for the County of Chowan at the Court House in Edenton on the 2nd Monday in December next; then and there to render to the said Benjamin Coffield his debt, damages and costs as aforesaid; and you at that day returned on the said writ to you directed, that you had levied on Negro boy named Joe and forborne by the Plaintiffs. We do therefore command you, that you again expose to sale the property aforesaid, by you levied on, so that you have the money aforesaid before our Justices of our Inferior Court of Pleas and Quarter Sessions, to be held at the Court House in Edenton on the 2nd Monday in March next; to render to the said Benjamin Coffield for his debt, damages and costs as aforesaid. Herein fail not, and have you then and there this writ. Witness James Norfleet, Clerk of the said Court, at Edenton the 13th day of December in the XXX6 year of the Independence of the said State, Anno Dom. 1811.
Jas. Norfleet, Clk

Recd the 9th March 1812 Satisfaction of the within Execution.
Benj. Coffield

Judgments 35.0.0 Int from 12th September 1811	
Damage	1.16.6
Former Clk	1.15.3
J.N. Clerk	0.6.9
J.N. Atto	2
J.S. Shff	0.18.0
	4.19.0

****

Daniel Leggett Vs. Joel Moon
Civil Action [1811]
Chowan County Records

Daniel Leggett Vs. Joel Moon

The Pltff charges the Deft sold him a Negro **[?]** as a good Negro and of Good Character not liable to run away and in **[?]** of Good fame all of which is false to his damage accordingly to wit
HN Vail Pltff Atto

Daniel Leggett Vs Joel Moon

Executed by Summons deliver to Bartia & by service aforesaid by Moon **[Moor]** TL Hart[?]

State of North Carolina
To the Sheriff of Edgecombe County, Greeting:
You are hereby commanded to summon John Bartia & Britain Moore personally to be and appear before the Judges of our Superior Court of Law, held at the Court House in Edenton, on the first Monday after the fourth Monday in March then and there to testify and the truth to say, in behalf of Pltff in a certain matter of controversy in the said Court depending, and then and there to be tried, wherein Daniel Leggett is Plaintiff, and Joel Moon is Defendant; and this you shall in no wise omit,

under the penalty by law enjoined. Witness H.A. Donaldson Clerk of the said Court, in Edenton the **[Smudged]** day after the 4th Monday in Septr in the XXX6 year of our Independence, Anno Dom. 1811.
Hy A. Donaldson, Clk

Daniel Leggett Vs Joel Mohun
Subpoena
Executed on Amos Rayner & Service Excepted
Of Jon Blount
By Jno Rascoe

Service Excepted, John L. Blount
I hereby Deputize John Rascoe to Execute this writ given under my hand and seal this 20th March 1812, Baldy Ashburn (Seal)

State of North Carolina
To the Sheriff of Bertie County, Greeting:
You are hereby commanded to summon Amos Rayner & John L. Blount personally to be and appear before the Judges of our Superior Court of Law, held at the Court House in Edenton, on the first Monday after the fourth Monday in March then and there to testify and the truth to say, in behalf of the Pltff in a certain matter of controversy in the said Court depending, and then and there to be tried, wherein Daniel Leggett is Plaintiff, and Joel Moon is Defendant; and this you shall in no wise omit, under the penalty by law enjoined. Witness H.A. Donaldson, Clerk of the said Court, in Edenton, the 1st Monday after the 4th Monday in the XXXV6 year of our Independence, Anno Dom. 1811.
Hy. A. Donaldson, Clk

Leggett Vs Mohun
Subp for Defndt
Thos Walker
Chowan Supr Court
March Term 1812
Washington County

State of North Carolina
To the Coroner of Washington County, Greeting:

Chowan County
Civil Actions

You are hereby commanded to summon Thomas Walker personally to be and appear before the Judges of our Superior Court of Law, held at the Court House in Edenton, on the first Monday after the fourth Monday in March next, then and there to testify and the truth to say, in behalf of the Defendant in a certain matter of controversy in the said Court depending, and then and there to be tried, wherein Daniel Leggett is Plaintiff, and Joel Mohun is defendant; and this you shall in no wise omit, under the penalty by law enjoined. Witness Henry A. Donaldson, Clerk of the said Court, in Edenton the 3rd day of October in the XXX1th year of our Independence, Anno Dom. 1811
Hy. A. Donaldson, Clk

Service Accepted
Luke Leggett
Service Accepted
M. Hardy

State of North Carolina
To the Sheriff of Washington County, Greeting:
You are hereby commanded to summon Luke Leggett Junr. & Miles Hardy personally to be and appear before the Judge of the Superior Court of Law, at Edenton, on the first Monday after the fourth Monday in Septr next; then and there to testify and the truth to say in behalf of the Plaintiff in a certain matter of controversy in the said Court depending, and then and there to be tried, wherein Danl Leggett is Plaintiff, and Joel Mohun is Defendant. And this you shall in no wise omit, under the penalty by law enjoined. Witness Henry A. Donaldson, Clerk of the said Court, at Edenton, the 31st day of March in the XXXVth year of our Independence, Anno Dom. 1812.
Hy. A. Donaldson, Clk

Leggett Vs Mohun
To Chowan Supr Court
April Term 1812

State of North Carolina
To the Sheriff of Bertie County, Greeting:
You are hereby commanded to summon William R. Bozman personally to be and appear before the Judges of our Superior Court of Law, held at the

Court House in Edenton, on the first Monday after the fourth Monday in **[Blank]** then and there to testify and the truth to say in behalf of Pltff in a certain matter of controversy in the said Court depending, and then and there to be tried, wherein Danl Leggett is Plaintiff, and Joel Moon is Defendant; and this you shall in no wise omit, under the penalty by law enjoined. Witness H. A. Donaldson, Clerk of the said Court, in Edenton, the 1st Monday after the 4th Monday in Septr in the XXXV6 year of our Independence, Anno Dom. 1811.
Hy. A. Donaldson, Clk

Daniel Leggett Vs Joel Moon
Subp for Pltff
To Spring Term 1813
Executed, Baldy Ashburn**[?]**, Shff

State of North Carolina
To the Sheriff of Bertie County, Greeting:
You are hereby commanded to summon John Harris & Benj. Williams personally to be and appear before the Judge of the Superior Court of Law, at Edenton, on the first Monday after the fourth Monday in March next; then and there to testify and the truth to say in behalf of Daniel Leggett in a certain matter of controversy in the said Court depending, and then and there to be tried, wherein Daniel Leggett is Plaintiff, and Joel Moon is Defendant. And this you shall in no wise omit, under the penalty by law enjoined. Witness Duncan McDonald, Clerk of the said Court, at Edenton, the 5th day of October in the XXXII year of our Independence, Anno Dom. 1812
D McDonald, Clk

15
Daniel Leggett Vs Joel Moon
Transcript
To Chowan Superior Court
Washington County

This may Certify that the foregoing is a true transcript of the record in the Suit Daniel Leggett Vs Joel Moon
Test, John Walker C. S. C

State of North Carolina

Be it remembered that at a Superior Court of Law held for the County of Washington at the Court House at Lees Mills on the fifth Monday after the fourth Monday in September one thousand Eight hundred and Eleven came before the honourable Judge of our said Court Daniel Leggett by his Attorney Abner N. Vail Esqr. And brings his Suit against Joel Moon in the following Words

State of North Carolina

To the Sheriff of Bertie County Greeting you are hereby commanded to take the body of Joel Moon if to be found in your bailiwick, and him safely keep so that you have him before the Judges of our Superior Court of Law at the Next Court to be held for the County of Washington at the Court House at Lees Mills on the fifth Monday after the fourth Monday in September next then and there to answer unto Daniel Leggett of a Plea of Tresspass on the Case &c. damage Four hundred pounds. Herein fail not, and have you then and there this writ. Witness John Walker, Clerk of the said Court at Lees Mills the 1st day of May in the XXXV year of our Independence Anno Dom. 1811. Issued 10th day of August, John Walker C.S. C.

September Term 1811 On Motion Ordered upon reason shewn on affidavit filed that this Cause be transmitted to Chowan Superior Court.

Bill of Cost	
Attorney A.N. P.	£2.0.0
Sheriff B. Ashburn	0.7.6
Tax fee	0.10.0
John Walker C.S.C.	0.19.6
Removal	1.0.0
	£4.17.0

Joel Moon
Affidavit

I Certify that upon this Affdt this cause is removed to Chowan
S. Downing for John Walker, Clk

Daniel Leggett Vs Joel Mhoon

Chowan County Civil Actions

Washington Supt Court of Law
October Sessions 1811

The Defendant in this cause duly sworn deposeth and saith that the Plaintiff being a resident of this County & the Defendant a total Stranger, the Pltff on account of his extensive acquaintance & relations as well as an account of his being an intriguing & designing man and his having acted as a Public Officer for several years and his undue influence over the minds of many, he this Defendant believes that he does not stand an equal chance to have Justice done him in said County.

This defendant further states his belief that the Pltff's cause of action (if any there be) frivolous & malicious & that had it not been for the causes aforesaid the Suit would never have been instituted.

Joel Moon
Sworn to before S Downing
John Walker, Clk

****

Samuel Hyman Vs. William Slade
Civil Action [1811]
Chowan County Records

Samuel Hyman vs Wm. Slade
Vends Expons
March Term 1811
Forborn by the Atto
E. Hoskins, Shff

State of North Carolina

To the Sheriff of Chowan County, Greeting:

Whereas we by our writ have commanded you, that of the goods and chattels, lands and tenements of William Slade Esqr. In your bailiwick, you should cause to be made the sum of Eighty Eight Pounds which Samuel Hyman recovered agt him for damage & the sum of Four Pounds two Shillings for costs, whereof the said William Slade is convicted and liable, as appears to us of record, besides your own fees for this service; and that you should have those monies before the Justices of our Inferior Court of Pleas and Quarter Sessions, at our next Court, to be held for the County of Chowan at the Court House in Edenton on the 2nd Monday in Septr. Next;

then and there to render to the said Samuel Hyman his debt, damages and costs as aforesaid; and you at that day returned on the said writ to you directed, that you had levied on one Negroe woman Carry & one small mulatto Girl & forborne. We do therefore command you, that you again expose to sale the property aforesaid, by you levied on, so that you have the money aforesaid before our Justices of our Inferior Court of Pleas and Quarter Sessions, to be held at the Court House in Edenton on the 2nd Monday in March next; to render to the said Samuel Hyman for his debt, damages and costs as aforesaid. Herein fail not, and have you then and there this writ. Witness Elisha Norfleet, Clerk of the said Court, at Edenton the 15th day of December in the XXXVth year of the Independence of the said State, Anno Dom. 1810. Issued the 11th day of Jany 1811.
E. Norfleet, Clk

Judgment	£88
Clerk	2.2
Atto WAL	2

Samuel Hyman Vs William Slade
Vends Expons
June Term 1811

Forborne by the Pltff's Atto Cost Satisfied & paid in the Office Clks & Atty, E. Hoskins, Shff

State of North Carolina
To the Sheriff of Chowan County, Greeting:
We commanded you, that of the goods and chattels, lands and tenements of William Slade Esqr. & you levied on Negroe woman Carry & small Mulatto Girl & forborne, you will again expose to sale the said property (if to be found in your bailiwick) you cause to be made the sum of Eighty Eight Pounds which Samuel Hyman lately in our County Court of Pleas and Quarter Sessions, held for Chowan County, at the Court House in Edenton, recovered against William Slade for Debt as also the sum of Four Pounds Eight shillings & 9d for his damages, costs and charges in the said Suit expended, whereof the said William Slade is convicted and liable as to us appears of record. And have you the said monies before the Justices of our said Court, on the second Monday in June next, then and there to

render to the said Samuel Hyman his debt, costs and charges aforesaid. Herein fail not, and have you then and there this writ. Witness Elisha Norfleet, Clerk of the said Court, at Edenton, the 14th day of March in the XXXVth year of our Independence, Anno Dom. 1811
E. Norfleet, Clk

****

Frederick Creecy Vs. Thomas Vail
Civil Action [1811]
Chowan County Records

28
Fredr. Creecy Vs Fred: Vail & als
Vends Expons
September Term 1810
Forborne by the Pltff
E. Hoskins, Shff

State of North Carolina
To the Sheriff of Chowan County, Greeting:
Whereas we by our writ have commanded you, that of the goods and chattels, lands and tenements of Frederick Vail & Thomas Vail in your bailiwick, you should cause to be made the sum of Fifty Pounds with Int. from 15th June 1809, which Frederick Creecy Recovered agt. Them, whereof the said Frederick & Thomas are convicted and liable as appears to us of record, besides your own fees for this service; and that you should have those monies before the Justices of our Inferior Court of Pleas and Quarter Sessions, at our next Court, to be held for the County of Chowan, at the Court House in Edenton, on the second Monday in June then next; then and there to render to the said Fredrick Creecy his debt, damages and costs as aforesaid; and you at that day returned on the said writ to you directed, that you had levied on Negroes Rachel, & boy Jim & forborne. We do therefore command you, that you again expose to sale the property aforesaid, by you levied on, so that you have the money aforesaid before our Justices of our Inferior Court of Pleas and quarter Sessions, to be held at the Court House in Edenton, on the second Monday in September next; to render to the said Frederick Creecy for his debt, damages and costs as aforesaid. Herein fail not, and have you then and there this writ. Witness

Elisha Norfleet, Clerk of the said Court, at Edenton, the 16th day of June in the XXXVth year of the Independence of the said State, Anno Dom. 1810.
E. Norfleet, Clk

Judgment £50 with Interest from 15th June 1809 till paid

Clerk	£1.0.3
Damage	1.12.6

Mr. Edmund Hoskins
Sir, You are perfectly at Liberty to dispose of Negroe man Tom in Edenton to satisfy Fred. Creecy's Execution
John Dickinson
15th June 1810

69
Frederic Creecy, Assignee Vs Thomas Vail
Vends Expons
March Term 1811

Satisfied & paid Amt. of Judgt to Wm. A. Littlejohn as pr order inclosed also Atto fee, Clks fee paid in the Office, E. Hoskins, Shff

State of North Carolina
To the Sheriff of Chowan County, Greeting:
Whereas we by our writ have commanded you, that of the goods and chattels, lands and tenements of Thomas Vail in your bailiwick, you should cause to be made the sum of One hundred & Thirty Seven Pounds, ten shillings Debt & the sum of Twenty three pounds three shillings & nine pence which Frederick Creecy, Assignee &c Recovered agt. Thomas Vail & whereof the said Thomas Vail is convicted and liable, as appears to us of record, besides your own fees for this service; and that you should have those monies before the Justices of our Inferior Court of Pleas and Quarter Sessions, at our next Court, to be held for the County of Chowan at the Court House in Edenton on the 2nd Monday in **[Blank]** next; then and there to render to the said Frederick Creecy his debt, damages and costs aforesaid; and you at that day returned on the said writ to you directed, that you had levied on two Negroes Rachel & Jim & forborne by the Executor. We do therefore command you, that you again expose to sale the property

aforesaid, by you levied on, so that you have the money aforesaid before our Justices of our Inferior Court of Pleas and Quarter Sessions, to be held at the Court House in Edenton on the 2nd Monday in March next; to render to the said Frederick Creecy for his debt, damages and costs aforesaid. Herein fail not, and have you then and there this writ. Witness Elisha Norfleet, Clerk of the said Court, at Edenton the XVth day of December in the XXXVth year of the Independence of the said state, Anno Dom. 1810.
Issued the 2nd day of Feby 1811.
E. Norfleet, Clk

Rec'd Edenton 15th March 1811 from Edm'd Hoskins, Shff one hundred & Sixty Pounds five shillings in full of the Judgt. Named within & four Dollars, Atto fee.
William A Littlejohn by J W Littlejohn

Judgment	£137.10.0
Interest	18.11.3
Interest on £137.10 till pd from 12th September 1810	
Clerk	£2.2.0
Atto	2
Sheriff	0.10.6
	£4.12.6

53
Fred: Creecy Vs Fred & Thomas Vail
Vends Expons
June Term 1811
Forborne by the Pltff
E. Hoskins, Shff

State of North Carolina
To the Sheriff of Chowan County, Greeting:
Whereas we by our writ have commanded you, that of the goods and chattels, lands and tenements of Frederick & Thomas Vail in your bailiwick, you should cause to be made the sum of Fifty Pounds with Int. which Frederick Creecy Recovered against them for Debt and thirty two shillings & six pence Damage, whereof the said Frederick Vail & Thomas Vail are convicted and liable, as appears to us of record, besides your own fees for this service; and that you should have those monies before the

Justices of our Inferior Court of Pleas and Quarter Sessions, at our next Court, to be held for the County of Chowan at the Court House in Edenton on the 2nd Monday in **[Blank]** next; then and there to render to the said Frederick Creecy for his debt, damages and costs as aforesaid; and you at that day returned on the said writ to you directed, that you had levied on Negroe Girl Rachel & Boy Jim and forborne. We do therefore command you, that you again expose to sale the property aforesaid, by you levied on, so that you have the money aforesaid before our Justices of our Inferior Court of Pleas and Quarter Sessions, to be held at the Court House in Edenton on the 2nd Monday in June next; to render to the said Frederick Creecy for his debt, damages and costs as aforesaid. Herein fail not, and have you then and there this writ. Witness Elisha Norfleet, Clerk of the said Court, at Edenton the 4th day of March in the XXXVth year of the Independence of the said state, Anno Dom. 1811.
E. Norfleet, Clk

Judgment £50 Int. from 15th June 1809 till paid

Damage	1.12.6
Clerk	0.6.9
	2.8.0

37
Fred: Creecy Vs Fred. & Thos Vail
Vends Expons
September Term 1811
Forborne by thr Pltff
E. Hoskins, Shff

State of North Carolina
To the Sheriff of Chowan County, Greeting:
Whereas we by our writ have commanded you, that of the goods and chattels, lands and tenements of Frederick & Thomas Vail in your bailiwick, you should cause to be made the sum of Fifty Pounds with Onterest, which Frederick Creecy Recovered agt. Them for debt and the sum of two Pounds six Shillings Damage & Costs, whereof the said Frederick Vail & Thomas Vail are convicted and liable, as appears to us of record, besides your own fees for this service; and that you should have those monies before the Justices of our Inferior Court of Pleas and quarter Sessions, at our next Court, to be held for the County of Chowan at the

Court House in Edenton on the 2nd Monday in **[Blank]** next; then and there to render to the said Frederick Creecy his debt, damages and costs aforesaid; and you at that day returned on the said writ to you directed, that you had levied on Negroe Girl Rachel & Boy Jim and forborne. We do therefore command you, that you again expose to sale the property aforesaid, by you levied on, so that you have the money aforesaid before our Justices of our Inferior Court of Pleas and Quarter Sessions, to be held at the Court House in Edenton on the 2nd Monday in September next; to render to the said Frederick Creecy for his debt, damages and costs as aforesaid. Herein fail not, and have you then and there this writ. Witness Elisha Norfleet, Clerk of the said Court, at Edenton the 12th day of June in the XXXVth year of the Independence of the said state, Anno Dom. 1811.
E. Norfleet, Clk

Judgment £50 with Interest from 15th June 1809 till paid	
Damages	1.12.6
Clerk	0.13.9

66
Fredk Creecy Vs Fredk & Thos Vail
Issued 24th October
December Term 1811
Suspended by the Pltff
E. Hoskins, Shff

State of North Carolina
To the Sheriff of Chowan County, Greeting:
Whereas we by our writ have commanded you, that of the goods and chattels, lands and tenements of Thomas and Frederick Vail in your bailiwick, you should cause to be made the sum of Fifty Pounds which Frederick Creecy Recovered against him for debt as also the Sum of two pounds six shillings, Damage & costs whereof the said Thomas and Frederick are convicted and liable, as appears to us of record, besides your own fees for this service; and that you should have those monies before the Justices of our Inferior Court of Pleas and Quarter Sessions, at our next Court, to be held for the County of Chowan at the Court House in Edenton on the 2nd Monday in September next; then and there to render to the said Frederick Creecy his debt, damages and costs as aforesaid; and you at that day returned on the said writ to you directed, that you had levied on Negro

girl Rachael and Negro boy Jim and forborne by the Plaintiff. We do therefore command you, that you again expose to sale the property aforesaid, by you levied on, so that you have the money aforesaid before our Justices of our Inferior Court of Pleas and Quarter Sessions, to be held at the Court House in Edenton on the 2nd Monday in December next; to render to the said Frederick Creecy for his debt, damages ans costs as aforesaid. Herein fail not, and have you then and there this writ. Witness Elisha Norfleet, Clerk of the said Court, at Edenton the 2nd Monday of September in the XXX6 year of the Independence of the said state, Anno Dom. 1811.
E. Norfleet, Clk

Judgment £50 Int. from 15th June 1809
Damage 1.12.6
Clerk 1.0.6

70
Frederick Creecy Vs Frederick Vail & als
Vends Expons
66.4
Issued [?] January
March Term 1812
Suspended, E. Hoskins, Shff

State of North Carolina
To the Sheriff of Chowan County, Greeting:
Whereas we by our writ have commanded you, that of the goods and chattels, lands and tenements of Frederick and Thomas Vail in your bailiwick, you cause to be made the sum of Fifty Pounds which Frederick Creecy Recovered against them for Debts as also £2.13 Cost & damage whereof the said Fredrk and Thomas are convicted and liable, as appears to us of record, besides your own fees for this service; and that you should have those monies before the Justices of our Inferior Court of Pleas and Quarter Sessions, at our next Court, to be held for the County of Chowan at the Court House in Edenton on the 2nd Monday in December next; then and there to render to the said Frederick Creecy his debt, damages and costs as aforesaid; and you at that day returned on the said writ to you directed, that you had levied on Negro girl Rachael and Negro boy Jim and suspended by the Plaintiffs. We do therefore command you, that you again expose to

sale the property aforesaid, by you levied on, so that you have the money aforesaid before our Justices of our Inferior Court of Pleas and Quarter Sessions, to be held at the Court House in Edenton on the 2nd Monday in March next; to render to the said Frederick Creecy for his debt, damages and costs as aforesaid. Herein fail not, and have you then and there this writ. Witness James Norfleet, Clerk of the said Court, at Edenton the 13th day of Decemr. In the XXX6 year of the Independence of the said state, Anno Dom. 1811.
Jas. Norfleet, Clk

Judgments £50 Int. from 15th June 1809

Damage	1.12.6
E.N. former Clk	1.0.6
J. N. Clerk	0.6.9

28
Frederick Creecy Vs Frederick Vail & als
Vends Expons
70.5
Issued 10th April
June Term 1812

Judgt settled with the Pltff by the Defendant Suspended
E. Hoskins, Shff

State of North Carolina
To the Sheriff of Chowan County, Greeting:
Whereas we by our writ have commanded you, that of the goods and chattels, lands and tenements of Frederick Vail and Thomas Vail in your bailiwick, you should cause to be made the sum of Fifty pounds which Frederick Creecy Recovered against them for debt & also the sum of £2.13 cost and damage whereof the said Frederick & Thomas are convicted and liable, as appears to us of record, besides your own fees for this service; and that you should have those monies before the Justices of our Inferior Court of Pleas and Quarter Sessions, at our next Court, to be held for the County of Chowan at the Court House in Edenton on the 2nd Monday in March next; then and there to render to the said Frederick his debt, damages and costs as aforesaid; and you at that day returned on the said writ to you directed, that you had levied on negroe girl Rachael and negroe

boy Jim and suspended by the Plaintiffs. We do therefore command you, that you again expose to sale the property aforesaid, by you levied on, so that you have the money aforesaid before our Justices of our Inferior Court of Pleas and Quarter Sessions, to be held at the Court House in Edenton on the 2nd Monday in June next; to render to the said Frederick Creecy for his debt, damages and costs as aforesaid. Herein fail not, and have you then and there this writ. Witness James Norfleet, Clerk of the said Court, at Edenton the 12th day of March in the XXX6 year of the Independence of the said State, Anno Dom. 1812.
Jas. Norfleet, Clk

Judgment £50 from 15th June 1809	
Damage	£1.12.6
EN former Clk	1.0.6
JN Clk	13.6
	£3.6.6

****

Richard Baker & J. Coffield Vs. Isaac Baker et als
Civil Action [1813]
Chowan County Records

Richd Baker, Assignee & J. Coffield, Plaintiff in Fact Vs Isaac Baker als
Chowan Sup Court
March Term 1814
To hand 17th Feb 1814
Satisfied the cost & fifty one dollars thirty five cents of the debt
Lewis Watters, Shff
Hertford

State of North Carolina
To the Sheriff of Hertford County, Greeting:
Whereas, we by our writ commanded you, that of the goods and chattels, lands and tenements of Isaac Baker & David Ralls (in your bailiwick) you should cause to be made the sum of Forty eight Pounds 8/7 which lately in our Superior Court of Law at Edenton, Richard Baker, Assignee recovered against them for debt and also the further sum of Five Pounds seven & 6d for the costs and charges by him in his Suit in that behalf expended, whereof the said Isaac Baker & David Ralls are convicted and liable as to

us appears of record; besides your own fees for that service, and that you should have the said money before the Judge of our said Court, at Edenton, on the first Monday after the fourth Monday of March next, after the 1st day of October in the year of our Lord one thousand eight hundred and thirteen to render to the said Richard Baker his damages, costs and charges aforesaid: And you at that day returned on the said writ, that you had levied the same on Two Negroes the property of David Ralls which remain in your hands unsold. By reason of the forbearance of the Pltff. We do therefore command you, that you expose to sale the goods and chattels by you so as aforesaid levied upon, so that you have the said money and 6 ¼ shillings for accruing costs, before the Judge of our said Court, at Edenton, on the first Monday after the fourth Monday of March next, and we do command you further, that of the goods and chattels, lands and tenements of the said Isaac Baker & Rich Ralls in your bailiwick, you cause to be made the residue of the said Debt, damages, costs and charges, and that you have the said money before the Judge of our said Court, at Edenton, on the day aforesaid, to render to the said Richd Baker his damages, costs and charges aforesaid; and have you then and there this writ. Witness Duncan McDonald, Clerk of our said Court, at Edenton, the 8th day of October in the XXXVIII year of our Independence, anno Dom 1813.
Duncan McDonald, Clk

Rec'd £25.13.6 of the Deft, 4.6.6 cost
Rec'd from D McDonald Clk Fifty one Dolls of the above
Thos Coffield

Judgment £48.8.7 with Interest from 7th October 1811 till paid

DMcD	1.6.6
Do	1.0.0
Shff	1.1
Atto	2
	£5.7.6

****

Wm. Jackson Vs. Nathaniel Bond
Civil Action [1812]
Chowan County Records

Wm Jackson Vs N. Bond

Subpoena
Immediately
Executed, Jas Skinner, Shff

State of North Carolina

To the Sheriff of Chowan County, Greeting:

You are hereby commanded to summon John Coffield personally to be and appear before the Justices of our County Court of Pleas and Quarter Sessions, at the Court House in Edenton, immediately, then and there to testify and the truth to say, in behalf of Wm Jackson in a certain matter of controversy in the said Court depending, and then and there to be tried, wherein Wm Jackson is Plaintiff, and Nath Bond, Exor is Defendant; and this you shall in no wise omit, under the penalty by law enjoined. Witness James Norfleet, Clerk of the said Court at Edenton, the 15th day of December in the XXX7th year of our Independence, Anno Dom. 1812.
Jas Norfleet, Clk

Warrant &c	14
1 Continuance	3
6 Subpo	9.6
D & Exon	11.3
	£1.17.3
Atto TDM	1.6.8
J.J. Shff	0.9.0
EH	0.6.0
	£3.18.11

Wm Jackson Vs N. Bond, Exor
Subpoena
Immediately
Executed, Jas. Skinner, Shff

State of North Carolina

To the Sheriff of Chowan County, Greeting:

You are hereby commanded to summon Henry P Bennett personally to be and appear before the Justices of our County Court of Pleas and Quarter Sessions, at the Court House in Edenton, immediately, then and there to testify and the truth to say, in behalf of Wm Jackson in a certain matter of controversy in the said Court depending, and then and there to be tried,

wherein Wm Jackson is Plaintiff, and Nathl. Bond, Exor is Defendant; and this you shall in no wise omit, under the penalty by law enjoined. Witness James Norfleet, Clerk of the said Court at Edenton, the 15th day of December in the XXX7 year of our Independence, Anno Dom. 1812.
Jas Norfleet, Clk

Wm Jackson Vs N. Bond, Exor
Subpoena
Immediately
Executed, Jas Skinner, DShff

State of North Carolina
To the Sheriff of Chowan County, Greeting:
You are hereby commanded to summon Seth Parker, Junr. Personally to be and appear before the Justices of our County Court of Pleas and Quarter Sessions, at the Court House in Edenton, immediately, then and there to testify and the truth to say, in behalf of Wm Jackson in a certain matter of controversy in the said Court depending, and then and there to be tried, wherein Wm Jackson is Plaintiff, and Nath Bond, Exor is Defendant; and this you shall in no wise omit, under the penalty by law enjoined. Witness James Norfleet, Clerk of the said Court at Edenton, the 15th day of December in the XXX7th year of our Independence, Anno Dom. 1812.
Jas Norfleet, Clk

****

J.B. Skinner Vs. Wm. Gregory
Civil Action [1812]
Chowan County Records

JB Skinner Vs Wm Gregory
Vends Expons
Chowan Supr Court
September Term 1812
Rec'd [?], [?], Grice, Shff
Forborne by Plaintiff
Charles Grice, Shff
Pasquotank

State of North Carolina

To the Sheriff of Pasquotank County, Greeting:

Whereas, we by our writ commanded you, that of the goods and chattels, lands and tenements of William Gregory (in your bailiwick) you should cause to be made the sum of Seven Hundred and twenty Pounds two Shillings and eight pence which lately in our Superior Court of Law at Edenton, Joseph B. Skinner recovered against him for debt and damages and also the sum of Five pounds four Shillings and eleven pence for the costs and charges by him in his Suit in that behalf expended, whereof the said William Gregory is convicted and liable as to us appears of record; besides your own fees for that service, and that you should have the said money before the Judges of our said Court, at Edenton, on the first Monday after the fourth Monday of March next, after the 4th day of October in the year of our Lord one thousand eight hundred and eleven to render to the said Joseph B. Skinner his debt, damages, costs and charges aforesaid: And you at that day returned on the said writ, that you had levied the same on Ten Negroes (to wit) York a Cooper, Robert, Allida, Phillis, Smart, Molly & Child, Luvinia, Eliza, & Louisa which remain in your hands unsold. We do therefore command you, that you expose to sale the goods and chattels by you so as aforesaid levied upon, so that you have the said money and 9 ¼ shillings for accruing costs, before the Judges of our said Court, at Edenton, on the first Monday after the fourth Monday of September next, and we do command you further, that of the goods and chattels, lands and tenements of the said William Gregory in your bailiwick, you cause to be made the residue of the said debt, damages, costs and charges, and that you have the said money before the Judges of our said Court, at Edenton, on the day aforesaid, to render to the said Joseph B. Skinner his debt, damages, costs and charges aforesaid; and have you then and there this writ. Witness Henry A. Donaldson, Clerk of our said Court, at Edenton, the 4th day of April in the XXXVIth year of our Independence, Anno Dom. 1812.

Hy. A. Donaldson, Clk

Debt £657.13.4 To Draw Interest from 5th October 1811 til paid

Damages		62.9.4
T.H.S. late Clk		1.6.6
HHD, Clk		0.15.3
Do Accruing		0.9.3
Do Witness	6.8 1.11.2	2.17.8
Atto JBS		2

Shff 0.16.6

****

Rogers & Lambert Vs. J.W. Langley et als
Civil Action [1812]
Chowan County Records

R. & Lambert Vs J.W. Langley & als
Vends Expons
Chowan S. Court
September Term 1812
Chowan

State of North Carolina
To the Sheriff of Chowan County, Greeting:
Whereas, we by our writ commanded you, that of the goods and chattels, lands and tenements of James W Langley & William Slade (in your bailiwick) you should cause to be made the sum of One Hundred and eighty Eight Pounds Fourteen Shillings which lately in our Superior Court of Law at Edenton, Rogers & Lambert, Assignees Recovered against them for Debt and Damages and also the further sum of Five Pounds Seven Shillings and five pence for the costs and charges by them in their Suit in that behalf expended, whereof the said James W. Langley & William Slade are convicted and liable as to us appears of record; besides your own fees for that service, and that you should have the said money before the Judges of our said Court, at Edenton, on the first Monday after the fourth Monday of March next, after the 4th day of October in the year of our Lord one thousand eight hundred and eleven to render to the said Rogers & Lambert their Debt, damages, costs and charges aforesaid: And you at that day returned on the said writ, that you had levied the same on all the Household furniture and horses, one Gig, one Negro man & one Negro Woman named Carry which remain in your hands unsold. We do therefore command you, that you expose to sale the goods and chattels by you so as aforesaid levied upon, so that you have the said money and 6 ¾ shillings for accruing costs, before the Judges of our said Court, at Edenton, on the first Monday after the fourth Monday of September next, and we do command you further, that of the goods and chattels, lands and tenements of the said James W & William in your bailiwick, you cause to be made the residue of the said Debt, damages, costs and charges, and that you have

the said money before the Judges of our said Court, at Edenton, on the day aforesaid, to render to the said Rogers & Lambert their debt, damages, costs and charges aforesaid; and have you then and there this writ. Witness Henry A. Donaldson, Clerk of our said Court, at Edenton, the 1st day of April in the XXXVIth year of our Independence, Anno Dom. 1812.
Hy. A. Donaldson, Clk

The Debt & damages accept £13.9.9 paid on a Former Exr to JBS – say on 15th April 1812 – All Former Costs paid
H.A.D. , Clk 6.9

Octr 22nd 1812 received the above balance of this Execution (viz) £13.9.9 in full
Jos. B. Skinner

****

Joseph Bozman Vs. Wm. Slade & als
Civil Action [1812]
Chowan County Records

Joseph Bozman Vs Wm. Slade & als
Vends Expons
20.2
Issued 22nd Octr.
December Term 1812.

Satisfied & paid the Pltff his Judgt as pr receipt on this Vend Expons – Clk & Atto fees paid in the office
E. Hoskins, Shff

State of North Carolina
To the Sheriff of Chowan County, Greeting:
Whereas we by our writ have commanded you, that of the goods and chattels, lands and tenements of William Slade and Henry Flury in your bailiwick, you should made to be caused the sum of Sixty one Pounds 17/ which Joseph Bozman Recovered agt. Him for debts as also the Sum of £4.5.9 Cost &c, whereof the said William Slade and Henry Flury are convicted and liable, as appears to us of record, besides your own fees for this service; and that you should have those monies before the Justices of

our Inferior Court of Pleas and Quarter Sessions, at our next Court, to be held for the County of Chowan at the Court House in Edenton on the 2nd Monday in September next; then and there to render to the said Joseph Bozman his debt, damages and costs as aforesaid; and you at that day returned on the said writ to you directed, that you had levied on One Negro man and one mare and suspended by the Plaintiff. We do therefore command you, that you again expose to sale the property aforesaid, by you levied on, so that you have the money aforesaid before our Justices of our Inferior Court of Pleas and Quarter Sessions, to be held at the Court House in Edenton on the second Monday in December next; to render to the said Joseph Bozman for his debt, damages and costs as aforesaid. Herein fail not, and have you then and there this writ. Witness James Norfleet, Clerk of the said Court, at Edenton the 16th day of September in the XXXIIth year of the Independence of the said State, Anno Dom. 1812.
Jas. Norfleet, Clk

Rec'd 27 decr. 1812 from Edmd Hoskins, Shff, the within Judgt & Int in full, Joseph Bozman

Debt £61 17 Int on £46.7.1 from 6th Apl. 1811

Clerk	£2.2.0
Atto JBS	2
Shff EH	10.6
	£4.12.6

****

Wm. Thompson & als Vs. Thomas Small als
Civil Action [1812]
Chowan County Records

Wm Thompson & als Vs. Thos Small & als
Vends Expons
7.2
December Term 1812
No Sale for want of Bidders
Jas Skinner, DShff

State of North Carolina
To the Sheriff of Chowan County, Greeting:

Chowan County
Civil Actions

Whereas we by our writ have commanded you, that of the goods and chattels, lands and tenements of Thomas Small and William Small in your bailiwick, you should cause to be made the sum of Two pounds 10/1d Amt. of Wm. Thompson, Micajah Bunch; and Richard Bonds Wit. Tickets in 2 Indictments agt. Them at March Term last, whereof the said Thomas and William Small are convicted and liable, as appears to us of record, besides your own fees for this service; and that you should have those monies before the Justices of our Inferior Court of Pleas and quarter Sessions, at our next Court, to be held for the County of Chowan at the Court House in Edenton on the 2nd Monday in September next; then and there to render to the said William, Micajah & Richard their debt, damages and costs as aforesaid; and you at that day returned on the said writ to you directed, that you had levied on a mare and bed the property of Thomas Small and not sold for want of bidders. We do therefore command you, that you again expose to sale the property aforesaid, by you levied on, so that you have the money aforesaid before our Justices of our Inferior Court of Pleas and Quarter Sessions, to be held at the Court House in Edenton on the 2nd Monday in Decemr. Next; to render to the said William, Micajah & Richard for his debt, damages and costs aforesaid. Herein fail not, and have then and there this writ. Witness James Norfleet, Clerk of the said Court, at Edenton the 16th day of September in the XXXVIIth year of the Independence of the said State, Anno Dom. 1812. Issued 26th Oct.
Jas Norfleet, Clk

Clerk 13/6 to be paid by Plaintiffs

William Thompson	1.2.3
Micajah Bunch	14.10
Richard Bond	13
	£2.10.1

****

Henry Gilliam Vs. Thomas Vail et als
Civil Action [1812]
Chowan County Records

Henry Gilliam Vs. Thomas Vail & als
Vends Expons
45.3
December Term 1812

Judgt forborne, Cost Satisfied
E. Hoskins, Shff

State of North Carolina

To the Sheriff of Chowan County, Greeting:

Whereas we by our writ have commanded you, that of the goods and chattels, lands and tenements of Thomas Vail and Samuel Gregory in your bailiwick, you should cause to be made the sum of Fifty pounds 11/ for debt and £3.4.6 Cost &c which Henry Gilliam Recovered against them whereof the said Thomas and Samuel are convicted and liable, as appears to us of record, besides your own fees for this Service; and that you should have those monies before the Justices of our Inferior Court of Pleas and Quarter Sessions, at our next Court, to be held for the County of Chowan at the Court House in Edenton on the 2nd Monday in September next; then and there to render to the said Henry Gilliam his debt, damages and costs as aforesaid; and you at that day returned on the said writ to you directed, that you had levied on one Negro boy named Jim & not sold for want of bidders. We do therefore command you, that you again expose to sale the property aforesaid, by you levied on, so that you have the money aforesaid before our Justices of our Inferior Court of Pleas and Quarter Sessions, to be held at the Court House in Edenton on the 2nd Monday in December next; to render to the said Henry Gilliam for his debt, damages and costs as aforesaid. Herein fail not, and have you then and there this writ. Witness James Norfleet, Clerk of the said Court, at Edenton the 16th day of September in the XXXV year of the Independence of the said State, Anno Dom. 1812. Issued 26th Oct.
Jas Norfleet, Clk

Debt £50.11 Int. from 16th Oct 1810 – 3.10.8 Int.	
EN former Clk	1.4
J.N. Clerk	1.6.3
Atto J.J.	2
Shff EH	1.1
	£5.11.3

Henry Gilliam Vs Thomas Vail & als
Vends Expons
March Term 1813
Satisfied & Paid, Ebenezer Paine

Pr Receit filed
E. Hoskins, Shff

State of North Carolina

To the Sheriff of Chowan County, Greeting:

Whereas we by our writ have commanded you, that of the goods and chattels, lands and tenements of Thomas Vail and Saml. Gregory in your bailiwick, you should cause to be made the sum of Fifty pounds 11/ for Debt and £5.11.3 cost &c which Henry Gilliam Recovered against them whereof the said Thomas & Samuel are convicted and liable, as appears to us of record, besides your own fees for this service; and that you should have those monies before the Justices of our Inferior Court of Pleas and Quarter Sessions, at our next Court, to be held for the County of Chowan at the Court House in Edenton on the 2nd Monday in December next; then and there to render to the said Henry Gilliam his debt, damages and costs as aforesaid; and you at that day returned on the said writ to you directed, that you had levied on one Negro boy named Jim and Judgment Forborne & cost Satisfied. We do therefore command you, that you again expose to sale the property aforesaid, by you levied on, so that you have the money aforesaid before our Justices of our Inferior Court of Pleas and Quarter Sessions, to be held at the Court House in Edenton on the 2nd Monday in March next; to render to the said Henry Gilliam for his debt, damages and costs aforesaid. Herein fail not, and have you then and there this writ. Witness James Norfleet, Clerk of the said Court, at Edenton the 14th day of December in the XXXII year of the Independence of the said State, Anno Dom. 1812.
Jas Norfleet, Clk

Debt £50.11 Int. from 16th Oct 1810
Clk £0.6.9

****

Joseph Bryan Vs. Nathaniel Bissell
Civil Action [1812]
Chowan County Records

Jos. H. Bryan Vs. N.C. Bissell
Vends Expons
12.2

Chowan County
Civil Actions

Issued 22nd Octr
December Term 1812
Judgt Forborne by Jas Iredell
Cost Satisfied
E. Hoskins, Shff

State of North Carolina
To the Sheriff of Chowan County, Greeting:
Whereas we by our writ have commanded you, that of the goods and chattels, lands and tenements of Nathaniel C. Bissell in your bailiwick, you should cause to be made the sum of one hundred and eighteen Pounds 18/ 1d which Joseph H. Bryan Recovered against him for debt, as also the Sum of £4.15.9 cost and charges whereof the said Nathaniel C. Bissell is convicted and liable, as appears to us of record, besides your own fees for this service; and that you should have those monies before the Justices of our Inferior Court of Pleas and Quarter Sessions, at our next Court, to be held for the County of Chowan at the Court House in Edenton on the 2nd Monday in September next; then and there to render to the said Joseph H. Bryan his debt, damages and costs as aforesaid; and you at that day returned on the said writ to you directed, that you had levied on Negro boy George and forborne by Plaintiffs Attorney. We do therefore command you, that you again expose to sale the property aforesaid, by you levied on, so that you have the money aforesaid before our Justices of our Inferior Court of Pleas and Quarter Sessions, to be held at the Court House in Edenton on the 2nd Monday in December next; to render to the said Joseph H. Bryan for his debt, damages and costs aforesaid. Herein fail not, and have you then and there this writ. Witness James Norfleet, Clerk of the said Court, at Edenton the 16th day of September in the XXXIIth year of the Independence of the said State, Anno Dom. 1812.
Jas Norfleet, Clk

Debt £118.18.1 Int from 29th Octr. 1811

Clerk	£2.12.0
Atty JJ	2
Shff E.H.	10.6
	£5.2.6

Jos. H. Bryan Vs N. C. Bissell
Vends Expons

Chowan County
Civil Actions

March Term 1813
Suspended under the Act of Assembly
E. Hoskins, Shff

State of North Carolina

To the Sheriff of Chowan County, Greeting:

Whereas we by our writ have commanded you, that of the goods and chattels, lands and tenements of Nathaniel C Bissell in your bailiwick, you should cause to be made the sum of One hundred and Eighteen Pounds 18/1 which Jos H Bryan Recovered against him for Debt as also the Sum of £5.2.6 cost Whereof the said Nathl C Bissell is convicted and liable, as appears to us of record, besides your own fees for this service; and that you should have those monies before the Justices of our Inferior Court of Pleas and Quarter Sessions, at our next Court, to be held for the County of Chowan at the Court House in Edenton on the 2nd Monday in December next; then and there to render to the said Joseph H. Bryan his debt, damages and costs as aforesaid; and you at that day returned on the said writ to you directed, that you had levied on Negro Boy George and forborne by Pltffs Attorney, cost satisfied. We do therefore command you, that you again expose to sale the property aforesaid, by you levied on, so that you have the money aforesaid before the Justices of our Inferior Court of Pleas and Quarter Sessions, to be held at the Court House in Edenton on the 2nd Monday in March next; to render to the said Jos H Bryan for his debt, damages and costs as aforesaid. Herein fail not, and have you then and there this writ. Witness James Norfleet, Clerk of the said Court, at Edenton the 14th day of Decr. In the XXXII year of the Independence of the said State, Anno Dom. 1812.
Jas Norfleet, Clk

Judgmt £118.18.1 Int from 29th Oct
Clk 0.6.9

State of North Carolina }
Chowan County }

Know all men by these presents that we Nathaniel C Bissell, Charles Bissell and John Beasley are held and firmly bound unto Jos. H. Bryan in the sum of one hundred & twenty eight pounds Eleven Shillings & 8d good and lawful Money of the State aforesaid, to be paid to the said Joseph H.

Bryan his Executors, Administrators & Assigns, for which payment well and truly to be made we bind our selves our and each of our Heirs Executors and Assigns firmly by these presents, Sealed with our seals and dated this 10th day of March 1813.

The Condition of the above obligation is such, That whereas an Execution hath issued from the County Court of Chowan at the instance of the above named Joseph H Bryan against the above bounden Nathaniel C Bissell for the above mentioned sum of One Hundred and twenty eight pounds eleven Shillings & 8d and the above bounden Charles Bissell and John Beasley have become Securities for the suspention of the said Execution, for a time therein mentioned. Now if the above bounden Nathaniel C. Bissell, shall on or before the first day of February 1814, pay or cause to be paid to the said Joseph H Bryan his Executors or Assigns the above sum of one Hundred & twenty eight Pounds 11/8 for which Execution hath issued as aforesaid Then the above Obligation to be Void, otherwise to remain in full force & Virtue.
Signed Sealed & Delivered in the presence of
Nath C Bissell (Seal)
Charles Bissell (Seal)
Jn Beasley (Seal)

****

Officers Vs. Samuel McGuire et als
Civil Action [1813]
Chowan County Records

The Officers Vs S. McGuire & als
Vends Expons
Chowan Supr Court
March Term 1813
No Sale for want of Bidders
James Skinner, Shff

State of North Carolina
To the Sheriff of Chowan County, Greeting:
Whereas, we by our writ commanded you, that of the goods and chattels, lands and tenements of Samuel Mcguire, Miles Welch and John Leary (in your bailiwick) you should cause to be made the sum of Fifteen Pounds

15/5d which lately in our Superior Court of Law at Edenton, was adjudged agt. Them for cost and charges in the Suit Joseph Rogers against Samuel McGuire in that behalf expended, whereof the said Samuel McGuire, Miles Welch and John Leary are convicted and liable as to us appears of record; besides your own fees for that service, and that you should have the said money before the Judges of our said Court, at Edenton, on the first Monday after the fourth Monday of October next, after the 4th Monday of March in the year of our Lord one thousand eight hundred and twelve to render to the Officers of Court, costs and charges aforesaid: And you at that day returned on the said writ, that you had levied the same on Negro boy Jack the property of Miles Welch and not sold for want of time which remain in your hands unsold. We do therefore command you, that you expose to sale the goods and chattels of the Sd. Myles by you so as aforesaid levied upon, so that you have the said money and 6/9 shillings for accruing costs, before the Judges of our said Court, at Edenton, on the first Monday after the fourth Monday of September next, and we do command you further, that of the goods and chattels, lands and tenements of the said Saml, Miles and John in your bailiwick, you cause to be made the residue of the said costs and charges, and that you have the said money before the Judges of our said Court, at Edenton, on the day aforesaid, to render to the said Officers costs and charges aforesaid; and have you then and there this writ. Witness Duncan McDonald, Clerk of our said Court, at Edenton, the 1st day after the 4th in Septr. In the XXX7th year of our Independence, Anno Dom. 1813.
Duncan McDonald

HAD former Clk	2.2.6
D McD Clerk	0.6.9
Atto J.N.	4.0.0
Cost Below	8.12.11
	£15.2.2

****

Officers of the Court Vs. Norman King
Civil Action [1813]
Chowan County Records

Officers of the Court Vs. Norman King
Vends Expons

Chowan County
Civil Actions

Issued 11th October
December Term 1813
No sale for want of Bidders
Jas Skinner, DShff

State of North Carolina

To the Sheriff of Chowan County, Greeting:

Whereas we by our writ have commanded you, that of the goods and chattels, lands and tenements of Norman King in your bailiwick, you should cause to be made the sum of twenty Five Pounds 11/11 which was adjudged to him in his Suit Vs Jno Coffield for cost &c whereof the said Norman King is convicted and liable, as appears to us of record, besides your own fees for this service; and that you should have those monies before the Justices of our Inferior Court of Pleas and Quarter Sessions, at our next Court, to be held for the County of Chowan at the Court House in Edenton on the 2nd Monday in September next; then and there to render to the said Officers of Court his debt, damages and costs aforesaid; and you at that day returned on the said writ to you directed, that you had levied on Boy Joe and not sold for want of Bidders but satisfied Twenty five Dollars. We do therefore command you, that you again expose to sale the property aforesaid, by you levied on, so that you have the money aforesaid before our Justices of our Inferior Court of Pleas and Quarter Sessions, to be held at the Court House in Edenton on the 2nd Monday in December next; to render to the said Officers of Court for his debt, damages and costs as aforesaid. Herein fail not, and have you then and there this writ. Witness James Norfleet, Clerk of the said Court, at Edenton the 16th day of September in the XXXVI year of the Independence of the said State, Anno Dom. 1813.

James Norfleet, Clk

Clk	£0.6.9
E. Jones, Wit.	2.16.8
Tickets filed by J Coffield	10.5.3
	13.8.8

Officers of Court Vs Norman King
Vends Expons
Issued 20th January
March Term 1814

No Sale for want of Bidders
Jas Skinner, DShff

State of North Carolina
To the Sheriff of Chowan County, Greeting:
Whereas we by our writ have commanded you, that of the goods and chattels, lands and tenements of Norman King in your bailiwick, you should cause to be made the sum of Twenty five pounds 11/11 which was adjudged to him in his Suit against John Coffield for cost, whereof the said Norman King is convicted and liable, as appears to us of record, besides your own fees for this service; and that you should have those monies before the Justices of our Inferior Court of Pleas and Quarter Sessions, at our next Court, to be held for the County of Chowan at the Court House in Edenton on the 2nd Monday in December next; then and there to render to the said Officers of Court his debt, damages and costs as aforesaid; and you at that day returned on the said writ to you directed, that you had levied on Boy Joe and not sold for want of bidders, But satisfied Twenty five Dollars. We do therefore command you, that you again expose to sale the property aforesaid, by you levied on, so that you have the money aforesaid before our Justices of our Inferior Court of Pleas and Quarter Sessions, to be held at the Court House in Edenton on the 2nd Monday in March next; to render to the said Officers of Court for his debt, damages and costs aforesaid. Herein fail not, and have you then and there this writ. Witness James Norfleet, Clerk of the said Court, at Edenton the 16th day of December in the XXXVII year of the Independence of the said State, Anno Dom. 1813.
James Norfleet, Clk

Clk	$1.35
E. Jones, Wit	5.67
Tickets filed by J Coffield	20-52
	3

Officers of Court Vs Norman King
Vends Expons
Issued 1st july
September Term 1814
Forborne by the Pltf, Clks fees paid
James R [?] Shff

Chowan County Civil Actions

State of North Carolina

To the Sheriff of Chowan County, Greeting:

Whereas we by our writ have commanded you, that of the goods and chattels, lands and tenements of Norman King in your bailiwick, you should cause to be made the sum of Twenty five pounds 11/11 which was adjudged to him for cost in his Suit against John Coffield, whereof the said Norman King is convicted and liable, as appears to us of record, besides your own fees for this service; and that you should have those monies before the Justices of our Inferior Court of Pleas and Quarter Sessions, at our next Court, to be held for the County of Chowan at the Court House in Edenton on the 2nd Monday in June next; then and there to render to the said Officers of Court their debt, damages and costs aforesaid; and you at that day returned on the said writ to you directed, that you had levied on Boy Joe & not sold for want of Bidders But satisfied Twenty five Dollars. We do therefore command you, that you again expose to Sale the Property aforesaid, by you levied on, so that you have the money aforesaid before our Justices of our Inferior Court of Pleas and Quarter Sessions, to be held at the Court House in Edenton on the 2nd Monday in September next; to render to the said Officers of Court for his debt, damages and costs as aforesaid. Herein fail not, and have you then and there this writ. Witness James Norfleet, Clerk of the said Court, at Edenton the 16th day of June in the XXXVII year of the Independence of the said State, Anno Dom. 1814.
James Norfleet, Clk

Clk	2.85
E. Jones, Wit.	5.67
Tickets by Jno Coffield	20.52

Officers of Court Vs Norman King
Vends Expons
December Term 1814
Satisfaction for all but Coffields Ticket
James R Bent, Shff

State of North Carolina

To the Sheriff of Chowan County, Greeting:

Whereas, we by our writ commanded you, that of the goods and chattels, lands and tenements of Norman King (in your bailiwick) you should cause

to be made the sum of Twenty five pounds 11/11 which lately in our Court of Pleas and Quarter Sessions, held for the County of Chowan, the Officers of Court Recovered against him in his Suit Vs John Coffield as also the sum of **[Blank]** for costs and charges by him in said Suit in that behalf expended, whereof the said Norman King is convicted and liable as to us appears of record; besides your own fees for that service, and that you have the said money before the Justices of our said Court, at Edenton, the second Monday of September next, in the year of our Lord one thousand eight hundred and 14 to render to the said Officers of Court damages, costs and charges aforesaid; and you at that day returned on the said writ that you had levied the same on Boy Joe and not sold for want of bidders but satisfied Twenty five Dollars & Clerks fees satisfied. We do therefore command you, that you expose to sale the goods and chattels of Norman King by you so as aforesaid levied upon, so that you have the said money, and six shillings and nine pence for accruing costs, before the Justices of our said Court, at Edenton, on the second Monday of Decr. next; and we do command you further, that of the goods and chattels, lands and tenements of the said Norman King (in your bailiwick) you cause to be made the residue of the damages, costs and charges, and that you have the said money before the Justices of our said Court, at Edenton, on the day aforesaid, to render to the said Officers of Court damages, costs and charges aforesaid; and have you then and there this writ. Witness James Norfleet, Clerk of the said Court, at Edenton, the 16th day of September in the 39th year of our Independence, and in the year of our Lord one thousand eight hundred and fourteen.
James Norfleet, Clk

E. Jones, Wit.	$5.67
Clerk	67
Tickets filed by J Coffield	20.52

State of North Carolina
To the Sheriff of Chowan County, Greeting:
Whereas, we by our writ commanded you, that of the goods and chattels, lands and tenements of Norman King (in your bailiwick) you should cause to be made the sum of Twenty Five pounds 11/11 which lately in our County Court of Pleas and Quarter Sessions, held fro the County of Chowan, the Officers of Court Recovered against him in his Suit Vs John Coffield for costs and charges by him in said Suit in that behalf expended,

whereof the said Norman King is convicted and liable as to us appears of record; besides your own fees for that service, and that you have the said Money before the Justices of our said Court, at Edenton, the second Monday of September next, in the year of our Lord one thousand eight hundred and 14 to render to the said Officers of Court damages, costs and charges aforesaid; and you at that day returned on the said writ that you had levied the same on Boy Joe and not sold for want of bidders but satisfied Twenty five Dollars & Clerks fees Satisfied. We do therefore command you, that you expose to sale the goods and chattels of Norman King by you so as aforesaid levied upon, so that you have the said Money, and six shillings and nine pence for accruing costs, before the Justices of our said Court, at Edenton, on the second Monday of Decr. Next; and we do command you further, that of the goods and chattels, lands and tenements of the said Norman King (in your bailiwick) you cause to be made the residue of the damages, costs and charges, and that you have the said money before the Justices of our said Court, at Edenton, on the day aforesaid, to render to the said Officers of Court damages, costs and charges aforesaid; and have you then and there this writ. Witness James Norfleet, Clerk of the said Court, at Edenton, the 16th day of September in the 39th year of our Independence, and in the year of our Lord one thousand eight hundred and fourteen.
James Norfleet, Clk

E. Jones Wit	$5.67
Clerk	67
Ticket filed by J Coffield	20.52

Officers of Court Vs Norman King
Vends Expons
March Term 1815
Forborne
James R. Bent, Shff

State of North Carolina
To the Sheriff of Chowan County, Greeting:
Whereas, we by our writ commanded you, that of the goods and chattels, lands and tenements of Norman King (in your bailiwick) you should cause to be made the sum of twenty five pounds which lately in our County Court of Pleas and Quarter Sessions, held for the County of Chowan the

Officers of Court recovered against him in his Suit Vs Coffield in his Suit in that behalf expended, whereof the said Norman is convicted and liable as to us appears of record; besides your own fees for that service, and that you have the said money before the Justices of our said Court, at Edenton, the second Monday of Decr next, in the year of our Lord one thousand eight hundred and 14 to render to the said Officer of Court damages, costs and charges aforesaid; and you at that day returned on the said writ that you had levied the same on Boy Joe and not sold for want of bidders but satisfied all but Jno Coffield's Wit Ticket. We do therefore command you, that you expose to sale the goods and chattels of Norman King by you so as aforesaid levied upon, so that you have the said money, and six shillings and nine pence for accruing costs, before the Justices of our said Court, at Edenton, on the second Monday of March next; and we do command you further, that of the goods and chattels, lands and tenements of the said Norman King (in your bailiwick) you cause to be made the residue of the damages, costs and charges, and that you have the said money before the Justices of our said Court, at Edenton, on the day aforesaid, to render to the said Officers damages, costs and charges aforesaid; and have you then and there this writ. Witness James Norfleet, Clerk of the said Court, at Edenton, the 14th day of Decr. In the 39th year of our Independence, and in the year of our Lord one thousand eight hundred and 14.
James Norfleet, Clk

Ticket filed by Coffield	$20.52
Clk	67

Officers of Court Vs Norman King
Vends Expons
June Term 1815

Satisfied & Pd the Pltf Mr. Coffield by Thomas Browrigg Esqr
James R Bent, Shff

State of North Carolina
To the Sheriff of Chowan County, Greeting:
Whereas, we by our writ commanded you, that of the goods and chattels, lands and tenements of Norman King (in your bailiwick) you should cause to be made the sum of Twenty five pounds which lately in our County

Court of Pleas and Quarter Sessions, held for the County of Chowan, the Officers of Court recovered against him for costs and charges in his Suit Vs Coffield in that behalf expended, whereof the said Norman King is convicted and liable as to us appears of record; besides your own fees for that service, and that you have the said money before the Justices of our said Court, at Edenton, the second Monday of March next, in the year of our Lord one thousand eight hundred and 15 to render to the said Officers costs and charges aforesaid; and you at that day returned on the said writ that you had levied the same on Boy Joe and not sold for want of bidders but satisfied all but Jno Coffield's Wit Ticket. We do therefore command you, that you expose to sale the goods and chattels of Norman King by you so as aforesaid levied upon, so that you have the said money, and six shillings and nine pence for accruing costs, before the Justices of our said Court, at Edenton, on the second Monday of June next; and we do command you further, that of the goods and chattels. Lands and tenements of the said Norman King (in your bailiwick) you cause to be made the residue of the damages, costs and charges, and that you have the said money before the Justices of our said Court, at Edenton, on the day aforesaid, to render to the said Officers of Court damages, costs and charges aforesaid; and have you then and there this writ. Witness Will Norfleet, Deputy Clerk of the said Court, at Edenton, the 16th day of March in the 39th year of our Independence, and in the year of our Lord one thousand eight hundred and fifteen.
Will Norfleet, DClk

Tickets filed by Jno Coffield $20.52
J.N. former Clk 67
W N DClk 67

****

Beasley & Norcom Vs. Eliza Gray
Civil Action [1813]
Chowan County Records

Beasley & Norcom Vs Eliza Gray
Chowan Sup Court
March Term 1814
Suspended by the Pltff
E. Hoskins, Shff

Chowan County
Civil Actions

Chowan

State of North Carolina

To the Sheriff of Chowan County, Greeting:

Whereas, we by our writ commanded you, that of the goods and chattels, lands and tenements of Eliza Gray (in your bailiwick) you should cause to be made the sum of One hundred and six Pounds nineteen & 4d which lately in our Superior Court of Law at Edenton Beasley & Norcom Recovered against her for Debt also, Four Pounds twelve Shillings for the costs and charges by them in their Suit in that behalf expended, whereof the said Eliza Gray is convicted and liable as to us appears of record; besides your own fees for that service, and that you should have the said Money before the Judge of our said Court, at Edenton, on the first Monday after the Fourth Monday of Septr next, after the 1st day of April in the year of our Lord one thousand eight hundred and thirteen to render to the said Beasley & Norcom his debt, damages, costs and charges aforesaid: And you at that day returned on the said writ, that you had levied the same on Two Negroes Phoebe & Penny on the Tavern adjoining Mr. Horniblows & on Sundry Lotts on Queen Street which remain in your hands unsold.By forbearance of the Plaintiff. We do therefore command you, that you expose to sale the goods and chattels, Lands and tenements by you so as aforesaid levied upon, so that you have the said money and 6 & ¼ shillings for accruing costs, before the Judge of our said Court, at Edenton, on the first Monday after the Fourth Monday of March next, and we do command you further, that of the goods and chattels, lands and tenements of the said Eliza Gray in your bailiwick, you cause to be made the residue of the said Debt, damages, costs and charges, and that you have the said money before the Judge of our said Court, at Edenton, on the day aforesaid, to render to the said Beasley & Norcom their debt, damages, costs and charges aforesaid; and have you then and there this writ. Witness Duncan McDonald, Clerk of our said Court, at Edenton, the 8th day of October in the XXXVIII year of our Independence, Anno Dom. 1813.

D McDonald, Clk

Judgment £106.19.4 £81.19.4 to bear Int. from 14th February 1811 till paid
£25 to bear Interest from 19 June 1812 till paid

H AD	£1.4
DMcD	19.6
Shf	10.6
Atto	2

£4.12

****

James Jackson Vs. Nathaniel Bond
Civil Action [1813]
Chowan County Records

James Jackson
Subpoena
Nathl Bond
Mary Bond
Executed by Jas Skinner, DShff

State of North Carolina
To the Sheriff of Chowan County, Greeting:
You are hereby commanded to summon Mary Bond personally to be and appear before the Judge of our Superior Court of Law, to be held at the Court House in Edenton, on the first Monday after the Fourth Monday in Septr. Then and there to testify and the truth to say, in behalf of James Jackson in a certain matter of controversy in the said Court depending, and then and there to be tried, wherein James Jackson is Plaintiff, and Nat Bond is Defendant. And this you shall in no wise omit, under the penalty by law enjoined. Witness Duncan McDonald, Clerk of the said Court, at Edenton, the 1st day of April in the XXXVII year of our Independence, Anno Dom. 1813.
D McDonald, Clk

James Jackson Vs Nat Bond
For John Hoskins
Executed by
Jas. S. M [?]

State of North Carolina
To the Sheriff of Chowan County, Greeting:
You are hereby commanded to summon John Hoskins personally to be and appear before the Judge of our Superior Court of Law, held at the Court House in Edenton, on the first Monday after the fourth Monday in March next, then and there to testify and the truth to say in behalf of Jas Jackson

in a certain matter of controversy in the said Court depending, and then and there to be tried, wherein Jas Jackson is Plaintiff and Nat Bond is Defendant. And this you shall in no wise omit, under the penalty by law enjoined. Witness Duncan McDonald, Clerk of the said Court, at Edenton, the 4th day of October in the XXXIII year of our Independence, Anno Dom. 1813.
D McDonald, Clk

Jas Jackson
Nathl Bond
Subpoena, Immediately
Executed
Jas Skinner, DShff

State of North Carolina
To the Sheriff of Chowan County, Greeting:
You are hereby commanded to summon Henry Flury & Eli Bertee personally to be and appear before the Judge of our Superior Court of Law, held at the Court House in Edenton, on the first Monday after fourth Monday in Septr. Next, then and there to testify and the truth to say in behalf of Jas Jackson in a certain matter of controversy in the said Court depending, and then and there to be tried, wherein Jas Jackson is Plaintiff, and Nat Bond is Defendant. And this you shall in no wise omit, under the penalty by law enjoined. Witness Duncan McDonald, Clerk of the said Court, at Edenton, the 5th day of October in the XXXIII year of our Independence, Anno Dom. 1813.
D McDonald, Clk

James Jackson
Nathl Bond
Subpoena
Norman King
Executed by Jas Skinner, DShff

State of North Carolina
To the Sheriff of Chowan County, Greeting:
You are hereby commanded to summon Norman King personally to be and appear before the Judge of our Superior Court of Law in Edenton, on the

first Monday after the Fourth Monday in Septr, then and there to testify and the truth to say, in behalf of James Jackson in a certain matter of controversy in the said court depending, and then and there to be tried, wherein Jas Jackson is Plaintiff and Nat Bond is Defendant. And this you shall in no wise omit, under the penalty by law enjoined. Witness Duncan McDonald, Clerk of the said Court, at Edenton the 5th day of October in the XXXIII year of our Independence, Anno Dom. 1813.
D McDonald, Clk

Jackson Vs N. Bond
Subpoena for Wm. Walton
Executed by E. Hoskins, Shff

State of North Carolina
To the Sheriff of Chowan County, Greeting:
You are hereby commanded to summon William Walton personally to be and appear before the Judge of our Superior Court of Law, held at the Court house in Edenton, on the first Monday after the fourth Monday in March next, then and there to testify and the truth to say in behalf of Jas. Jackson in a certain matter of controversy in the said Court depending, wherein Jas. Jackson is Plaintiff and Nat Bond is Defendant. And this you shall in no wise omit, under the penalty by law enjoined. Witness Duncan McDonald, Clerk of the said Court, at Edenton, the 4th day of October in the XXXVIII year of our Independence, Anno Dom. 1813.
D McDonald, Clk

James Jackson
Nat Bond
Subpoena
Lewis Bond
Executed by Jas Skinner, DShff

State of North Carolina
To the Sheriff of Chowan County, Greeting:
You are hereby commanded to summon Lewis Bond personally to be and appear before the Judge of our Superior Court of Law, to be held at the Court House in Edenton, on the first Monday after the fourth Monday in Septr., then and there to testify and the truth to say, in behalf of James

Jackson in a certain matter of Controversy in the said Court depending, and then and there to be tried, wherein James Jackson is Plaintiff, and Nat Bond is Defendant. And this you shall in no wise omit, under the penalty by law enjoined. Witness Duncan McDonald, Clerk of the said Court, at Edenton, the 1st day of April in the XXXVII year of our Independence, Anno Dom. 1813.
D McDonald, Clk

James Jackson Vs Nat Bond
Subpoena
Tho Satterfield
Executed by E. Hoskins, Shff

State of North Carolina
To the Sheriff of Chowan County, greeting:
You are hereby commanded to summon Thomas Satterfield personally to be and appear before the Judge of our Superior Court of Law, to be held at the Court House in Edenton, on the first Monday after the fourth Monday in Septr then and there to testify and the truth to say, in behalf of Nathaniel Bond in a certain matter of controversy in the said Court depending, and then and there to be tried, wherein James Jackson is Plaintiff, and Nat Bond is Defendant. And this you shall in no wise omit, under the penalty by law enjoined. Witness Duncan McDonald, Clerk of the said Court, at Edenton, the 1st day of April in the XXXVII year of our Independence, Anno Dom. 1813
D McDonald, Clk

Jas Jackson Vs Nathl Bond
Sobpoena
For Absalom H Pritchard
Served, Jos S MKeel, Dep, Shff

State of North Carolina
To the Sheriff of Chowan County, Greeting:
You are hereby commanded to summon Absalom Pritchard personally to be and appear before the Judge of our Superior Court of Law, held at the Court House in Edenton, on the first Monday after the fourth Monday in March next, then and there to testify and the truth to say in behalf of Jas.

Jackson in a certain matter of controversy in the said Court depending, and then and there to be tried, wherein Jas. Jackson is Plaintiff, and Nat Bond is Defendant. And this you shall in no wise omit, under the penalty by law enjoined. Witness Duncan McDonald, Clerk of the said Court, at Edenton, the 4th day of October in the XXXVIII year of our Independence, Anno Dom. 1813.
D McDonald, Clk

Jas. Jackson Vs Nat Bond
Subpoena for Reuben Small
Served by Jos. S. Mckeel, Dep Shff

State of North Carolina
To the Sheriff of Chowan County, Greeting:
You are hereby commanded to summon Reuben Small personally to be and appear before the Judge of our Superior Court of Law, held at the Court House in Edenton, on the first Monday after the fourth Monday in March next, then and there to testify and the truth to say in behalf Nat Bond in a certain matter of controversy in the said Court depending, and then and there to be tried, wherein Jas Jackson is Plaintiff and Nat Bond is Defendant. And this you shall in no wise omit, under the penalty by law enjoined. Witness Duncan McDonald, Clerk of the said Court, at Edenton, the 4th day of October in the XXXVIII year of our Independence, Anno Dom.. 1813
D McDonald, Clk

Jas. Jackson Vs Nat Bond
Subpoena for Exum Simpson
Executed by Jos S McKeel, Dep Shff

State of North Carolina
To the Sheriff of Chowan County, Greeting:
You are hereby commanded to summon Exum Simpson personally to be and appear before the Judge of our Superior Court of Law, held at the Court House in Edenton, on the first Monday after the fourth Monday in March next, then and there to testify and the truth to say in behalf of Nat Bond in a certain matter of controversy in the said Court depending, and then and there to be tried, wherein Jas. Jackson is Plaintiff and Nat Bond is

Defendant. And this you shall in no wise omit, under the penalty by law enjoined. Witness Duncan McDonald, Clerk of the said Court, at Edenton, the 4th day of October in the XXXVIII year of our Independence, Anno Dom. 1813.
D McDonald, Clk

Jas Jackson Vs Nat Bond
Subpoena for James Skinner
Executed by Jos S. McKeel, Dep. Shff

State of North Carolina
To the Sheriff of Chowan County, Greeting:
You are hereby commanded to summon James Skinner personally to be and appear before the Judge of our Superior Court of Law, held at the Court House in Edenton, on the first Monday after the fourth Monday in March next, then and there to testify and the truth to say in behalf of Nat Bond in a certain matter of controversy in the said Court depending, and then and there to be tried, wherein Jas Jackson is Plaintiff and Nat Bond is Defendant. And this you shall in no wise omit, under the penalty by law enjoined. Witness Duncan McDonald, Clerk of the said Court, at Edenton, the 4th day of March in the XXXVIII year of our Independence, Anno Dom. 1813.
D McDonald, Clk

Service Accepted
Jas Jackson Vs Nat Bond
Executed by Jas Skinner, Shff

State of North Carolina
To the Sheriff of Chowan County, Greeting:
You are hereby commanded to summon Ben Small Junr. Personally to be and appear before the Judge of our Superior Court of Law, held at the Court House in Edenton, on the first Monday after the fourth Monday in March next, then and there to testify and the truth to say in behalf of Nat Bond in a certain matter of controversy in the said Court depending, and then and there to be tried, wherein Jas Jackson is Plaintiff and Nat Bond is Defendant. And this you shall in no wise omit, under the penalty by law enjoined. Witness Duncan McDonald, Clerk of the said Court, at Edenton,

the 4th day of March in the XXXVIII year of our Independence, Anno Dom. 1813
D McDonald, Clk

Jas Jackson Vs Nat Bond
Subp for Elizabeth Beasley
Served by Jos. S. Mckeel, Dep. Shff

State of North Carolina
To the Sheriff of Chowan County, Greeting:
You are hereby commanded to summon Elisabeth Beasley personally to be and appear before the Judge of our Superior Court of Law, held at the Court House in Edenton, on the first Monday after the fourth Monday in March next, then and there to testify and the truth to say in behalf of Nat Bond in a certain matter of controversy in the said Court depending, and then and there to be tried, wherein Jas Jackson is Plaintiff and Nat Bond is Defendant. And this you shall in no wise omit, under the penalty by law enjoined. Witness Duncan McDonald, Clerk of the said Court, at Edenton, the 4th day of March in the XXXVIII year of our Independence, Anno Dom. 1813.
D McDonald, Clk

Jas Jackson Vs Nat Bond
Subp for Alex Small
Served by Jos. S. McKeel, Dep. Shff

State of North Carolina
To the Sheriff of Chowan County, Greeting:
You are hereby commanded to summon Alex Small personally to be and appear before the Judge of our Superior Court of Law, held at the Court House in Edenton, on the first Monday after the fourth Monday in March next, then and there to testify and the truth to say in behalf of Nat Bond in a certain matter of controversy in the said Court depending, and then and there to be tried, wherein Jas Jackson is Plaintiff and Nat Bond is Defendant. And this you shall in no wise omit, under the penalty by law enjoined. Witness Duncan McDonald, Clerk of the said Court, at Edenton, the 4th day of March in the XXXVIII year of our Independence, Anno Dom. 1813

D McDonald, Clk

Jackson vs Bond
Service Accepted
Northampton October 4th 1813
Harrison Boyce

State of North Carolina
To the Sheriff of Northampton County, Greeting:
You are hereby commanded to summon Harrison Boyce personally to be and appear before the Judge of our Superior Court of Law, to be held at the Court House in Edenton, on the first Monday after the fourth Monday in Septr. Then and there to testify and the truth to say, in behalf of Nathaniel Bond in a certain matter of controversy in the saud Court depending, and then and there to be tried, wherein James Jackson is Plaintiff, and Nat Bond is Defendant. And this you shall in no wise omit, under the penalty by law enjoined. Witness Duncan McDonald, Clerk of the said Court, at Edenton, the 1st day of April in the XXXVII year of our Independence, Anno Dom. 1813
D Mcdonald, Clk

Jackson Vs. N Bond
Subp for Thos Beasley
Executed by E. Hoskins, Shff

State of North Carolina
To the Sheriff of Chowan County, Greeting:
You are hereby commanded to summon Tho Beasley personally to be and appear before the Judge of our Superior Court of Law, held at the Court House in Edenton, on the first Monday after the Fourth Monday in March next, then and there to testify and the truth to say in behalf of Jas Jackson in a certain matter of controversy in the said Court depending, and then and there to be tried, wherein Jas Jackson is Plaintiff and Nat Bond is Defendant. And this you shall in no wise omit, under the penalty by law enjoined. Witness Duncan McDonald, Clerk of the said Court, at Edenton, the 4th day of March in the XXXVIII year of our Independence, Anno Dom. 1813
D McDonald, Clk

Jas Jackson Vs Nat Bond
Subp for Josiah Buchies
Executed by Jos. S. McKeel, Dep. Shff

State of North Carolina
To the Sheriff of Chowan County, Greeting:
You are hereby commanded to summon Josiah Bacchies personally to be and appear before the Judge of our Superior Court of Law, held at the Court House in Edenton, on the first Monday after the fourth Monday in March next, then and there to testify and the truth to say in behalf of Nat Bond in a certain matter of controversy in the said Court depending, and then and there to be tried, wherein Jas Jackson is Plaintiff, and Nat Bond is Defendant. And this you shall in no wise omit, under the penalty by law enjoined. Witness Duncan McDonald, Clerk of the said Court, at Edenton, the 4th day of October in the XXXVIII year of our Independence, Anno Dom. 1813.
D McDonald, Clk

Jas. Jackson Vs Nat Bond
Service Accepted
Excepted by Abs H Pritchard

State of North Carolina
To the Sheriff of Chowan County, Greeting:
You are hereby commanded to summon Absalom Pritchard personally to be and appear before the Judge of our Superior Court of Law, held at the Court House in Edenton immediately next; then and there to testify and the truth to say in behalf of Deft. In a certain matter of controversy in the said Court depending, and then and there to be tried, wherein Jas Jackson is Plaintiff, and Nat Bond Defendant. And this you shall in no wise omit, under the penalty by law enjoined. Witness Duncan McDonald, Clerk of the said Court, at Edenton, the 5th day of April in the XXXVIII year of our Independence, Anno Dom. 1814
D McDonald, Clk

Jas. Jackson Vs Nat Bond

Chowan County Civil Actions

Subp for Elizabeth Simpson
Service Jos. S. McKeel, Dep. Shff

State of North Carolina
To the Sheriff of Chowan County, Greeting:
You are hereby commanded to summon Elisabeth Simpson, wife of Evan personally to be and appear before the Judge of our Superior Court of Law, held at the Court House in Edenton, on the first Monday after the fourth Monday in March next, then and there to testify and the truth to say in behalf of Nat Bond in a certain matter of controversy in the said Court depending, and then and there to be tried, wherein Jas. Jackson is Plaintiff and Nat Bond is Defendant. And this you shall in no wise omit, under the penalty by law enjoined. Witness Duncan McDonald, Clerk of the said Court, at Edenton, the 4th day of March in the XXXVIII year of our Independence, Anno Dom. 1813
D McDonald, Clk

Service Accepted
Wm. Thompson

State of North Carolina
To the Sheriff of Chowan County, Greeting:
You are hereby commanded to summon Wm Thompson personally to be and appear before the Judge of our Superior Court of Law, held at the Court House in Edenton March next, then and there to testify and the truth to say in behalf of Defdt. In a certain matter of controversy in the said Court depending, and then and there to be tried, wherein Jas Jackson is Plaintiff and Nat Bond is Defendant. And this you shall in no wise omit, under the penalty by law enjoined. Witness Duncan McDonald, Clerk of the said Court, at Edenton, the 5th day of April in the XXXVIII year of our Independence, Anno Dom. 1814.
D McDonald, Clk

Jas Jackson Vs Nat Bond
Subp for Lydia Sanderlin
Executed Jos S. Mckeel, Dep. Shff

State of North Carolina

Chowan County
Civil Actions

To the Sheriff of Chowan County, Greeting:
You are hereby commanded to summon Lydia Sanderlin personally to be and appear before the Judge of our Superior Court of Law, held at the Court House in Edenton, on the first Monday after the fourth Monday in March next, then and there to testify and the truth to say in behalf of Nat Bond in a certain matter of controversy in the said Court depending, and then and there to be tried, wherein Jas. Jackson is Plaintiff, and Nat Bond is Defendant. And this you shall in no wise omit, under the penalty by law enjoined. Witness Duncan McDonald, Clerk of the said Court, at Edenton, the 4th day of October in the XXXVIII year of our Independence, Anno Dom. 1813.
D McDonald, Clk

Service Excepted
Edmd Jones

State of North Carolina
To the Sheriff of Chowan County, Greeting:
You are hereby commanded to summon Edm Jones personally to be and appear before the Judge of our Superior Court of Law, held at the Court House in Edenton, on the first Monday after the fourth Monday in March next, then and there to testify and the truth to say in behalf of Deft. In a certain matter of controversy in the said Court depending, and then and there to be tried, wherein Jas Jackson is Plaintiff and Nat Bond is Defendant. And this you shall in no wise omit, under the penalty by law enjoined. Witness Duncan McDonald, Clerk of the said Court, at Edenton, the 5th day of April in the XXXVIII year of our Independence, Anno Dom. 1814.
D McDonald, Clk

****

James Jackson Vs. Nathaniel Bond
Civil Action [1814]
Chowan County Records

James Jackson Vs Nathaniel Bond
March Term 1813
Executed by E. Hoskins, Shff

Chowan County
Civil Actions

JBS

State of North Carolina

To the Sheriff of Chowan County, Greeting:

You are hereby commanded to summon Ben Hassell personally to be and appear before the Judge of our Superior Court of Law, held at the Court House in Edenton, on the first Monday after the fourth Monday in March next, then and there to testify and the truth to say in behalf of Defd. In a certain matter of controversy in the said Court depending, and then and there to be tried, wherein Jas Jackson is Plaintiff and Nat Bond is Defendant. And this you shall in no wise omit, under the penalty by law enjoined. Witness Duncan McDonald, Clerk of the said Court, at Edenton, the 5th day of April in the XXX[?] year of our Independence, anno Dom. 1814

D. McDonald, Clk

Security for the costs of this Suit.

Test, N[?]

Henry Hurdle

Writ	1.4
Con 3p 23 [?]	1.14.6
Trans 10/ Trans 1.5	1.15
	4.13.6
Shff	3.19.6
Atto	2
	£10.13

State of North Carolina

To the Sheriff of Chowan County, Geeeting:

You are hereby commanded to take the body of Nathaniel Bond (if to be found in your County) and him safely keep, so that you have him before the Judge of the Superior Court of Law, to be held for the County of Chowan, at the Court House in Edenton, on the first Monday after the fourth Monday of March next, then and there to answer unto James Jackson of a plea that he render unto him a certain negro woman Slave named Annis of the value of three hundred pounds which from him he unjustly detains to his damage three hundred pounds. Herein fail not, and have you then and there this writ. Witness Duncan McDonald, Clerk of

our said Court, at Edenton, the tenth day of October 1812 and in the XXXVII year of our Independence. Issued the 11th day of February 1813.
D. McDonald, Clk

James Jackson maketh oath that in the Suit now depending in this Honorable Court wherein he is Plaintiff and Nathaniel Bond is Defendant and in the Suit at his instance against John Bond, the Defendants are persons of very extensive and powerful connections in the County of Chowan, that he has been informed and does conscientiously believe since the institution of the aforesaid suits, the Defendants, have used their influence to excite the prejudices of many of the Citizens of the County against this deponant personally, and against his claim & the subject matter of controversy depending inso much that he verily believes he cannot have justice fairly and impartially administered to him in the said County -- he therefore prays the aforesaid Suits may be removed to some adjacent County
Sworn to in open Court 7th April
James Jackson
D. McDonald, Clk

****

Joseph B. Skinner Vs James & William Jones
Civil Action [1814]
Chowan County Records

Joseph B. Skinner Vs James & William Jones
Vends Expons
Cho Sup Court
March Term 1815
To hand 13th Decr. 1814

Exposed the within named negroes to public Sale & not sold for want of bidders, Lewis Walters, Shff

State of North Carolina
To the Sheriff of Hertford county, Greeting:
Whereas, by our writ commanded you, that of the goods and chattels, lands and tenements of James Jones and William Jones (in your bailiwick) you

should cause to be made the sum of Thirteen hundred and Eighty two pounds 4/6 which lately in our Superior Court of Law at Edenton, Joseph B. Skinner Recovered against them for debt and damages Sustained by him by reason of the detention of that debt also the further sum of four pounds 16/3 for the costs and damages by him in his Suit in that behalf expended, whereof the said James Jones and William Jones are convicted and liable as to us appears of record; besides your own fees for that service, and that you should have the said money before the Judge of our said Court, at Edenton, on the first Monday after the fourth Monday of Sept. next, after the 5th day of March in the year of our Lord one thousand eight hundred and fourteen to render to the said Joseph Skinner damages, costs and charges aforesaid: And you at that day returned on the said writ, that you had levied the same on Negroes Bob, Allen & Price which remain in your hands unsold for want of bidders. We do therefore command you, that you expose to sale the goods and chattels by you so as aforesaid levied upon, so that you have the said money and **[Blank]** shillings for accruing costs, before the Judge of our said Court, at Edenton, on the first Monday after the fourth Monday of March next, and we do command you further, that of the goods and chattels, lands and tenements of the said James Jones and William Jones in your bailiwick, you cause to be made the residue of the said Debt, damages, costs and charges, and that you have the said money before the Judge of our said Court, at Edenton on the day aforesaid, to render to the said Joseph B Skinner damages, costs and charges aforesaid; and have you then and there this writ. Witness Duncan McDonald, Clerk of our said Court, at Edenton, the 5th day of October in the XXX9th year of our Independence, Anno Dom. 1814
D. McDonald, Clk

Judgment £1382.4.6 Int. from 31st December 1810 till paid

H.A.D.	1.8.6
DMD	1.7.4
Atto JBS	2
	£4.16.3

£500 of the above has been Rec'd on a former Execution 4th March 1813, also £400 on the 31st Decr. 1813

Joseph B. Skinner, Assignee Vs James & Wm. Jones
Vends Expons
Chowan Sup Court

September Term 1815
To hand 10th August 1815

Again exposed the within named negroes to sale, which still remain unsold for want of bidders
Lewis Walters, Shff, Hertford

State of North Carolina
To the Sheriff of Hertford County, Greeting:
Whereas, we by our writ commanded you, that of the goods and chattels, lands and tenements of James Jones and William Jones (in your bailiwick) you should cause to be made the sum of Thirteen hundred and eighty two pounds 4/6 which lately in our Superior Court of Law at Edenton, Joseph B. Skinner Recovered against them for Debt & Damages sustained by him by reason of the detention of that debt, also the further sum of Five Pounds 5/6 for the costs and charges by him in his Suit in that behalf expended, whereof the said James and William Jones are convicted and liable as to us appears of record; besides your own fees for that service, and that you should have the said money before the Judge of our said Court, at Edenton, on the first Monday after the fourth Monday of Septr. Next, after the 5th day of March in the year of our Lord and 14 to render to the said Joseph B. Skinner his damages, costs and charges aforesaid: And you at that day returned on the said writ, that you had levied the same on Negroes Bob, Allen & Price which remain in your hands unsold for want of bidders. We do therefore command you, that you expose to sale the goods and chattels by you so as aforesaid levied upon, so that you have the said money and **[Blank]** shillings for accriung costs, before the Judge of our said Court, at Edenton, on the first Monday after the fourth Monday of September next, and we do command you further, that of the goods and chattels, lands and tenements of the said James and William Jones in your bailiwick, you cause to be made the residue of the said Debt, damages, costs and charges, and that you have the said money before the Judge of our said Court, at Edenton, on the day aforesaid, to render to the said Joseph B. Skinner damages, costs and charges aforesaid; and have you then and there this writ. Witness Duncan McDonald, Clerk of our said Court, at Edenton, the 5th day of April in the XXXIX year of our Independence, Anno Dom. 1815.
D McDonald, Clk

Judgment £1382.4.6 Interest from 31st Decr 1810 till paid

H.A.D. former Clk	1.8.6
DMcD Clk	1.17.2
Atto J.B.S.	2
	£5.5.6

£500 has been rec'd on a former Exr. 9th March 1813 also £400 on 31st Decr. 1813.

Jos B. Skinner Vs. Jas & Howell Jones
Vends Expons
Chowan County Court
March Term 1816

Rec'd 7th March 1816 sale advertised at Pitch Landing David Harrells store & Court House. No Sale for want of bidders.
Jas. Copland, Shff, Hertford

State of North Carolina
To the Sheriff of Hertford County, Greeting:
Whereas, we by our writ commanded you, that of the goods and chattels, lands and tenements of James Jones and William Jones (in your bailiwick) you should cause to be made the sum of Thirteen hundred and eighty two Pounds 4/16 which lately in our Superior Court of Law at Edenton, Joseph B. Skinner Recovered against them for debt & damages sustained by them by reason of the detention of that debt also the further sum of Five pounds 11/19 for the costs and charges by him in his suit in that behalf expended, whereof the said James & William Jones are convicted and liable as to us appears of record; besides your own fees for that service, and that you should have the said money before the Judge of our said Court, at Edenton, on the first Monday after the fourth Monday of Septr next, after the 5th day of March in the year of our Lord one thousand eight hundred and 14 to render to the said Joseph B. Skinner his damages, costs and charges aforesaid: And you at that day returned on the said writ, that you had levied the same on Negroes Bob, Allen and Prince which remain in your hands unsold. We do therefore command you, that you expose to sale the goods and chattels by you so as aforesaid levied upon, so that you have the said money and **[Blank]** shillings for accruing costs, before the Judge of our said Court, at Edenton, on the first Monday after the fourth Monday of March next, and we do command you further, that of the goods and chattels, lands and tenements of the said James Jones & Wm Jones in your

bailiwick, you cause to be made the residue of the said debt, damages, costs and charges, on the day aforesaid, to render to the said Joseph B. Skinner his damages, costs and charges aforesaid; and have you then and there this writ. Witness Duncan McDonald, Clerk of our said Court, at Edenton, the 5th day of October in the 40 yrea of our Independence, Anno Dom. 1815
D McDonald, Clk

Judgment £1382.4.6 Interest from 31st Decr 1810 till Paid
HAD 1.8.6
DMcD Clk 2.3.3
Atto JBS 2
£500 of the above has been rec'd 9th March 1813 also £400 31st Decr 1813.

****

Thomas Coffield Vs. Sarah Elliot
Civil Action [1814]
Chowan County Records

Tho Coffield Vs Sarah Elliot
Subp for Edm. Jones
Septr Term 1814
Executed by James R. Bent, Shff

State of North Carolina
To the Sheriff of Chowan County, Greeting:
You are hereby commanded to summon Edmund Jones personally to be and appear before the Judge of our Superior Court of Law, held at the Court House in Edenton, on the first Monday after the fourth Monday in Septr next, then and there to testify and the truth to say in behalf of Sarah Elliot in a certain matter of controversy in the said Court depending, and then and there to be tried, wherein Tho Coffield is Plaintiff and Sarah Elliot is Defendant. And this you shall in no wise omit, under the penalty by law enjoined. Witness Duncan McDonald, Clerk of the said Court, at Edenton, the 5th day of April in the XXXVIII year of our Independence, Anno Dom. 1814
D McDonald, Clk

Chowan County
Civil Actions

John Coffield Vs Sarah Elliott
Subpo for Wm Hall
Executed by James R Bent, Shff

State of North Carolina
To the Sheriff of Chowan County, Greeting:
You are hereby commanded to summon Wm Hall personally to be and appear before the Judge of our Superior Court of Law, held at the Court House in Edenton immediately next, then and there to testify and the truth to say in behalf of plaintiff in a certain matter of controversy in the said Court depending, and then and there to be tried, wherein John Coffield is Plaintiff, and Sarah Elliott is Defendant. And this you shall in no wise omit, under the penalty by law enjoined. Witness Duncan McDonald, Clerk of the said Court, at Edenton, the 3rd day of October in the 40th year of our Independence, Anno Dom. 1815
D McDonald, Clk

Tho Coffield Vs Sarah Elliott
Subp for Robert Wheaton & John Moore
Chowan Sup Court
Sept 1814
Executed by Myles Elliott, Shff
Perquimans

State of North Carolina
To the Sheriff of Perquimans County, greeting:
You are hereby commanded to summon John Moore personally to be and appear before the judge of our Superior Court of Law, held at the Court House in Edenton, on the first Monday after the fourth Monday in Septr next, then and there to testify and the truth to say in behalf of Sarah Elliott in a certain matter of controversy in the said Court depending, and then and there to be tried, wherein Tho Coffield Plaintiff, and Sarah Elliott is Defendant. And this you shall in no wise omit, under the penalty by law enjoined. Witness Duncan McDonald, Clerk of the said Court, at Edenton, the 5th day of April in the XXXVIII year of our Independence, Anno Dom. 1814
D McDonald, Clk

Chowan County
Civil Actions

Thomas Coffield Vs Sarah Elliott
Subp for Wm Sanders & Wm Hall
Executed on Wm Sanders & Wm Hall
Not to be found
James R. Bent, Shff

State of North Carolina
To the Sheriff of Chowan County, Greeting:
You are hereby commanded to summon William Sanders & Wm. Hall personally to be and appear before the Judge of our Superior Court of Law, held at the Court House in Edenton, on the first Monday after the fourth Monday in September next, then and there to testify and the truth to say in behalf of Thomas Coffield in a certain matter of controversy in the said Court depending, and then and there to be tried, wherein Thomas Coffield is Plaintiff, and Sarah Elliott is Defendant. And this you shall in no wise omit, under the penalty by law enjoined. Witness Duncan McDonald, Clerk of the said Court, at Edenton, the **[Blank]** day of **[Blank]** in the year oof our Independence, anno Dom.
D. McDonald, Clk.

Thomas Coffield Vs Sarah Elliott
Subpoena
Executed by Myles Elliott, Shff

State of North Carolina
To the Sheriff of Perquimans County, Greeting:
You are hereby commanded to summon Robert Wheaton personally to be and appear before the Judge of our Superior Court of Law, held at the Court House in Edenton, on the first Monday after the fourth Monday in Septr next, then and there to testify and the truth to say in behalf of Tho Coffield in a certain matter of controversy in the said Court depending, and then and there to be tried, wherein Tho Coffield is Plaintiff, and Sarah Elliott is Defendant. Witness Duncan McDonald, Clerk of the said Court, at Edenton, the 5th day of April in the XXXVIII year of our Independence, anno Dom. 1814
D McDonald, Clk

State of North Carolina } Ss

Chowan County
Civil Actions

Chowan County }

Sarah Elliott, late of the County of Perquimans and State aforesaid, was summoned to answer to Thomas Coffield of the County of Chowan and State aforesaid of a plea that she render unto him four certain negro Slaves of the value of One thousand pounds which she unjustly detains to herself; and whereupon the said Thomas Coffield by Joseph Skinner his Attorney declares, that whereas she the said Sarah procured and obtained possession on the **[Blank]** day of **[Blank]** one thousand eight hundred and **[Blank]** at the County of Perquimans aforesaid of the negro Slaves of the said Thomas following to wit, negro Jim of the value of four hundred pounds, negro Trease of the value of two hundred pounds, negro Jack of the value of Two hundred pounds, and negro Squire of the like value of two hundred pounds, to be redelivered to the said Thomas whenever the same should be required: Nevertheless the said Sarah though often requested, hath not yet delivered the said negroes to the said Thomas, but hitherto hath and still doth refuse to deliver the same; Whereupon the said Thomas declares that he is injured and damaged to the value of **[Blank]** and thereof he brings proof &c.

Thos. Coffield Vs Sarah Elliott
Subp for Robt Wheaton
Chowan Supr. Court, 1814
Executed by Myles Elliott, Shff

State of North Carolina
To the Sheriff of Perquimans County, Greeting:
You are hereby commanded to summon Robert Wheaton personally to be and appear before the Judge of our Superior Court of Law, held at the Court House in Edenton, on the first Monday after the fourth Monday in Septr next, then and there to testify and the truth to say in behalf of Sarah Elliott in a certain matter of controversy in the said Court depending, and then and there to be tried, wherein Tho Coffield is plaintiff, and **[Blank]** is Defendant. And this you shall in no wise omit, under the penalty by law enjoined. Witness Duncan McDonald, Clerk of the said Court, at Edenton, the 5th day of April in the XXXVIII year of our Independence, Anno Dom. 1814
D McDonald, Clk

Chowan County
Civil Actions

Thos Coffield Vs Sarah Elliott
Subp for Eli Brinkley
Chowan Supr Court, 1814
Executed by Myles Elliott, Shff

State of North Carolina
To the Sheriff of Perquimans County, Greeting:
You are hereby commanded to summon Eli Brinkley personally to be and appear before the Judge of our Superior Court of Law, held at the Court House in Edenton, on the first Monday after the fourth Monday in Septr next, then and there to testify and the truth to say in behalf of Sarah Elliott in a certain matter of controversy in the said Court depending, and then and there to be tried, wherein Tho Coffield is Plaintiff, and Sarah Elliott is Defendant. And this you shall in no wise omit, under the penalty by law enjoined. Witness Duncan McDonald, Clerk of the said Court, at Edenton, the 5th day of April in the XXXVIII year of our Independence, Anno Dom. 1814
D McDonald, Clk

Tho Coffield Vs Sarah Elliott
Subp for Wm. Simmons & Eli Brinkley
Chowan Sep 1814
Executed by Myles Elliott, Shff
Perquimans

State of North Carolina
To the Sheriff of Perquimans County, Greeting:
You are hereby commanded to summon William Simones Senr. Personally to be and appear before the Judge of ou Superior Court of Law, held at the Court House in Edenton, on the first Monday after the fourth Monday in Septr next, then and there to be tried, wherein Tho Coffield is Plaintiff, and Sarah Elliott is Defendant. And this you shall in no wise omit, under the penalty by law enjoined. Witness Duncan McDonald, Clerk of the said Court, at Edenton, the 5th day of April in the XXXVIII year of our Independence, Anno Dom. 1814.
D McDonald, Clk

Chowan County
Civil Actions

Thos Hosea, Shff
Bill of Sale to Thos Coffield
Fees paid 6/

Perquimans }
County Court }

February Term at Hertford 1809 & this Bill of sale was acknowledged In Open Court & ordered to be Registered
John Wood, Clk

Registered in the Registers Office of Perquimans County the 4th day of May A.D. 1809
Test, Gab White, Regr.

Know all men by these presents that **[Smudged]** of and in satisfaction for an execution from Coffield against Justus Leary and Townsend Elliott and for and in consideration of the sum of one hundred and sixty Six Pounds nine shillings and three pence to me in hand paid the Receipt of which I do hereby acknowledge have this day bargained, Sell and deliver unto Thomas Coffield of Chowan County all the right, title and interest which Townsend Elliot had in and to the following Negroes Viz. Jim, Jack, Trease and Squire, also two horses, one Cow, as witness my hand and Seal this fifteenth day of August 1808.
Witness, Jas. Norfleet
Ackwd, Thos Hosea, Shff (Seal)
Perqt County

Tho Coffield Vs Sarah Elliott
Subp for Wm Felton
Chowan Sept Term 1814
Executed by Myles Elliott, Shff
Perquimans

State of North Carolina
To the Sheriff of Perquimans County, Greeting:
You are hereby commanded to summon William Felton personally to be and appear before the Judge of our Superior Court of Law, held at the Court House in Edenton, on the first Monday after the fourth Monday in Septr next, then and there to testify and the truth to say in behalf of Sarah

Elliott in a certain matter of controversy in the said Court depending, and then and there to be tried, wherein Thomas Coffield is Plaintiff, and Sarah Elliott is Defendant. And this you shall in no wise omit, under the penalty by law enjoined. Witness Duncan McDonald, Clerk of the said Court, at Edenton, the 5th day of April in the XXXVIII year of our Independence, Anno Dom. 1814
D McDonald, Clk

Thomas Coffield Vs Sarah Elliott
Detinue
Chowan Sup Court
March Term 1814
Executed by Myles Elliott, Shff

State of North Carolina
To the Sheriff of Perquimans County, Greeting:
You are hereby commanded to take the body of Sarah Elliott (if to be found in your County) and her safely keep, so that you have her before the Judge of the Superior Court of Law, to be held for the County of Chowan, at the Court House in Edenton, on the first Monday after the fourth Monday of March next, then and there to answer unto Thomas Coffield of a plea that she render unto him negroes Jim of the value of £400 Trease of the value of £200 Jack of the value of £200 and Squire of the value of £200 which from him she unjustly detains to her Damage Three hundred pounds. Herein fail not, and have you then and there this writ. Witness Duncan McDonald, Clerk of our said Court, at Edenton, the 1st Monday after the 4th Monday in Septr 1813 and in the XXX8th year of our Independence. Issued the 28th day of feby 1814.
D McDonald, Clk

Thomas Coffield vs Sarah Elliott

State of North Carolina, Chowan County
To William Blount Esqr, Justice of the peace for Perquimans County
Know ye, That we reposing especial trust and confidence in your fidelity and prudent circumspection, do command, authorise and empower you, or any of you, that at such time and place as you shall appoint, you call and

cause to come before you, that at such time and place as you shall appoint, you call and cause to come before you William Felton & others & them diligently examine on the Holy Evangelists of Almighty God, what they know in and about a certain matter of dispute now at issue in the Superior Court of Law, made in a cause, wherein Thomas Coffield is Plaintiff, and Sarah Elliott is Defendant, as well on the part of the Plaintiff as the Defendant, and such examination and deposition by you so taken, you are to send closed up under your seal, to our said Court, to be held for the County of Chowan, at the Court House in Edenton, on the first Monday after the fourth Monday in Septr. Next; and this you shall in no wise omit. Witness Duncan McDonald, Clerk of the said Court at Edenton, the 5th day of April in the XXXVIIth year of the Independence of the said State, Anno Dom. 1814.
D McDonald, Clk

12th August 1814, Edm Hoskins
[Note: First line of this document creased and torn.]

Then in the possession of said Elliott claimed by them was clear from him after Elliotts paying the sum with the Interest.
Question - Was it after the Sale of Townsend Elliotts property, that Thos. & John Coffields purchased, that you had that Execution of Fredk Creecys
Answer: It was.
Question: Did you understand the **[?]** them as above Mentioned, to allude to Thos Coffield and his father.
Answer: I did.
William Felton Senr.
The above was sworn to before me the 27th of Augt. 1814
Will Blount

Mr. Thomas Coffield, Sir, I shall attend at the Storehouse of Mr. William Creecy in Perquimans County near Bethel Meeting house on Saturday 27th this inst between the hours of ten & twelve Oclock for the purpose of taking the deposition of William Felton in a Suit now pending in the Superior Court of Chowan County wherein Thos. Coffield is Plaintiff & Sarah Elliott is Defendant, of which you will take notice & govern yourself Accordingly
12th of August 1814
J. Mixon for Sarah Elliott

The above was sworn to before me the 27th of Augt 1814
Will. Blount

State of North Carolina }
Perquimans County }

Agreeable to a Commission from Superior Court to me directed I have proceeded to take the deposition of William Felton as follows. Viz. This Deponant Saith in the year of 1811 he as Depty Shff Leveyed an Execution on Townsend Elliotts Property in favour of Frederick Creecy, and Thos. Coffield appeared at the day of Sale, and should Several Instruments of writing claiming said property, he told him he would Sell Townsend Elliotts write, Said Thomas Cofield paid the money and cost, said Cofield then showed him an amount in writing with the Execution he then paid the Sum of about nine hundred Dollars, saying we have **[Note: Next line creased.]** Elliott, the property, then in possession of said Elliott claimed by them was clear from him after Elliotts paying the sum with the Interest.

Question: Was it after the sale of Townsend Elliotts property, that Thos. & John Cofields purchases, that you had that Execution of Fredk. Creecys.
Answer: It was.

Question: Did you understand the **[?]** them as above mentioned, to allude to Thos Cofield and his father.
Answer: I did.
William Felton, Senr.
The above was sworn to before me the 27th of Augt 1814
Will. Blount

Mr. Thomas Coffield, Sir on Saturday the 2nd day of July next between the hours of ten & twelve Oclock I shall attend at the Storehouse of William Creecy Esqr. in Perquimans County near Bethel Meeting House to take the Depositions of William Felton and John Moore relative to a Suit in the Superior Court of Chowan County wherein Thomas Coffield is Plaintiff and Sarah Elliott is Defendant, of which you will take Notice and govern yourself Accordingly
13th of June 1814, Edm Hoskins, Shff

[Note: Next line creased and torn.] Jack, Joe, Sam, Trease, Venus and Squire

by the Defendant: Did you ever hear of any Notice by **[Note: next line creased and torn]** Elliotts property at that time.
Answer: I did not.

How far did you live from Mr T. Elliotts.
Answer: About a quarter of a mile, you were a Acting Constable at that time.
Answer: I was.
Was those negroes Present when sold.
Answer: Neither of them were.
Were there any Cattle and horses sold.
Answer: There was.
Were they present.
Answer: They were not.
John Moore
Will Blount: Sworn to before me the 2nd day of July 1814.
Will. Blount

State of North Carolina }
Perquimans County }

From the Superior Court to me directed I have proceeded to take the deposition of Mr. John Moore as follows -- Viz. This Deponant Saith that about the Spring of 1808 he was at Mr. Townsend Elliotts Mill, and I was sent for to go to the house of Mr. T. Elliott, when He went, John Cofield & Thos. Cofield, thos **[?]** Moore and his son in law was at Mr. T. Elliotts, and John Cofield **[?].** I did not want to purchase some property And Mr. T. Elliotts negroes was offered for sale, and purchased by Thos. And John Coffield, the names of the negroes were Jim, Jack, Joe, Sam, Trease, Venus and Squire.

By the Defendant.
Did you ever hear of any Notice by Advr **[Note: rest of line is Creased.]** T. Elliotts property at that time.
Answer: I did not.
How far did you live from Mr. T. Elliotts.
Answer: About a quarter of a mile.
You were an Acting Constable at that time.
Answer: I was.
Was those Negroes present when sold.
Answer: Neither of them were.

Were there any cattle and horses sold.
Answer: There was.
Were they present.
Answer They were not.
John Moore
Sworn to before me the 2nd day of July 1814.
Will. Blount

Ely Brinkley's Certificates for Octr. & March Terms
£3.13.4

John Coffield Vs Sarah Elliott

Chowan Superior Court }April Term 1815
These are to certify, That Eli Brinkley hath attended this Court 5 days this term as a witness for the defendant

Attending 5 days at 10 Shillings per day	2.10
Travelling 18 miles at six shillings per thirty miles	6
Ferriages	
Certificate and Probate	8
	2.16.8

Sworn to before me
D McDonald, Clk

Wm Felton's Certificate
£1.10.8

Thos Coffield Vs Sarah Elliott

Chowan Superior Court } October Term 1815
These are to certify, That William Felton hath attended this Court 2 days this term as a witness for the Defendant

Attending 2 days at 10 shillings per day	1
Travelling 30 miles at 10 shillings per thirty miles	10
Ferriages	
Certificate and probate	8
	1.10.8

Sworn to before me

Duncan McDonald, Clk

Wm Felton's Certificate
£3.8.8
1.8.8
4.1.4

Thos Coffield vs. Sarah Elliott

Chowan Superior Court} April Term, 1815
These are to certify, That William Felton hath attended this Court 5 days this term as a witness for the Deft.

Attending 5 days at 10 shillings per day	2.10
Travelling 30 miles at 10 shillings per thirty miles	10
Ferriages	
Certificate and Probate	8
	3.0.8

Sworn to before me
Duncan McDonald, Clk

Wm Felton's Certificates
£1.0.8

Thomas Coffield Vs Sarah Elliott

Chowan Superior Court } October Term 1814
These are to certify, That William Felton hath attended this Court 1 day this term as a witness for the Defendant

Attending 5 days at 10 shillings per day	10
Travelling 18 miles at 10 shillings per thirty miles	10
Ferriages	
Certificate and Probate	8
	1.0.8

Sworn to before me
D. McDonald, Clk

John Moore's Certificate

£2.16.8
1.6.8
4.3.4

Thomas Coffield Vs Sarah Elliott

Chowan Superior Court } April Term 1815
These are to certify, That John Moore hath attended this Court 5 days this term as a witness for the Defendant.

Attending 5 days at 10 shillings per day	2.10
Travelling 18 miles at 10 shillings per thirty miles	6
Ferriages	
Certificate and Probate	8
	2.16.8

D. McDonald, Clk

E. Jones Certificate
£0.14.2

Tho. Coffield Vs Sarah Elliott

Chowan Superior Court } October Term 1815
These are to certify, That Edwd. Jones hath attended this Court 2 days this term as a witness for the Defendant.

Attending 2 days at 6 shillings per day	12
Travelling 8 miles at six shillings per thirty miles	1.6
Ferriages	
Certificate and Probate	8
	1.4.2

Sworn to before me
D. McDonald, Clk

Eli Brinkley
Certificates
£1.7.2

Tho. Coffield Vs. Sarah Elliott

Chowan County
Civil Actions

Chowan Superior Court } Chowan Superior Court
These are to certify, that Eli Brinkley hath attended this Court 2 days this term as a witness for the Defdt

Attending 2 days at 10 shillings per day	1
Travelling 18 miles at 10 shillings per thirty miles	6.4
Ferriages	
Certificate and Probate	8
	£1.7.2

Sworn to before me
D McDonald, Clk

R Wheaton's Certificate
£1.10.8

Tho Coffield Vs. Sarah Elliott

Chowan Superior Court } October term 1814
These are to certify, that Robert Wheaton hath attended this Court 2 days this term as a witness for the defd.

Attending 2 days at 10 shillings per day	£1.0.0
Travelling 30 miles at 1o shillings per thirty miles	10
Ferriages	
Certificate and Probate	8
	1.10.8

Sworn to before me
D McDonald, Clk

Wm Simone's Certificate
£1.5.8

Tho. Coffield Vs. Sarah Elliott

Chowan Superior Court } October Term 1815
These are to certify, That Will Simons Senr. Hath attended this Court 2 days this term as a witness for the Defdt.

Attending 2 days at 10 shillings per day	0.1.0
Travelling 15 miles at 10 shillings per thirty miles	0.5.0
Ferriages	

Certificate and Probate 8
1.5.8

Sworn to before me
D McDonald, Clk

John Moore's Certificate
£1.6.8

Thomas Coffield Vs. Sarah Elliott

Chowan Superior Court } Oct Term 1814
These are to certify, that John Moore hath attended this Court 2 days this term as a witness for the Defdt

Attending 2 days at 10 shillings per day	0.1.0
Travelling 18 miles at 10 shillings per thirty miles	0.0.6
Ferriages	
Certificate and Probate	8
	1.6.8

Sworn to before me
D McDonald, Clk

Wm Simon's Certificates
For Octr & March terms
£4.4.4

Tho Coffield Vs. Sarah Elliott

Chowan Superior Court } October Term 1814
These are to certify, That William Simons hath attended this Court 2 days this term as a witness for the Defd.

Attending 2 days at 10 shillings per day	1
Travelling 15 miles at 10 shillings per thirty miles	5
Ferriages	
Certificate and Probate	8
	1.5.8

Sworn to before me
D McDonald, Clk

Chowan County
Civil Actions

Tho Coffield Vs Sarah Elliott

Chowan Superior Court } March Term 1815
These are to certify, That Will Simons hath attended this Court 5 days this term as a witness fro the Defd.

Attending 5 days at 10 shillings per day	2.10.0
Travelling 15 miles at 10 shillings per thirty miles	5
Ferriages	
Certificate and Probate	8
	2.15.8

Sworn to before me
D McDonald, Clk

John Moore's Certificate
£1.6.8

Tho. Coffield Vs. Sarah Elliott

Chowan Superior Court } October Term 1815
These are to certify, that Jno Moore hath attended this Court 2 days this term as a witness for the defdt

Attending 2 days at 10 shillings per day	1
Travelling 18 miles at 10 shillings per thirty miles	6
Ferriages	
Certificate and Probate	8
	1.6.8

Sworn to before me
D McDonald, Clk

Edmd Jones Certificate
£1.12.2
14.2
2.6.4

Tho Coffield Vs Sarah Elliott

Chowan Superior Court } March Term 1815

These are to certify, That Edmund Jones hath attended this Court 5 days this term as a witness for the defdt.

Attending 5 days at 6 shillings per day	1.10
Travelling 8 miles at six shillings per thirty miles	1.6
Ferriages	
Certificate and Probate	8
	1.12.2

Sworn to before me
D McDonald, Clk

Edmd Jone's Certificate
£0.14.2

Tho Coffield Vs. Sarah Elliott

Chowan Superior Court } Septr Term 1814
These are to certify, That Edmd Jones hath attended this Court 2 days this term as a witness for the Defd.

Attending 2 days at 6 shillings per day	12
Travelling 8 miles at six shillings per thirty miles	1.6
Ferriages	
Certificate and Probate	8
	0.14.2

Sworn to before me
D McDonald, Clk

Eli Brinkley's Certificate

Thomas Coffield Vs. Sarah Elliott

Chowan Superior Court } October Term 1814
These are to certify, That Eli Brinkley hath attended this Court 1 day this term as a witness for the Defendant.

Attending 1 day at 10 shillings per day	£0.10
Travelling 18 miles at 10 shillings per thirty miles	6
Ferriages	
Certificate and Probate	8

0.16.8

Sworn to before me
D McDonald, Clk

William Hall's Certificate

Thomas Coffield Vs. Sarah Elliott

Chowan Superior Court } October Term 1815
These are to certify, that William Hall hath attended this Court 1 day this term as a witness for the Pltf.

Attending 1 day at 6 shillings per day	6
Travelling 26 miles at six shillings per thirty miles	5.3
Ferriages	
Certificate and Probate	8
	0.11.11

Sworn to before me
D McDonald, Clk

Witness Tickets filed by Jeremiah Mixon
Tho. Coffield Vs. Sarah Elliott

****

Cullen Cotton Vs. Lewis Powell
Civil Action [1814]
Chowan County Records

Cullen Vs. Lewis Powell
Depos L. Roby
Superior Court
Bertie County

Pursuant to the annexed commission to me directed, at the Store House of William Britton of Bertie County, on the thirteenth day of August One Thousand Eight hundred and Fourteen, both parties being present, namely Lewis Powell agent for Cullen Cotton, and Lewis Powell, I proceeded to take the following deposition of Luke Raiby, being Twenty five years of age who having been first sworn upon the Holy Evangelists, to depose the truth, the whole truth, and nothing but the truth Between the said parties named in the said commission, deposeth and saith as follows, to Wit -- That Cullen Cotton, had a negro woman named Pat and a Boy child, and some time in the month of December in the year 1812, the said negroes was missing one night, and the next night I went down to Lewis Powells, the defendant, and found said negroes in his kitchen - Cullen Cotton, ordered the negroes to open the door and after they refused to do it - Lewis Powell was called up, and Cullen Cotton asked him if his negroes was not in the kitchen, and Lewis Powell said that they was and that he forewarned him from taking them away.

Question by the Plaintiff's Agent: Were you called on by Cullen Cotton, some time before the negroes was missing to ride down with him to Lewis Powells on some business.
Answer: Yes and I went down with him and Mr. Wall.

Question 2nd by ditto: After Mr Wall and Lewis Powell, had done the business they had to do, did you not hear Mr Wall proclaim in the presence of Lewis Powell that he was then clear of the world, except a small account which he owed in Murfreesboro, which Mr Wall, said that the order that Lewis Powell gave him would discharge that debt as well as money.
Answer: As to his saying that it is true, but whether Mr. Lewis Powell was present or not, I am not certain.

1st Question by Lewis Powell, the Defendant - Mr. Raiby, don't you recollect the night that you came to my house that you tried to get into my kitchen previous to my knowing of it.
Answer: Mr. Cullen Cotton directed the negroes to open the door and they would not.

2nd Question by ditto: When Cullen Cotton asked me if his negroes was there & says I what negroes, says he Pat, says I yes
Answer: I don't recollect that the negroes was named.

3rd Question by ditto: Was you on the same side of the house that Cullen Cotton mentioned about the negroes the first time myself and Stephen Murdaugh, was on the other side of the house, Cullen Cotton then called us both over in the yard where you and him was, Cullen Cotton then repeated the same words to him again, by saying you say my negroes are here, and you replyed that they were, and that you did forewarn him from taking them away, and Cullin Cotton then asked you if his negro fellow which he had hired of Turner Rutland was not there, and you said that he was not that he knowed of - and you and Cullin Cotton went in to look for him.

4th Question by ditto: When I went to the door did I not order my negroes to open the door, did I not order my negroes to open the door immediately.
Answer: I do not recollect that you did

5th Question by ditto: Do you know how Cullin Cotton, came by the possession of said negroes.
Answer: The first time of my seeing the negroes or knowing there was such negroes, I saw them at Cullen Cottons house.

3rd question by the Plaintiff's Agent: Do you know anything about Cullen Cotton's buying a negro Boy Child of Mr Wall, which was supposed to be the child of the said negro woman pat, which you saw at Cullen Cottons.
Answer: I heard Mr Wall tell Cullen Cotton a few days before he went away that the negro wench and child was more than he was able to give all his children round and that Cullen Cotton gave him a horse for the child.

6th Question by the Defendant: What do you suppose that horse to be worth in cash.
Answer: I suppose about fifty five or sixty Dollars.

7th Question by ditto: How old do you suppose that horse to have been.
Answer: Mr Chester, the man who brought him here, called him Eight years old, how much older or younger, he was I do not know.

4th Question by Plaintiff's agent: Was you present when Cullen Cotton paid Mr Wall for the little negro by delivering to him the horse.
Answer: I was not present when he delivered him the horse, for the horse was sent to him.

5th Question by ditto: Whither did you not understand, that the order mentioned, was given Mr Wall by Mr Powell, for the swap in negroes.
Answer: I understand it was.

8th Question by the Defendant, what negroes were they that we swaped.

Answer: As to what negroes they was I do not know, but I understand from Mr Wall that they were both at your house and further this deponant saith not.

Sworn before me on the time and at the place above specifyed.
Wm Brittain, J.P.

Cullen Cotton Vs Lewis Powell
Executed by Isaac Carter, Shff

State of North Carolina
To the Sheriff of **[Blank]** County, Greeting:
You are hereby commanded to summon Silas Parker Senr. Personally to be and appear before the Judge of our Superior Court of Law, to be held for the county of Bertie, at the Court House in Windsor, on the fourth Monday after the fourth Monday in September next, then and there to testify and the truth to say in behalf of Cullen Cotton in a certain matter of controversy in the said Court depending, and then and there to be tried, wherein Cullen Cotton is Plaintiff, and Lewis Powell is Defendant. And this you shall in no wise omit, under the penalty by law enjoined. Witness Simon Turner, Clerk of the said Court, at Windsor.
Simon Turner, Clk

Cullen Cotton Vs Lewis Powell
Spa for Pltff
Luke Raby
To Bertie Supr Ct, April Term 1814
Executed by Jas Grimes, DShff

State of North Carolina
To the Sheriff of Bertie County, Greeting;
You are hereby commanded to summon Luke Raby personally to be and appear before the Judge of the Superior Court of Law and Equity at the next Court, to be held for the County of Bertie at the Court House in Windsor on the 4th Monday after the 4th Monday in March next; then and there to testify and the truth to say in behalf of the Pltff in a certain matter of controversy in the said Court depending, and then and there to be tried, wherein Cullen Cotton is Plaintiff and Lewis Powel is Defendant. And this

you shall in no wise omit, under the penalty by law injoined. Witness Simon Turner, Clerk of the said Court, at Office the 25th day of Oct in the 38th year of our Independence, Anno Dom. 1813.
Simon Turner, Clk

State of North Carolina
To Wm. Britton
Know ye, That we, reposing especial trust and confidence in your fidelity and prudent circumspection, do command, authorise and empower you, or any of you, that at such time and place as you shall appoint, you call and cause to come before you Luke Raiby and him diligently examine on the Holy Evangelists of Almighty God, what he may know in and about a certain matter of dispute now at issue in our Superior Court of Law and equity, made in a cause, wherein Cullen Cotton is Plaintiff, and Lewis Powell is Defendant, and such examination and deposition by you so taken, you are to send closed up under your seal, to our said Court, to be held for the county of Bertie, at the Court House in Windsor, on the fourth Monday after the fourth Monday in September next; and this you are in no wise to omit. Witness Simon Turner, Clerk of our said Court, at Windsor, the 26th day of April in the XXX7th year of our Independence, Anno Dom, 1814
Simon Turner, Clk

Cullin Cotton Vs Lewis Powell
Spa for Defdt
To Bertie Supr Ct, Octr Term 1814
Executed by Lewis Walters, Shff

State of North Carolina
To the Sheriff of Hertford County, Greeting:
You are hereby commanded to summon Isaac Carter personally to be and appear before the Judge of the Superior Court of Law and Equity at the next Court to be held for the County of Bertie at the Court House in Windsor on the 4th Monday after the 4th Monday in March next, then and there to testify and the truth to say in behalf of the Defendant in a certain matter of controversy in the said Court depending, and then and there to be tried, wherein Cullen Cotton is plaintiff and Lewis Powell is Defendant. And this you shall in no wise omit, under the penalty by law enjoined.

Witness Simon Turner, Clerk of the said Court, at Office the 25th day of April in the XXXVIII year of our Independence, anno Dom. 1814.
Simon Turner, Clk

Cullen Cotton Vs. Lewis Powell
Spa for Pltff, Henry Wall
Immediately, To Bertie Supr Ct.
April Term 1815
Executed by Thos Ruftin

State of North Carolina
To the Sheriff of Bertie County, Greeting:
You are hereby commanded to summon Henry Wall personally to be and appear before the Judge of our Superior Court of Law, held at the Court House in Windsor, immediately, then and there to testify and the truth to say in behalf of the Plaintiff in a certain matter of controversy in said Court depending, and then and there to be tried, wherein Cullen Cotton is Plaintiff and Lewis Powell is Defendant. And this you shall in no wise omit, under the penalty by law enjoined. Witness Simon Turner, Clerk of the said Court, at Windsor, the 24th day of April in the XXXIX year of our Independence, Anno Dom. 1815
Simon Turner, Clk

Executed by Jesse Deams, DShff
For Isaac Carter, Shff

State of North Carolina
To the Sheriff of Hertford County, Greeting:
You are hereby commanded to summon Goddin Cotton personally to be and appear before the Judge of our Superior Court of Law, held at the Court House in Edenton, on the first Monday after the fourth Monday in March next, then and there to testify and the truth to say in behalf of Lewis Powell in a certain matter of controversy in the said Court depending, and then and there to be tried, wherein Cullen Cotton is Plaintiff and Lewis Powell is Defendant. And this you shall in no wise omit, under the penalty by law enjoined. Witness Duncan McDonald, Clerk of the said Court, at Edenton, the 5th day of October in the XLI year of our Independence, Anno Dom. 1816.

D McDonald, Clk

Cotton Vs Powell
Subp, Polly Cotton
Executed by Baldy Ashburn, Shff
By Tho Ruffin, DShff

State of North Carolina
To the Sheriff of Bertie County, Greeting:
You are hereby commanded to summon Polly Cotton personally to be and appear before the Judge of our Superior Court of Law, held at the Court House in Edenton, on the first Monday after the fourth Monday in March next, then and there to testify and the truth to say in behalf of L. Powell in a certain matter of controversy in the said Court depending, and then and there to be tried, wherein Cullen Cotton is Plaintiff and Lewis Powell is Defendant. And this you shall in no wise omit, under the penalty by law enjoined. Witness Duncan McDonald, Clerk of the said Court, at Edenton, the 5th day of October in the XLI year of our Independence, Anno Dom. 1816
D McDonald, Clk

Cullen Cotton vs Lewis Powell
Executed by Jesse Deanes, DShff
For Isaac Carter, Shff

State of North Carolina
To the Sheriff of Hertford County, Greeting:
You are hereby commanded to summon Thomas Deans personally to be and appear before the Judge of our Superior Court of Law, to be held for the County of Bertie, at the Court House in Windsor, on the fourth Monday after the fourth Monday in September next, then and there to be tried, wherein Cullen Cotton is Plaintiff and Lewis Powell is Defendant. And this you shall in no wise omit, under the penalty by law enjoined. Witness Simon Turner, Clerk of the said Court, at Windsor, the 22nd day of April in the XL year of our Independence, Anno Dom. 1816.
Simon, Turner, Clk

Chowan County
Civil Actions

Executed by Isaac Carter, Shff

State of North Carolina
To the Sheriff of Hertford County, Greeting:
You are hereby commanded to summon Isaac Carter personally to be and appear before the Judge of our Superior Court of Law, held at the Court House in Edenton, on the first Monday after the fourth Monday in March next, then and there to testify and the truth to say in behalf of L. Powell in a certain matter of controversy in the said Court depending, and then and there to be tried, wherein Cullen Cotton is Plaintiff and Lewis Powell is Defendant. And this you shall in no wise omit, under the penalty by law enjoined. Witness Duncan McDonald, Clerk of the said Court, at Edenton, the 5th day of October in the XLI year of our Independence, Anno Dom. 1816.
D McDonald, Clk

Executed by Jesse Deanes, DShff
For Isaac Carter, Shff

State of North Carolina
To the Sheriff of Hertford County, Greeting:
You are hereby commanded to summon Dolly Carter personally to be and appear before the Judge of our Superior Court of Law, held at the Court House in Edenton, on the first Monday after the fourth Monday in March next, then and there to testify and the truth to say in behalf of Lewis Powell in a certain matter of controversy in the said Court depending, and then and there to be tried, wherein Cullen Cotton is Plaintiff, and Lewis Powell is Defendant. And this you shall in no wise omit, under the penalty by law enjoined. Witness Duncan McDonald, Clerk of the said Court, at Edenton, the 5th day of October in the XLI year of our Independence, Anno Dom. 1816.
D McDonald, Clk

Cotton Vs. Powell
Subpa for James Usher, Dolly Carter,
Goddin Cotton & Isaac Carter
Service Accepted, Isaac Carter
Hertford

Chowan County
Civil Actions

State of North Carolina

To the Sheriff of Hertford County, Greeting:

You are hereby commanded to summon James Usher personally to be and appear before the Judge of our Superior Court of Law, held at the Court House in Edenton, on the first Monday after the fourth Monday in March next, then and there to testify and the truth to say in behalf of L. Powell in a certain matter of controversy in the said Court depending, and then and there to be tried, wherein Cullen Cotton is Plaintiff and Lewis Powell is Defendant. And this you shall in no wise omit, under the penalty by law enjoined. Witness Duncan McDonald, Clerk of the said Court, at Edenton, the 5th day of October in the XLI year of our Independence, Anno Dom. 1816.

D McDonald, Clk

Cullen Cotton Vs Lewis Powell
Subp for Luke Raby
Executed by James R Bent, Shff

State of North Carolina

To the Sheriff of Chowan County, Greeting:

You are hereby commanded to summon Luke Raby personally to be and appear before the Judge of our Superior Court of Law, held at the Court House in Edenton, on the first Monday after the fourth Monday in March next, then and there to testify and the truth to say in behalf of Cullen Cotton in a certain matter of controversy in the said Court depending, and then and there to be tried, wherein Cullen Cotton is Plaintiff and Lewis Powell is Defendant. And this you shall in no wise omit, under the penalty by law enjoined. Witness Duncan McDonald, Clerk of the said Court, at Edenton, the 31st day of March in the XL year of our Independence, Anno Dom. 1817.

D McDonald, Clk

State of North Carolina

To John Wheeler & George Gordon

Know ye, That we reposing especial trust and confidence in your fidelity and prudent circumspection, do command, authorise and empower you, or any of you, that at such time and place as you shall appoint, you call and

cause to come before you Godwin Cotton, Isaac Carter, Hillary Morriss & Joel Jackson diligently examine on the Holy Evangelists of Almighty God, what they know in and about a certain matter of dispute now at issue in the Superior Court of Law, made in a cause, wherein Cullen Cotton is Plaintiff and Lewis Powell is Defendant, as well on the part of the Plaintiff as the Defendant, and such examination and deposition by you so taken, you are to send cloed up under your seal, to our said Court, to be held for the County of Chowan, at the Court House in Edenton, on the first Monday after the fourth Monday in March next; and this you are in no wie to omit. Witness Duncan McDonald, Clerk of the said Court at Edenton, the 4th day of October in the **[Torn]** of the Independence of the said State, Anno Dom 1817
D McDonald, Clk

Pursuant to the annexed Commission to us directed at the Indian Queen Tavern in Murfreesborough, on the Eighth day of December 1817 between the Hours of ten Oclock in the forenoon and five in the afternoon, We proceeded to take the Deposition of Godwin Cotton of Lawful Age to be read in evidence in the Suit Specified in the said Commission, who being duly Sworn on the Holy Evangelists of Almighty God to depose the truth, the whole truth and nothing but the truth between the said parties, deposeth and Saith.

That the Signature of John Wall to the Mortgage hereto annexed from the said John Wall to Lewis Powell is, as he verily believes the hand writing of said John Wall.

Question by the Commissioners: Are you well acquainted with the Hand Writing of John Wall, & have you seen him write.
Answer: I am acquainted with his writing & have seen him write.

And this deponant further Saith, that sometime before the said John Wall removed to the State of Tennessee, he heard some Conversation between the said Wall and Lewis Powell, & the said Lewis Powell in the Conversation said to the said John Wall, you have sent the Negro Pat to Cullen Cottens and you know that I have a Mortgage on the said Negro Patt, and she is my Negro untill you pay off the Mortgage, -- The said John Wall answered that his wife sent her when he was from home.

Question by the Defendt.: On the day you heard this Conversation between us, was not Cullen Cotton & Luke Rabee at my House that day.
Answer: They were

Question by the Defendant: Did you hear on that day, Mr. John Wall sell a negro Child of Patt's, to Cullen Cotton
Answer: I did not

And this deponant further Saith that the said Lewis **[Rest of Document is missing.]**

Pursuant to the annexed Commission to us directed at the Indian Queen Tavern in Murfreesborough, on the Eighth day of December 1817 between the Hours of ten oclock in the forenoon and five in the afternoon We proceeded to take the deposition of Isaac Carter of Lawful age to be read in evidence in the Suit Specified in the said Commission, who being duly Sworn on the Holy Evangelists of Almighty God to depose the truth the whole truth and nothing but the truth between the said parties deposeth & Saith

Question by the Defendant: Is not the Mortgage given by John Wall to me for the Negroes Pat & others in the hand writing of John Wall.
Answer: believe that all except a few words at the beginning is the hand writing of John Wall

Question by the Justices: Are you acquainted with the hand writing of John Wall
Answer: I am well acquainted with his Hand Writing

And further this deponant Saith not Sworn to and Subscribed before us on the day and at the place above Specified.
Isaac Carter, G Jordan, J.P.
John Wheeler

Joel Jackson of Lawful Age being duly Sworn deposeth and Saith.
That he heard John Wall say, that Cullen Cotton, the night before he Started to Tennessee gave him the said Wall a Horse to help him out.

Question by Defendt: What Kind of Horse was it.
Answer: Not more than five Dollars

And further this deponant Saith not.
Sworn to and Subscribed before us on the day and at the place Specified in the foregoing Deposition
His
Joel X Jackson
Mark
G Jordan, JP
John Wheeler

Pursuant to the annexed commission to us directed at the Indian Queen Tavern in Murfreesborough, on the 8th Decr 1817 between the Hours of 10 Oclock in the forenoon & five in the Afternoon We proceeded to take the deposition of Hillary Morris of Lawful age to be read in Evidence in the Suit Specified in the said Commission, who being duly sworn on the Holy Evangelists of Almighty God to depose the truth, the whole truth and nothing but the truth bewteen the said parties deposeth & Saith

Question by the Defnt: Have you not heard John Wall say that he had borrowed considerable Sums fro the Deft. & that he the said John Wall had mortgaged some property as Security therefore.
Answer: I have heard him Sd. Wall say that Lewis Powell had been very friendly to him & that he had assisted him at different times when he the said Wall had been distressed for want of Money & that he the deponant had about Fifty Dollars himself from Sd. Powell for a debt that Sd Wall owed him Sd Powell for a debt - that Sd. Wall owed him & further this deponant saith not.

Sworn to & Subscribed before us on the day and at the place above Specified
H. Morris
G Gordon, J.P.
John Wheeler

Wall
To John Wall, Bill of Sale

Powell, Con. B. Sale
J. Carter

Received of the within [?] two hundred and twenty five Dollars
By Me, L. Powell

State of North Carolina
Hertford County

Know all men by these presents that John Wall of the County and State aforesaid have bargained Sold and Delivered Unto Lewis Powell of the aforesaid County and State four Negroes to Wit, Fred, Pat, Dil, and Riney, for the Valuable Consideration of five Hundred Dollars and the titel of Sd Slaves to the said Lewis Powell I bind my Self, my Heirs, Executors or Administrators Ever to Warrant & defend In Witness Whearof I have hearunto affixt my hand and Seal this 9th Day of June 18**[Torn]**

The Condition of the above bill of Sale is such that the said John Wall pay unto the said Lewis Powell the full Sum of five Hundred Dollars With Lawful Interest from this day, then the above Bill of Sale to be Void.
Signed & Sealed in presence of
Test, John Wall (Seal)

North Carolina }August Court 1813
Hertford County }

There being no Subscribing Witnesses, the signature of John Wall to the within Conditional Bill of Sale was proved by Isaac Carter, and ordered to be registered
Test, Jos P. Cu[?]

Cotton Vs Powell
Subpa for Hillary Morris
To the [?] Term 1818
Executed by John M. Cotton
Dep. Shff

State of North Carolina

To the Sheriff of Chowan County, Greeting:
You are hereby commanded to summon Hillary Morris personally to be and appear before the Judge of our Superior Court of Law Now Holding in

the County of Chowan, at the Court House in Edenton, on the first Monday after the fourth Monday in March, then and there to testify and the truth to say in behalf of the Plaintiff in a certain matter of controversy in the said Court depending, and then and there to be tried, wherein Cullen Cotton is Plaintiff and , and Lewis Powell is defendant. And this you shall in no wise omit, under the penalty by law enjoined. Witness Duncan McDonald, Clerk of the said Court, at Edenton, the 1st day of April in the XLV year of our Independence, Anno Dom. 1818
D McDonald, Clk

Cotton Vs Powell
Executed by M. Cotton
Dpt. Shff

Mr. Cullen Cotton

Sir, You will take notice that on Monday the Eighth day of December Next, at the Indian Queen Tavern, in the Town of Murfreesborough Hertford County, State of North Carolina between the Hours of Ten Oclock in the forenoon and five in the afternoon, I shall procced to take the Depositions of Godwin Cotton, Isaac Carter & James Usher, to be read in evidence in a Suite now depending in Chowan Superior Court, Wherein Cullen Cotton is Plaintiff and I am Defendant, when and where you may attend and cross examine if you think proper.
October 1st 1817
Lewis Powell.

Certificate
Cullen Vs Lewis Powell
Bertie

State of North Carolina }January Term AD 1816
Raleigh } Supreme Court

Cullen Cotton Vs. Lewis Powell
Case agreed, Bertie

It is the Judgment of the Supreme Court that there be a new trial -- The Mortgage as between the parties to this suit is proper evidence - and a

conveyance in writing is required bt Act of 1806 -- let it be entered accordingly
Certified by WM Robards, C.S.C.

****

John Coffield Vs. Abner Vail
Civil Action [1816]
Chowan County Records

At the Instance of Sundry Executions against Thomas Vail I proceeded to levy on the following Property left in the possession of said Vail the 21st Septr 1818.

Negro Woman Phillis
Dr Man Quibey
Dr. Dr. Moses
Woman Rachel & Child
Negro Man Jon -- also the plantation where at said Vail at present resided -- N. B. the above Excr [?]
Ja R Bent, Shff in Decr Term 1818

John Coffield Vs. Abner Vail & others
Ven Exp
Chowan Sup Court
March Term 1817
B. Phillips, Shff
Washington

I advertised the property Levied on at the House of George Nichols, at the house of Silas Lang, at the house of Daniel Bateman, and at the Court House of my County to be Sold at the Defendants house, and I atended the sale on the day and offered the property for sale at the Defendants house and could not sell for want of Bidders.

State of North Carolina
To the Sheriff of Washington County, Greeting:
Whereas, we by our writ commanded you, that of the goods and chattels, lands and tenements of Abner N Vail & Edward Vail (in your bailiwick)

you should cause to be made the sum of Two hundred and seventy dollars & 70/100 which lately in our Superior Court of Law at Edenton, John Coffield recovered against him for Debt and damages also the further sum of twelve Dolls 80/100 for the costs and charges by him in his Suit in that behalf expended, whereof the said Abner N Vail & Edwd Vail are convicted and liable as to us appears of record: besides your own fees for that service, and that you should have the said money before the Judge of our said Court, at Edenton, on the first Monday after the fourth Monday of September next, after the 5th day of April in the year of our Lord one thousand eight hundred and 16 to render to the said John Coffield his damages, costs and charges aforesaid: And you at that day returned on the said writ, that you had levied the same on a Negro girl named Venus, one horse & chair, and all the rest of the property of the Defendant which remain in your hands unsold. We do therefore command you, that you expose to sale the goods and chattels by you so as aforesaid levied upon so that you have the said money and **[Blank]** Shillings for accruing costs, before the Judge of our said Court, at Edenton, on the first Monday after the fourt Monday of March next, and we do command you further, that of the goods and chattels, lands and tenements of the said Abner N Vail & Edwd Vail in your bailiwick, you cause to be made the residue of the said Debt, damages, costs and charges, and that you have the said Money before the Judge of our said Court, at Edenton, on the day aforesaid, to render to the said John Coffield his damages, costs and charges aforesaid; and have you then and there this writ. Witness Duncan McDonald, Clerk of our said Court, at Edenton, the 5th day of October.
D. McDonald, Clk

Judgt $270.70 with Interest from 1st Febr 1813 till paid.

DMcD	6.60
Atto	4
Shff	2.15
	$12.80

John Coffield Vs. Abner Vail & others
Van Exp
26
Chowan Sup Court
September Term 1814
Washington

I Thos Vail do hereby certify that this Execution was transferred to me and that I have received the full benefit of the bid of Thos B Haryhten[?] for negroe girl Venus mentioned in the Sheriffs levy & return as above
Thomas Vail

State of North Carolina
To the Sheriff of Washington County, Greeting:
Whereas, we by our writ commanded you, that of the goods and chattels, lands and tenements of Abner N Vail and Edward Vail (in your bailiwick) you should cause to be made the sum of Two hundred and Seventy Dollars 70/100 which lately in our Superior Court of Law at Edenton, John Coffield recovered against them for Debt and Damages also the further sum of Thirteen dollars 72/100 for the costs and charges by him in his Suit in that behalf expended, whereof the said Abner N and Edward Vail are convicted and liable as to us appears of record; besides your own fees for that service, and that you should have the said money before the Judge of our said Court, at Edenton, on the first Monday after the fourth Monday of September next, after the 5th day of April in the year of our Lord one thousand eight hundred and 16 to render to the said John Coffield his Debt, damages, costs and charges aforesaid: And you at that day returned on the said writ, that you had levied the same on a Negro Girl named Venus one Horse and chair, and all the rest of the property of the Defendant which remain in your hands unsold. We do therefore command you, that you expose to sale the goods and chattels, lands and tenements of the said money and **[Blank]** shillings for accruing costs, before the Judge of our said Court, at Edenton, on the first Monday after the fourth Monday of September next, and we do command you further, that of the goods and chattels, lands and tenements of the said Abner N and Edward Vail in your bailiwick, you cause to be made the residue of the said damages, costs and charges, and that you have the said money before the Judge of our said Court, at Edenton, on the day aforesaid, to render to the said John Coffield his damages, costs and charges aforesaid; and have you then and there this writ. Witness Duncan McDonald, Clerk of our said Court, at Edenton, the 5th day of April in the 41st year of our Independence, Anno Dom. 1817.
D McDonald, Clk

Judgment $270.70 with Interest from 1 February 1813 till paid.
DMcD, Clk 7.57
Shff 2.15

Atto	4
	$13.72

John Coffield Vs. Abner N Vail & others
Ven Expon
Chowan Sup Court
March T. 1818
Washington

Advertized the property levied on at the tavern of Wm. Wadbey & Saml Skinner & at the Court House of my County to be sold at the Defendants house, I atended on the day advertized, and ofered the property for sale and could not sell for want of Bidders.

The Negro girl Venus mentioned within, was sold on the 27th Sep 1816 for One hundred and fifty dollars by Tho. B. Haughton for Tho Vail, as per Execution returnable to September Term 1817

State of North Carolina
To the Sheriff of Washington County, Greeting:
Whereas, we by our writ commanded you, that of the goods and chattels, lands and tenements of Abner N. Vail and Edward Vail (in your bailiwick) you should cause to be made the sum of Two hundred and Seventy dollars 10/100 which lately in our Superior Court of Law at Edenton, John Coffield recovered against them for debt and damages also the further Sum of Fourteen dollars & 64/100 for the costs and charges by him in his suit in that behalf expended, whereof the said AN Vail and Edward Vail are convicted and liable as to us of record; besides your own fees for that service, and that you should have the said money before the Judge of our said Court, at Edenton, on the first Monday after the fourth Monday of Sep next, after the 5th day of April in the year of our Lord one thousand eight hundred and 16 to render to the said John Coffield his damages, costs and charges aforesaid: And you at that day returned on the said writ, that you had levied the same on a Negro Girl named Venus, one Horse and chair, and all the rest of the property of defendant which remains in your hands unsold for want of bidders. We do therefore command you, that you expose to sale the goods and chattels by you so as aforesaid levied upon, so that you have the said money and **[Blank]** shillings for accruing costs, before the Judge of our said Court, at Edenton, on the first Monday after

the fourth Monday of March next, and we do command you further, that of the goods and chattels, lands and tenements of the said A N Vail & Edward Vail in your bailiwick, you cause to be made the residue of the said damages, costs and charges, and that you have the said money before the Judge of our said Court, at Edenton, on the day aforesaid, to render to the said John Coffield his Debt, damages, costs and charges aforesaid; and have you then and there this writ. Witness Duncan McDonald, Clerk of our said Court, at Edenton, the 4th day of October in the 4th year of our Independence, Anno Dom. 1817.
D McDonald, Clk

Judgment $270.70 with Interest from 1st Febr 1813 till paid

D McDonald	8.49
Shff	2.15
Atto	4
	$14.64

Rec'd full satisfaction for a Judg which John Coffield recovered against Abner N Vail and Edward Vail in Chowan Superior Court this October 2nd 1817
Thomas Vail

****

Wood & Hastings Vs. James Jones et als
Civil Action [1816]
Chowan County Records

Wood & Hastings Vs. James Jones
Ven Expon
Chowan Sup. Court
September T. 1815
Hertford

Again exposed the within named negros to sale which still remain unsold for want of bodders
Lewis Walters, Shff, to hand 10th August 1815

State of North Carolina.

Chowan County
Civil Actions

To the Sheriff of Hertford County, Greeting:
Whereas, we by our writ commanded you that of the goods and chattels, lands and tenements of James Jones, John Cooper and Mills Jernigan (in your bailiwick) you should cause to be made the sum of Twelve hundred and twelve dollars and 82 cents. Which lately in our Superior Court of Law at Edenton, Wood & Hastings recovered against them for Debt & Damages sustained by them by reason of the detention of that Debt, also the further sum of Ten dollars & ninety two cents for the costs and charges by them in their Suit in that behalf expended, whereof the said James, John and Mills are convicted and liable as to us appears of record; besides your own fees for that service, and that you should have the said money before the judge of our said Court, at Edenton, on the first Monday after the fourth Monday of Sept next, after the 5th day of March in the year of our Lord one Thousand eight hundred and 14 to render to the said Wood & Hastings their Debt, damages, costs and charges aforesaid: And you at that day returned on the said writ, that you had levied the same on Negroes Philip, Jack & Ned which remain in your hands unsold for want of Bidders. We do therefore command you, that you expose to sale the goods and chattels by you so as aforesaid levied upon, so that you have the said money and **[Blank]** shillings for accruing costs, before the Judge of our said Court, at Edenton, on the first Monday after the fourth Monday of September next, and we do command you further, that of the goods and chattels, lands and tenements of the said James, John, & Mills in your bailiwick, you cause to be made the residue of the said Debt, damages, costs and charges, and that you have the said money before the Judge of our said Court, at Edenton, on the day aforesaid, to render to the said Wood & Hastings Debt, damages, costs and charges aforesaid; and have you then and there this writ. Witness Duncan McDonald, Clerk of our said Court, at Edenton, the 5th day of April in the XXXIX year of our Independence, Anno Dom. 1815
D McDonald, Clk

Debt & Damages $1212.82 $1105.87 to bear Interest from 4th October 1813 till paid

DMcD, Clk	5.87
Shff	1.5
Atto	4
	$10.92

£350 has been Rec'd on a former Exr. 31 Decr. 1813

Wood & Hastings Vs James Jones & Others
Chowan Sup Court
March Term 1816
Hertford

Rec'd 7th March 1816, sale advertised at Pitch Landing, David Han**[?]** store & Court House. No sale for want of Bidders
Jas Copeland, Shff

State of North Carolina
To the Sheriff of Hertford County, greeting:
Whereas, we by our writ commanded you, that of the goods and chattels, lands and tenements of James Jones, John Cooper and Mills Jernigan (in your bailiwick) you should cause to be made the sum of twelve hundred and twelve dollars and eighty two cents which lately in our Superior Court of Law at Edenton, Wood & Hastings recovered against them for debt and damages sustained by them by reason of the detention of that debt also the further sum of Eleven dolls 54/100 for the costs and charges by them in their Suit in that behalf expended, whereof the said James, John & Mills are convicted and liable as to us appears of record; besides your own fees for that service, and that you should have the said money before the Judge of our said Court, at Edenton, on the first Monday after the fourth Monday of Sepr. Next, after the 5th day of March in the year of our Lord one thousand eight hundred and 14 to render to the said Wood & Hastings their debt, damages, costs and charges aforesaid: And you at that day returned on the said writ, that you had levied the same on Negroe Philip, Jack & Ned which remain in your hands unsold for want of Bidders. We do therefore command you, that you expose to sale the goods and chattels by you so as aforesaid levied upon, so that you have the said money and **[Blank]** shillings for accruing costs, before the Judge of our said Court, at Edenton, on the first Monday after the fourth Monday of March next, and we do command you further, that of the goods and chattels, lands and tenements of the said James, John & Mills in your bailiwick, you cause to be made the residue of the said debt, damages, costs and charges, and that you have the said money before the Judge of our said Court, at Edenton, on the day aforesaid, to render to the said Wood & Hastings their debt, damages, costs and charges aforesaid; and have you then and there this

writ. Witness Duncan McDonald, Clerk of our said Court, at Edenton, the 6th day of October in the 40th year of our Independence, Anno Dom. 1815.
D McDonald, Clk

Debt & Damages $1272.82 $1105.87 to bear Interest from 4th October 1813 till Paid.

DMcD, Clk	6.49
Shff	1.5
Atto	4
	$11.54

Wood & Hastings Vs James Jones
Ven Expon
Chowan Sup Court
Septem Term 1816
Satisfied
Hertford

State of North Carolina
To the Sheriff of Hertford County, Greeting:
Whereas, we by our writ commanded you, that of the goods and chattels, lands and tenements of James Jones, John Cooper and Mills Jernigan (in your bailiwick) you should cause to be made the sum of Twelve hundred & twelve dollars & 83/100 which lately in our superior Court of Law at Edenton, Wood & Hastings recovered against them for Debt and damages, sustained by them by reason of the detention of that debt also the further sum of 12 16/100 for the costs and charges by them in their Suit in that behalf expended, whereof the said James, John and Mills are convicted and liable as to us appears of record; besides your own fees for that service, and that you should have the said money before the Judge of our said Court, at Edenton, on the first Monday after the fourth Monday of Sepr next, after the 5th day of March in the year of our Lord one thousand eight hundred and 14 to render to the said Wood & Hastings their debt, damages, costs and charges aforesaid: And you at that day returned on the said writ, that you had levied the same on Negroes Philip, Jack and Ned which remain in your hands unsold for want of Bidders. We do therefore command you, that you expose to sale the goods and chattels by you so as aforesaid levied upon, so that you have the said money and **[Blank]** shillings for accruing costs, before the Judge of our said Court, at Edenton, on the first Monday

after the fourth Monday of September next, and we do command you further, that of the goods and chattels, lands and tenements of the said James, John & Mills in your bailiwick, you cause to be made the residue of the said Debt, damages, costs and charges, and that you have the said money before the Judge of our said Court, at Edenton, on the day aforesaid, to render to the said Wood & Hastings their Debt, damages, costs and charges aforesaid; and have you then and there this writ. Witness Duncan McDonald, Clerk of our said Court, at Edenton, the 5th day of April in the 40th year of our Independence, Anno Dom. 1816
DMcDonald, Clk

Decr. 31st 1813 Seven hundred dollars was paid the Pltff, Atto Jos. B. Skinner upon this Execution by James Jones
Jos. B. Skinner, Atto

For the value received as the Attorney of the Pltffs & Transfer this Execution to Wm. Jones
J.B. Skinner

The Costs of this Execution have been paid to Jos. B. Skinner by William Jones.

Debt & Dam $1212.82 Interest on 1105.87 from 4th October 1813 till paid

D McDonald, Clk	7.11
Shff	1.5
Atto	4
	$12.16

Wood & Hastings Vs James Jones & others
Ven Ex
Chowan Sup Court
September T. 1817
Hertford

The within named property is not to be found but Leavyed on two Tracks of Land, one Tract whereon Doctor William Jones now lives, allso one Tract adjoining the lands of Eliza Askew, Jacob Rhoads & others but Came to hand too late to advertise and sell Lands.

Decr 31st 1813 Seven hundred dolls was Paid to Pltffs Atto, Jos B. Skinner upon this execution by James Jones.

For value Rec'd as the Attorney of the Pltffs I transferred the Execution to Wm Jones
Signed JB Skinner

The Cost amt. to 12.16 is paid by Wm Jones to JB Skinner
J. Carter, Shff, by Matt Deanes, DShff

State of North Carolina
To the Sheriff of Hertford County, Greeting:
Whereas, we by our writ commanded you, that of the goods and chattels, lands and tenements of James Jones, John Cooper and Mills Jernigan (in your bailiwick) you should cause to be made the sum of Twelve hundred and twelve dollars and eighty three cents which lately in our Superior Court of Law at Edenton, Wood & Hastings recovered against them for debt and damages, sustained by them by reason of the detention of that debt also the further sum of Thirteen dolls 8/100 for the costs and charges by them in their Suit in that behalf expended, whereof the said James, John and Mills are convicted and liable as to us appears of record; besides you own fees for that service, and that you should have the said money before the Judge of our said Court, at Edenton, on the first Monday after the fourth Monday of September next, after the 5th day of March in the year of our Lord one thousand eight hundred and Fourteen to render to the said Wood & Hastings their debt, damages, costs and charges aforesaid: And you at that day returned on the said writ, that you had levied the same on Negroes Philip, Jack and Ned which remain in your hands unsold for want of Bidders. We do therefore command you, that you expose to sale the goods and chattels, Lands and tenements by you so as aforesaid levied upon, so that you have the said money and **[Blank]** Shillings for accruing costs, be for the Judge of our said Court, at Edenton, on the first Monday after the fourth Monday of September next, and we do command you further, that of the goods and chattels, lands and tenements of the said James, John & Ned in your bailiwick, you cause to be made the residue of the said Debt, damages, costs and charges, and that you have the said money before the Judge of our said Court, at Edenton, on the day aforesaid, to render to the said Wood & Hastings their Debt, damages, costs and charges aforesaid; and have you then and there this writ. Witness

Duncan McDonald, Clerk of our said Court, at Edenton, the 5th day of April in the X41 year of our Independence, Anno Dom. 1817.
D McDonald, Clk

Debt & Damages $1212.82 with Int from 4 October 1813 till Paid

DMcD, Clk	$8.3
Shff	1.5
Atto	4
	$13.8

****

Thomas White Vs. Woolsy Hathaway
Civil Action [1817]
Chowan County Records

Tho White Vs Woolsey Hathaway
Ven Expo
All sold to Sattisfy Executions
Chowan Sup Court
March T. 1818
Nothing to be found By me, Edmd [?]
For Henry At[?]
Tyrell

State of North Carolina
To the Sheriff of Tyrell County, Greeting:
Whereas, we by our writ commanded you that of the goods and chattels, lands and tenements of Woolsy Hathaway (in your bailiwick) you should cause to be made the sum of One hundred and Seventy Nine Dolls 83/100 which lately in our Superior Court of Law at Edenton, Thomas White recovered against him for Debt, also the further sum of six pounds 2/9 for the costs and charges by him in his Suit in that behalf expended, whereof the said Woolsey Hathaway is convicted and liable as to us appears of record; besides your own fees for that service, and that you should have the said money before the Judge of our said Court, at Edenton, on the first Monday after the fourth Monday of Septemr next, after the 5th day of October in the year of our Lord one thousand eight hundred and 17 to render to the said Thomas White his Debt, damages, costs and charges

aforesaid: And you at that day returned on the said writ, that you had levied the same on one Old negro man named Ned and on one Mare, on the back of an older Execution which remains in your hands unsold for want of Bidders. We do therfore command you, that you expose to sale the goods and chattels, lands and tenements of the said Woolsey Hathaway in your bailiwick, you cause to be made the residue of the said Debt, damages, costs and charges, and that you have the said money before the Judge of our said Court, at Edenton, on the day aforesaid, to render to the said Tho White his Debt, damages, costs and charges aforesaid; and have you then and there this writ. Witness Duncan McDonald, Clerk of our said Court, at Edenton, the 4th day of October in the 41st year of our Independence, Anno Dom. 1817
DMcD, Clk

Judgment $179.83 with Interest from 3rd October 1816 till Paid

DMcD, Clk	£3.11.3
Shff	10.6
Atto	2
	£6.1.9

****

Josiah Collins, Jr. Vs. Louis Leroy et als
Civil Action [1817]
Chowan County Records

Josiah Collins Junr., Jno Gray Blount & Tho Trotter
[?] Josiah Collins Junr. Vs. Louis Leroy & others
Chowan Sup Court
March T. 1818
Beaufort

State of North Carolina
To the Sheriff of Beaufort County, Greeting:
Whereas, we by our writ commanded you, that of the goods and chattels, lands and tenements of Louis Leroy, William L. Lavender and William Ross (in your bailiwick) you should cause to be made the sum of Two thousand five hundred Pounds which lately in our Superior Court of Law at Edenton Josiah Collins Junr. recovered against them for debt, also the

further sum of Seven pounds 6/3 for the costs and damages by him in his Suit in that behalf expended, whereof the said Louis, William L &William are convicted and liable as to us appears of record; besides your own fees for that service, and that you should have the said money before the Judge of our said Court, at Edenton, on the first Monday after the fourth Monday of March next, after the 1st day of April in the year of our Lord one thousand eight hundred and 18 to render to the said Josiah Collins Junr. His debt, damages, costs and charges aforesaid: And you at that day returned on the said writ, that you had levied the same on Ship Ellen with every thing appertaining to her a quantity of Household & Kitchen furniture & Negros Gabriel, David, Hampton, Susan[?], Randall, Ned, Stephen, Samuel, Nan, Amy & Easop which remain in your hands unsold. We do therefore command you, that you expose to sale the goods and chattels by you so as aforesaid levied upon, so that you have the said money and 9/3 shillings for accruing costs, before the Judge of our said Court, at Edenton, on the first Monday after the fourth Monday of March next, and we do command you further, that of the goods and chattels, lands and tenements of the said William, Louis & William L. in your bailiwick, you cause to be made the residue of the said Debt, damages, costs and charges, and that you have the said money before the Judge of our said Court, at Edenton, on the day aforesaid, to render to the said Josiah Collins Junr. His Debt, damages, costs and charges aforesaid; and have you then and there this writ. Witness Duncan McDonald, Clerk of our said Court, at Edenton, the 4th day of October in the 42nd year of our Independence, Anno Dom. 1817
D McDonald, Clk

Endorsed on formia Execution as follows Vizt
16th April 1816 By this sum passed by Mister Tredwell & Thomas this day to the credit of Jos Collins Junr (being in part of this Execution) Three Thousand two hundred & fifty Dollars $3250

!6th June By this sum passed by M. Tredwell & [?] this day to the Credit of Josiah Collins Junr being in part of this Execution Eighteen hundred and seventy Dollars $1870
D McDonald, Clk

Judgment 2500 with Interest from 20th October 1813 till Paid
Att Cost Paid

Accruing £9.3

John Gray Blount & Tho Trotter, Assignees of Jos Collins Junr.
Vs. Louis Leroy & others
Ven Exp
Chowan Sup Court
Septem T. 1818
Beaufort

State of North Carolina
To the Sheriff of Beaufort County, Greeting:
Whereas, we by our writ commanded you, that of the goods and chattels, lands and tenements of Louis Leroy, William L Lavender, William Ross and Samuel Ralston (in your bailiwick) you should cause to be made the sum of Two thousand five hundred Pounds which lately in our Superior Court of Law at Edenton, Josiah Collins Junr recovered against them for debt, also the further sum of seven pounds 6/3 for the costs and charges by him in his Suit in that behalf expended, whereof the said louis, William, William L & Samuel are convicted and liable as to us appears of record; besides your own fees for that service, and that you should have the said money before the Judge of our said Court, at Edenton, on the first Monday I after the fourth Monday of September next, after the 1st day of April in the year of our Lord one thousand eight hundred and 18 to render to the said Josiah Collins Junr. Damages, costs and charges aforesaid: And you at that day returned on the said writ, that you had levied the same on Ship Ellen with every thing appertaining to her & quantity of household and kitchen furniture, and Negroes Gabriel, David, Hampton, Susan, Randall, Ned, Stephen, Samuel, Judith, Nan, Doll, Amy & Easop which remain in your hands unsold. We do therefore command you, that you expose to sale the goods and chattels by you so as aforesaid levied upon, so that you have the said money and 18/6 shillings for accruing costs, before the Judge of our said Court, at Edenton, on the first Monday after the fourth Monday of September next, and we do command you further, that of the goods and chattels, lands and tenements of the said Louis, William, Will L. & Samuel in your bailiwick, you cause to be made the residue of the said Debt, damages, costs and charges, and that you have the said money before the Judge of our said Court, at Edenton, on the day aforesaid, to render to the said Josiah Collins Junr his debt, damages, costs and charges aforesaid; and have you then and there this writ. Witness Duncan McDonald, Clerk

of our said Court, at Edenton, the 4th day of April in the 43rd year of our Independence, Anno Dom. 1818.
D McDonald, Clk

Sold in Conjunction with No 27
Allen Grist, Shff

Judgment £2500 with Interest from 20th October 1813 till paid.
Cost paid on a Forma Execution
Accruing) 0.8.6

John Grey Blount & Tho Trotter, Assignees of Josiah Collins Junr
Vs Louis Leroy
Ven Exp
Chowan Sup Court
Septem T. 1818
Sold in Conjunction with No. 27
Allen Grist, Shff
Beaufort

State of North Carolina
To the Sheriff of Beaufort County, Greeting:
Whereas, we by our writ commanded you, that of the goods and chattels, lands and tenements of Louis Leroy (in your bailiwick) you should cause to be made the sum of Eight hundred pounds 10/ which lately in our Superior Court of Law at Edenton, Josiah Collins Junr recovered against him for Debt, also the further sum of Five Pounds 14/9 for the costs and charges by him in his Suit in that behalf expended, whereof the said Louis Leroy is convicted and liable as to us appears of record; besides your own fees for that service, and that you have the said money before the Judge of our said Court, at Edenton, on the first Monday after the fourth Monday of September next, after the 1st day of April in the year of our Lord one thousand eight hundred and 18 to render to the said Josiah Collins Junr. His debt, damages, costs and charges aforesaid: And you at that day returned on the said writ, that you had levied the same on Ship Ellen with every thing appertaining to her a quantity of household and kitchen furniture and negroes Gabriel, David, Hampton, Susan, Randall, Ned, Stephen, Samuel, Judith, Nan, Doll, Amy & Easop which remain in your

hands unsold. We do therefore command you, that you expose to sale the goods and chattels by you so as aforesaid levied upon, so that you have the said money and 18/6 shillings for accruing costs, before the Judge of our said Court, at Edenton, on the first Monday after the fourth Monday of September next, and we do command you further, that of the goods and chattels, lands and tenements of the said Louis Leroy in your bailiwick, you cause to be made the residue of the said Debt, damages, costs and charges, and that you have the said money before the Judge of our said Court, at Edenton, on the day aforesaid, to render to the said Josiah Collins Junr. His Debt, damages, costs and charges aforesaid; and have you then and there this writ. Witness Duncan McDonald, Clerk of our said Court, at Edenton, the 4th day of April in the 43rd year of our Independence, Anno Dom. 1818
D McDonald, Clk

Judgt £800.10.7 with Interest from 20th October 1813 till paid
All Cost on a Forma Execution Paid
Accruing £18.6

****

Joseph Manning Vs James R. Bent
Civil Action [1817]
Chowan County Records

Joseph Manning } Chowan Sup Co. of Law
Vs James R. Bent } October Term 1818

Joseph Manning complains of James R. Bent in custody &c. for that whereas heretofore to wit on the 3rd day of January 1817 at Chowan County aforesaid at the special instance and request of the said James R. Bent, the said Joseph Manning bargained with the said James R. Bent, the said Joseph Manning bargained with the said James to purchase a negro slave named Lo[?] for the price of Ninety dollars, and the said James then & there well knowing the said negro woman slave to be unsound, diseased & of no value, by falsely and fraudulently affirming the said negro woman slave to be sound & healthy, deceitfully sold then and there the said slave to the said Joseph Manning for the price or sum above mentioned to be hereafter paid by the said Joseph Manning - Whereas in truth & in fact the

said slave Sassy at the time of the said sale thereof was unsound diseased & of no value and the said James then and there well knew the same - and the said slave was of no use to the said Joseph but shortly thereafter died of her disease - Whereby the said Joseph saith he hath sustained damage as in the writ & thereupon he brings his Suit
Skinner & Iredell, Attorneys.

Joseph Manning Vs James R. Bent
Case
April Term 1818
Executed by Thomas Vail, Coroner

I am security for the costs of this writ according to act of Assembly
J.W. Littlejohn (Seal)

State of North Carolina
To the Coroner of Chowan County, Greeting:
You are hereby commanded to take the body of James R. Bent (if to be found in your County, and him safely keep, so that you have him before the Judge of the Superior Court Law, to be held for the County of Chowan, at the Court House in Edenton, on the first Monday after the fourth Monday in March next, then and there to answer unto Joseph Manning of a plea of trespass on the case &c damage &c one hundred pounds. Herein fail not; and have you then and there this writ. Witness Duncan McDonald, Clerk of our said Court, at Edenton, the second day of October 1817 and in the XL11nd year of our Independence. Issued the 17th day of March 1818
D McDonald, Clk

Executed for Thos Vail, Coroner
John Mcfattor, Dep Shff
Manning } Subp

State of North Carolina
To the Coroner of Chowan County, Greeting:
You are hereby commanded to summon James Norcom personally to be and appear before the Judge of our Superior Court of Law, to be held for the County of Chowan, at the Court House in edenton, on the first Monday

after the fourth Monday in Sept next, then and there to testify and the truth to say in behalf of Plf in a certain matter of controversy in the said Court depending, and then and there to be tried, wherein Jos Manning is Plaintiff, and JR Bent is Defendant. And this you shall in no wise omit, under the penalty by law enjoined. Witness Duncan McDonald, Clerk, of the said Court, At Edenton, the 4th day of April in the XII[?] year of our Independence, Anno Dom 1818.
D McDonald, Clk

Executed for Thomas Vail, Coroner
John McCottor, Dep. Shff

State of North Carolina
To the Coroner of Chowan County, Greeting:
You are hereby commanded to summon Eliza Brooks personally to be and appear before the judge of our Superior Court of Law, to be held for the County of Chowan, at the Court House in Edenton, on the first Monday after the fourth Monday in Sept next, then and there to testify and the truth to say in behalf of Plf in a certain matter of controversy in the said Court depending, and then and there to be tried, wherein Jos Manning is Plaintiff and JR Bent is Defendant. And this you shall in no wise omit, under the penalty by law enjoined. Witness Duncan McDonald, Clerk of the said Court, at Edenton, the 4th day of April in the XLII year of our Independence, Anno Dom. 1818
D McDonald, Clk

Manning Vs Bent
Subp
Maria Chapman
Executed for Thos. Vail, Coroner
John McCottor, Dep. Shff

State of North Carolina
To the Coroner of Chowan County, Greeting:
You are hereby commanded to summon Maria Chapman personally to be and appear before the Judge of our Superior Court of Law, to be held for the County of Chowan, at the Court House in Edenton, on the first Monday after the fourth Monday in Sept next, then and there to testify and the truth

to say in behalf of Plf in a certain matter of Controversy in the said Court depending, and then and there to be tried, wherein Jos Manning is Plaintiff, and JR Bent is Defendant. And this you shall in no wise omit, under the penalty by law enjoined. Witness Duncan McDonald, Clerk, of the said Court, at Edenton, the 4th day of April in the XLII year of our Independence, Anno Dom. 1818.
D McDonald, Clk

Jno Squire
Executed for Thomas Vail, Coroner
John McCottor, Dep. Shff

State of North Carolina
To the Coroner of Chowan County, Greeting:
You are hereby commanded to summon John Squires personally to be and appear before the Judge of Our Superior Court of Law, to be held for the County of Chowan , at the Court House in Edenton, on the first Monday after the fourth Monday in Septr next, then and there to testify and the truth to say in Behalf of Jos Manning in a certain matter of controversy in the said Court depending, and then and there to be tried, wherein Jos Manning is Plaintiff, and Jas R. Bent is Defendant. And this you shall in no wise omit, under the penalty by law enjoined. Witness Duncan McDonald, Clerk of the said Court, at Edenton, the 4th day of April in the XXII year of our Independence, Anno Dom. 1818.
D McDonald, Clk

Jos Manning Vs Ja R. Bent
Subpoena for B. Elliot
Executed for Thos. Vail, Coroner
John M:Cotter, Dep. Shff

State of North Carolina
To the Coroner of Chowan County, Greeting:
You are hereby commanded to summon Benjamin Elliott personally to be and appear before the Judge of our Superior Court of Law, to be held for the County of Chowan, at the Court House in Edenton, on the first Monday after the fourth Monday in Sept next, then and there to testify and the truth to say in behalf of James R. Bent in a certain matter of controversy in the

said Court depending, and then and there to be tried, wherein Joseph Manning is Plaintiff and Ja R. Bent is Defendant: And this you shall in no wise omit, under the penalty by law enjoined. Witness Duncan McDonald, Clerk of the said Court, at Edenton, in the XL year of our Independence, Anno Dom. 1818
D McDonald, Clk.

Jos Manning Vs Ja R. Bent
Subp for Jos Bozman
Executed for Thos. Vail, Coroner
John M: Cotter, Dep. Shff

State of North Carolina
To the Coroner of Chowan County, Greeting:
You are hereby commanded to summon Joseph Bozman personally to be and appear before the Judge of our Superior Court of Law, to be held for the County of Chowan, at the Court House in Edenton, on the first Monday after the fourth Monday in September next, then and there to testify and the truth to say in behalf of Ja. R. Bent in a certain matter of controversy in the said Court depending, and then and there to be tried, wherein Jos Manning is Plaintiff and Ja. R. Bent is Defendant. And this you shall in no wise omit, under the penalty by law enjoined. Witness Duncan McDonald, Clerk of the said Court, at Edenton in the XL year of our Independence, Anno Dom. 1818.
D McDonald, Clk

Jos Manning Vs Ja R. Bent
Subp for Charles Sturtivent
Executed for Thomas Vail, Coroner
John M: Cotter, Dep. Shff

State of North Carolina
To the Coroner of Chowan County, Greeting:
You are hereby commanded to summon Charles Stertivent personally to be and appear before the Judge of our Superior Court of Law, to be held for the County of Chowan, at the Court house in Edenton, on the first Monday after the the fourth Monday in September next, then and there to testify and the truth to say in behalf of James R. Bent in a certain matter of

controversy before the said Court depending, and then and there to be tried, wherein Joseph Manning is Plaintiff and Ja. R. Bent is Defendant. And this you shall in no wise omit, under the penalty by law enjoined. Witness Duncan McDonald, Clerk of the said Court, at Edenton, in the XL year of our Independence, Anno Dom. 1818.
D McDonald, Clk

Jos Manning Vs Ja R Bent
Subp for Henry Flury
Executed for Thos. Vail, Coroner
John M: Cottor, Dep. Shff

State of North Carolina
To the Coroner of Chowan County, Greeting:
You are hereby commanded to summon Henry Flury personally to be and appear before the judge of our Superior Court of Law, to be held for the County of Chowan, at the Court House in Edenton, on the first Monday after the fourth Monday in Sept next, then and there to testify and the truth to say in behalf of Ja. R. Bent in a certain matter of controversy in the said Court depending, and then and there to be tried, wherein Jos. Manning is Plaintiff and Ja R. Bent is Defendant. And this you shall in no wise omit, under the penalty by law enjoined. Witness Duncan McDonald, Clerk of the said Court, at Edenton, in the XL year of our Independence, Anno Dom. 1818.
D McDonald, Clk

Chowan superior Court }
Octo Term AD 1818 }

Manning Vs Bent

The Defendant maketh oath that on the trial of the cause He expected to be able to prove by Joseph Bozman a witness examined in the Cause that he had heard [?] had not purchased the Slave on this affiants representations but on information derived from Flury that the Witness actually heard the Plaintiff make the Declaration, But that the Witness had informed him that owing to his confusion he forgot the conversation on his examination and that his confusion in part proceeded from the Plaintiff &

shaking his head at him when the Questions were put to him and the Witness has told this affiant that since the Trial he has had a conversation with Manning in which he owned that he had made the declaration above stated -- This affiant further says he has since the Trial discovered two Witnesses who are able to prove that Manning was cautioned not to purchase the slave and answered that he knew her as well as any person & that she only wanted a Master.
Sworn to in Open Court
D McDonald, Clk
Ja R. Bent

Manning Vs Bent

Chowan Superior Court
Septr term 1818

These are to Certify, that Jno Squires hath attended this Court 4 days this term as a witness for the Pltff
Attending 4 days at 6 shillings per day 1.4
Travelling **[Blank]** miles at **[Blank]** shillings per thirty miles
Certificate and Probate 8
1.4.8

Sworn to before me,
D McDonald, Clk

Jos Manning Vs Jas R. Bent

Chowan Superior Court
Septr term 1818

These are to certify, That Eliza Brooks hath attended this Court 2 days this term as a witness for the Pltff
Attending 2 days at 6 shillings per day 12
Travelling **[Blank]** miles at **[Blank]** shillings per thirty miles
Ferriages
Certificate and Probate 8
12.8

Sworn to before me

D McDonald, Clk

Joseph Manning vs Jas. R. Bent

Chowan Superior Court
Septr Term 1818

These are to certify, that Maria Chapman hath attended this Court 2 days this term as a witness for the Pltff

Attending 2 days a 6 shillings per day	12
Travelling **[Blank]** miles at **[Blank]** shillings per thirty miles	
Ferriages	
Certificate and Probate	8
	12.8

Sworn to before me
D McDonald, Clk

****

Josiah Collins Junr. Vs. William Jones
Civil Action [1818]
Chowan County Records

Jos. Collins Junr. Vs Wm. Jones & others
Vand Exp
Chowan Sup Court
April Term 1819
Hertford

State of North Carolina
To the Sheriff of Hertford County, Greeting:
Whereas, we by our writ commanded you, that of the goods and chattels, lands and tenements of William Jones and Howell Jones (in your bailiwick) you should cause to be made the sum of Seven hundred and twenty dollars, Interest from 10th June 1816 till Paid which lately in our Superior Court of Law at Edenton, Josiah Collins Junr. Recovered against them for debt, also the further sum of Two pounds 10/6 for the costs and charges by him in his suit in that behalf expended, whereof the said William and Howell Jones are convicted and liable as to us appears of

record; besides your own fees for that service, and that you should have the said money before the Judge of our said Court, at Edenton, on the first Monday after the 5th Monday of March next, after the 4th day of April in the year of our Lord one thousand eight hundred and 18 to render to the said Josiah Collins Junr. His damages, costs and charges aforesaid: And you at that day returned on the said writ, that you had levied the same on Three Negroes which remain in your hands unsold for want of bidders. We do therefore command you, that you expose to sale the goods and chattels by you so as aforesaid levied upon, so that you have the said money and 9/3 shillings for accruing costs, before the Judge of our said Court, at Edenton, on the first Monday after the 5th Monday of March next, and we do command you further, that of the goods and chattels, lands and tenements of the said William & Howell Jones in your bailiwick, you cause to be made the residue of the said Debt, damages, costs and charges, and that you have the said money before the Judge of our said Court at Edenton, on the day aforesaid, to render to the said Josiah Collins Junr. Damages, costs and charges aforesaid; and have you then and there this writ. Witness Duncan McDonald, Clerk of our said Court, at Edenton, the 4th day of April in the 43rd year of our Independence, Anno Dom. 1818.
D McDonald, Clk

Advertised the said property for sale on the 19th March at the Court House in Winton in the District of Col. Jones at Barfields and one on the Road from Winton to Murfreesboro, No Sale for want of Bidders.
Isaac Carter, Shff by Reddick Cross, DS.

Debt	$720.00
Ints	110.70
	830.70
Court Charges	11.5
Coms & Exe	25.79
	$863.54

Judgment $720 with Int from 10th June 1816 till Paid

DMcD, Clk	2.9.6
Shff	1.1
Atto	2
	5.10.6

Josiah Collins Junr. Vs. Will. Jones & others
Vand Exp
Chowan Sup Court
September T. 1819
Satisfied June 25th 1819
Ja. Copeland, Shff
Hertford

State of North Carolina

To the Sheriff of Hertford County, Greeting:

Whereas, we by our writ commanded you, that of the goods and chattels, lands and tenements of William Jones and Howell Jones (in your bailiwick) you should cause to be made the sum of Seven hundred & twenty dollars, with Interest from 10th June 1816 till paid which lately in our Superior Court of Law at Edenton, Josiah Collins Junr. Recovered against them fro Debt also the further sum of Ten Pounds 9/9 for the costs and charges by him in his suit in that behalf expended, whereof the said William & Howell Jones are convicted and liable as to us appears of record; besides your own fees for that service, and that you should have the said money before the Judge of our said Court, at Edenton on the Second Monday after the fifth Monday of March next, after the 4th day of April in the year of our Lord one thousand eight hundred and 18 to render to the said Josiah Collins Junr. His damages, costs and charges aforesaid: And you at that day returned on the said writ, that you had levied the same on Three Negroes which remain in your hands unsold for want of Bidders. We do therefore command you, that you expose to sale the goods and chattels by you so as aforesaid levied upon, so that you have the said money and 18/6 shillings for accruing costs, before the Judge of our said Court, at Edenton, on the Second Monday after the fourth Monday of September next, and we do command you further, that of the goods and chattels, lands and tenements of the said William & Howell Jones in your bailiwick, you cause to be made the residue of the said Debt, damages, costs and charges, and that you have the said money before the Judge of our said Court, at Edenton, on the day aforesaid, to render to the said Josiah Collins Junr. His Debt, costs and charges aforesaid; and have you then and there this writ. Witness Duncan McDonald, Clerk of our said Court, at Edenton, the 8th day of April in the 43rd year of our Independence, anno Dom. 1819.

D McDonald, Clk

Rec'd Eight hundred & fifty one dollars forty in full of the above Judgment and Interest from the Sheriff Oct 2nd 1819 for Josiah Collins
James Moffat, Atto

Rec'd the Clerk & Attos fees from the Shff £4.18.9
D McDonald, Clk

Judgment $720 with Int from 10th June 1816 till paid

DMcD, Clk	2.18.9
Shff	1.1
Atto	2
	£5.19.9

****

Sawyer & Norcom Vs. Joseph Sutton
Civil Action [1818]
Chowan County Records

Sawyer Vs. Norcom
Vend Expons
September Term 1818
Satisfied
John McCottor, Dep. Shff

State of North Carolina
To the Sheriff of Chowan County, greeting:
Whereas, we by our writ commanded you, that of the goods and chattels, lands and tenements of Joseph Sutton (in your bailiwick) you should cause to be made the sum of Seventy Three Dollars and Ninety Cents, which lately in our County Court of Pleas and Quarter Sessions, held for the County of Chowan, Sawyer & Norcom recovered against him for Debt, as also the sum of Nine Dollars and Twenty four Cents for costs and charges by them in their Suit in that behalf expended, whereof the said Joseph Sutton is convicted and liable as to us appears of record; besides your own fees for that service; and that you have the said money before the Justices of our said Court, at Edenton, the Second Monday of March next after the Second Monday of December, in the year of our Lord one thousand eight hundred and seventeen, to render to the said Sawyer & Norcom Debt, damages, costs and charges aforesaid; and you at that day returned on the

same writ that you had levied the same on a Field of Wheat next Mr Nail's, and on a subsequent Vendtition Exponas you had further levied on a Negro Boy called Jefferson which remain in your hands unsold. We do therefore command you, that you expose to sale the goods and chattels of Joseph Sutton by you so as aforesaid levied upon, so that you have the said money, and Six shillings and Nine pence for accruing costs, before the Justices of our said Court, at Edenton, on the second Monday of September next; and we do command you further, that of the goods and chattels, lands and tenements of the said Joseph Sutton (in your bailiwick) you cause to be made the residue of the Debt, damages, costs and charges, and that you have the said money before the Justices of our said Court, at Edenton, on the day aforesaid, to render to the said Sawyer & Norcom, Debt, damages, costs and charges aforesaid; and have you then and there this writ. Witness William Norfleet, Clerk of the said Court, at Edenton, the 10th day of June in the XL year of our Independence, and in the year of our Lord one thousand eight hundred and Eighteen.
William Norfleet, Clk.

Edenton 19th September 1818 Rec'd Thirty Three Dollars & 6/100 in full for the Within judgment and Interest $33.6
MC Sawyer et al, Plaintiff

Judgment $73.90 Int from jan 1st 1814. Payment made March 10th 1818, of $50, Clk 67 Cents.

****

Beasley's Executor Vs. John Haughton
Civil Action [1818]
Chowan County Records

Beasley's Executor Vs John Haughton
Vend Exponas
Sattisfyed
Edmund Alexander, DShff

State of North Carolina
To the Sheriff of Tyrell County, Greeting:
Whereas, we by our writ commanded you, that of the goods and chattels, lands and tenements of John Haughton (in your bailiwick) you should

cause to be made the sum of One Hundred and Two Dollars and Sixty four Cents which lately in our County Court of Pleas and Quarter Sessions, held for the County of Chowan, Beasley's Executors recovered against him for Debt, Twelve Dollars and Eighty four Cents for costs and charges by him in his Suit in that behalf expended, whereof the said John Haughton is convicted and liable as to us appears of record; besides your own fees for that service, and that you have the said money before the Justices of our said Court, at Edenton, the Second Monday of March next, after the 2nd Monday of December in the year of our Lord one thousand eight hundred and Seventeen, to render to the said Beasley's Executors Debt, damages, costs and charges aforesaid; and you at that day returned on the said writ that you had levied the same on One Negro Boy by the name of Isaac which remain in your hands unsold. We do therefore command you, that you expose to sale the goods and chattels of John Haughton by you so as aforesaid levied upon, so that you have the said money, and nine shillings and three pence for accruing costs, before the Justices of our said Court, at Edenton, on the second Monday of June next; and we do command you further, that of the goods and chattels, lands and tenements of the said John Haughton (in your bailiwick) you cause to be made the residue of the Debt, damages, costs and charges, and that you have the said money before the Justices of our said Court, at Edenton, on the day aforesaid, to render to the said Beasley's Executors Debt, damages, costs and charges aforesaid; and have you then and there this writ. Witness William Norfleet, Clerk of the said Court, at Edenton, the 12th day of March in the 42nd year of our Independence, and in the year of our Lord one thousand eight hundred and Eighteen
William Norfleet, Clk

Judgment $102.64 Int. from 1st Jan 1815

Clks	$8.71
Shff	1.05
Att J.J.	4
	$13.76

J.W. Littlejohn Vs John Haughton
Vend Exponas
Advertised an no Sale for want of Bidders
Edmund Alexander, DShff
For Henry [?], Shff

Chowan County
Civil Actions

June Term 1818

State of North Carolina

To the Sheriff of Tyrell County, Greeting:

Whereas, we by our writ commanded you, that of the goods and chattels, lands and tenements of John Haughton (in your bailiwick) you should cause to be made the sum of Seventy Six Dollars and Ninety five Cents which lately in our County Court of Pleas and Quarter Sessions, held for the County of Chowan, John W. Littlejohn recovered against him for Debt as also the sum of Fourteen Dollars and Seventy Cents for costs and charges by him in his suit in that behalf expended, whereof the said John Haughton is convicted and liable as to us appears of record; besides your own fees for that service, and that you have the said money before the Justices of our said Court, at Edenton, the second Monday of March next, after the 2nd Monday of December in the year of our Lord one thousand eight hundred and Seventeen, to render to the said John W. Littlejohn Debt, damages, costs and charges aforesaid; and you at that day returned on the said writ that you had levied the same on one Negro Boy Isaac and some Horses which remain in your hands unsold. We do therefore command you, that you expose to sale the goods and chattels of John Haughton by you so as aforesaid levied upon, so that you have the said money, and Nine shillings and three pence for accruing costs, before the Justices of our said Court, at Edenton, on the second Monday of June next; and we do command you further, that of the goods and chattels, lands and tenements of the said John Haughton (in your bailiwick) you cause to be made the residue of the Debt, damages, costs and charges, and that you have the said money before the Justices of our said Court, at Edenton, on the day aforesaid, to render to the said John W. Littlejohn Debt, damages, costs and charges aforesaid; and have you then and there this writ. Witness William Norfleet, Clerk of the said Court, at Edenton, the 12th day of March in the 42nd year of our Independence, and in the year of our Lord one thousand eight hundred and Eighteen.

William Norfleet, Clk.

Judgment $76.95 Int. from Decr. 10th 1817

Damages	$5.88
Clk	4.69
D. Shff, W.F.	1.05
Att JBS	4
	$15.62

Beasley's Executors Vs John Haughton
Vend Exp
September Term 1818

State of North Carolina

To the Sheriff of Tyrell County, Greeting:

Whereas, we by our writ commanded you, that of the goods and chattels, lands and tenements of John Haughton (in your bailiwick) you should cause to be made the sum of One Hundred and Two Dollars and sixty four cents which lately in our County Court of Pleas and Quarter Sessions, held for the County of Chowan, Beasley's Executors recovered against him for debt as also the sum of twelve Dollars anf Fifty Nine Cents, for costs and charges by them in their suit in that behalf expended, whereof the said John Haughton is convicted and liable as to us appears of record; besides your own fees for that service; and that you have the said money before the Justices of our said Court, at Edenton, the second Monday of March next after the second Monday of December in the year of our Lord one thousand eight hundred and Seventeen, to render to the said Beasley's Executors Debt, damages, costs and charges aforesaid; and you at that day returned on the said writ that you had levied the same on One Negro Boy by the name of Isaac which remain in your hands unsold. We do therefore command you, that you expose to sale the goods and chattels of John Haughton by you so as aforesaid levied upon, so that you have the said money, and 18 shillings and five pence for accruing costs, before the Justices of our said Court, at Edenton, on the second Monday of September next; and we do command you further, that of the goods and chattels, lands and tenements of the said John Haughton (in your Bailiwick) you cause to be made the residue of the Debt, damages, costs and charges, and that you have the said money before the Justices of our said Court, at Edenton, on the day aforesaid, to render to the said Beasley's Executors Debt, damages, costs and charges aforesaid; and have you then and there this writ. Witness William Norfleet, Clerk of the said Court, at Edenton, the 10th day of June in the XL year of our Independence, and in the year of our Lord one thousand eight hundred and Eighteen. Issued the 14th day of July 1818.
William Norfleet, Clk

Judgment $102.64 Int. 1st Jan 1815
Clks $9.38

Shff	1.05
Att JJ	4
	$14.43

John W. Littlejohn Vs John Haughton
Vend Exponas
September term 1818
Advertised, no sale for want of a Bidder
Jno B. Beasley for **[Faded]** Alexander, Shff

State of North Carolina
To the Sheriff of Tyrell County, Greeting:
Whereas, we by our writ commanded you, that of the goods and chattels, lands and tenements of John Haughton (in your bailiwick) you should cause to be made the sum of Seventy Six Dollars and Ninety five Cents, which lately in our County Court of Pleas and Quarter Sessions, held for the County of Chowan, John W. Littlejohn recovered against him for Debt, as also the sum of Fourteen Dollars and Seventy Cents for costs and charges by said John W. Littlejohn in his suit in that behalf expended, whereof the said John Haughton is convicted and liable as to us appears of record; besides your own fees for that service; and that you have the said money before the Justices of our said Court, at Edenton, the second Monday of March next after the second Monday of December, in the year of our Lord one thousand eight hundred and seventeen, to render to the said John W. Littlejohn his Debt, damages, costs and charges aforesaid; and that you at that day returned on the said writ that you had levied the same on. One Negro Boy Isaac, and some Horses which remain in your hands unsold. We do therefore command you, that you expose to sale the goods and chattels of John haughton by you so as aforesaid levied upon, so that you have the said money, and Eighteen shillings and Six pence for accruing costs, before the Justices of our said Court, at Edenton, on the second Monday of September next; and we do command you further, that of the goods and chattels, lands and tenements of the said John Haughton (in your bailiwick) you cause to be made the residue of the said Debt, damages, costs and charges, and that you have the said money before the Justices of our said Court, at Edenton, on the day aforesaid, to render to the said John W. Littlejohn his Debt, damages, costs and charges aforesaid; and have you then and there this writ. Witness William norfleet, Clerk of the said Court, at Edenton, the 10th day of June in the XL year of our

Independence, and in the year of our Lord one thousand eight hundred and Eighteen
William Norfleet, Clk

Judgment $76.95 Int from Dec. 10th 1817	
Damages	$5.61
Clk	5.01
D. Shff W.F.	1.05
Att JBS	4
	$16.54

****

Officers of the Court Vs Michael Wilder
Civil Action [1818]
Chowan County Records

Officers of the Court Vs Michael Wilder
Ca. Sa.
September Term 1818
Forborne
John M: Cottor, Dep. Shff

State of North Carolina
To the Sheriff of Chowan County, Greeting:
You are hereby commanded to take the body of Michael Wilder, if to be found in your bailiwick, and him safely keep, so that you have him before the Justices of the County Court of Pleas and Quarter Sessions, to be held for the County of Chowan, at the Court House in Edenton, on the second Monday in September next, then and there to satisfy the Officers of the Court the sum of Seven Dollars and Seventy Seven Cents for Costs on Indictment of Negro Jack, the property of the said Michael Wilder, and accruing Costs since. Herein fail not, and have then and there this writ. Witness William Norfleet, Clerk of our said Court, at Edenton, the 10th day of June in the XLII year of our Independence, Anno Dom. 1818. Issued the 18th day of July 1818.
William Norfleet, Clk.

Clk	$4.06
Shff	1.05

Att MH	2.66
	$7.77

****

Officers of the Court Vs. Mills Hill
Civil Action [1818]
Chowan County Records

Officers of the Court Vs Mills Hill
Fi Fa
March Term 1819
Forborn by the Pltff
JR Bent, Shff

State of North Carolina
To the Sheriff of Chowan County, Greeting:
We command you, that of the goods and chattels, lands and tenements of Mills Hill (if to be found in your bailiwick) you cause to be made the sum of Seven Dollars and eighty Cents which was lately in our County Court of Pleas and Quarter Sessions held for Chowan County, at the Court House in Edenton, adjudged to him on his Petition for sale of a Negro for costs and charges in the said suit expended, whereof the said Mills Hill is liable, as appears to us of record. And have you the said monies, besides your fees for this service, before our said Court, at Edenton aforesaid, on the second Monday in March next, then and there to render to the Officers of the Court costs and charges aforesaid. herein fail not, and have you then and there this writ. Witness William Norfleet, Clerk of the said Court, the 16th day of December, Anno Dom. 1818.
William Norfleet, Clk.

Petition & Copy	80
3 Continuances	90
Order & Report	60
Dismission & Execution	1.20
	$3.50
D. Shff JMG	30
Att MH	4
	$7.80

Chowan County
Civil Actions

Officers of the Court Vs Mills Hill
Fi Fa
June Term 1819
Satisfyed
JR Bent, Shff

State of North Carolina

To the Sheriff of Chowan County, Greeting:

We command you, that of the goods and chattels, lands and tenements of Mills Hill (if to be found in your bailiwick) you cause to be made the sum of Eight Dollars and Forty Seven Cents which was lately in our County Court of Pleas and Quarter Sessions held for the Chowan County, at the Court House in Edenton, adjudged to him on his Petition for sale of a Negro for costs and charges in the said suit expended, whereof the said Mills Hill is liable, as appears to us of record. And have you the said monies, besides your fees for this service, before our said Court, at Edenton aforesaid, on the second Monday in June next, then and there to render to the Officers of the Court costs and charges aforesaid. Herein fail not, and have you then and there this writ. Witness William Norfleet, Clerk of the said Court, the 10th day of March Anno Dom. 1819.
William Norfleet, Clk

Clk	$4.17
D. Shff JMG	30
Att MH	4
	$8.47

****

Officers of the Court Vs. William Hurdle
Civil Action [1818]
Chowan County Records

Officers of the Court Vs William Hurdle
Fi Fa
March Term 1818
Satisfyed
J R. Bent, Shff

Chowan County
Civil Actions

State of North Carolina
To the Sheriff of Chowan County, greeting:
We command you, that of the goods and chattels, lands and tenements of William Hurdle (if to be found in your bailiwick) you cause to be made the sum of Six Dollars which was lately in our County Court of Pleas and Quarter Sessions held for Chowan County, at the Court House in Edenton, adjudged to him on the Petition of William Hurdle & als to the Court for Division of Negroes for costs and charges in the said suit expended, whereof the said William Hurdle is liable, as appears to us of record. And have you the said monies, besides your fees for this service, before our said Court, at Edenton aforesaid, on the second Monday in March next, then and there to render to the Officers of the Court costs and charges aforesaid. Herein fail not, and have you then and there this writ. Witness William Norfleet, Clerk of the said Court, the 16th day of december, Anno Dom.1818
William Norfleet, Clk

Received of William Hurdle my fees for filing petition in Chowan County Court for division of negroes &c - Decr. 1818
Jos. B. Skinner

Order for Petition	20
Dittoi for Division	20
Report	40
Dismission & Execution	1.20
	2
P Himself Att JBS	4
	$6

****

Enoch Sawyer Vs. John McCottor
Civil Action [1819]
Chowan County Records

Enoch Sawyer Vs. John McCottor
Vend Exp
June Term 1819
Negroes Claimed & Sold by E. Hoskins
Ja. R. Bent Shff

State of North Carolina

To the Sheriff of Chowan County, Greeting:

Whereas, we by our writ commanded you, that of the goods and chattels, lands and tenements of John McCottor (in your bailiwick) you should cause to be made the sum of Two Hundred Dollars which lately in our County Court of Pleas and Quarter Sessions, held for the County of Chowan, Enoch Sawyer recovered against him for Debt as also the sum of Twenty-One Dollars and Ninety-one Cents for costs and charges by him in his suit in that behalf expended, whereof the said John McCottor is convicted and liable as to us appears of record; besides your own fees for that service; and that you have the said money before the Justices of our said Court, at Edenton, the second Monday of March next after the 2nd Monday of December, in the year of our Lord one thousand eight hundred and Eighteen, to render to the said Enoch Sawyer his Debt, damages, costs and charges aforesaid; and you at that day returned on the said writ that you had levied the same on Negroes Bob and Sylvia which remain in your hands unsold. We do therefore command you, that you expose to sale the goods and chattels of John Mcottor by you so as aforesaid levied upon, so that you have the said money, and Six Shillings and Nine pence for accruing costs, before the Justices of our said Court, at Edenton, on the second Monday in June next; and we do command you further, that of the goods and chattels, lands and tenements of the said John McCottor (in your bailiwick) you cause to be made the residue of the Debt, damages, costs and charges, and that you have the said money before the Justices of our said Court, at Edenton, on the day aforesaid; and have you then and there this writ. Witness William Norfleet, Clerk of the said Court, at Edenton, the 10th day of March in the XLIII year of our Independence, and in the year of our Lord one thousand eight hundred and nineteen.

William Norfleet, Clk

Judgment $200 Int. from 10th June 1818

Damages	$12
Clk	5.53
Shff	1.05
Att JBS	4
	$22.58

Enoch Sawyer Vs John McCottor

Chowan County Civil Actions

Vend Exp
December Term 1819
Forborn by the Pltff
J. R. Bent, Shff

State of North Carolina

To the Sheriff of Chowan County, Greeting;

Whereas, we by our writ commanded you, that of the goods and chattels, lands and tenements of John McCottor (in your bailiwick) you should cause to be made the sum of Two Hundred Dollars which lately in our County Court of Pleas and Quarter Sessions, held for the County of Chowan, Enoch Sawyer recovered against him for Debt as also the sum of Twenty one Dollars and Ninety one Cents for costs and charges by him in his suit in that behalf expended, whereof the said John McCottor is convicted and liable as to us appears of record, besides your own fees for that service; and that you have the said money before the Justices of our said Court, at Edenton, the second Monday of March next after the 2nd Monday of December in the year of our Lord one thousand eight hundred and Eighteen, to render to the said Enoch Sawyer his Debt, damages, costs and charges aforesaid; and you at that day returned on the said writ that you had levied the same on Negroes Bob and Sylvia which remain in your hands unsold. We do therefore command you, that you expose to sale the goods and chattels of John McCotter by you so as aforesaid levied upon, so that you have the said money, and 20 Shillings and three pence for accruing costs, before the Justices of our said Court, at Edenton, on the second Monday of December next; and we do command you further, that of the goods and chattels, lands and tenements of the said John McCottor (in your bailiwick) you cause to be made the residue of the Debt, damages, costs and charges, and that you have the said money before the Justices of our said Court, at Edenton, on the day aforesaid, to render to the said Enoch Sawyer his Debt, damages, costs and charges aforesaid; and have you then and there this writ. Witness William Norfleet, Clerk of the said Court, at Edenton, the 2nd Monday of september in the XLIV year of our Independence, and in the year of our Lord one thousand eight hundred and Nineteen.

William Norfleet, Clk

Judgment $200 Int. From 10th June 1818

Damages	$12
Clk	6.87

Shff	1.05
Att JBS	4
	$23.92

Officers of the Court Vs. Negro Bob
December Term 1819

State of North Carolina
To the Sheriff of Chowan County, Greeting:
You are hereby commanded to take the body of Negro Bob, the property of Edmd Hoskins if to be found in your bailiwick, and him safely keep, so that you have him before the Justices of the County Court of Pleas and Quarter Sessions, to be held for the County of Chowan, at the Court House in Edenton, on the second Monday in December next; then and there to satisfy the Officers of the Court the Sum of Eleven Dollars and Eleven Cents, for Costs on an Indictment for Petit Larceny whereof the said Negro Bob, the property of edmd Hoskins is Liable. Herein fail not, and have you then and there this writ. Witness William Norfleet, Clerk of our said Court, at Edenton, the 2nd Monday of September in the XLIV year of our Independence, Anno Dom. 1819.
William Norfleet.

Indictment	60
Capias	1.00
Subpoenas	60
Det & Ex	1.12
	$3.30
Shff 1.05 do by AH 1.20	2.25
Witnesses Jacob Munns	.98
Freda Munns, Senr	1.02
Freda Munns Junr	1.02
Delilah Ashley	1.02
Charles Jordan	1.50
	$11.11

****

John McCottor Vs. Thomas Myers & Allen Laseter
Civil Action [1819]

Chowan County Civil Actions

Chowan County Records

John McCottor Vs Thomas Myers & Allen Laseter
Declaration

North Carolina } Superior Court of Law
} Spring Term 1819

Chowan Towit

John McCottor complains of Thomas Myers and Allen Laseter being in the custody of the Sheriff &c of a Plea of Trespass. For that whereas the said Thomas Myers and Allen Laseter, on the **[Blank]** day of **[Blank]** in the year of our Lord **[Blank]** with force and arms, at Edenton in the County aforesaid, made an assault on a certain Negro woman Rose then and still being the servant and Slave of the said John McCottor, towit at Edenton in the County aforesaid and then and there beat, Bruised, wounded and ill treated the said Rose, insomuch that by means thereof, the said Rose then and there because and was sick, sore, lame and disordered and so remained and continued for a long space of time, towit from thence hitherto during all which time, he the said John McCottor last and was deprived of the labour and service of his said servant Rose and of all benefit and advantage which might and would otherwise have arisen and earned to him from such labor and service, towit at Edenton in the County aforesaid. And other wrongs to the said John McCottor then and there did against the peace of the State and to the damage of the said John McCottor (as said in the writ) and therefore he brings suit &c.

A. M **[?],** Attorney for Plaintiff.

****

Clerk Vs. Thomas Waff
Civil Action [1819]
Chowan County Records

Clerk Vs Thomas Waff
December Term 1819
Satisfied
H. Wills, D.C.

State of North Carolina

To the Sheriff of Chowan County, Greeting:
We command you, that of the goods and chattels, lands and tenements of Thomas Waff (if to be found in your bailiwick) you cause to be made the sum of Two Dollars and Thirty Cents which was lately in our County Court of Pleas and Quarter Sessions, held for Chowan County, at the Court House in Edenton, adjudged to him on his petition for Sale and Division of Negroes for costs and charges in the said Suit expended, whereof the said Thomas Waff is liable as to us appears of record. And have you the said monies before the Justices of our said Court, on the second Monday in December next, then and there to render to the said Clerk costs and charges aforesaid. Herein fail not, and have you then and there this writ. Witness William Norfleet, Clerk of the said Court, at Edenton, the second Monday of September in the XLIV year of our Independence, Anno Dom. 1819.
William Norfleet, Clk

Order for Petition	20
1 Continuance	30
Order for sale & Report	60
Dismission & Ex	1.20
	$2.30

****

William Coffield Vs. George Bozman
Civil Action [1819]
Chowan County Records

William Coffield, Assignee Vs. George Bozman
December Term 1819
Satisfied
For Ja R Bent, Shff
Thos Hathaway

State of North Carolina
To the Sheriff of Chowan County, Greeting:
Whereas, we by our writ commanded you, that of the goods and chattels, lands and tenements of George Bozman (in your bailiwick) you should cause to be made the sum of Six Hundred and Twenty Five Dollars, which lately in our Court of Pleas and Quarter Sessions, held for the County of Chowan, William Coffield, Assignee recovered against him for debt as

also the sum of Eight Dollars and Fifty seven Cents for costs and charges by him in his suit in that behalf expended, whereof the said George Bozman is convicted and liable as to us appears of record, besides your own fees for that service; and that you have the said money before the Justices of our said Court, at Edenton, the second Monday of September next after the 2nd Monday of June in the year of our Lord one thousand eight hundred and nineteen, to render to the said William Coffield, Assignee, debt, damages, costs and charges aforesaid; and you at that day returned on the said writ that you had levied the same on Negroes Sam & Jenny, one elegant Gig, one Half Oil Factory, Three Shares Steam Boat Stock which remain in your hands unsold. We do therefore command you, that you expose to sale the goods and chattels of the said George Bozman by you so as aforesaid levied upon, so that you have the said money, and Six Shillings and Nine pence for accruing costs, before the Justices of our said Court, at Edenton, on the second Monday of December next; and we do command you further, that of the goods and chattels, lands and tenements of the said George Bozman (in your Bailiwick) you cause to be made the residue of the said debt, damages, costs and Charges, and that you have the said money before the Justices of our said Court, at Edenton, on the day aforesaid, to render to the said William Coffield Debt, damages, costs and charges aforesaid, and have you then and there this writ. Witness William Norfleet, Clerk of the said Court, at Edenton, the 2nd Monday of September in the XLIV year of our Independence, and in the year of our Lord one thousand eight hundred and nineteen.
William Norfleet, Clk

Edenton decr. 14th 1817 rec'd the Amount of the within Vend Exponas and Interest
Wm Coffield

Judgment $625 Int from 1st Dec. 1818
Payment made Sept term 1819 $184.29. Former Costs and Commissions paid
Clk 67 cents

****

John B. Blount Vs. George Williams
Civil Action [1819]
Chowan County Records

Chowan County
Civil Actions

John B. Blount, Assignee Vs. George Williams
Ven Expon
The former Sheriff cannot Produce any property of the Defendant
Jas Copeland, Shff by **[?]** DShff
Chowan Sup Court
September Term 1817
Rec'd Augt. 13th 1817
Hertford

No Property to be found belonging to George Williams whereof I can make the debts & costs within mentioned
James Copeland, Shff by Carr Darden, DShff

State of North Carolina

To the Sheriff of Chowan County, Greeting:

Whereas, we by our writ commanded you, that of the goods and chattels, lands and tenements of George Williams (in your bailiwick) you should cause to be made the sum of Six hundred Seventy dollars, with Int from 26th March 1817 till Paid which lately in our Superior Court of Law at Edenton, John B. Blount, Assignee recovered against him for Debt, also the further sum of Two Pounds 3/6 for the costs and charges by him in his suit in that behalf expended, whereof the said George Williams is convicted and liable as to us appears of record; besides your own fees for that service, and that you should have the said money before the Judge of our said Court, at Edenton, on the first Monday of March next, after the **[Blank]** day of **[Blank]** in the year of our Lord one thousand eight hundred and **[Blank]** to render to the said John B. Blount his Debt, damages, costs and charges aforesaid: And you at that day returned on the said writ that you had levied the same on Three Negroes which remain in your hands unsold for want of Bidders. We do therefore command you, that you expose to sale the goods and chattels by you so as aforesaid levied upon, so that you have the said money and 93 shillings for accruing costs, before the Judge of our said Court, at Edenton, on the second Monday after the fourth Monday of September next, and we do command you further, that of the goods and chattels, lands and tenements of the said George Williams in your bailiwick, you cause to be made the residue of the said Debt, damages, costs and charges, and that you have the said money before the Judge of our said Court, at Edenton, on the day aforesaid, to render to the said John B. Blount his Debt, damages, costs and charges aforesaid; and

have you then and there this writ. Witness Duncan McDonald, Clerk of our said Court, at Edenton, the 6th day of April in the 43rd year of our Independence, Anno Dom. 1819
P . McDonald, DY Clk

Judg $670 with Int. from 26th March 1817 till Paid
Executors hand been issued against Boon Felton and Howell Jones, for the above sum; either of them being satisfied, this to be void except as to the Court Tax)

D McDonald	£2.13
Shff	10.6
Atto	2
	£5.3.6

****

John B. Blount Vs. Howell Jones
Civil Action [1819]
Chowan County Records

John B. Blount, Assignee Vs Howell Jones
Vend Expo
Chowan Sup Court
September T. 1819
Rec'd Augt 13th 1819
Hertford

The Defendant has no property to be found subject to this Execution the former Sheriff says he had none at the time of the former returns
Jas Copeland, Shff

State of North Carolina
To the Sheriff of Hertford County, Greeting:
Whereas, we by our writ commanded you, that of the goods and chattels, lands and tenements of Howell Jones (in your bailiwick) you should cause to be made the sum of Six hundred & Seventy dollars, with Int. from 26th March 1817 till paid which lately in our Superior Court of Law at Edenton, John B. Blount, Assignee recovered against him for Debt, also the further sum of Five Pounds 3/6 for the costs and charges by him in his suit in that behalf expended, whereof the said Howell Jones is convicted and liable as

to us appears of record; besides your own fees for that service, and that you should have the said money before the Judge of our said Court, at Edenton, on the second Monday after the fourth Monday of March next, after the **[Blank]** day of **[Blank]** in the year of our Lord one thousand eight hundred and **[Blank]** to render to the said John B. Blount his Debt, damages, costs and charges aforesaid: And you at that day returned on the said writ, that you had levied the same on Three Negroes which remain in your hands unsold for want of Bidders. We do therefore command you, that you expose to sale the goods and chattels, lands and tenements of the said Howell Jones in your bailiwick, you cause to be made the residue of the said Debt, damages, costs and charges, and that you have the said money before the Judge of our said Court, at Edenton, on the day aforesaid, to render to the said John B. Blount his Debt, damages, costs and charges aforesaid; and have you then and there this writ. Witness Duncan McDonald, Clerk of our said Court, at Edenton, the 6th day of April in the 43rd year of our Independence, Anno Dom. 1819.
D McDonald.

Judgment $670 with Int. from 26th March 1817 till paid.
Executors have been issued against George Williams, & Boon Felton for the above sum; either of them being satisfied this to be void and of no effect (except as to Court Fees)

D Mcdonald	£2.13
Shff	10.6
Atto	2
	£5.3.6

****

John B. Blount Vs. Nathaniel Bissell
Civil Action [1819]
Chowan County Records

John B. Blount Vs Nathl. C. Bissell
Vend Expo
December Term 1819
Fofborne by the Plaintiff
Fo Jas. R. Bent
Tho Hathaway

Chowan County
Civil Actions

State of North Carolina

To the Sheriff of Chowan County, Greeting:

Whereas, we by our writ commanded you, that of the goods and chattels, lands and tenements of Nathaniel C. Bissell (in your bailiwick) you should cause to be made the sum of Sixty Six Dollars and seventy two cents which lately in our County Court of Pleas and Quarter Sessions, held for the County of Chowan, John B. Blount recovered against him for Debt as also the sum of Twelve Dollars and Fifty Nine Cents for costs and charges by him in his suit in that behalf expended, whereof the said Nathaniel C. Bissell is convicted and liable as to us appears of record, besides your own fees for that service; and that you have the said money before the Justices of our said Court, at Edenton, the second Monday of June next after the 2nd Monday of March in the year of our Lord one thousand eight hundred and nineteen to render to the said John B. Blount his Debt, damages, costs and charges aforesaid; and you at that day returned on the same writ you had levied the same on Negro Woman Molly and Man Sam which remain in your hands unsold. We do therefore command you, that you expose to sale the goods and chattels of Nathaniel C. Bissell by you so as aforesaid levied upon, so that you have the said money, and 13 shillings and six pence for accruing costs, before the Justices of our said Court, at Edenton, on the second Monday of December next; and we do command you further, that of the goods and chattels, lands and tenements of the said Nathaniel C. Bissell (in your bailiwick) you cause to be made the residue of the debt, damages, costs and charges, and that you have the said money before the justices of our said Court, at Edenton, on the day aforesaid, to render to the said John B. Blount, debt, damages, costs and charges aforesaid; and have you then and there this writ. Witness William Norfleet, Clerk of the said Court, at Edenton, the 2nd Monday of September in the XLIV year of our Independence, and in the year of our Lord one thousand eight hundred and nineteen.

William Norfleet, Clk

Judgment $72 Int. from 17th Nov 1815

Clk	$8.24
D. Shff W.F.	1.05
Att JBS	4
	$13.26

****

Chowan County
Civil Actions

John B. Blount & als Vs. Boon Felton
Civil Action [1819]
Chowan County Records

John B. Blount, Assignee & als Vs. Boon Felton
Vend Exp
Chowan Superior Court
March Term 1820
Rec'd feby 9th 1820
Auction agreeable to Law
No Sale for want of a Bidder
Jas Copeland, Shff
Hertford

State of North Carolina

To the Sheriff of Hertford County, Greeting:

Whereas, we by our writ commanded you, that of the goods and chattels, lands and tenements of Boon Felton (in your bailiwick) you should cause to be made the sum of Six hundred and seventy dolls, with Int from 26th March Aprill till paid which lately in our Superior Court of Law at Edenton, John B. Blount, Assignee recovered against him for Debt, also the further sum of £5.12.9 for the costs and charges by him in his suit in that behalf expended, whereof the said Boon Felton is convicted and liable as to us appears of record; besides your own fees for that service, and that you should have the said money before the Judge of our said Court, at Edenton, on the first Monday after the fourth Monday of **[Blank]** next, after the **[Blank]** day of **[Blank]** in the year of our Lord one thousand eight hundred and **[Blank]** to render to the said John B. Blount his Debt, damages, costs and charges aforesaid: And you at that day returned on the said writ, that you had levied the same on Three Negroes which remain in your hands unsold for want of Bidders. We do therefore command you, that you expose to sale the goods and chattels by you so as aforesaid levied upon, so that you have the said money and **[Blank]** shillings for accruing costs, before the Judge of our said Court, at Edenton, on the second Monday after the fourth Monday of March next, and we do command you further, that of the goods and chattels, lands and tenements of the said Boon Felton in your bailiwick, you cause to be made the residue of the said damages, costs and charges, and that you have the said money before the Judge of our said Court, at Edenton, on the day aforesaid, to render to the

said John B. Blount his Debt, damages, costs and charges aforesaid; and have you then and there this writ. Witness Duncan McDonald, Clerk of our said Court, at Edenton, the 10th day of October in the 44th year of our Independence, Anno Dom. 1819
D McDonald, Clk

Judgment $670 with Int. from 26th March 1817 till paid
Executions have been issued against Howell Jones & George Williams, either being satisfied discharged this (except as to Court fees)

D McDonald	3.2.3
Shff	10.6
Atto	2
	£5.12.9

****

John B. Blount Vs. Abner Harrell
Civil Action [1819]
Chowan County Records

Jno. B. Blount, Assignee Vs Abner Harrell
Vend Exp
Chowan Sup Court
Septem T. 1819
Satisfied
Jas Copeland, Shff by W.B. Wynns, DShff
Hertford

State of North Carolina
To the Sheriff of Hertford County, Greeting:
Whereas, we by our writ commanded you, that of the goods and chattels, lands and tenements of Abner Harrell (in your bailiwick) you should cause to be made the sum of One hundred & twenty two dollars, with Interest from 8th August 1817 till paid which lately in our Superior Court of Law at Edenton, John B Blount, Assignee recovered against him for Debt, also the further sum of Five pounds 3/6 for the costs and charges by him in his suit in that behalf expended, whereof the said Abner Harrell is convicted and liable as to us appears of record; besides your own fees for that service; and that you should have the said money before the Judge of our said Court, at Edenton, on the second Monday after the fourth Monday of

March next, after the **[Blank]** day of **[Blank]** in the year of our Lord one thousand eight hundred and **[Blank]** to render to the said John B. Blount, Assignee his Debt, damages, costs and charges aforesaid: And you at that day returned on the said writ, that you had levied the same on One Negro which remains in your hands unsold for want of Bidders. We do therefore command you, that you expose to sale the goods and chattels by you so as aforesaid levied upon, so that you have the said money and 9/3 shillings for accruing costs, before the Judge of our said Court, at Edenton, on the second Monday after the fourth Monday of September next, and we do command you further, that of the goods and chattels, lands and tenements of the said Abner Harrell in your bailiwick, you cause to be made the residue of the said Debt, damages, costs and charges, and that you have the said money before the Judge of our said Court, at Edenton, on the day aforesaid, to render to the said John B Blount his debt, damages, costs and charges aforesaid; and have you then and there this writ. Witness Duncan McDonald, Clerk of our said Court, at Edenton, the 6th day of Aprill in the 43rd year of our Independence Anno Dom. 1819.
D. McDonald, Clk

Rec'd the Amot. Of this Execution and the [?] due thereon
[?] 23rd Oct 1819
JB Blount

Debt	$122.00
Interest	15.86
Court Charges	9.30
	$147.16

judgment $122 with Interest from 8th August 1817 till paid
Execution has issued against James Strines[?] for the above sum, it being satisfied, this to br void (except as to the Court Tax)

D McDonald, Clk	2.13
Shff	10.6
Atto	2
	5.3.6

John B. Blount, Assignee Vs Boon Felton
Ven Exp
Chowan Sup Court

Chowan County Civil Actions

March T. 1820
Rec'd Feby 9th 1820
Jas Copeland, Shff
Hertford

Advertised agreeable to law, no sale for want of bidders

State of North Carolina

To the Sheriff of Hertford County, greeting:

Whereas, we by our writ commanded you, that of the goods and chattels, lands and tenements of Boon Felton (in your bailiwick) you should cause to be made the sum of One hundred and Seventy dollars, with Interest from 1st June 1818 till Paid which lately in our Superior Court of Law at Edenton, John B Blount, Assignee recovered against him for Debt, also the further sum of £5 for the costs and charges by him in his suit in that behalf expended, whereof the said Boon Felton is convicted and liable as to us appears of record; besides your own fees for that service, and that you should have the said money before the Judge of our said Court, at Edenton, on the first Monday after the fourth Monday of **[Blank]** next, after the **[Blank]** day of **[Blank]** in the year of of our Lord one thousand eight hundred and **[Blank]** to render to the said John B Blount, Assignee damages, costs and charges aforesaid: And you at that day returned on the said writ, that you had levied the same on Four Negroes which remain in your hands unsold for want of Bidders. We do therefore command you, that you expose to sale the goods and Chattels by you so as aforesaid levied upon, so that you have the said money and **[Blank]** shillings for accruing costs, before the Judge of our said Court, at Edenton, on the second Monday after the fourth Monday of March next, and we do command you further that of the goods and chattels, lands and tenements of the said Boon Felton in your bailiwick, you cause to be made the residue of the said Debt, damages, costs and charges, and that you have the said money before the Judge of our said Court, at Edenton, on the day aforesaid, to render to the said John B Blount his Debt, damages, costs and charges aforesaid; and have you then and there this writ. Witness Duncan McDonald, Clerk of our said Court, at Edenton, the 10th day of October in the 44th year of our Independence, Anno Dom. 1819.
D McDonald, Clk

Judge $170 with Interest from 1st June 1818 till Paid

Executions has issued against G. W Sess[?], It being satesfied, discharges this, (except as to the Court fees)

D McDonald, Clk	2.9.6
Shff	10.6
Atto	2
	£5

****

John McCottor Vs Thomas Myers et als
Civil Action [1819]
Chowan County Records

John McCottor Vs Tho Myres &c
Subp for Charles Taylor
Executed, James R. Bent, Shff
By A Howe

State of North Carolina
To the Sheriff of Chowan County, Greeting:
You are hereby commanded to summon Charles Taylor personally to be and appear before the Judge of our Superior Court of Law, to be held for the County of Chowan, at the Court House in Edenton Immediately next, then and there to testify and the truth to say in behalf of Plaintiff in a certaim matter of controversy in the said Court depending, and then and there to be tried, wherein John McCottor is Plaintiff and Tho Myres & others are Defendants. And this you shall in no wise omit, under the penalty by law enjoined. Witness Duncan McDonald, Clerk of the said Court, at Edenton, the 12th day of October in the XLIV year of our Independence, Anno Dom. 1819.
D McDonald, Clk

Jno McCottor Vs Tho Myres & others
Subp
John Boyd
Executed Jos Rea[?]

State of North Carolina
To the Sheriff of Chowan County, greeting:

You are hereby commanded to summon John Boyd personally to be and appear before the Judge of our Superior Court of Law, to be held for the County of Chowan, at the Court House in Edenton Immediately next, then and there to testify and the truth to say in behalf of Plaintiff in a certain matter of controversy in the said Court depending, and then and there to be tried, wherein John McCottor is Plaintiff and Tho Myres & others are Defendants. And this you shall in no wise omit, under the penalty by law enjoined. Witness Duncan McDonald, Clerk of the said Court, at Edenton, the 12th day of October in the XLIV year of our Independence, Anno Dom. 1819
D McDonald, Clk

McCottor Vs Tho Myres & others
Subp
Chas Taylor
Executed
Ja R. Bent, Shff

State of North Carolina
To the Sheriff of Chowan County, Greeting:
You are hereby commanded to summon Charles Taylor personally to be and appear before the Judge of our Superior Court of Law, to be held for the County of Chowan, at the Court House in Edenton Immediately next, then and there to testify and the truth to say in behalf of Tho Myres & others in a certain matter of controversy in the said Court depending, and then and there to be tried, wherein Jno McCottor is Plaintiff and Tho Myres & others are Defendants. And this you shall in no wise omit, under the penalty by law enjoined. Witness Duncan McDonald, Clerk of the said Court, at Edenton, the 11th day of October in the XIXII year of our Independence, Anno Dom. 1819.
D McDonald, Clk

McCottor Vs Tho. Myres & others
Subp
Jonah Overton
Executed
Ja R. Bent, Shff

Chowan County
Civil Actions

State of North Carolina

To the Sheriff of Chowan County, Greeting:

You are hereby commanded to be and appear before the Judge of our Superior Court of Law, to be held for the County of Chowan, at the Court House in Edenton, Immediately next, then and there to testify and the truth to say in behalf of Defendant in a certain matter of controversy in the said Court depending, and then and there to be tried, wherein Jno McCottor is Plaintiff and Tho Myres & others are Defendants. And this you shall in no wise omit, under the penalty by law enjoined. Witness Duncan McDonald, Clerk of the said Court, at Edenton, the 11th day of October in the XLIV year of our Independence, Anno Dom. 1819.

D McDonald, Clk

John McCottor Vs Allen Laseter & Thomas Myers
Writ
Tres V& Arms
To Spring Term 1819
Executed
Ja R. Bent, Shff
AM Gatlin

I agree to be Security for the costs of this writ agreeable to act of Assembly
Tho T Charleson (Seal)

State of North Carolina

To the Sheriff of Chowan County, Greeting:

You are hereby commanded to summon Allen Lasseter and Thomas Myers (if to be found in your County,) and them safely keep, so that you have them before the Judge of the Superior Court of Law, to be held for the County of Chowan, at the Court House in Edenton, on the second Monday after the fourth Monday in March next; then and there to answer unto John McCottor in a Plea of Trespass vi et armis to damage one hundred and fifty dollars &c &c. Herein fail not, and have you then and there this writ. Witness Duncan McDonald, Clerk of our said Court, at Edenton, the 4th day of October 1818 and in the XL year of our Independence. Issued the 24th day of March 1819.

D McDonald, Clk

Writ Tax & S 1.4

Dete 7/6 Subp 6/	13.6
Ex 3/9	3.9
	£5.14.3

****

Richard Wood Vs. Josiah Flowers et als
Civil Action [1819]
Chowan County Records

Richard Wood Vs Josiah Flowers & als
Detinue
Rec'd in my Office
20th September 1819
D McDonald, Clk
Transmitted to Chowan Supr Court of Law

A Transcript in the Suit Wherein Richard Wood is Plaintiff and Josiah Flowers & Francis Ward are Defendants
General Issue

Tyrell County Superior Court of Law September Term 1819, An Affidavit of Josiah Flowers.

Ordered by the Honorable Court that the within Suit be transferred to Chowan County Superior Court of Law agreeable to act of the general Assembly in like Cases made and Provided
Test Robert Wynns, Clk

These are to certify that the within is a true copy taken from the records in this Office Given under my hand and Seal of Office this 16th day of September Anno Dom. 1819
Test Robt Wynne, Clk

A Transcript in the Suit Where in Richard Wood is Plaintiff and Josiah Flowers & Francis Ward is Defendants

State of North Carolina

Chowan County
Civil Actions

To the Sheriff of Washington County, Greeting: You are hereby Commanded to take the bodies of Josiah Flowers and Francis Ward If to be found in your County and them safely keep so that you have them before the Judge of Our Superior Court of Law held at the Court House in Columbia, Tyrell County on the first Monday in September next, then and there to answer unto Richard wood of a Plea that they render to him negro fellow Slave Named March of the value of five hundred Pounds negro - Temp of the Value of five hundred Pounds Which they unjustly detain to his damage One Thousand Pounds and this you shall in no wise omit under the penalty by law enjoined, Witness Robert Wynne, Clerk of the said Court at Columbia the first day of March in the XLIIIrd year of our Independence Anno Dom. 1819. Issued the 4th March 1819 A.N. Vail Atto Robt Wynne, Clk

I Bind myself Securety for the cost of this Writ should the Plaintiff fail to prosecute the same with Efect as Witness my hand and Seal this 4th day of March 1819 - Wm D Coakley (Seal)
A.N. Vail
Returned Executed to September Term Anno Dom 1819.
B. Phelps, Shff by A.M. Hardison, DShff

Bill of Cost in Tyrell Supr Court of Law	
Sheriff of Washington	£1.0.0
Clerk of Tyrell Supr Court	1.13.6
Tax due to Clk	10.0
	£3.3.6

Josiah Flowers et als
Detinue
Richd Wood
From Washington Co.
To Chowan County
Oct 4th 1819

Be it remembered, that at the Spring Term 1919 of Washington County Superior Court of Law, Josiah Flowers & others, brought their Writ into Court, against Richard Wood, in the following words (See a Copy of the Writ hereunto annexed Marked "A"); that the said writ being returned not executed; an alias writ was issued & returned to the Fall term 1819,

Executed, (a Copy of which writ is also annexed marked "B"); that at the Fall Term 1819 Richd Wood, filed his Affidavit for the removal of the suit to some other County, a Copy of which affidavit is also annexed marked "C"; And that thereupon it was ordered by the Court that the suit be remoned for Trial to Chowan County -
Commission to Georgia 40 days notices Comissions Mutual.
Given under my hand & Seal of Office Oct 4th 1819.

"A"

State of North Carolina
To the Sheriff of Tyrell County, Greeting:
You are hereby commanded to take the body of Richard Wood, if to be found in your bailiwick, & him safely keep, so that you have him before the Judge of our Superior Court of Law, to be held for Washington County, at the Court House in said County on the second Monday of March next, then and there to answer unto Josiah Flowers & Wife Harriet, James Wood & Wife, Deborah & Francis Ward, of a Plea that he render unto them Certain Negroes to wit, Mark of the Value of fifteen hundred dollars, Bet of the value of one thousand Dollars, & Tempe of the value of one thousand Dollars, which he unjustly detains to their damage Three thousand dollars. Herein fail not & have you then and there this writ. Witness Thomas Turner, Clerk of our said Court at the Court House the fifth Monday after the fourth Monday of September on the XLIII year of American Independence. Issued Feb 18th 1819
"Too late to hand" J Beasly, DShff
Tho Turner, Clk

"B"

State of North Carolina
To the Sheriff of Tyrell County, Greeting:
You are hereby commanded as you have been Commanded to take the body of Richd Wood, (if to be found in your bailiwick) and him safely keep so that you have him before the Judge of our Superior Court of Law at our next Court to be held for Washington County on the second Monday of September next, then and there to answer unto Josiah Flowers & Wife Harriet, James Wood & Wife Deborah and Francis Ward, of a Plea that he render certain negroes to wit, Mark of the value of Fifteen Hundred

Dollars, Bet of the value of one thousand Dollars and Tempe of the value One thousand dollars, which he unjustly detains to their damage three thousand dollars. Herein fail not, and have you then and there this writ. Witness Thomas Turner Clk of our said Court, at the Court House in said County the second Monday of March in the XLIII year of the Independence of the United States. Issued June 2nd 1819.
Signed Tho Turner, Clk
Exd, Jno Beasly, DShff for Henry Alexander, Shff

We do hereby bind ourselves, agreeably to Act of Assembly, that the Plaintiff shall prosecute this suit; and in Case of failure of such Prosecution, shall pay to the Defendant, all such costs & damages as shall be awarded against him, as Witness our hands & Seals
Witness Tho Turner
Signed Jno Pike (Seal)

Josiah Flowers Vs Richd Wood
Sep Term 1819.

The Defendant makes Oath that the Pltff lives in the County of Washington & has a number of relations to whom he is related by marriage and verily does believe that Justice cannot be done him in this County, Owing to the above influence - The Defendant further deposeth that Josiah Flowers is a man of influence as he verily believes, and verily does believe it will be exerted to obtain and unjust Verdict.
Sworn to in Open Court
Signed Richd Wood
Test Tho Turner, Clk

State of North Carolina
Washington County

I Thomas Turner Clerk of the Superior Court in & for said County, do hereby certify that the preceding Copy of the Writs marked "A" & "B", copy of Affidavit marked "C" copy of Jno Pikes bond as security for the costs of the suit on the part of the Pltff; Copy of the Shff Return on the two writs aforesaid, are truly taken from the records in this Office. Given under my hand & Seal of Office Oct 4th 1819

Cost
Writ 10/ Security & Entering }
Security 4/ tax 10/ }
2 Seals 5/ Removal 10/ } 1.19.0
Jno Beasly DShff Arrest 7.6
£2.6.6

Oct 4th 1819 Rec'd of Josiah Flower four dollars & sixty five cents the above costs
Tho Turner, Clk

****

John B. Blount Vs. James Spiers
Civil Action [1819]
Chowan County Records

Jno B. Blount Vs James Spiers
Vend Exp
Chowan Sup Court
September T. 1819
Cost Satisfied
Jas Copeland, Shff
By WB Wynnes, DShff

State of North Carolina

To the Sheriff of Hertford County, Greeting:

Whereas, we by our writ commanded you, that of the goods and chattels, lands and tenements of James Spiers (in your bailiwick) you should cause to be made the sum of One hundred & twenty two dollars, with Int. from August 1st 1819 till Paid, which lately in our Superior Court of Law at Edenton, John B. Blount recovered against him for Debt, also the further sum of Five pounds 3/6 for the costs and charges by him in his suit in that behalf expended, whereof the said James Spiers is convicted and liable as to us appears of record; besides your own fees for that service, and that you should have the said money before the Judge of our said Court, at Edenton, on the second Monday after the fourth Monday of March next, after the **[Blank]** day of **[Blank]** in the year of our Lord one thousand eight hundred and **[Blank]** to render to the said John B. Blount, Assignee damages, costs and charges aforesaid: And you at that day returned on the said writ, that

you had levied the same on One Negro which remains in your hands unsold for want of Bidders. We do therefore command you, that you expose to sale the goods and chattels by you so as aforesaid levied upon, so that you have the said money and #/3 shillings for accruing costs, before the Judge of our said Court, at edenton, on the second Monday after the fourth Monday of September next, and we do command you further, that of the goods and chattels, lands and tenements of the said James Spiers in your bailiwick, you cause to be made the residue of the said Debt, damages, costs and charges, and that you have the said money before the Judge of our said Court, at Edenton, on the day aforesaid, to render to the said John B Blount, Assignee damages, costs and charges aforesaid; and have you then and there this writ. Witness Duncan McDonald, Clerk of our said Court, at Edenton, the 6th day of April in the 43rd year of our Independence, Anno Dom. 1819
D McDonald, Clk

Judgment $122 with Int. from 8th August 1817 till Paid
Execution has issued against Abner Harrell for the above sum, it being satisfied, this to be void (except as to the Court fees)

D McDonald, Clk	£2.13
Shff	10.6
Atto	2
	£5.3.6

****

John Little &. John W. Littlejohn Vs. John Bond & als
Civil Action [1819]
Chowan County Records

John Little & Jno W. Littlejohn Vs. John Bond & als
Dend Expo
December Term 1819
Forborne by Mr. Little
Ja. R. Bent, Shff

State of North Carolina
To the Sheriff of Chowan County, Greeting:
Whereas, we by our writ commanded you, that of the goods and chattels, lands and tenements of John M. Bond and Nathaniel Bond (in your

bailiwick) you should cause to be made the sum of Four Hundred and Seventy five Dollars & Fifty Cents, which lately in our County Court of Pleas and Quarter Sessions, held for the County of Chowan, John Little and John W. Littlejohn recovered against them for Debt as also the sum of Nine Dollars and Fifty Seven Cents for costs and charges by them in their suit in that behalf expended, whereof the said John M. Bond and Nathaniel Bond, are convicted and liable as to us appears of record, besides your own fees for that service; and have you the said money before the Justices of our said Court, at Edenton, the second Monday of September next after the 2nd Monday of June in the year of our Lord one thousand eight hundred and Nineteen, to render to the said John Little and John damages, costs and charges aforesaid; and you at that day returned on the said writ that you had levied the same on Negroes John belonging to John Bond, and Isom, belonging to Nathaniel Bond which remain in your hands unsold. We do therefore command you, that you expose to sale the goods and chattels of John M Bond and Nathaniel Bond by you so as aforesaid levied upon, so that you have the said money, and Six shillings and Nine pence for accruing costs, before the Justices of our said Court, at Edenton, on the second Monday of December next; and we do command you further, that of the goods and chattels, lands and tenements of the said John M. Bond and Nathaniel Bond, (in your bailiwick) you cause to be made the residue of the Debt, damages, costs and charges, and that you have the said money before the Justices of our said Court, at Edenton, on the day aforesaid, to render to the said John Little and John W. Littlejohn Debt, damages, costs and charges aforesaid; and have you then and there this writ. Witness William Norfleet, Clerk of the said Court, at Edenton, the 2nd Monday of september; in the XLIVth year of our Independence, and in the year of our Lord one thousand eight hundred and Nineteen.
William Norfleet, Clk

Judgment $475.50 Int. from 9th July, 1818

Clk	$4.19
Shff	2.05
Att JJ	4
	$10.24

****

Rachael Hare Vs. Henry Gilliam
Civil Action [1819]

Chowan County Civil Actions

Chowan County Records

State of North Carolina
To the Sheriff of Chowan County, Greeting:
You are hereby commanded to summon Jeremiah & Lemuel Sutton personally to be and appear before the judge of our Superior Court of Law, to be held for the County of Chowan, at the Court House in Edenton, on the second Monday after the fourth Monday in September next, then and there to testify and the truth to say in behalf of the Plaintiff in a certain matter of controversy in the said Court depending, and then and there to be tried, wherein Rachael Hare is Plaintiff and Henry Gilliam is Defendant. And this you shall in no wise omit, under the penalty by law enjoined. Witness Duncan McDonald, Clerk of the said Court, at Edenton, the 2nd Monday after the 4th Monday of **[?]** in the XLIII year of our Independence, Anno Dom 1819.
D McDonald, Clk

State of North Carolina
To the Sheriff of Chowan County, Greeting:
You are hereby commanded to summon Vincent Parsons personally to be and appear before the judge of our Superior Court of Law, to be held for the County of Chowan, at the Court House in Edenton, on the first Monday after the fourth Monday in **[Blank]** next, then and there to testify and the truth to say in behalf of Rachael Hare in a certain matter of controversy in the said Court depending, and then and there to be tried, wherein Rachael Hare is Plaintiff, and Henry Gilliam is Defendant. And this you shall in no wise omit, under the penalty by law enjoined. Witness Duncan McDonald, Clerk of the said Court, at Edenton, the 16th day of October in the XLIV year of our Independence, Anno Dom. 1819
D McDonald, Clk

Rachael Hare Vs Henry Gilliam
Subp
Tho H. Leary
Executed by Ja. R. Bent, Shff

State of North Carolina
To the Sheriff of Chowan County, Greeting:

Chowan County
Civil Actions

You are hereby commanded to summon Tho. H. Leary personally to be and appear before the Judge of Superior Court of Law, to be held for the County of Chowan, at the Court House in Edenton Immediately next, then and there to testify and the truth to say in behalf of Defendant in a certain matter of controversy in the said Court depending, and then and there to be tried, wherein Rachael Hare is Plaintiff and Henry Gilliam is Defendant. And this you shall in no wise omit, under the penalty by law enjoined. Witness Duncan McDonald, Clerk of the said Court, at Edenton, the 12th day of October in the XLIV year of our Independence, Anno Dom. 1819.
D McDonald, Clk

James & Sampson Guthrie
Summons
Executed on James Guthrie
W Long, Shff

State of North Carolina
To the Sheriff of Anson County, Greeting:
You are hereby commanded to summon Sampson Guthrie & James Guthrie personally to be and appear before the Judge of our Superior Court of Law, to be held for the County of Chowan, at the Court House in Edenton, on the second Monday after the fourth Monday in March next, then and there to testify and the truth to say in behalf of Henry Gilliam in a certain matter of controversy in the said Court depending, and then and there to be tried, wherein Rachael Hare is Plaintiff and Henry Gilliam is Defendant. And this you shall in no wise omit, under the penalty by law enjoined. Witness Duncan McDonald, Clerk of the said Court, at Edenton, the 15th day of Octr in the XLIII year of our Independence, Anno Dom. 1819.
D McDonald, Clk

Rachael Hare Vs Henry Gilliam
Subp
Jno M. Bond
Executed, J.R. Bent, Shff

State of North Carolina
To the Sheriff of Chowan County, Greeting:

Chowan County
Civil Actions

You are hereby commanded to summon John M. Bond personally to be and appear before the Judge of our Superior Court of Law, held at the Court House in Edenton, on the 2nd Monday after the fourth Monday in March next, then and there to testify and the truth to say in behalf of Rachael Hare in a certain matter of controversy in the said Court depending, and then and there to be tried, wherein Rachael Hare is Plaintiff, and H. Gilliam is Defendant. And this you shall in no wise omit, under the penalty by law enjoined. Witness Duncan McDonald, Clerk of the said Court, at Edenton, the 10th day of Octr in the 44th year of our Independence, Anno Dom. 1819.
D McDonald, Clk

Rachael Hare Vs H. Gilliam
Executed, J.R. Bent, Shff

State of North Carolina
To the Sheriff of Chowan County, Greeting:
You are hereby commanded to summon George Bozman personally to be and appear before the Judge of our Superior Court of Law, to be held for the County of Chowan, at the Court House in Edenton, on the second Monday after the fourth Monday in Septr. Next, then and there to testify and the truth to say in behalf of Defendant in a certain matter of controversy in the said Court depending, and then and there to be tried, wherein Henry Gilliam is Plaintiff and Rachael Hare is Defendant. And this you shall in no wise omit, under the penalty by law enjoined. Witness Duncan McDonald, Clerk of the said Court, at Edenton, the 12th day of October in the XLI[?] year of our Independence, Anno Dom. 1819.
D McDonald, Clk

Rachel Hare Vs. H. Gilliam
To April Term 1819
Executed By Jno. Burrus[?], DShff

State of North Carolina
To the Sheriff of Gates County, Greeting:
You are hereby commanded to summon Simon Stalling[?] & John Branch personally to be and appear before the Judge of our Superior Court of Law, to be held for the County of Chowan, at the Court House in Edenton, on

the second Monday after the fourth Monday in March next, then and there to testify and the truth to say in behalf of Defendant in a certain matter of controversy in the said Court depending, and then and there to be tried, wherein Rachael Hare is Plaintiff and H. Gilliam is Defendant. And this you shall in no wise omit, under the penalty by law enjoined. Witness Duncan McDonald, Clerk, of the said Court, at Edenton, the 17th day of March in the XLIII year of our Independence, Anno Dom. 1819.
D McDonald, Clk

Rachael Hare Vs H. Gilliam
To April Term 1819
Executed by Jno. Burnas[?], DShff

State of North Carolina
To the Sheriff of Gates County, Greeting:
You are hereby commanded to summon Simon Stalling & John Branch personally to be and appear before the Judge of the Superior Court of Law, to be held for the County of Chowan, at the Court House in Edenton, on the second Monday after the fourth Monday in March next, then and there to testify and the truth to say in behalf of Defendant in a certain matter of controversy in the said Court depending, and then and there to be tried, wherein Rachael Hare is Plaintiff and Henry Gilliam is Defendant. And this you shall in no wise omit, under the penalty by law enjoined. Witness Duncan McDonald, Clerk of the said Court, at Edenton, the 17th day of March in the XLIII year of our Independence, Anno Dom. 1819
D McDonald, Clk

Rachael Hare Vs. Henry Gilliam
Subp
To Fall Term 1819
Executed, Jas. R. Bent, By Abraham Howell

State of North Carolina
To the Sheriff of Chowan County, Greeting:
You are hereby commanded to summon Lemuel Sutton personally to be and appear before the Judge of our Superior Court of Law, to be held for the County of Chowan, at the Court House in Edenton, on the second Monday after the fourth Monday in September next, then and there to

testify and the truth to say in behalf of the Plaintiff in a certain matter of controversy in the said Court depending, and then and there to be tried, wherein Rachael Hare is Plaintiff and Henry Gilliam is Defendant. And this you shall in no wise omit, under the penalty by law enjoined. Witness Duncan McDonald, Clerk of the said Court, at Edenton, the 2nd Monday of March in the XLIII year of our Independence, Anno Dom. 1819.
D McDonald, Clk

Rachael Hare Vs. Henry Gilliam
In the Suit Concerning a Negroe
Actrin Detinue
To Fall Term 1819
Executed, B Phelps, Shff
By Alex Hardison, Dep.

State of North Carolina
To the Sheriff of Washington County, Greeting:
You are hereby commanded to summon William Ramsey personally to be and appear before the Judge of our Superior Court of Law, to be held for the County of Chowan, at the Court House in Edenton, on the second Monday after the fourth Monday in Sept next, then and there to testify and the truth to say in behalf of Rachael Hare in a certain matter of controversy in the said Court depending, and then and there to be tried, wherein Rachael Hare is Plaintiff and Henry Gilliam is Defendant. And this you shall in no wise omit, under the penalty by law enjoined. Witness, Duncan McDonald, Clerk of the said Court, at Edenton, the 5th day of April in the XLIII year of our Independence, Anno Dom. 1819.
D McDonald, Clk

Chowan Superior Court of Law
Rachael Hare Vs Henry Gilliam

The Plaintiff complains of the Defendant in custody &c of [?] Vi et armis &c for that on the day of **[Blank]** at **[Blank]** an assault did make upon her with force and arms & he did beat, wound, abuse & threaten her without any lawful cause by which her life was desparate of to her damage &c **[Blank]** £ whereupon she produces Suit &c
L. Martin, Atto for Pltff.

Chowan County Court of Law
Rachael Hare Vs Henry Gilliam

The Plaintiff complains of the Defendant in custody &c for that the Plaintiff was the owner of a certain Negro man named **[Blank]** at **[Blank]** on the **[Blank]** day of **[Blank]** which she lost &c &c of the value of **[Blank]** and that the Defendant afterwards came to said Negro man named Dave otherwise called Jo by finding on the day of **[Blank]** and Plaintiffs well knowing the property of the said Dave which she called Joe to be in the Plaintiff unlawfully detained him and the Plaintiff applied to Defendant to give up said Negro Dave otherwise called Joe to her and the Plaintiff refused and still does refuse to deliver him up, but **[?]** declares said Negroe Dave otherwise called Jo to her damages $1000 whereupon she produces Suit.
L. Martin, Atto for Plaintiff.

Rachael Hare Vs Henry Gilliam
L. Martin Plaintiffs Attorney

Removal from Washington to Chowan County demanded by Plaintiff & [?] Jan 24th 1819
Tho Turner, Clk

This bond Rec'd into office Sept 21st 1818
Tho Turner[?]

A True Copy, Test, Tho Turner, Clk
Bill of Cost in Washington Superior Court

Turner, Clk, Writ 10/ Seal 2/6	12.6
1 Security & Entering the same	4
Tax 10/ Removal & transcript 10/	1.00
Lewis Eure, DShff	1.16.6
Arrest 7/6 Bail bond 2/6	10
	2.66

Memo The Clks fees and tax an unpaid - perhaps the Shffs fees are unpaid also.

Chowan County
Civil Actions

Rachael Hare Vs Henry Gilliam
L. Martin, Plaintiff's Attorney
J. Iredell Defendants Attorney

Removal from Washington to Chowan County, demanded by Plaintiff & Detered Jan 24th 1819
Tho Turner, Clk

Copy of this Writ marked "A"
State of North Carolina
To the Sheriff of Gates County, Greeting:
You are hereby commanded to take the body of Henry Gilliam (if to be found in your bailiwick) & him safely keep so that you have him before the Judge of our Superior Court of Law to be held for Washington County, at the Court House in said County on the fifth Monday after the fourth Monday of March next, then and there to render unto Rachael Hare negro man Dave otherwise called Joe of the value of One thousand dollars, which he unjustly detains from her to her damage five hundred dollars- Herein fail not; and have you then and there this writ. Witness Thomas Turner, Clerk of our said Court, at the Court House the fifth Monday after the fourth Monday of September in the XLII year of American Independence being 1817
Tho Turner, Clk

I James Galling, Shff do assign the within obligation to Rachael Hare to be sued agreeable to the Statute in such cases made & provided this 11th of decr. 1817
Signed James Galling, Shff, A True Copy
Test Tho Turner, Clk

The Original of this writ is endorsed in the following words
"Rachael Hare Vs Henry Gilliam, Detinue
To Spring Term 1817
Exed, Lewis Eure DShff for Jas. Galling, Shff
Leonard Martin, Atto
Test, Tho Turner, Clk

Chowan County
Civil Actions

Copy of Bail Bond filed with the writ
"State of North Carolina

Gates County

Know all men by these presents that we Henry Gilliam & Will Gatling are held and firmly bound unto James Galling, Sheriff of the County aforesaid in the sum of Two thousand dollars, to be paid unto Mr said Jas. Galling Sheriff his heirs or assigns; To which payment well and truly to be made we do bind ourselves, our heirs, Exers & Admrs jointly & severall firmly by these presents, Sealed with our Seals and dated 11th Decr 1817.

The Condition of the above obligation is such that if the above bounden Henry Gilliam do make his personal appearance before the Judge of the Superior Court of Law & Equity held for Washington County at the Court House in said County on the fifth Monday after the fourth Monday of March next, To answer unto Rachael Hare, & not to depart without leave had & obtained by the said Court, then the above obligation to be void, otherwise to remain in full force and virtue

Henry Gilliam (Seal)
William Gatling (Seal)
Signed, Sealed & delivered in the presence of
Attest Lewis Eure

I James Galling, Sheriff do assign the within obligation & Condition to Rachael Hare to be sued for agreeable to the statute in such Cases made and provided this 11th day of Decr. 1817
James Galling, Shff
A True Copy
Test Tho Turner, Clk

(The following words are endorsed on the said writ)
Rachael Hare Vs Henry Gilliam
To Spring Term
Executed by Lewis Eure, DShff
For Jas Galling, Shff
Leonard Martin, a True Copy
Test, Tho Turner, Clk

State of North Carolina

Chowan County
Civil Actions

Be it remembered that at the Superior Court of Law began & held for Washington County at the Court House in said County on the fifth Monday after the fourth Monday of March in the year of our Lord one thousand eight hundred & eighteen, Rachael Hare, by her Attorney Leonard Martin brought into Court her writ against Henry Gilliam in the following words; see a Copy of the Writ annexed marked A; That upon motion, It was ordered by the Court, that the Plaintiff give security for Costs in four Months; That this order was Complied with on the 21st September 1818, the Plaintiff filing on that day a bond in the following words, see a Copy of the bond annexed, marked B: That at the succeedeng term of the said Court of Law began & held for Washington County on the fifth Monday after the fourth Monday of September AD 1818, The Defendant Henry Gilliam pleaded to the said action " Non defunct, Stat lims," to which pleas the Plaintiff replied and issue was joined: That then, upon motion of Leonard Martin, Pltff's Atty, "It was ordered by the Court that this Cause be removed for Trial to Chowan County, Mr Martin being present & vouching for the Consent of Mr Iredell.
In Testimony whereof I Thomas Turner Clerk of the said Court have hereunto set my hand & Seal of Office, January 23rd 1819.
Tho Turner, Clk.

Rachael Hare Vs Henry Gilliam
Chowan Sup Court
October Term 1819

Henry Gilliam maketh oath that the negro mentioned in the annexed affidavit which Mr Parsons examined since the trial is the same negro which Mrs. Hare claimed as hers & to which the testimony of Mr Sutton, a witness examined at the trial, refers so far as related to what he stated of the negro in possession of this Deponant.
H. Gilliam
Sworn to in open Court 16th Oct 1819
D McDonald, Clk

Rachael Hare Vs Henry Gilliam
Action of Detinue
Chowan Supr Court
October Term 1819

Vincent Parsons who was sworn as a Witness in this case maketh oath that he was well acquainted with the negro slave which Mrs. Hare claimed in this suit, having been informed by her that it was the same negro she bought in Anson County & having been summoned by her to prove the identity of the negro - that on the trial of this suit Deponent thought from the description given by the other witnesses that the negro in possession of the Defendant was the same negro - but that since the trial he hath seen & examined the negro in possession of Mr. Gilliam & who is now before the Court st that he may be identified to be the same Mrs Hare claimed and he is perfectly satisfied this is not the negro Mrs Hare purchaded in Anson & which she has always told him was the one for which she brought suit - that Deponant is satisfied he never saw the negro now in possession of Mr Gilliam untill [?] this trial.
Sworn to in open Court, 11th October 1819
Vincent Parsons
D McDonald, Clk.

Copy of Bail Bond filed with the aforesaid Writ

State of North Carolina }
Gates County]

Know all men by these presents that we Henry Gilliam and William Gatling are held & firmly bound unto James Galling, Sheriff of the County aforesaid in the sum of Two Thousand dollars to be paid unto the Sd. James Galling, Sheriff his heirs or assigns: To which payment well and truly to be made we do bind our selves, our heirs, Exers and Admins. Jointly and severally, firmly by these presents, sealed with our seals and dated this 11th Decr. 1817.

The Condition of the above obligation is such that if the above bounden Henry Gilliam do make his personal appearance before the Judge of the Superior Court of Law & Equity held for the County of Washington at the Court House in said County on the fifth Monday after the fourth Monday of March next, to answer unto Rachael Hare & not to depart without leave had and obtained by the said Court, then the above obligation to be void, otherwise to remain in full force & virtue - Signed, Sealed & Delivered in the presence of
Attest, Lewis Eure

H Gilliam (Seal)
William Gatling (Seal)

Copy of Bond for costs Marked "B"

Know all men by these presents that we Rachael Hare & Thomas Fagan & Demsey Marriner are held and firmly bound unto Henry Gilliam in the sum of one hundred dollars, for the which payment well and truly to be made we do hereby bind ourselves our & each of our heirs, executors & Administrators jointly & severally firmly by these presents, Sealed with our seals and dated May 18th 1818.

The condition of the above obligation is such that whereas the said Rachael Hare hath brought a suit in Washington County Superior Court of Law to the last Spring Term of said Court, against the said Henry Gilliam in an action of Detinue; now if the aforesaid Rachael Hare, shall prosecute said suit with effect, or in case she fail therein shall well and truly pay to the Defendant in said suit all such costs & damages as shall be awarded against him, then the above obligation shall be void; otherwise to remain in full force & virtue. Witness our hands & Seals the day & year above written
Rachael Hare (Seal)
Thomas Satterfield (Seal)

Copy Marked "B"

Know all men by these presents that We Rachael Hare, Thomas Fagan and Demsey Marriner are held & firmly bound unto Henry Gilliam in the sum of One hundred dollars - for the which payment well and truly to be made, we do hereby bind ourselves, our & each of our Heirs, Executors & Administrators jointly & severally firmly by these presents-Sealed with our Seals and dated May 18th 1818.

The Condition of the above obligation is such that whereas the said Rachael Hare hath brought a suit in Washington County Superior Court of Law to the last Spring Term of said Court against said Henry Gilliam in an action of Trespass Vi et Armis; now if the said Rachael Hare shall prosecute said suit with effect; & in case she fail therein, shall well and truly pay to the Defendant in said Suit all such costs & damages, as

shall be awarded against him then the above obligation to be void, otherwise remain & be in full force and virtue - Witness our hands & Seals the day and year above written
Test
Rachael Hare (Seal)
Thomas Satterfield (Seal)
D Marriner (Seal)
Rec'd this bond into Office Sept. 21st 1818
Tho Turner, Clk
A True Copy of the Original
Test, Tho Turner, Clk

Bill of cost in Washington Supr Court
Turner Clk, Writ 10/ Seal 2/6, 2 Securities & Entering the same $/ 10/
Removal of the cause & transcript 10/ 2.06
Lewis Eure DShff Arrest 1-7/6 Bail Bond 2/6 10
£2.10.6
Memo The Clks fees & tax, (& perhaps the Shff's fees also)

State of North Carolina

Be it remembered that heretofore, to wit, That at the Superior Court of Law began and held for Washington County at the Court House in said County on the fifth Monday after the fourth Monday of March in the year of our Lord one thousand eight hundred & eighteen, Rachael Hare by her Attorney Leonard Martin brought into Court her Writ against Henry Gilliam in the following words; See a Copy of the writ annexed marked A: that upon motion, It was ordered by the Court that the Plaintiff give security for costs I four months; That this order was complied with on the 21st September 1818 - the Plaintiff filing on that day a bond in the following words; see Copy of the Bond annexed marked B: That at the succeeding term of the said Court, namely at the Superior Court of Law began & held for Washington County on the fifth Monday after the fourth Monday of September AD 1818, the Defendant Henry Gilliam pleaded to the said action a Genl. Issue, justification, mot, man, imp Stat Lims to which pleas the Plaintiff replied and issue was joined: That then upon motion of Leonard Martin Pltff's Attorney, "It was ordered by the Court That this Cause be removed for trial to Chowan County, Mr Martin being present and vouching for the consent of Mr. Iredell.

In Testimony whereof I Thomas Turner Clerk of the Court aforesaid have hereunto set my hand & Seal of Office January 23rd 1819.
Tho Turner, Clk

Gates. Vill 10th April 1820

D McDonald Esquire

Dr. Sir Inclosed you will receive Mr. L. Martin's Receipt for amt. Mrs. Hare's Judgt & his fee in said Suit the balance of Cost in that Case I will pay you when I shall be in Town & not long first Martin has agreed to Dismiss the Suit that is now Agt. Me in Favr. Mrs. Hare. Should he not direct you to do so Mention to Genl. Iredell that he agreed before several Gentlemen that I need not attend [?] the Negro being Convinced that the right is in a Mr. Gray who was at our Court last week, This will therefore be bound for the Court of this Term.
I am yours with Respect &c.
H. Gilliam.

L. Martin's Receipt for R Hare, Judgt.

Rec'd from Henry Gilliam thirty three Dollars Specie for a Judgt that Rachael Hare Obtd. Agt. Him in the Supr Court at Edenton at last Octr Term for an Assault &c Aprl 1820.
Leonard Martin, Atto for Plaintiff, also my fee in this Suit.
L. Martin.

Chapter Three

Chowan County

Miscellaneous Records

North Carolina State Archives
Chowan County Records
Records of Slaves and Free Persons of Color
C.R.024.928.27

Fragment of Document

Recd. Edenton Decr. 3rd the sum of One hundred **[Torn]** in full of all Accounts

****

Fragment of Document

Jef, Ben, Will, Pattey, Edmon, John, Mary, Jude; One White Hors, one Rone Dito, and all his House Hold furniture Consisting tabels, Desks and Chears and sundry other to tedious to Menchene was levied on by Felton

****

Chowan County Miscellaneous Records

Weapon Permits for Slaves

Jas. Horniblow
Bond for his Negroe to Carry a Gun
Septr. 1791

State of No. Carolina

Know all Men by these presents that we John Horniblow & Edmund Blount are held and firmly Bound unto William Barritz Esquire Acting Chairman and the rest of the Justices for Chowan County in the sum of fifty pounds -- to which payment well and truly to be made we bind ourselves our heirs, Exors and Admrs. Jointly and severally firmly by these presents, Sealed with our Seals & dated this 14th day of September 1791.

The Condition of the above obligation is such that if a certain Negroe Called Jim the property of the aforesaid John Horniblow who is allowed to Carry a gun on his Masters Land by the County Court of Chowan shall well & truly demean himself and do no injury to any person whatsoever with the Sd. gun then this Obligation to be Void or Else to remain in full force & virtue.
Jno Horniblow (Seal)
Edmd Blount (Seal)
Signed, Sealed & Delivered In the Presence of
Jos. Blount.

****

Weapon Permits for Slaves

S. Tredwell to the Court
Bond for Negro Dundee to carry a gun

State of No. Carolina }
Chowan County }

Know all Men by these presents that We Samuel Tredwell, & Jacob Blount are held and firmly Bound unto Samuel Dickinson Chairman of the County Court of Chowan in the sum of Two Hundred and fifty

Pounds to which payment well & truly to be made and done, We bind ourselves our heirs, Executors & Administrators Jointly and severally firmly by these presents, Sealed with Our Seals and dated this 15th day of March 1793.

The Condition of the above obligation is such that if a Certain Negroe Called Dundee the property of the said Samuel Tredwell, who is allowed to Carry a Gun on his Masters Land by the County Court of Chowan, shall will and truly demean himself and do no Injury with his said Gun to any person or persons whatever then this obligation to be Void or else to remain in full force & Virtue.
Saml. Tredwell (Seal)
Jacob Blount (Seal)
Signed, Sealed & Delivered in the presence of;
Jos. Blount

****

Sale of Slave

Order for Edmund Blount, Esqr.
Executed so says Ed. Blount, Sheriff

State of North Carolina }June County Court
Chowan County } Anno Dom 1783

Ordered that John Smith Deliver a Negroe Man by Name of Jack to the Sheriff, the said Negroe was put in his Charge some years past by the County Court of Chowan, and the Sheriff Sell the said Negroe at Publick Sale for Six Months Credited Taking Bond with appreved Security
Test, James Blount, CCC
Issued 1st day of June 1783

Acct. of Sale of Negroe Jack, 1783

Acct of the Sale of Negro Jack Sold at Vendue on the 28th Day of August 1783 By Order of the Worshipfull Court of Chowan County.

Negro Jack --- To Mr. Francis Hardy £152.10

Comm --- at 2/ P.Ct. £3.16.3 } 4.12.3
Cash for Punch to Mr. Gray -16- }
Net Amount £147.17.9
Ed. Blount, Sheriff

****

Hiring of Slaves

March ye 25th 1760
Nathaniel Matthias to Hire of Negro Dick one year att £9 proclamation money.

To the Intrest for Sd. money Two years £1 : 1 10.1
1:10
8:11
Credits by £1:6:8 money Sent by John Hunter
To four Shillings for feriage makes 1:10
Errors Excepted

Sarah Hunter Personally Appeared before me this day and made Oath on the Holy Evengelist of Almighty God that the above accompt is Just and True
July ye 16th 1763
Elisha Hunter

****

Hiring of Slaves

Mr Peter Copland Dr.
To Samuel Swift

1760
To hire of a Negro Girl Esther from the 29th of July to the 10th of November ----- 104 days £5.4.0

****

Chowan County
Miscellaneous Records

Hiring of Slaves

Peter Johnston to Henry Bonner	Dr
To the Hire of a Negro boy Year @ 35	£1.17.4
Virginia Currency Pr Year in proclamation	
To the hire of a Negro girl 4 months @ 38	12.8
P year & pay her leveys	
To Your Part of her Leveys	4.8
	£2.14.8
Cr Sundrys	£-3-
	2.11.8

Chapter Four

Chowan County

Miscellaneous Records - CRX

North Carolina State Archives
CRX Miscellaneous Records, Box #4
Chowan County, North Carolina
1699- 1865

State Vs. Negroe Grainge
Criminal Action [1783]
Inciting Slaves to Murder
Chowan County Records

To the Sheriff of Chowan County, Greeting

You are hereby Authorized and Ordered to Summon Three Justices of the Peace for said for said County & Four Freeholders, Owners of Slaves to meet at the Court House on Monday the first day of December next at the Hour of Ten Oclock in the forenoon, in order to hold a Court for the Trial of Negroe Grainge the property of Jennings Baker of Virginia for the attrocious Crime of endeavouring to stir up the Slaves for the Diabolical purpose of Murdering their Masters and Mistresses, and for so doing this

shall be your Sufficient Authority Given under my hand at Edenton this 30th day of Novr. 1783
Michl. Payne, JP

State of North Carolina }
Chowan County }

The Justices & Freeholders, as Ordered above to be Summoned met at the Court House in Edenton on the Tryal of Negro Grainge the Property of Jennings Baker of Virginia, December 1st 1783, Present

Thomas Benbury }
Charles Johnson } Esqrs Justices
Michael Payne }

William Bennett }
William Littlejohn }
George Gray } Freeholders
John Mushrom }

The Court Accordingly Qualified agreeable to the several Acts of Assembly & Proceed to Tryal & On Examining the Testimony The Court Do Adjudge & Pass Sentence that the said Grainge, shall have Both his Ears Cut off, & have two hundred Stripes well laid on his Bare Back, at the Gards Jale

Tho Benbury, Chas Johnson, Michl. Payne, Geo Gray, John Mushrowe, William Bennett & Wm. Littlejohn

****

Presentment, Grand Jury of Chowan
Emancipation of the Blacks, 1795

North Carolina } December Term 1795
Chowan County }

The Jurors for the State & County aforesaid present that the Country is reduced to a situation of great peril & Danger in Consequence of the

Chowan County
Miscellaneous Records - CRX

Proceedings of the Society of People called Quakers -- That the idea of Emancipation amongst Slaves is Publicly held out to them & encouraged by the Conduct of the Quakers -- that the minds of the Slaves are not only greatly corrupted & alienated from the Service of their Masters, But run aways are protected, harboured & encouraged by them Arsons are Committed without a possibility of Discovery.

The Grand Jury are so perfectly sensible of the infatuated enthusiasm of the Quakers as to partial & General Emancipation, that they see a present alarm amongst the minds of the people & forsee a prospect of eminent Danger to impend by the influence & disguising attempt of the Quakers to this purpose which unless prevented in due time must burst with destruction around the Citizens of the State.

The Grand Jury reflecting upon the miserable havoc & Massacre which have lately taken place in the West [?] in Consequence of Emancipation; knowing the opinion of the Northern States; of the many hundred there and Slaves around them; & of the infatuated enthusiasm of Men calling themselves religious, who are amongst them, conceive it a duty which they owe to themselves, their familys & their Country to present this existing & alarming evil & to present the people called Quakers & their Abettors as the authors of the common Mischief in this quarter of the State where independent of foreign Opinion; emancipation is publickly held out by the Quakers to the Negroes & private funds established in support of it.

The Grand Jury present that speedy & resolute Measures ought to be adopted by the good sense & Spirit of the people, in order to prevent that common appeal to arms in their own Defense, which at present appears to be almost, if not altogether necessary.

John Little, Foreman, James Bond, Wm. Jones, Robert Egan, Willis Wilder, James Woodward, Wm Goodwin, Joshua White, Chs. Laughrey, .Masan Miller, Josiah Hurdell, JP Faricaults, John Backam.

****

Negro Welcomes Petition for Emancipation
To March Term 1800

State of North Carolina } March Term 1800
Chowan County }

Chowan County
Miscellaneous Records - CRX

To the Worshipful County Court of Pleas and Quarter Sessions for the County aforesaid.

Humbly Complaining Sheweth to Your Worships, Your Petitioner Reuben Long, That your Petitioner is possessed of a Certain Negro Man Slave Named Welcome, who has Served Your Petitioner for many Years Past with great honesty, Fidelity, and Industry, and that his general Conduct and past Services of the said Slave Is desirous of having him Emancipated, and Prays that Your Worships will extend to him the benefits of the Act of Assembly in such care made and Provided.

And your Petitioner as in duty bound shall ever Pray &c

Reuben Long
John R McThey

We whose names are hereunto Subscribed do Certify that we have long known Negro Welcome at present the Property of Mr. Reuben Long, and that he has always as far as we know or believe Behaved himself as a faithful and Industrious Slave, and that his general Conduct has been highly Meritorious, we therefore take the Liberty to recommend him to the Worshipful the Justices of the County Court of Pleas and Quarter Sessions of the County of Chowan as a Proper Object of Emancipation, and which we Submit to their Consideration.
15 day of February 1800

Michl. Payne the oldest, Jas. Hathaway, Thos. Bissell, Wm. Rombough, John Little, Alexr Millen, Saml. Tredwell, Myles O Malley, Honore Neil, Joseph Bozman, Henry Cheshire, Thomas **[Faded],** Reuben Long, John Russel McThey, Wm. Satterfield, Chas. Roberts, Saml. Hoskins, John Fife, Fredr. **[Faded],** John Beasley, Geo. Wilkinson, Thos **[Faded],** Wm Carter, Thos Satterfield, Hendn. Standin, Jno Cheshire, J. B. Williams, Geo Morgan, Charles Sanders, John Luten, W. Slade, Edward **[Faded],** Stephen **[Faded],** Thomas Dunkin, Henry **[?],** Peter P. Laurence, Francis **[Faded],** Sam Butler, Thos. Iredell, Edmd Hoskins

****

State Vs. Negroe Titus
Criminal Action [1785]
Breaking out of Jail
Chowan County Records

Chowan County
Miscellaneous Records - CRX

Trial of Negroe Titus
July 26th 1785

State of North Carolina }
Chowan County }

At a Court Called & held at the Court House in Edenton on Tuesday the 26th day of July 1785 for the trial of a negroe Slave called Titus the Property of Mr. Josiah Collins for breaking open the publick Goal of Sd. County & letting out several prisoners therein confined

Present
Samuel Dickinson }
Michael Payne } Esqrs Justices
Joseph Blount }

William Bennett }
William Righton } Freeholders
Joseph Whidbee } Owners of Slaves
Michael McTheil }

After Examining the Evidence do adjudge and order that the Constable carry the said Negroe Titus to the Public Whipping Post and there give One Hundred Lashes on his Bare Back & to have his ears cutt off.

L. Dickinson, Michl. Payne, Jos. Blount, Wm. Righton, Willm. Bennett, Joseph Whedbee & Michael McTheil.

****

Coroner's Inquest

State of North Carolina }
Bertie County }

Inquisition Indented,
Taken at the House of Samuel Maer, in the County aforesaid, the Eighth Day of May in the Year of our Lord one Thousand Seven hundred & Ninety six, before me Benjn. Williams one of the States Coroners for the

Sd. County, upon View of the Body of Negro Sarah late the property of Samuel Maer of the State and County aforesaid, then and there lying Dead; and upon the Oath of Thomas Rasco, Edmund Dunstone, William Yeats, William Smithwick, John Smithwick, Alexander Legett, Abraham Avis, John Reed, Stephen Soans, James Rasco, Matthew Willey, Solomon Weston, Luke Warburton, Thomas Ryan, Edward Ryan, John Johnston, and Peter Yeats, good and Lawfull men of the Parish of Society in the said County who being Charged & Sworn to Enquire how, and in what manner, the Sd. Negro Sarah by her Death Came; upon their Oaths, do say that on the Sixth Day of said year and month afsd. The said Negro Sarah was brought home to her said Master from being Runaway. Her Sd. Master, gave her some Correction and During which time she resisted her said Master very much which occasioned her to be very much fatigued and then Sd. Sarah went into a Millpond and washed her head and feet in Cold water whilst in a very great prespiration which we Expect Caused a sudden stagnation of the Blood and Caused a sudden appoplex to Ensue and the next day Expired, which act we the said Jurors do term a Mischance in Testimony whereof, as well & the said Coroner; as the Jurors aforesaid, to this Inquisition have severally put our Seals, the Day, Year, and place first above mentioned.
Stephan Soans, Jas. Rascoe, Matthias Willey, Solomon Weston, Luke Warburton, Thos. Ryan, Edward Ryan, John Johnston, Benjn. Williams, Coroner, Thos Rascoe, Ed Dunston, William Yeats, Wm. Smithwick, John Smithwick, Alex Legett, Abraham Avis, John Reed & Peter Yeats.

****

State Vs. Negro Juba
Criminal Action [1780]
Felony
Chowan County Records

Chowan County Court Orders

State of North Carolina } November 13th Anno Dom 1780
Chowan County }

At a Court Called & held on Tryal, on Negro Juba for a felony the property of Joseph Underhill esqr.

Present the Worshipfull
Thomas Bonner }
William Hoskins }
Edward Vail }Gentlemen Freeholders
George Gray }

The Court accordingly Proceeded on the Tryal of the Prisoner Juba & it is Ordered that the Sheriff of the said County take the aforesaid Prisoner to the Publick Whipping post & there Nail his Ears thereto & sever them from his head & then to have one hundred Stripes well laid on his Bare Back.
Thos Bonner, Tho Benbury, Michl. Payne, Wm. Littlejohn, Geo Gray, Willm. Hoskins & Edwd Vail.

Appendix A
Glossary of Legal Terms

Appendix A

Glossary of Legal Terms

[Definition of legal terms appearing in transcriptions within this book are derived from *Black's Law Dictionary*.]

A & B (Assault & Battery): The unlawful touching of another individual without excuse or justification.

Action of Trover: A remedy to recover the value of personal property wrongfully converted by another person or persons to his own use.

Affiant: An individual who creates and subscribes an affidavit. Interchangeable with deponent.

Agent: An individual authorized by another to act in place of another person.

Alias Capias: The issuance of a second writ.

Assignee: An individual who receives an assignment. An individual whom the law vests the right; Executor or Administrator.

Attachment: The legal seizing of someones property to comply with a writ or judicial order to satisfy a judgment not yet rendered.

Atrix: Female Plaintiff.

Appendix A
Glossary of Legal Terms

Bailiwick: A given area over which a bailiff or sheriff has authority or jurisdiction.

Calaboose: An old term for jail or prison. From the Spanish word, "*calabozo*."

Capias: A general name for different types of writs requiring an officer to detain someone in custody.

Certiori: A writ issued by a superior court to an inferior court for the purpose of an investigation into irregularities.

Commission: A warrant issued by a government empowering an individual to do certain acts.

Commissioner: An individual to whom a commission is directed by a government or a court.

Decree: In equity, a sentence or order of the court after considering the case.

Deposition: A pretrial discovery method by which one party, through their attorney asks oral questions of the other party.

Dimunition of the Record: A phrase stating that the record delivered from an inferior court to a superior court for review is incomplete.

Determination: A decision given by a court implying an ending of a controversy or suit.

Enfeoff: A gift of hereditaments to another.

Equity Courts: Courts that deliver justice according to the system of equity. Equity courts are sometimes called, "Courts of Chancery."

Esquire: A title given to sheriffs, justices of the peace, and barristers at law.

Et als: Latin term meaning "and others."

Appendix A
Glossary of Legal Terms

Ex Parte: Done for, or on the application of, one party only.

Execution: The carrying out of an act to its completion.

Exemplifications: An official transcript or certified copy of a document retrieved from public records to be used as evidence.

False Imprisonment: An individual who is placed in detention without his consent, and without lawful authority.

Fi Fa (Fieri Facias): A writ requiring a sheriff to satisfy a judgment levied from a debtors property.

Forma Execution: The prescribed form of execution..

Forma Pauperis: A provision made for a poor person to have their day in court without liability for fees or costs.

Free Persons of Color: Term applied to all persons not part of the white race, including Indians.

F.W.C.: Free woman of color: Term applied to all persons not part of the white race, including Indians. The term was not used much after the Civil War.

Goal (Gaol): An obsolete English term for prison or Jail.

Guardian: An individual invested with power for caring for someone who is incapable of handling their own affairs.

Guardian ad litem: A special guardian appointed by the Court to represent an infant or unborn person.

Gaurnished: A furnishing or garnishment.

Hue & Cry: A loud outcry to pursue felons (robbers and murderers), and all who heard it were bound to join in the pursuit.

Habeas Corpus: A writ commonly directed to a sheriff ordering him to deliver a prisoner, or an individual who is to be detained. The purpose is to test the legality of the detention, and not whether the individual is guilty or innocent

Inops Consilli: Without legal counsel.

Injunction: A court order prohibiting an individual from committing a certain act, or ordering an individual to undo an injury.

Indenture: A contract by which bonds and debentures are issued stating the form of bond, maturity date, amount of issue, descriptions of assets, interest rates and various other terms.

Inquest: An inquisition by a coroner, sometimes accompanied by a jury to investigate the death of someone who has been killed, or died under suspicious circumstances.

Next Friend: An individual who acts for the benefit of an infant; or a person who is not able to look after his own business or interests. It is similar to guardian ad litem.

Ne Exeat: A writ that forbids an individual to flee the country, state or jurisdiction of the court.

Nol Pros (Nolle Prosequi): The prosecuting attorney will no longer prosecute the case.

Non Compus Mentes: Incompetent, or not of sound mind.

Non Suit: A judgment against the plaintiff when he is unable to prove his case.

Outlaw: In English law, an individual who has been banned from the protection of the law.

Partition: The dividing of lands owned by joint tenants or tenants in common.

Prima Facie: A fact supposedly to be true unless disproved by evidence to the contrary.

Appendix A
Glossary of Legal Terms

Recognizance: An obligation of an individual, before a magistrate, that he will perform some act required by law.

Referee: An individual who is referred by the court in a cause pending to listen to the testimony and parties involved and return a report to the court.

Replevin: A legal action giving the owner or person entitled the right to repossession of property from someone who has wrongfully taken or detains his property.

Subpoena: An order to appear at a specific time to testify upon a matter.

Solicitor: The chief law officer in a government body.

Special Venire: To appear in court, or citizens from whom a jury is selected. A Special Venire is usually called for a protracted case.

Surety: An individual who is primarily liable for payment of debt, or for the performance of obligation of another.

Statute of Limitations: Statutes of the Federal Government and States that set a given amount of time for which certain actions can be brought forth.

Severalty: Individuals who own real or personal property without other persons sharing in the ownership.

Struck Off: In the language of an auctioneer, by the fall of his hammer, property is to be "Struck Off," which signifies the bidder is entitled to property after paying for it.

Scifa: Abbreviation for "Scire Facias."

Scire Facias: A judicial writ requiring a debtor to appear and show cause why judgment against him should not be revived. An order to show cause why mortgaged property should not be sold to satisfy a debt.

Slave: An individual who has no freedom and is subject to another in whole. His person and services are completely under the control of another. He belongs to his Master, and his industry and labor are not his own. His Master may sell or dispose of his person.

Appendix A
Glossary of Legal Terms

True Bill of Indictment: An endorsement issued by a grand jury upon finding sufficient evidence for a criminal charge.

Trespass: The unlawful interference with another's rights or property.

Tenants in Common: Tenants who hold the same property (including Slaves) together by several and distinct titles.

Trustee: An individual who is chosen or appointed by law to execute a Trust.

Testamentary Trustee: An individual chosen or appointed to fulfill or carry out a trust created by a Will.

Tax District: A district to which a tax is ratably apportioned, and levied upon its population.

Venditioni Exponas: In Latin - You expose to sale. The sale is usually directed by the sheriff.

Venire Facias: A writ directed to the sheriff to command that he cause twelve good and lawful men to come to court on a given day to serve as jurors.

Vi et Armis: The use of Force and Arms.

Writ: A judicial order that is written for a specific act, or giving power to another to have it done.

Writ of Detinue: An order to recover, in specie, the property or chattels from an individual who acquired them lawfully, but retains the property without lawful right.

Writ of Venire: A command to appear in court, or citizens from whom a jury is selected.

Appendix A
Glossary of Legal Terms

Writ of Replevin: An order giving the owner or person entitled the right to repossession of property from someone who has wrongfully taken or detains his property.[3]

[3] Henry Campbell, M.A., ***Black's Law Dictionary***, 6th ed. (St. Paul, Minn.: West Publishing Company, 1990.)

Table of Cases

Civil and Criminal Actions

Cases

Ann Anderson Vs Samuel Kerr
Civil Action [1782]
Chowan County Records ________ 30

Beasley & Norcom Vs. Eliza Gray
Civil Action [1813]
Chowan County Records ________ 219

Beasley's Executor Vs. John Haughton
Civil Action [1818]
Chowan County Records ________ 294

Benj. Coffield & Fred Creecy Vs. John Dickinson
Civil Action [1810]
Chowan County Records ________ 140

Benjamin & John Coffield Vs. Thomas Vail
Civil Action [1810]
Chowan County Records ________ 144

Benjamin Coffield Vs. James W. Langley
Civil Action [1808]
Chowan County Records ________ 98

Table of Cases
Civil and Criminal Actions

Benjamin Coffield Vs. John B. Bennet
Civil Action [1802]
Chowan County Records ________________ 51

Benjamin Coffield Vs. Josiah Skinner
Civil Action [1808]
Chowan County Records ________________ 104

Benjamin Coffield Vs. Norman King
Civil Action [1811]
Chowan County Records ________________ 183

Benners Vail Vs William Blair
Civil Action [1810]
Chowan County Records ________________ 134

Caleb Winslow Vs. James Sowell
Civil Actions [1807]
Chowan County Records ________________ 78

Charles Roberts Vs. Arthur Howe
Civil Action [1807]
Chowan County Records ________________ 54

Charles Roberts, Sheriff Vs. Negro Dick
Civil Action [1801]
Chowan County Records ________________ 49

Clendening & Adams Vs. Henry A. Donaldson
Civil Action [1810]
Chowan County Records ________________ 155

Clerk Vs. Thomas Waff
Civil Action [1819]
Chowan County Records ________________ 306

Cross Vs. Mumford
Civil Action [1809]
Chowan County Records ________________ 116

Table of Cases
Civil and Criminal Actions

Cullen Cotton Vs. Lewis Powell
Civil Action [1814]
Chowan County Records ____________ 254

Daniel Leggett Vs. Joel Moon
Civil Action [1811]
Chowan County Records ____________ 184

Daniel McClannen Vs. John B. Griffin
Civil Actions [1804]
Chowan County Records ____________ 57

Edward Tilghman Vs. James Granbery
Civil Action [1803]
Chowan County Records ____________ 55

Edwin Lisles Vs. John B. Hunter
Civil Actions [1807]
Chowan County Records ____________ 63

Elizabeth Patterson Vs. Michael McKeel
Civil Action [1791]
Chowan County Records ____________ 33

Elliot Vs. Stallings
Civil Action [1810]
Chowan County Records ____________ 142

Enoch Sawyer Vs. John McCottor
Civil Action [1819]
Chowan County Records ____________ 302

Frederick Creecy Vs. Thomas Vail
Civil Action [1811]
Chowan County Records ____________ 191

Gardner Vs. Dickinson
Civil Action [1811]
Chowan County Records ____________ 157

Table of Cases
Civil and Criminal Actions

Gray & Blount Vs. James Langley
Civil Action [1808]
Chowan County Records ______ 103

Henry A. Donaldson Vs. Charles Haughton
Civil Action [1811]
Chowan County Records ______ 175

Henry Gilliam Vs. Thomas Vail et als
Civil Action [1812]
Chowan County Records ______ 206

Henry Harramond Vs. Daniel Young
Civil Action [1796]
Chowan County Records ______ 42

Henry Wills Vs William Blair
Civil Action [1810]
Chowan County Records ______ 127

Herbert Pride Vs. John Drew the Elder ______ 87

Icabod Jordan Vs. Levendure
Civil Action [1798]
Chowan County Records ______ 45

J.B. Skinner Vs. Wm. Gregory
Civil Action [1812]
Chowan County Records ______ 201

Jackson Hoyle Vs John Dickinson
Civil Action [1809]
Chowan County Records ______ 112

James Jackson Vs. Nathaniel Bond
Civil Action [1814]
Chowan County Record ______ 231

Table of Cases
Civil and Criminal Actions

James Jackson Vs. Nathaniel Bond
Civil Action [1813]
Chowan County Records ______ 221

James Ming Vs. Thomas Saterfield
Civil Action [1810]
Chowan County Records ______ 141

James Saterfield Vs. John Norcom et als
Civil Action [1811]
Chowan County Records ______ 171

James W. Langley Vs. Edward Reily
Civil Action [1811]
Chowan County Records ______ 174

Job Parker Vs. Reuben Small
Civil Action [1810]
Chowan County Records ______ 147

John B. Blount & als Vs. Boon Felton
Civil Action [1819]
Chowan County Records ______ 313

John B. Blount Vs. Abner Harrell
Civil Action [1819]
Chowan County Records ______ 314

John B. Blount Vs. George Williams
Civil Action [1819]
Chowan County Records ______ 308

John B. Blount Vs. Howell Jones
Civil Action [1819]
Chowan County Records ______ 310

John B. Blount Vs. James Spiers
Civil Action [1819]
Chowan County Records ______ 324

Table of Cases
Civil and Criminal Actions

John B. Blount Vs. Nathaniel Bissell
Civil Action [1819]
Chowan County Records ______ 311

John Coffield Vs. Abner Vail
Civil Action [1816]
Chowan County Records ______ 268

John Coffield Vs. Jesse Hassell
Civil Action [1810]
Chowan County Records ______ 120

John Haughton Vs. Thomas Vail
Civil Action [1810]
Chowan County Records ______ 119

John Little &. John W. Littlejohn Vs. John Bond & als
Civil Action [1819]
Chowan County Records ______ 325

John McCottor Vs Thomas Myers et als
Civil Action [1819]
Chowan County Records ______ 317

John McCottor Vs. Thomas Myers & Allen Laseter
Civil Action [1819]
Chowan County Records ______ 305

John Oxley Vs. David Gaskins et als
Civil Action [1807]
Chowan County Records ______ 59

John Robinson Vs. Henry O'Neal
Civil Actions [1782]
Chowan County Records ______ 27

John Vs. John Johnston
Civil Action [1797]
Chowan County Records ______ 44

Table of Cases
Civil and Criminal Actions

Jordan Vs. Winham
Civil Actions [1757]
Chowan County Records ____ 23

Joseph B. Skinner Vs James & William Jones
Civil Action [1814]
Chowan County Records ____ 233

Joseph B. Skinner Vs. Henry A. Donaldson als
Civil Action [1810]
Chowan County Records ____ 154

Joseph Blount Vs James Hathaway
Civil Action [1808]
Chowan County Records ____ 107

Joseph Bozman Vs. Wm. Slade & als
Civil Action [1812]
Chowan County Records ____ 204

Joseph Bryan Vs. Nathaniel Bissell
Civil Action [1812]
Chowan County Records ____ 208

Joseph Manning Vs James R. Bent
Civil Action [1817]
Chowan County Records ____ 283

Josiah Collins Junr. Vs. William Jones
Civil Action [1818]
Chowan County Records ____ 290

Josiah Collins Vs. Arthur Howe
Civil Action [1807]
Chowan County Records ____ 60

Josiah Collins Vs. John Leary Jr.
Civil Action [1807]
Chowan County Records ____ 76

Table of Cases
Civil and Criminal Actions

Josiah Collins Vs. John McCrae et als
Civil Actions 1807]
Chowan County Records ______ 94

Josiah Collins, Jr. Vs. Louis Leroy et als
Civil Action [1817]
Chowan County Records ______ 279

Knox Vs. Johnson et als
Civil Action [1811]
Chowan County Records ______ 177

Lewis Bond Vs. Benajah Nicholls et als
Civil Actions [1807]
Chowan County Records ______ 67

Lewis Bond Vs. Reuben Small
Civil Action [1809]
Chowan County Records ______ 110

Littlejohn Blount Vs. Lewis Bond
Civil Action [1808]
Chowan County Records ______ 96

Margaret Norfleet Vs. James Jones
Civil Action [1809]
Chowan County Records ______ 113

Mason Miller Vs. Honore Neil
Civil Action [1800]
Chowan County Records ______ 48

McCotter & Muil Vs. John Dickinson
Civil Action [1811]
Chowan County Records ______ 172

Nathan Creecy Vs. Simion Simons
Civil Actions [1807]
Chowan County Records ______ 95

Table of Cases
Civil and Criminal Actions

Nathaniel Brinn Vs. Jethro Benton et als
Civil Actions [1802]
Chowan County Records ____ 53

Nehemiah Batemans Vs. William Rombough
Civil Action [1804]
Chowan County Records ____ 56

Nixen Carter & Co. Vs. John Shaw als
Civil Action [1810]
Chowan County Records ____ 151

Officers of the Court Vs Michael Wilder
Civil Action [1818]
Chowan County Records ____ 299

Officers of the Court Vs. Mills Hill
Civil Action [1818]
Chowan County Records ____ 300

Officers of the Court Vs. Norman King
Civil Action [1813]
Chowan County Records ____ 212

Officers of the Court Vs. William Hurdle
Civil Action [1818]
Chowan County Records ____ 301

Officers Vs. Evans et als
Civil Action [1809]
Chowan County Records ____ 114

Officers Vs. John McFarland et als
Civil Action [1807]
Chowan County Records ____ 61

Officers Vs. Samuel McGuire et als
Civil Action [1813]
Chowan County Records ____ 211

Table of Cases
Civil and Criminal Actions

Phillip McGuire & Benjamin Coffield Vs. John Dickinson
Civil Action [1808]
Chowan County Records ________________ 99

Rachael Hare Vs. Henry Gilliam
Civil Action [1819]
Chowan County Records ________________ 326

Reuben Small Vs. Samuel McGuire
Civil Action [1811]
Chowan County Records ________________ 178

Richard Baker & J. Coffield Vs. Isaac Baker et als
Civil Action [1813]
Chowan County Records ________________ 198

Richard Wood Vs. Josiah Flowers et als
Civil Action [1819]
Chowan County Records ________________ 320

Robert Bowne Vs. Reuben Small
Civil Action [1810]
Chowan County Records ________________ 121

Robert Jordan Vs. Samuel Dickinson
Civil Action [1806]
Chowan County Records ________________ 58

Rogers & Lambert Vs. J.W. Langley et als
Civil Action [1812]
Chowan County Records ________________ 203

Samuel Hyman Vs. William Slade
Civil Action [1811]
Chowan County Records ________________ 189

Samuel Tredwell Vs. James W. Langley
Civil Action [1811]
Chowan County Records ________________ 162

Table of Cases
Civil and Criminal Actions

Sarah Hoskins Vs. William Badham
Civil Action [1799]
Chowan County Records ____________ 47

Sawyer & Norcom Vs. Joseph Sutton
Civil Action [1818]
Chowan County Records ____________ 293

Smith Vs. Jeffreys
Civil Action [1795]
Chowan County Records ____________ 41

Solomon King Vs. Daniel Marshal
Civil Action [1759]
Chowan County Records ____________ 25

State Vs. Isaac, a Negro
Criminal Action [1797]
Chowan County Records
Taken up as Emancipated ____________ 11

State Vs. Negro John
Criminal Action [1787]
Chowan County Records
Murder ____________ 4

State Vs. William Jackson
Criminal Action [1817]
Chowan County Records
Crime not Given ____________ 20

State Vs. Bet, a Slave
Criminal Action [1796]
Chowan County Records
Arson ____________ 11

State Vs. Daniel Leary
Criminal Action [1794]
Chowan County Records
Assault ____________ 6

Table of Cases
Civil and Criminal Actions

State Vs. Elizabeth Plummer
Criminal Action [1785]
Chowan County Records
Trading with a Slave ______ 4

State Vs. Henry D. Watson
Criminal Action [1783]
Chowan County Records
Selling Liquor to a Slave ______ 2

State Vs. Jacob Dowdey
Criminal Action [1783]
Chowan County Records
Trading with a Negro ______ 3

State Vs. Negro Dick
Criminal Action [1800]
Chowan County Records
Taken up as Emancipated ______ 13

State Vs. Negro Frank
Criminal Action [1782]
Chowan County Records
Felony (Assault) ______ 2

State Vs. Negro Jack
Criminal Action [1814]
Chowan County Records
Hiring his own Time ______ 19

State Vs. Negro Juba
Criminal Action
Felony
Chowan County Records ______ 352

State Vs. Negro Peter
Criminal Action [1797]
Chowan County Records
Hiring his own Time ______ 12

Table of Cases
Civil and Criminal Actions

State Vs. Negro Rages
Criminal Action [1794]
Chowan County Records
Breaking & Entering ____ 7

State Vs. Negro Sam
Criminal Action [1777]
Chowan County Records
Felony ____ 1

State Vs. Negro Toney
Criminal Action [1812]
Chowan County Records
Felony ____ 17

State Vs. Negro Will
Criminal Action [1800]
Chowan County Records
Felony ____ 15

State Vs. Negroe Grainge
Criminal Action [1783]
Inciting Slaves to Murder
Chowan County Records ____ 347

State Vs. Negroe Titus
Criminal Action [1785]
Breaking out of Jail
Chowan County Records ____ 350

State Vs. Negroes July, Jack & James
Criminal Action [1790]
Chowan County Records
Breaking & Entering ____ 5

State Vs. Rufus Stafford
Criminal Actions [1795]
Chowan County Records
Trading with Slaves ____ 7

Table of Cases
Civil and Criminal Actions

State Vs. Thomas Simmons
Criminal Action [1795]
Petty Larceny ________ 8

Stephen Smith Vs. William Harris
Civil Action [1811]
Chowan County Records ________ 180

Swift Vs. Copland
Civil Action [1760]
Chowan County Records ________ 24

Thomas Coffield Vs. Sarah Elliot
Civil Action [1814]
Chowan County Records ________ 237

Thomas Harramond Vs. James De Camp
Civil Action [1791]
Chowan County Records ________ 39

Thomas Harramond Vs. William McDonald
Civil Action [1790]
Chowan County Records ________ 32

Thomas Saterfield Vs. James Bond
Civil Action [1808]
Chowan County Records ________ 109

Thomas Stewart Vs. John Drew et als
Civil Action [1808]
Chowan County Records ________ 108

Thomas White Vs. Woolsy Hathaway
Civil Action [1817]
Chowan County Records ________ 278

Unknown Vs. Unknown
Civil Action [1798]
Chowan County Records ________ 46

Table of Cases
Civil and Criminal Actions

William Coffield Vs. George Bozman
Civil Action [1819]
Chowan County Records ________________ 307

William Gregory Vs. John B. Hunter et als
Civil Actions [1807]
Chowan County Records ________________ 68

William Littlejohn Vs. Moses Sumner
Civil Action [1809]
Chowan County Records ________________ 117

William Littlejohn Vs. Richard Michalls
Civil Action [1781]
Chowan County Records ________________ 26

William Saunders & Nathan Creecy Vs. Townsend Elliot
Civil Action [1808]
Chowan County Records ________________ 101

William Shaw Vs. John Norcom
Civil Action [1807]
Chowan County Records ________________ 93

William Wilson & Co. Vs Thomas C. Ferebe
Civil Action [1807]
Chowan County Records ________________ 77

Wm. Jackson Vs. Nathaniel Bond
Civil Action [1812]
Chowan County Records ________________ 199

Wm. Thompson & als Vs. Thomas Small als
Civil Action [1812]
Chowan County Records ________________ 205

Wood & Hastings Vs. James Jones et als
Civil Action [1816]
Chowan County Records ________________ 272

Index

A

Alexander
Edmund, DShff, 294, 295
Henry, Shff, 323
Allen
Nathaniel, Esquire, 3, 4
Nathl, 6
Nathl., Esqr., 5
Allens
Nathl., 171
Anderson
Anne, 30
Mrs. Ann, 31
Armistead
Mr., 43
Mr. John, 43
Arnestead
Mr. John, 71
Ashburn
B., Shff, 188
Baldy, 185, 187
Baldy, Shff, 260
William, 67
Ashley
Delilah, 305
Askew
Eliza, 276
Avis
Abraham, 352

B

Bacchies
Josiah, 229
Backam
John, 349
Badham
Mr. William, 47
William, 47
Bahama Islands, 44
Bailey
Gab., 62
Gabl., Shff, 152
Bailley
Gabl., Shff, 153
Baker
Isaac, 198, 199
Jennings, 348
Jennings of Virginia, 347
Richard, 198, 199
Richd, 198
Barker
Penelpoe, 6
Barnes
Richd, 144
Barrett
Henery P., 17
Barritz
William, Esqr., 5
William, Esquire, 342
Wm., 6
Bartia
John, 184
Bateman
Daniel, 268
Batemans
Nehemiah, 56, 57
Beasley
Docter, 61
Docter John, 55
Elisabeth, 227
Jn., 211
Jno. B., 298
John, 5, 210, 211, 350
Jos, Foreman, 6
Tho, 228
Thos., 228
Beasley & Norcom, 219, 220
Beasley's Executors, 297
Beasly
J., 322
Jno, DShff, 323, 324
Beckley
M., 111

Index

Benbury
Tho, 348, 353
Thomas, 348
Bennett
Henry, 19
Henry P., 200
Jno. B., 52
John, 51
John B., 51
Mr. John B., 52
William, 348, 351
Willm., 351
Bent
J R, 286
J.R., Shff, 301, 304, 328, 329
Ja R, 287
Ja R, Shff, 318
Ja R., 288
Ja. R., 286, 287, 288
Ja. R., Shff, 268, 302, 307, 318, 319, 325, 327
James R, 283, 284
James R., 141, 283, 284, 286, 287
James R., Shff, 215, 217, 218, 237, 238, 239, 262, 317
Jas R., 286
Jas. R., 141, 289, 290, 311
Jas. R., Shff, 330
JR, 285
JR, Shff, 300, 301
Benton
Jethro, 53
Miles, 53
Bertee
Eli, 222
Bethel Meeting House, 244, 245
Bissell
Charles, 210, 211
N.C., 208, 209
Nath C., 211
Nathaniel C, 209, 211, 312
Nathaniel C., 209, 210, 312
Nathl C, 210
Nathl. C., 311
Thos., 350
Black
Alex, 6
Alexander, 5
Alexr, 6
Mr., 33, 40, 42
Mr. Samuel, 43
Mrs., 33
Samuel, 33, 40, 42
Blair
Mr., 65, 130, 177
W., 73
Will, 129
Will, Clerk, 44
Will, Clk, 60, 62, 64, 66, 68, 69, 78, 88, 89, 90, 91
William, 64, 117, 128, 129, 130, 131, 132, 133, 134, 135, 136, 137, 138, 139, 140
William, Clerk, 60, 62, 66, 68, 69, 78, 88, 89, 90, 91
William, Esqr, 128, 129, 130, 134, 135, 136
Willm., 39
Wm, 93
Wm., 71, 72, 74, 76, 109, 116, 128, 136
Wm., Esqr, 134
Blauer
Mr, 58
Mr., 58
Blount
Ed, Shff, 343, 344
Ed., 38
Ed., Shff, 26, 28
Edmd, 6, 342
Edmund, 342, 343
Edmund, Esqr., 5
Jacob, 11, 342, 343
James, CCC, 27, 343
James, Clerk, 28
James, Clk, 28
Jas., Clerk, 30
Jas., Clk, 28, 29
Jesse, 13
Jno, 61
Jno B., 324
Jno. B., 314
John B, 141, 309, 311, 312, 313, 315, 316, 324
John B., 141, 309, 310, 311, 312, 313, 314, 315, 316, 324, 325
John Gray, 281
John Grey, 282
John L., 185
Jon, 185
Jos, 6, 108
Jos, Clk, 36
Jos., 40, 342, 343, 351
Jos., Clk, 32
Joseph, 3, 107, 351

Index

Joseph, Clerk, 34, 36, 39
Littlejohn, 97
Mr., 12, 96
Mr. Edmund, 38
Mr. Jno., 16
will, 245
Will, 244, 245, 246, 247
William, Esqr, 243

Bond
Col. John, 17
Henry, DShff, 5
James, 109, 110
James, Foreman, 349
Jas., 110
Jno, 18, 19
Jno M., 328
John, 112, 233, 325, 326
John M, 326
John M., 325, 326, 329
John, Prosecutor, 8
Lewis, 67, 97, 110, 111, 112, 223
Mary, 221
N., 199, 200, 201, 223
Nat, 221, 222, 223, 224, 225, 226, 227, 228, 229, 230, 231
Nat., 225, 226, 227, 229, 230, 232
Nath, 200
Nath., 201
Nathaniel, 224, 228, 231, 232, 233, 325, 326
Nathl, 201, 222, 224
Nathl., 221, 222
Richard, 206

Bonds
Richard, 206

Bonner
Henry, 345
Thomas, 353
Thos, 353

Boulton
Jona., 2
Jonathan, 2

Bowne
R H, 122
Robert H, 122, 123, 124, 125, 126, 127
Robert H., 121, 122, 123, 124, 125, 126, 127
Robt H., 126

Boyce
Harrison, 228
W.H., DShff, 9

Boyd
John, 152, 153, 317, 318

Bozman
George, 307, 308, 329
Jos., 287
Joseph, 204, 205, 287, 288, 350
William R., 186

Branch
Isacker, 9
John, 329, 330

Brice
Fanny, 40, 42
Nancy, 33, 40, 42, 43

Brick House
Plantation, 113

Brickhous
Matthew, 46

Brinkley
Eli, 241, 247, 249, 250, 253
Ely, 247

Brinn
Nathaniel, 53
Nathl., 53

Brittain
Wm., JP, 257

Britton
Wm., 258

Brooks
Eliza, 285, 289

Brown
Lewis, 50
Peter, Attorney, 50

Browrigg
Thomas, Esqr, 218

Bryan
Jos H, 210
Jos. H., 208, 209
Joseph H, 209, 210, 211
Joseph H., 210, 211

Bryands
A.S., 37

Buchies
Josiah, 229

Buckley
Moses, 112

Bull
Ethelred, 51

Bunch
M., 148
Micajah, 206
Mich, 151
Micj, 159

Bundey
Caleb, 11

Burns
Mr, 42

Mr., 33, 40, 42
Burrus
Jno, DShff, 329
Butler
Sam, 350
Saml, 6
Saml., 5
Samuell, 5
Bynum
William, 50, 51

C

Cabarrus
S., 4, 16
Stephen, 4
Stephen, Esquire, 4
Capt. Walk's Brig, 1
Carleton
J., 23
Carter
Dolly, 261
Isaac, 50, 258, 261, 263, 264, 266, 267, 291
Isaac, Shff, 257, 259, 260, 261
J, 266
J., Shff, 277
Nixen, 152, 153
Nixen R., 152
William, 5
Wm., 350
Chapman
Maria, 285, 290
Charleson
Tho T, 319
Charlton
J., Attorney, 24
Jasper, 24
Cheshire
Henry, 350
Jno, 350
Chester
Mr., 256
Clemons
John, 9
Clendening &
Adams, 154, 155, 156, 157
Clendining &
Adams, 156
Coakley
Wm. D., 321
Coffield
B., 144
Ben, 100, 141
Benj, 99, 100, 104, 105, 106
Benj., 52, 98, 99, 105, 106, 184
Benjamin, 51, 98, 99, 100, 105, 106, 140, 183
J, 216
J., 182, 198, 213, 214, 217
Jno, 213, 215
Jno., 174
John, 52, 101, 105, 120, 121, 123, 124, 125, 126, 127, 144, 174, 182, 200, 214, 215, 216, 238, 246, 247, 268, 269, 270, 271, 272
John, Senr., 17
Mr., 218
Mr. B., 52
Mr. John, 105
Mr. Thomas, 244, 245
T., 81, 82, 85, 86, 180
Tho, 86, 237, 238, 239, 240, 241, 242, 249, 250, 251, 252, 253, 254
Tho., 238, 239, 241
Thomas, 105, 239, 240, 242, 243, 244, 245, 248, 249, 251, 253, 254
Thos, 99, 100, 127, 199, 241, 245, 246, 247, 248
Thos., 178, 240, 242, 244
William, 307, 308
Wm., 308
Coffield’s
Jno., 219
Coffields
John, 244
Thos., 244
Cofield
John, 246
Thomas, 245
Thos, 245
Thos., 246
Cofields
John, 245
Thos., 245
Collins
Jos, 60
Jos, Junr., 280, 281
Jos., Junr, 290
Josiah, 61, 94, 95, 293
Josiah, Esqr., 5
Josiah, Junr., 76, 279, 280, 281, 282, 283, 290, 291, 292
Mr. Josiah, 351
Cooley

Mrs. Penelope, 5
Cooper
John, 273, 274, 275, 277
Copeland
Ja., Shff, 292
James, Shff, 309
Jas., Shff, 274, 309, 310, 313, 314, 316, 324
Copland
Jas., Shff, 236
Mr Peter, 344
Peter, 24, 25
Cottens
Cullen, 263
Cotter
John M, DShff, 287
John M, Shff, 286
Cotton
Cullen, 254, 255, 256, 257, 258, 259, 260, 261, 262, 263, 264, 267
Cullin, 256, 258
Goddin, 259, 261
Godwin, 50, 263, 267
Mr. Cullen, 255
Polly, 260
Cottor
John M, DShff, 288, 299
Creecy
Fred, 140, 192, 193, 194
Frederic, 192
Frederick, 141, 191, 192, 193, 194, 195, 196, 197, 198, 245
Fredk, 195
Fredr., 191
Fredrick, 191
Mr. William, 244
N., 101
Nathan, 96, 101, 102
William, 245
Creecys
Fredk, 244, 245
Cross
Edward, 116, 117
Edwd, 117
Reddick, DShff, 291
Richard, 117
Richard T, 117
Richard T., 116, 117
T., 117
Cumming
W., Attorney, 27

D

Darden
Carr, DShff, 309
Dawson
Penelope, 44
Deams
Jesse, DShff, 259
Deanes
Jesse, DShff, 260, 261
Matt, DShff, 277
Deans
Matt, DShff, 84, 85
Matt, Shff, 79, 80, 81
Thomas, 260
DeCamp
James, 39, 40, 42
Declughny
Marquis, 12
DeClughny
Marquis, 12
DeClugny
Marquis, 13
Demsey
Johnston, 59
Den
Jno, 45
Dickinson
Dr., 29
John, 99, 100, 112, 113, 140, 141, 157, 158, 160, 161, 172, 173, 192
L., 3, 351
Mrs. Eliz. P., 58
S., 4
Saml., 11, 58
Samuel, 4, 11, 58, 342, 351
Samuel, Esqr., 30
Dickson
John, 159
Doe
John, 47
Donaldson
H.A., 156
H.A., Clerk, 185, 187
Henry, 154
Henry A, 154, 155, 156, 171, 175, 176
Henry A, Clerk, 186
Henry A., 154, 155, 156, 175, 176
Henry A., Clerk, 181, 182, 202, 204
Hy A, 181
Hy A, Clk, 185
Hy A., Clk, 186

Hy. A., Clk, 182, 187, 202, 204
Dowdey
Jacob, 3
Downing
S., 188, 189
Drew
John, 87, 109
John the Elder, 87, 88, 90, 92
John, Junr., 108
John, the Elder, 87, 89, 91
John, The Elder, 90
Dunkin
Thomas, 350
Dunston
Ed, 352
Dunstone
Edmund, 352

E

Eellbeck
Jos. H., 6
Egan
Robert, 6, 349
Elder
John the Elder, 89, 91
John, the Elder, 91, 92
Elliot
B., 286
Ephrm., 20
Sarah, 237
Stephen, 20
Townsend, 101, 102, 242
Willis, 20
Elliott
Benjamin, 286
Elliott, 250
Miles, 143
Mr. T., 246
Myles, Junr., 144
Myles, Shff, 131, 132, 133, 136, 137, 138, 139, 140, 160, 161, 238, 239, 240, 241, 242, 243
Sarah, 238, 239, 240, 241, 242, 243, 244, 247, 248, 249, 250, 251, 252, 253, 254
Stephen, 144
T., 246
Townsend, 160, 161, 242
Willis, 144
Elliotts
Mr T, 246
Mr. T., 246
Townsend, 244, 245, 246
Emancipation, 349
Slave Welcome's Petition, 349
Etheridge
C., 58
Eure
Lewis, 334, 336
Lewis, DShff, 332, 333, 334, 338
Evans
Eden, 115

F

Fagan
Thomas, 337
Faricaults
JP, 349
Farrow
James, 34, 35
Felton
Bolling, DShff, 118
Boon, 310, 311, 313, 315, 316
William, 242, 244, 245, 247, 248
William, Senr., 244
Wm, 248
Wm, DShff, 129
Wm., 242, 247, 248
Wm., DShff, 128, 135
Fen
Richd, 45, 47
Ferebee
Thomas, 77
Thomas C., 77, 78
Fergason
William, JP, 43
Fetter
Balling, Shff, 115
Fife
Jno, Constable, 49
John, 16, 350
Flower
Josiah, 324
Flowers
Harriet, 322
Josiah, 320, 321, 322, 323
Flury
Henry, 95, 180, 181, 204, 222, 288
Fonville
John, 39
John, JP, 41
Forbes
Capt., 44

Captain Richard, 43
Forros
James, 3
Frazal
John, 36
Frizzell
John, 35
Fullington
John, 79, 80, 81, 82, 84, 85, 86, 99, 100

G

Galling
James, Shff, 333, 334, 336
Jas, Shff, 334
Jas., Shff, 333
Gardner
Henry, 157, 158, 159, 160, 161
Garrett
James, 3
Gaskins
David, 59
Gatlin
AM, 319
Gatling
Will, 334
William, 334, 336, 337
Gilliam
H, 329, 337
H., 329, 330, 335, 339
Henry, 206, 207, 208, 327, 328, 329, 330, 331, 332, 333, 334, 335, 336, 337, 338, 339
Mr., 336
Gilmore
T., Shff, 116
Goodman
David, 108, 109
Goodwin
Wm., 349
Gordon
G., JP, 265
George, 262
Gorham
H., 113
Granbery
James, 55
Granbury
James, Esqr., 55
Gray
Eliza, 219, 220
Geo, 348, 353
George, 348, 353
Jno. Gray, 279
Mr., 339, 344
Gray & Blount, 103, 104
Green
Wm H, Shff, 88, 91
Wm. H, Shff, 92
Wm. H., 89
Wm. H., Shff, 87, 108
Greens
Wm. H., 67
Gregory
Saml., 208
Samuel, 207
William, 68, 69, 70, 71, 72, 73, 74, 75, 152, 153, 202
Wm, 153
Wm., 152, 201
Grice
Charles, Shff, 201
Griffin
John B., 57
Grimes
Jas., DShff, 257
Grist
Allen, Shff, 282
Grist Mill, 101, 102
Guthrie
James, 328
Sampson, 328

H

Hall
Edward, 14, 49
William, 15, 49, 254
Wm., 14, 15, 238, 239
Halsephor
Will, 26
Halsey
William, Esqr., 25
Hambleton
Mr. John, 43
Hamelton
Mr. John, 43
Hamilton
Colo., 43
J., 11, 13, 16
J.H., 48
JH, 49
John, 43
Hardison
A.M., DShff, 321
Alex, DShff, 331
Hardy
M., 186
Miles, 186
Mr. Francis, 343
Mrs, 32, 40, 42
Mrs., 32, 33, 40, 42, 43
Hare
Mrs., 335, 336, 339

Index

R., 339
Rachael, 327, 328, 329, 330, 331, 332, 333, 334, 335, 336, 337, 338, 339
Harramond
Henry, 40, 42, 43, 44
Henry Senr., 42
Henry, Senr., 40
Tho. S., 39
Thomas, 32, 39
Thomas Lee, 40, 42
Thos. Lee, 42
Harrell
Abner, 314, 315, 325
N., 115
N., Clk, 51
Nathan, 115
Harrells
David, 236
Harriman
Henry, 32, 33
Thomas Lee, 33
Harrimond
Thomas Lee, 32
Harris
John, 187
William, 180, 181
Harromond
Henry, 43
Hassell
Ben, 232
Jesse, 120, 121
Jessey, 120
Hathaway
James, 107, 180, 181
James, Esqr., 107
Jas., 350
Tho., 311
Thos., 307
Woolsey, 278, 279
Haughton
John, 298
Haughton
Charles, 175, 176
Chas, 176
Chas., 175
Haughton, 175
James, 144
John, 119, 120, 294, 295, 296, 297, 298
Richd, 14
Tho. B., 271
Hayes
Polly, 9
Winefred, 9
Winifred, 10
Wm., Prosecutor, 8
Hentore
William, 177
Hewet
Joseph, 2
Hill
Mills, 300, 301
Hornblow
Mr., 220
Horniblow
Jas., 342
Jno, 342
John, 342
Horniblows
Mrs., 94
Hosea
Thos, 242
Thos, Shff, 242
Hoskins
E, Shff, 110, 122, 158, 163, 164, 166, 193, 223
E., 302
E., Shff, 20, 93, 98, 101, 102, 103, 105, 106, 107, 111, 112, 114, 119, 120, 121, 123, 125, 141, 149, 150, 157, 158, 162, 164, 165, 167, 168, 169, 171, 172, 173, 174, 175, 181, 189, 190, 191, 192, 194, 195, 196, 197, 204, 207, 208, 209, 210, 219, 224, 228, 231
Edm., 244
Edm., Shff, 245
Edmd, 305, 350
Edmd, Shff, 94, 104, 105, 110, 159, 193, 205
Edmnd, Shff, 175
Edmund, Shff, 108, 170
Edwd, Shff, 182
James, Shff, 94
John, 221
Mr Edm, 105
Mr. Edmund, 175, 192
Saml., 15, 350
Samuel, Foreman, 13
Sarah, 47
William, 353
Willm., 353
Howe
A., 317
Arthur, 54, 55, 60
Howell
Abraham, 330
Hoyle
Jackson, 112
Jackson S, 113

Jackson S., 113
Hunter
Elisha, 344
Henry, 68, 69, 70, 71, 72, 74, 75
Jno B., 64
John, 344
John B, 63, 64, 65, 66, 69, 70, 72, 75
John B., 63, 64, 66, 68, 70, 71, 72, 74, 75
Sarah, 344
Hurdell
Josiah, 349
Hurdle
Henry, 232
William, 301, 302
Hyman
Samuel, 189, 190, 191

I

Indian Queen Tavern, 263, 264, 265, 267
Inquisition by Coroner, 351
Iredell
J., Attorney, 333
Ja., 92, 180
Ja., Clk, 119
James, 105, 109
James, Clerk, 65, 70, 72, 73, 74, 93, 115, 117, 118
James, Clk, 75
Jas, Clk, 74, 109
Jas., 114, 115, 117, 209
Jas., Clk, 65, 70, 72, 73, 93
Mr., 335, 338
T., Attorney, 36
Thos., 34, 350
Thos., Attorney, 34

J

Jackson
James, 183, 221, 222, 223, 224, 228, 231, 232, 233
Jas, 222, 223, 225
Jas., 221, 222, 223, 224, 225, 226, 227, 228, 229, 230, 231, 232
Joel, 263, 264, 265
William, 17, 20, 21, 201
Wm, 200, 201
Wm., 144, 199, 200, 201
Jacocks
Jonathan, 108, 109
Jaffors
Christafor, 41
Jaffreys
Christafor, 41
Christopher, 41
Jeffreys
Christofor, 41
Jernigan
Mills, 273, 274, 275, 277
Jinnett
Joseph, 46
Johnson
Charles, 348
Chas, 348
Chas., JP, 2
Johnston
Gabriel, 44
John, 44, 352
Peter, 345
Sam, 44
Saml., Attorney, 24
Samuel, 44
Samuel, Esqr., 5
William H., 177
William W., 177
Jones
Col., 291
Docter William, 276
E, 216
E., 18, 213, 214, 215, 217, 249
Edm., 231, 237
Edmd, 18, 231, 253
Edmund, 18, 237, 253
Edwd, 249
Elisha, 44, 45
Howell, 290, 291, 292, 310, 311, 314
James, 114, 233, 234, 235, 236, 272, 273, 274, 275, 276, 277
James:, 234
Mr., 23
T., 158
Thomas, Clerk, 25, 26
Thos, Clk, 25, 26
Will., 292
William, 233, 234, 235, 236, 276, 290, 292

Wm, 277
Wm., 234, 236, 276, 277, 290, 349
Jordan
Charles, 24, 305
G, JP, 265
G., JP, 264
Icabod, 45
Jacob, 45
Robert, 58
Robt., 58

K

Kalbors
Robert, 41
Keating
R, 86
R., 85, 86
Robt., 86
Kelly
Mary, 2
Kerr
Mrs., 31
Samuel, 30, 31, 32
Samuel, Merchant, 30
Keys
James H., Attorney, 50
King
Norman, 183, 212, 213, 214, 215, 216, 217, 218, 219, 222
Solomon, 26
Thomas, 5
Knox
Andrew, 177, 178

L

Landings
Pitch Landing, 236, 274
Lang
Silas, 268
Langley
J.W., 203
James, 162
James W, 98, 163, 165, 166, 167, 168, 169, 171, 174, 203
James W., 98, 103, 104, 162, 163, 164, 165, 166, 167, 168, 169, 170, 174, 203
Jas W, 164, 175
Jas. W., 163, 174
Mr., 170
Langly
James W., 103
Jas., 98
Laseter
Allen, 306, 319
Lasseter
Allen, 319
Laughrey
Chs., 349
Laurence
Peter P., 350
Lavender
William L., 279, 281
Leary
Daniel, Cordwainer, 6
John, 211, 212
John Junr., 76
John, Junr., 76
Justus, 242
Tho H., 327
Tho. H., 328
Lee
Thomas, 33
Legett
Alex, 352
Alexander, 352
Leggett
Daniel, 184, 185, 186, 187, 188
Danl, 186
Danl., 187
Luke Junr., 186
Lenox
Rob, 24
Robert, 25
Robt, 25
Leroy
Louis, 279, 281, 282, 283
Lewis
Luten, 116, 117
Margaret, 116, 117
William W., 178
Lisles
Edwin, 63, 64, 65, 66
Little
John, 325, 326, 349, 350
John, Foreman, 8
Mr., 325
Littlejohn
J.W., 193, 284, 295
Jno. W., 325
John W, 296, 298, 326
John W., 296, 298, 326
William, 26, 27, 348
William A, 118

William A., 118, 193
Wm A, 170
Wm A., 170
Wm., 5, 348, 353
Wm. A., 192
Wm., JP, 7
Long
Mr. Reuben, 350
Reuben, 350
Reuben, Petition for Emancipation., 350
W., Shff, 328
Luten
John, 350
King, 180, 181

M

Maer
Samuel, 351, 352
Manning
Jos, 285, 286, 287
Jos., 285, 286, 287, 288, 289
Joseph, 283, 284, 287, 288, 290
Mardin
Thomas D., Solicitor, 20
Markham
Joshua, 41
Marriner
D., 338
Demsey, 337
Marsh
Cyrus, 6
Cyrus, Prosecutor, 6
Mr. Cyrus, 7
Marshal
Daniel, 26
Marten
PB, 86
Peter B., 85
Martin
L, Attorney, 332, 333
L., 339
L., Attorney, 331, 332
Leonard, 334, 335
Leonard, Attorney, 333, 335, 338, 339
Martha, 4
Mr L., 339
Mr., 335, 338
Wm, 168, 170
Wm., 167, 169
Matthews
George, 43
Mr. George, 43
Matthias
Nathaniel, 344
Thomas, 17
Thos, 18
Sawyer, 160
McCartney
Mrs., 44
McClannen
Daniel, 57
McCotter
John, 304
McCotter & Muil, 172, 173
McCottor
Jno., 317, 318, 319
John, 302, 303, 304, 306, 317, 318, 319
John, Dshff, 285
John, DShff, 286, 293
McCrae
Jno, 95
Jno., 94
McDonald
D, Clk, 199, 220, 221, 223, 225, 226, 228, 229, 231, 233, 234, 235, 237, 238, 239, 240, 241, 243, 247, 248, 249, 250, 251, 252, 253, 254, 272, 275, 280, 282, 283, 285, 286, 287, 288, 289, 290, 291, 292, 315, 316, 317, 318, 319, 320, 325, 327, 328, 329, 330, 331, 335, 336
D, Esquire, 339
D., Clk, 222, 226, 260, 261, 267, 269, 278
Duncan, 154, 212
Duncan, Clerk, 187, 199, 212, 220, 221, 222, 223, 224, 225, 226, 227, 228, 229, 230, 231, 232, 234, 235, 237, 238, 239, 240, 241, 243, 244, 259, 260, 261, 262, 263, 267, 269, 270, 272, 273, 275, 276, 278, 279, 280, 281, 283, 284, 285, 286, 287, 288, 311, 314, 315, 316, 317, 318, 319,

325, 327, 328, 329, 330, 331
Duncan, Clk, 199, 248
P, DClk, 310
William, 32
McFarland
John, 62
Mcfattor
John, DShff, 284
Mcguire
Samuel, 211
McGuire
Jn Phillip, 151
Phil, 148
Phill, 110
Phillip, 99, 100
S., 211
Saml., 53
Samuel, 179, 212
McKeal
Mr., 38
Mckeel
Jos S., DShff, 225
Jos. S., DShff, 227, 230
McKeel
Jos S, DShff, 226
Jos. S., DShff, 225, 227, 229, 230
M., 36
Michael, 34, 35, 36, 37, 38, 39
Michael, a Taylor, 34
Michl, 36, 38
Michl., 33, 35
Mr. Michl, 38
McKeell
Michel, 37
Mcottor
John, 303
McTheil
Michael, 351
McThey
John R., 350
Mhoon
Joel, 188
Michalls
Richard, 26
Mieres
Jack, 17
Millen
Alex, 8
Alexr., 350
Miller
A., 56
M., 48
Masan, 349
Mason, 48
Ming
James, 141, 142
Willy, 46
Mixon
J., 244
Jeremiah, 254
MKeel
Jos. S., DShff, 224
Moffat
James, Attorney, 293
Mohun
James, 59
Joel, 185, 186
Moon
Joel, 184, 185, 187, 188, 189
Moon, 187
Moore
Britain, 184
James, 115
James:, 115
Jno, 252
John, 238, 245, 246, 247, 248, 249, 251, 252
Mr. John, 246
Morgan
Geo, 350
J.P., 65
Morris
H., 265
Hillary, 265, 266
Morriss
Hillary, 263
Muel
James, 172
Muil
James, 173
Mumford
Robinson, 116, 117
Munns
Freda, Junr., 305
Freda, Senr., 305
Jacob, 305
Murdaugh
Stephen, 255
Mushrom
John, 348
Mushrowe
John, 348
Myers
Thomas, 306, 319
Myres
Tho, 317, 318, 319
Tho., 317, 318

N

Nail
Mr., 294
Nash
Caleb, 17, 148, 151
NC Counties
Anson, 328, 336
Beaufort, 279, 281, 282
Bertie, 67, 87, 88, 89, 91, 92, 108,

186, 188, 254, 257, 259, 260, 351
Cumberland, 116
Currituck, 77
Edgecombe, 184
Gates, 143, 330, 333
Hertford, 9, 50, 79, 80, 81, 82, 83, 84, 115, 118, 198, 233, 235, 236, 242, 258, 259, 260, 261, 262, 266, 267, 273, 274, 276, 277, 290, 292, 310, 313, 314, 316, 324
Martin, 63, 65, 68, 70, 71, 72, 74, 75
Northampton, 228
Pasquotank, 41, 62, 152, 153, 202
Perquimans, 102, 103, 128, 129, 130, 131, 132, 133, 134, 135, 136, 137, 139, 160, 161, 238, 239, 240, 241, 242, 243, 245
Tyrell, 43, 95, 278, 294, 297, 320, 322
Washington, 185, 186, 187, 188, 189, 268, 269, 271, 321, 322, 323, 331, 335, 337
NC Towns
Columbia, 321
Lees Mills, 188
Murfreesboro, 291
Murfreesborough, 263, 264, 265, 267
New Bern, 33
Newbern, 40, 42
Nixonton, 94
Plymouth, 43
Raleigh, 267
Windsor, 257, 258, 260
Winton, 50, 291
Neal
Abner, JP, 33
Neale
Abner, Esqr., 32
Neil
Hon., 48
Honore, 48, 350
Honore, Merchant, 48
James, 16
Jas., 17
New York Towns
City of New York, 30
Nicholls
B., 67
Benajah, 67
Binajah, 67
Nichols
George, 268
William, 175
Nixen Carter & Co., 153
Nixen Carter & Company, 153
Nixon Carter & Co, 152
Nixon Carter & Co., 153
Norcom
Edmund, 171
James, 284
John, 93, 94, 171
Norfleet
Abraham, 52
E, 9, 13, 81, 83, 97, 102, 114, 149
E, CC, 10
E, Clk, 54, 57, 121, 122, 125, 129, 130, 153, 169
E, CS, 173
E., 8, 53, 82, 84, 96, 98, 99, 100, 103, 104, 105, 106, 107, 110, 111, 112, 113, 120, 128, 138, 148, 150, 152, 157
E., CC, 9, 10, 12
E., Clk, 50, 52, 56, 61, 77, 79, 80, 85, 95, 123, 124, 131, 132, 135, 137, 141, 142, 151, 155, 158, 159, 163, 172, 173, 190, 191, 192, 193, 194, 195, 196
E., CS, 94, 164, 166, 167, 168, 177
Elisha, 100
Elisha, Clerk, 9, 10, 49, 52, 54, 56, 57, 61, 76, 79, 80, 81, 82, 83, 84, 85, 94, 95, 96, 97, 98, 99, 100, 101, 102, 104, 105, 106, 107, 110,

111, 112, 113, 114, 120, 121, 122, 123, 124, 125, 128, 129, 130, 131, 132, 134, 135, 136, 137, 141, 142, 148, 149, 150, 152, 153, 155, 156, 157, 158, 159, 162, 163, 164, 165, 166, 167, 168, 169, 170, 171, 173, 174, 176, 190, 191, 192, 193, 194, 195, 196
Elisha. Clerk, 151
J., 142
James, Clerk, 19, 20, 126, 127, 133, 138, 140, 160, 161, 183, 197, 198, 200, 201, 205, 206, 207, 208, 209, 210, 213, 214, 215, 216, 217, 218
James, Clk, 18, 20, 160, 161, 213, 214, 215, 216, 217, 218
Jas, 18, 150, 170, 175
Jas, Clk, 19, 126, 200, 201, 206, 207, 209
Jas., 149, 242
Jas., Clk, 19, 127, 133, 139, 140, 183, 197, 201, 205, 208, 210
Margaret, 114
Mr., 170
Mr. Elisha, Clerk, 54
Mr. James, 170
Will, DClk, 219
Will, Deputy Clerk, 219
William, 301
William, Clerk, 21, 294, 295, 296, 297, 299, 300, 303, 304, 305, 308, 312, 326
William, Clk, 21, 294, 295, 299, 301, 302, 303, 305, 307, 308, 312, 326
Norman
Henry, JP, 46
Northern States
Opinion of Slavery., 349

O

O Malley
Myles, 350
Odham
James, 115
O'Malley
Myles, 55
O'Neal
Henry, 27, 28, 29, 30
Henry, Planter, 27
O'Neil
Henry, 2
Overton
Jonah, 318
Oxley
John, 59, 60

P

Paine
Ebenezer, 207
Parishes
Parish of Society, 352
Parker
E., 84, 85, 86
Enoch, 79, 80, 81, 82, 86
Job, 147, 148, 149, 150, 151
Seth, Junr., 17, 201
Silas, Senr., 257
Parkers
Enoch, 86
Parshall
Benjamin, 29
Parsons
Mr., 335
Vincent, 327, 336
Paterson
Elizabeth, 37
Patterson
E., 36
Eliz., 33
Elizabeth, 34, 35, 36, 38, 39
Elizabeth, Widow, 34
Miss Elizabeth, 37
Mr., 37
Mrs. Elizabeth, 38, 39
Payne
Michael, 348, 351
Micheal, 4
Michl, 35, 348, 353
Michl, DShff, 35, 36

Michl, Esquire, 4
Michl, JP, 348
Michl, the oldest., 350
Michl., 5, 36, 351
Michl., JP, 3
Michl., Shff, 33
Perry
Elisha, 9
Robert, 9
Phelps
B., Shff, 321, 331
Phennery
Geo., Esqr., 44
Phenny
Mr., 44
Phillips
B., Shff, 268
Pike
Jno, 323
Pikes
Jno, 323
Plummer
Elizabeth, 4
Portsmouth, 31
Powel
Lewis, 257
Powell
L., 260, 261, 262, 266
Lewis, 254, 255, 257, 258, 259, 260, 261, 262, 263, 265, 266, 267
Mr., 256
Mr. Lewis, 255
Pride
Herbert, 87, 88, 89, 90, 91, 92, 93
Pritchard
Abs H., 229
Absalom, 224, 229
Absalom H., 224

Q

Quakers, 349

R

R. & Lambert, 203
Rabee
Luke, 264
Raby
Luke, 257, 262
Raiby
Luke, 254, 258
Mr., 255
Ralls
David, 198, 199
Rich, 199
Ralston
Samuel, 281
Ramcke
Doctor, 7
Ramsay
Henry, 65
Lisle H, 64
Lisle H., 63
Lisles H, 65
Ramsey
William, 331
Rasco
James, 352
Thomas, 352
Rascoe
Jas., 352
Jno, 185
John, 185
Thos, 352
Rayner
Amos, 185
Miles, 119
Reed
John, 352
Reily
Edward, 174, 175
Rennant
Francis, 170
Rhoads
Jacob, 276
Righton
William, 20, 351
Wm., 351
Robards
Wm., CSC, 268
Roberts
Charles, 16, 54, 55
Charles, Shff, 14, 49
Chas, 16, 350
Chas, Shff, 8, 9, 12, 13, 55, 56
Chas., Esqr., 16
Chas., Shff, 10, 12, 51
John M., 155
Mr., 54
Will, Shff, 61
William, 28, 29, 33, 35, 36
William, Shff, 34, 35
Wm., Shff, 96
RobertsJohn M., 156
Robinson
John, 28, 29, 30
John, Planter, 27
Rogers
Joseph, 212
Rogers & Lambert, 203, 204
Rombough
William, 56
Wm., 56, 350
Ross
William, 279, 281
Ruffin
Thos, DShff, 260

Ruftin
  Thos., 259
Russel
  John, 350
Rutland
  Turner, 256
Ryan
  Edward, 352
  Thomas, 352
  Thos., 352
Ryhton
  William, 20

S

Sanderlin
  Lydia, 230, 231
Sanders
  Charles, 350
  William, 239
  Wm, 102, 239
  Wm., 239
Saterfield
  James, 171
  Jas., 171
  Thomas, 110, 141, 142
  Thos, 109
Satterfield
  Tho, 224
  Thomas, 224, 337, 338
  Thos., 350
  Wm., 350
Satterwhite
  Thomas, 43
Saunders
  William, 102
  Wm, 101
  Wm., 101
Sawyer
  Enoch, 302, 303, 304
  M., 161
  Matthias E, 160
  Matthias E., 159, 161
  MC, 294
Sawyer & Norcom, 293, 294
Sedguike
  John, 46
Serimshell
  John, 1
Shaw
  John, 152, 153
  Shaw, 152
  William, 93, 94, 152, 153
  Wm, 93
  Wm., 93, 94
Ships
  Ship Ellen, 281, 282
Simmons
  Thomas, 10
  Wm., 241
Simon
  Wm., 251
Simone
  Wm., 250
Simones
  William, Senr., 241
Simons
  Elizabeth, 9
  Joseph, 10
  Joshua, 37
  Simion, 96
  Thomas, 9, 10
  Thos, 9
  Thos., 8, 9
  Will, 252
  Will, Senr., 250
  William, 251
Simpson
  E., 111
  Elisabeth, 230
  Elizabeth, 230
  Evan, 112, 230
  Exum, 225
Skenner
  Charles, 51
Skinner
  J B, Attorney, 156
  J.B., 276
  James, 226
  James, Shff, 178, 211
  Jas, DShff, 19, 213, 221, 222, 223
  Jas, Shff, 200, 226
  Jas., DShff, 126, 142, 183, 205, 214
  Jas., Shff, 125, 201
  JB, 201, 277
  Jos B, 105, 276, 277
  Jos B., 236
  Jos. B, Attorney, 276
  Jos. B., 154, 156, 204, 302
  Jos. B., Attorney, 276
  Jos., Clk, 58
  Joseph, 234, 240
  Joseph B, 155, 234
  Joseph B., 154, 155, 202, 233, 234, 235, 236, 237
  Joseph B., Attorney, 154
  Josiah, 104, 105, 106
  Saml., 271
  Thomas H, Clerk, 179

Index

Thos H, Clk, 143, 179
Thos H., Clerk, 178
Thos, Clerk, 143
W., 46
WJ, 45
SkinnerJ.B., 277
Slade
W., 15, 350
W., Attorney, 14, 47
William, 15, 189, 190, 203, 204
William, Attorney, 14
Wm., 189, 204
Wm., Attorney, 15
Slave
Tom, 99
Slaves
Abraham, 140
Abram, 133, 139
Allen, 234, 235, 236
Allida, 202
Amy, 280, 281, 282
Ann, 127
Annis, 232
Arthur, 84
Atlas, 133, 135, 136, 137, 138, 139, 140
Ben, 97, 133, 139, 140, 341
Bess, 56
Bet, 11, 322, 323
Betty, 31, 56, 127
Bob, 31, 234, 235, 236, 303, 304, 305
Carry, 190, 203
Cate, 31
Charles, 114
Cherry, 10
Child, 202
Cooper, 202
Dan, 69, 70, 71, 73, 74, 75
Daniel, 6
Dave, 55, 332, 333
David, 87, 90, 91, 92, 280, 281, 282
Davis, 89
Dick, 13, 14, 15, 49, 344
Dicks, 49
Dil, 266
Dinah, 46
Doll, 281, 282
Dundee, 342, 343
Easop, 280, 281, 282
Edmon, 139, 341
Edmund, 133, 140
Eliza, 202
Emancipation of., 348
Esther, 56, 154, 156, 157, 344
Exi, 87, 89, 90, 91, 92
Fanny, 31, 154, 156, 157
Frank, 2, 24, 56, 58
Fred, 266
Gabriel, 280, 281, 282
George, 3, 48, 49, 57, 58, 69, 70, 71, 73, 74, 75, 105, 106, 121, 209, 210
Grainge, 347, 348
Hamlett, 31
Hampton, 280, 281, 282
Hannah, 31
Henry, 154, 156, 157
Isaac, 11, 12, 31, 103, 295, 296, 297, 298
Isom, 326
Jack, 5, 6, 19, 20, 24, 27, 101, 102, 103, 110, 142, 212, 240, 242, 245, 246, 273, 274, 275, 277, 299, 343
Jacob, 98, 133, 139, 140
James, 5, 6
Jef, 128, 133, 341
Jeff, 139, 140
Jefferson, 294
Jenny, 308
Jim, 6, 120, 191, 192, 194, 195, 196, 198, 207, 208, 240, 242, 243, 246, 342
Jo, 332
Joan, 55
Joe, 10, 87, 89, 90, 91, 92, 103, 162, 163, 164, 165, 166, 167, 168, 169, 170, 183, 213, 214, 215, 216, 217, 218, 219, 245, 246, 333
John, 5, 128, 133, 134, 139, 140, 326, 341
John, a Taylor, 39
Jon, 268
Juba, 352, 353

Index

Jude, 133, 139, 140, 341
Judith, 281, 282
Lawrence, 180, 182
Lennon, 58
Lewis, 87, 89, 90, 91, 92
London, 171
Louisa, 202
Luke, 179
Luvinia, 202
March, 321
Mariah, 133, 139, 140
Mariam, 31
Marian, 133, 139, 140
Mark, 322
Mary, 128, 134, 341
Merrick, 63, 64, 66
Michael, 31
Miles, 76
Mills, 154, 156, 157
Milly, 31
Mingo, 47, 96
Mingoe, 27
Moll, 67
Molly, 202, 312
Moses, 268
Nan, 280, 281, 282
Nancy, 55, 158, 159, 172, 173, 175, 176
Ned, 33, 40, 42, 273, 274, 275, 277, 279, 280, 281, 282
Nelly, 172, 173
Pat, 133, 139, 140, 255, 263, 264, 266
Patt, 263, 264
Pattey, 341
Peggy, 158, 159, 172, 173
Penny, 220
Perthena, 58
Peter, 12, 13
Philip, 273, 274, 275, 277
Phillis, 202, 268
Phoebe, 220
Pomp, 133, 140
Pompy, 128, 134
Price, 234, 235
Prince, 33, 40, 42, 43, 236
Quibey, 268
Rachael, 120, 196, 197
Rachel, 191, 192, 194, 195, 268
Rages, 7
Ralfe, 113
Randall, 280, 281, 282
Reddick, 154, 156, 157
Robert, 202
Robin, 48, 49
Rose, 31, 121, 306
Salisbury, 31
Sam, 1, 87, 89, 90, 91, 92, 245, 246, 308, 312
Samuel, 280, 281, 282
Sandy, 5
Sarah, 352
Sassy, 284
Serener, 133, 139, 140
Simon, 122, 123, 124, 125, 148, 149, 150, 151
Smart, 202
Sook, 133, 139, 140
Squire, 111, 112, 123, 124, 125, 126, 127, 240, 242, 243, 245, 246
Step, 61
Stephen, 94, 280, 281, 282
Suck, 128, 129, 130, 131, 132
Suke, 133
Susan, 280, 281, 282
Sylvia, 303, 304
Taff, 31
Tamer, 67
Tempe, 322, 323
Tereza, 31
Titus, 351
Tom, 63, 64, 66, 100, 192
Toney, 17, 18, 19
Tony, 19
Trease, 240, 242, 243, 245, 246
Venus, 33, 40, 42, 245, 246, 269, 270, 271
Violet, 116, 117
Welcome, 350
West, 50
Will, 16, 17, 128, 133, 134, 139, 140, 341
York, 162, 163, 164, 165, 166, 167, 168, 169, 170, 202
Small

A., 52
Alex, 227
Ben, Junr., 226
R., 17, 178
Reuben, 17, 18, 19, 110, 111, 121, 122, 123, 124, 125, 126, 127, 147, 148, 149, 150, 151, 179, 225
Reuben, Esqr, 111, 121, 123, 149, 150
Reuben, JP, 17
Thomas, 206
Thos., 205
William, 206
Smith
John, 343
Step, 181
Stephen, 180, 181, 182
Smith & Shaw
Storehouse of., 5
Smithwick
H, 71
H., 63, 64, 65, 68, 70, 72
H., Shff, 74, 75
John, 352
William, 352
Wm, 352
Soans
Stephan, 352
Stephen, 352
Sowel
James, 100
Sowell
James, 79, 80, 81, 82, 83, 84, 85
James:, 81, 83
Jas, 81, 86
Jas., 80, 86
Spiers
James, 324, 325
Spruill
Samuel, 46
Squire
Jno., 286
Squires
Jno., 289
John, 286
Stafford
Rufus, 8
Rufus, Merchant, 8
Stalling
Simon, 143, 329, 330
Stallings
Nichl., 46
Nicholas, 46
Simon, 143
Standin
Hendn., 350
States
Georgia, 322
Philadelphia, 78
Tennessee, 263, 264
Stertivent
Charles, 287
Stewart
Thomas C, 108
Thomas C., 108, 109
Store
Mr William Creecy's Store, 244
Stores
David Harrells Store, 236
Store House of William Britton, 254
Stott
William, 62
Strines
James, 315
Sturtivent
Charles, 287
Sumner
Jethro, 53
Moses, 118
Sutton
Jeremiah, 327
Joseph, 293, 294
Lemuel, 327, 330
Mr., 335
Swift
Samuel, 25, 344

T

Taxsey
Elliot, 149
Joseph, 149
Nancy, 149
Taylor
Charles, 317, 318
Chas., 318
Thompson
Lewis, 177
Mr., 110, 111
William, 206
Wm, 230
Wm., 112, 205, 206, 230
Tilghman
Edward, 56
Edwd, 55
Tisdale
William, JP, 43
Tomlinson
Elizabeth, 33, 39, 40, 41, 43
Mrs Elizabeth, 42
Mrs Elizabeth, 32
Mrs., 44
Mrs. Elizabeth, 32, 40, 42

Townsend Elliotts
Mill, 246
Tredwell
James, 164
Mister, 280
S., 342
Saml, 164
Saml., 162, 165, 166, 175, 343, 350
Samuel, 162, 163, 164, 165, 166, 167, 168, 169, 170, 342, 343
Trotter
Tho., 281, 282
TrotterTho., 279
Turner
Simon, Clerk, 257, 258, 259, 260
Simon, Clk, 257, 258, 259, 260
Tho, Clk, 324, 333, 338, 339
Tho., 332
Tho., Clk, 322, 332, 333, 334, 335
Thomas, Clerk, 333, 335, 339

U

Underhill
Joseph, 352
Usher
James, 261, 267
James:, 262

V

Vail
A N, 271
A.N., 272, 321
A.N., Attorney, 321
Abner, 268, 269
Abner N, 269, 270, 271
Abner N., 268, 269, 270, 271, 272
B., 140
Benners, 134, 135, 136, 137, 138, 139, 140
Edward, 268, 270, 271, 272, 353
Edwd, 269, 353
Edwd., 269
Fred, 191, 193, 194
Frederick, 191, 193, 194, 195, 196, 197
Fredk, 195
H N, Attorney, 184
Jno., 44
John, 45
Tho., 271
Thomas, 119, 144, 191, 192, 193, 194, 195, 196, 197, 206, 207, 208, 268, 270, 272
Thomas, Coroner, 284, 285, 286, 287
Thos, 194, 195
Thos, Coroner, 284, 288
Thos., 270
Thos., Coroner, 285, 286, 287

W

Wadbey
Wm., 271
Waff
Thomas, 306, 307
Walker
John, Clerk, 188
John, Clk, 188, 189
John, CSC, 187, 188
Thomas, 186
Thos, 185
Walk's
Capt, 1
Wall
Henry, 259
John, 263, 264, 265, 266
Mr, 255, 256, 257
Mr., 255, 256
Mr. John, 264
Walters
Lewis, Shff, 84, 118, 233, 235, 258, 272
Walton
Holloday, 12
William, 223
Warburton
Luke, 352
Ward
Francis, 320, 321, 322
Watson
Henry, 27, 28
Henry D., 3
Henry Drake, 3
Wm., 28, 59
Watters
Lewis, Shff, 198
Welch
Miles, 211, 212

Weston
Solomon, 352
Wharton
Edward E., 41
Wheaton
R., 250
Robert, 238, 239, 240, 250
Robt., 240
Whedbee
Jos., 29
Joseph, 29, 351
Wheeler
John, 262, 264, 265
Whidbee
Joseph, 351
White
Caleb, 13, 14, 15
Caleb the Elder, 14
Caleb, the Elder, 14
Francis, 13, 14, 15
Gab., 242
James, 15
Joshua, 349
Mr. Francis, 15
Tho., 278, 279
Thomas, 278
Wm., 144
Wilder
Michael, 299
Willis, 349
Wilkins
Jos., 8, 9
Joseph, 9, 10
Joseph, Planter, 10
Thomas, 9
William, 28, 29, 30
Wilkinson
Geo., 350
Willey
Matthew, 352
Matthias, 352
William Wilson & Company, 77, 78
Williams
Benj., 187
Benjn., 351
Benjn., Coroner, 352
George, 309, 311, 314
J.B., 350
Mr., 58
Williamson
Richard, 50
Wills
H., 177, 306
Henry, 128, 129, 130, 131, 132, 133
Wilroy
John, 62
Wilson
William, 77
Winham
William, 24
Winslow
C., 86
Caleb, 79, 80, 81, 82, 83, 84, 85, 86, 100
Wood
Deborah, 322
James, 322
John, Clk, 242
Richard, 320, 321, 322
Richd, 321, 322, 323
Richd., 322, 323
Wood & Hastings, 272, 273, 274, 275, 276, 277
Woodward
James, 349
Wynne
Robert, Clerk, 321
Robt., Clk, 320, 321
Wynnes
WB, DShff, 324
Wynns
Robert, Clk, 320
W.B., DShff, 314

Y

Yeats
Peter, 352
William, 352
Young
Capt. Daniel, 44
Daniel, 42, 43
Mrs., 43

ABOUT THE AUTHOR

William L. Byrd, III has been involved in genealogical and historical research for more than thirty years. His primary areas of interest are Native Americans, African Americans, West Indians, East Indians and Moors in Virginia, North Carolina, and South Carolina.

He has been published by the *North Carolina Genealogical Society Journal*, the *Magazine of Virginia Genealogy*, *The Rowan County Register*, and *The South Carolina Magazine of Ancestral Research*. He has also co-authored articles with Sheila Stover in the *North Carolina Genealogical Society Journal*, *The Augustan Society Omnibus*, the *Pan-American Indian Association News*, and the *Eagle: New England's American Indian Journal*. He has received an "Award of Special Recognition" from The North Carolina Society of Historians in the category of "The History Article Award" for preserving North Carolina history.

He is a U.S. Army Veteran from the Vietnam era, and served with the U.S. Armed Forces overseas. He is currently retired, and resides with his family in Hickory, North Carolina.

☙ ❧

Other Heritage Books by William L. Byrd, III:

Against the Peace and Dignity of the State: North Carolina Laws Regarding Slaves, Free Persons of Color, and Indians

Bladen County, North Carolina Tax Lists: 1768 through 1774, Volume I

Bladen County, North Carolina Tax Lists: 1775 through 1789, Volume II

For So Long as the Sun and Moon Endure: Indian Records from the North Carolina General Assembly Sessions, & Other Sources

In Full Force and Virtue: North Carolina Emancipation Records, 1713-1860

North Carolina General Assembly Sessions Records: Slaves and Free Persons of Color, 1709-1789

North Carolina Slaves and Free Persons of Color: Chowan County, Volume One

North Carolina Slaves and Free Persons of Color: Chowan County, Volume Two

North Carolina Slaves and Free Persons of Color: Pasquotank County

North Carolina Slaves and Free Persons of Color: Perquimans County

Villainy Often Goes Unpunished: Indian Records from the North Carolina General Assembly Sessions, 1675-1789

Other Heritage Books by William L. Byrd, III and John H. Smith:

North Carolina Slaves and Free Persons of Color: Burke, Lincoln, and Rowan Counties

North Carolina Slaves and Free Persons of Color: Hyde and Beaufort Counties

North Carolina Slaves and Free Persons of Color: Iredell County

North Carolina Slaves and Free Persons of Color: Mecklenburg, Gaston, and Union Counties

North Carolina Slaves and Free Persons of Color: McDowell County

North Carolina Slaves and Free Persons of Color: Stokes and Yadkin Counties

www.ingramcontent.com/pod-product-compliance
Lightning Source LLC
Chambersburg PA
CBHW050427240426
43661CB00055B/2301

* 9 7 8 0 7 8 8 4 2 4 6 0 1 *